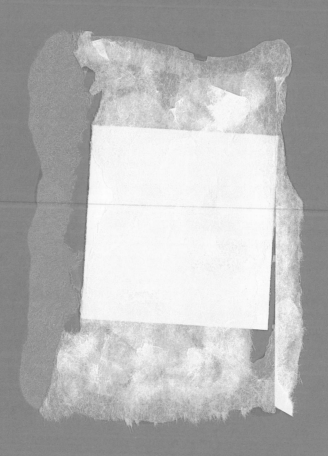

STARDUST

THE
DAVID BOWIE
STORY

STARDUST

THE
DAVID BOWIE
STORY

Henry Edwards and
Tony Zanetta

McGRAW-HILL BOOK COMPANY
New York   St. Louis   San Francisco
Hamburg   Mexico   Toronto

ISBN 0-07-072797-X

LIBRARY OF CONGRESS CATALOGING-IN-PUBLICATION DATA

Edwards, Henry.
    Stardust : the David Bowie story.
    1. Bowie, David.   2. Rock musicians—England—
Biography.   I. Zanetta, Tony.   II. Title.
ML420.B754E3   1986   784.5'4'00924 [B]   86-42552
ISBN 0-07-072797-X

Book design by Kathryn Parise

Contents

49234

PART FOUR
THE FALL OF ZIGGY STARDUST

PART FIVE
CHANGES

"Who wants the truth? That's what show business is for—to prove that it's not what you are that counts, it's what you think you are."

—Andy Warhol

Prologue

David Bowie's personal assistant Coco Schwab knew what David wanted better than anyone else. What David wanted was to have the past erased.

On July 11, 1983, Serious Moonlight, David's first tour in five years, settled down for a three-night stay in England's huge Milton Keynes Bowl. The tour was breaking the world attendance records set by the Rolling Stones.

In the audience sat Graham Rivens, a middle-aged owner of a Margate electrical supplies shop. In 1965, eighteen years before, Rivens had played bass guitar in a band called Davie Jones and the Lower Third. Eighteen-year-old Davie Jones became David Bowie.

Rivens watched as the audience cheered and screamed. The ritual was repeated everywhere as audience after audience paid tribute to the elegant, aristocratic man, at one time the very symbol of rock outrage—the king of glitter rock.

Rivens wanted to say hello to his old mate at the end of the show. He knew Davie Jones was a rock legend. He had seen David's face on the covers of *Time* and *Rolling Stone*; he had listened to his new album, *Let's Dance*, which had gone straight to the top of the world pop charts. But to Rivens Bowie would always be Davie Jones. At one time they had been close friends.

Backstage Rivens was cut off at the pass. There was no way he was going to be allowed anywhere near David.

Rivens, Davie Jones and the Lower Third, and the pain of nine years of early failure during the mid- and late-1960s were all part of the past Coco Schwab made sure had been erased.

Journalist Craig Copetas also attended an English concert. In the mid-1970s, Copetas believed that David was among his closest friends. Copetas and David had spent hours together in long, intimate conversation. Copetas had introduced David to William Burroughs, covered the meeting for *Rolling Stone*, and had been dispatched by David to Paris with a personal message for Jean Genet.

"May I say hello to David?" Copetas asked Schwab politely. Coco had accompanied him to Paris to search for Genet.

"No way!" Coco replied.

Copetas was also part of the past.

At the U.S. Festival in northern California, an agent, Maggie Abbott, made her way backstage. It was her singlehanded battle that had gotten David his first dramatic film role in *The Man Who Fell to Earth*. She had fought to have Schwab placed on the film's payroll.

But Coco barred her way; Abbott had also been erased.

Another backstage visitor at the U.S. Festival was Ava Cherry, a sumptuous black woman in her late twenties. As a teenager she had been involved with David in a torrid on-again off-again love affair that had stretched over three years.

Ava was definitely to be kept away from David.

As soon as the Serious Moonlight tour docked down in North America, David's ex-wife Angela was served with a restraining order ordering her not to go anywhere near the tour. David and Angela had been divorced for three years after a ten-year marriage. Angela blamed Coco for stealing David from her. Angela believes David feared she might do physical harm to Coco. She seemed incapable of facing the fact that she, too, had been erased.

In Australia, a local promoter invited an American manager, Michael Lippman, to attend a Serious Moonlight performance. Lippman had been one of David's four managers. David had lived in Lippman's Los Angeles house.

The day after the invitation was extended Lippman was informed that Coco had demanded that his name be struck from the list of invitees. Lippman had been erased.

David Robert Jones Bowie was driven by one overriding ambition: to stand center stage basking in the glow of a spotlight focused directly, solely on him. He was so persuasive that everyone who had ever loved him and helped him believed that he, too, was standing in that spotlight. To know David is to believe that one is sprinkled with the stardust that belongs to David alone.

The new and improved Serious Moonlight version of David offered a new and improved official version of his past. He seemed to have forgotten Rivens, Copetas, Abbott, Cherry, Angela, Lippman, and so many others who had once been his friends. But those who lived through his history had not forgotten him. Their moments with David were magical moments that had dramatically heightened their lives. They could not forget. Everyone who knew David felt compelled to relive his magical moment with him, to claim his rightful part in David's history.

Coco's zeal and dedication in helping David erase these people from his past was awesome, but no matter how hard she tried, she proved incapable of erasing David from their collective pasts. Once and for all, the record would be set straight.

PART I

THE
ELECTRIFIED
JUDY GARLAND

CHAPTER 1

The Prince

The parents, Peggy and John Jones, were an ordinary couple who kept their feelings strictly to themselves and were disinclined to share them even with each other. At her core Peggy craved upward mobility; John was cautious and frugal. It was a battleground of unfulfilled desires, and their only child inevitably became one of their pawns.

In many ways Peggy's marriage seemed to repeat the pattern of her mother, Margaret's, marriage. Margaret's respectable middle-class family was in the printing business. By marrying James Burns, a staunch Irish Catholic professional soldier, Margaret had doomed herself by marrying beneath her class.

While she dreamed of a life of gentility, picturing herself writing poems and reading Jane Austen, she would never have the resources or the opportunity to make her fantasies come true. Instead she found herself continually pregnant. Margaret and James Burns had six children, five girls and one boy. The prettiest of all was Mary Margaret, called Peggy.

Peggy was rebellious. Her rebellion was aimed at her father, James Burns, a staunch Irish Catholic and a professional soldier, who frequently beat her. In 1927, at the age of fourteen, to the displeasure of James Burns, she left school to work as a nursemaid. She couldn't wait to enter the world, where she expected her beauty to win her the life denied her mother Margaret. An uncle, Tom Burns, owned a stable. There she learned to ride, and she began to socialize with "ladies" and "gentlemen." Her dream seemed to be coming true.

Peggy remained a nursemaid for eight years. While she waited for Prince Charming to come along and rescue her from her menial existence, she bought pretty clothes and went dancing, enjoying the frivolity of it all.

Her quest for excitement led her to join Sir Oswald Mosley's Blackshirts. Peggy seemed to have no understanding of the political meaning of her actions. Mosley was England's most outspoken fascist; fired by hatred, the Blackshirts gathered for rallies and dances and were charged with an insane sense of excitement.

Despite her Blackshirt membership, she fell in love with James Rosenberg, a twenty-four-year-old Jew, son of a successful Parisian furrier. Soon she was pregnant. Rosenberg promised to marry her and then disappeared. On November 5, 1937, Peggy gave birth to a son, Terrance Burns, scandalizing both the household and the neighborhood. James and Margaret Burns had no choice but to take in their daughter's half-Jewish bastard child. They would raise Terry as a strict Roman Catholic, while Peggy was to be sent back to work.

With Britain's entry into World War II, all of England was swept up in the war effort. Peggy worked as a machinist. Still desperate to find the way out, she launched into an affair with a married man. Once again she became pregnant; once again she was abandoned. This child was a girl, and James Burns wanted no part of her. The baby was put up for adoption at the age of ten months.

At the age of thirty-three, with the war over for two years, Peggy got a job as a waitress-usherette at a restaurant-cinema. Then she met John Jones, a slight, blue-eyed, sandy-haired, quiet man.

John Jones was born in Yorkshire. His father had been a successful boot and shoe manufacturer, and John had received a good education. Early in his life his parents died, and he was raised by relatives. On his twenty-first birthday he received an inheritance of 2,000 pounds. He took the money and went to London. Attracted by show business, he became the proprietor of a small Soho nightclub called the Boop-A-Doop. There he met the singer Hilda Sullivan.

He opened a drinking club with her. A partner cheated him, and he lost what was left of his inheritance. John was haunted by the memory of his father, whose money he had lost.

In 1935 he took a steady job at Dr. Bernardo's Home for Boys. When he died in 1969, he had risen to chief administrator.

Some say John was a drinker. He also had a number of affairs.

In 1942, after nine years of marriage to Hilda he had an affair with a nurse, who became pregnant. She had a child, Annette. His sense of responsibility prevailed, and he adopted the baby girl.

When Peggy became pregnant again, Jones invited her to live with him; Hilda, charging adultery, sued him for divorce. David was born illegitimately on January 8, 1947.

Eight months later the divorce was final, and Peggy and John were married. Peggy Jones was finally a legal wife with a legitimate child.

Peggy and John's first home was in North London, a poor neighborhood. While her husband demanded thrift and order, Peggy had fantasies of upward mobility. Marriage encouraged those fantasies to run riot.

A tiny house was for sale in nearby Brixton. It was a step up, and Peggy wanted it. John capitulated.

Soon after David's birth the past reared its head. Peggy's father, James Burns, died of leukemia. Meanwhile, Peggy's mother had grown peculiar. The world had been cruel to her, and so she withdrew from it, living in a world of illusions. The symptoms were those of schizophrenia. Peggy's nine-year-old son, Terry, a handsome and precocious child, could not be left in the care of the dotty old woman. The only respectable thing to do was for Peggy and John to take the child in with them.

It was a decision that made each of them uncomfortable. To Peggy, the child represented the past she wanted to forget. To John, Terry was a constant reminder that other men had succumbed to Peggy's charms but had escaped the responsibility and cost of marriage. Terry was merely tolerated; neither parent seemed to love him. Instead they lavished their attention on David. He was the special one; he was their prince.

At the age of five David was sent to school. On the first day he was so terrified about being left alone that he urinated on the floor.

Terry adored David. The boys shared a bedroom, and David often slept in Terry's bed. Hungry for love, Terry could get it only from an innocent child who basked in the approval eagerly doled out by his older brother. On the one hand Terry played older and wiser brother with David; on the other he treated him as a peer, confiding in him his fear of John Jones. David could not help but identify with Terry's desperation, yet John Jones convinced David that he was far superior to Terry. The emotions aroused by these conflicting messages were too much for a young child to deal with; they had to be repressed. David had to be perfect—or the same thing that was happening to Terry might happen to him.

David's cousin Christine was a little older than he. When her mother became schizophrenic, she came to live with the Joneses, sleeping in the tiny bedroom on the second floor while David and Terry continued to share a larger room below. As if Terry's presence weren't enough of an irritant to John, Christine was yet another reminder of how victimized John was by his marriage. To David her arrival demonstrated the tenuousness of his roots: his mother's sister had gone mad, leaving her daughter homeless.

David, Terry, and Christine often played together. Terry proved a wonderful chess player and artist.

An evening ritual now began. As soon as he returned home after work John would send for David. He took a special interest in all of David's projects and really encouraged him to be a success. John wanted David to be an entertainer, and took him to lots of shows in his capacity as Dr. Bernardo's publicity director, introducing him to the stars who did benefits for his orphanage.

In 1956, Terry, eighteen, left home to do his National Service with the RAF. John Jones seemed glad to see him go; Peggy also seemed relieved. David felt abandoned and had no way to express his feelings. Clearly it was better—and safer—not to have any feelings at all.

This was the year Elvismania swept England. Six Elvis Presley hits would land in England's Top Twenty. Elvis was the antidote to the stultifying atmosphere in David's conventional, suburban, middle-class house. He conjured fantasies of the magical kingdom called America. English working-class teenagers of the 1950s refined their own concept of the American teenager to create a teenage culture of their own.

With *Elvis* and *America* David could shut out his turbulent inner world.

While working-class children liked Elvis's primal energy and basic feelings, David had a subtler response. The records were mysterious, made by a man who was full of unexpected and intriguing surprises. There was not one but many Elvises—the romantic hero, the tough guy, the sensualist. He was a singing actor with an infinite variety of roles. Elvis refused to be pinned down.

Sensing his son's interest in Presley, John Jones got David a small ukelele and then helped him build a string bass out of a plywood tea chest. David didn't learn how to play the instruments; he was deep in the fantasy of having them. Attempting to master them involved the risk of failure; more than anything he could not stand the threat of humiliation.

In 1957, the Jones family moved to the London suburb of Bromley. The new house was neither more spacious nor more attractive than the Brixton residence. But Bromley was a middle-class suburb, a step up. There were two bedrooms on the second floor. John knocked down the wall between them and gave the large new room to his prince. No one asked where Terry would sleep when he returned from the RAF.

David was sent to a new elementary school for his last year before high school. There he made two friends his own age. Geoffrey MacCormack and George Underwood were like surrogate brothers, replacing the absent Terry.

David was afraid of the violence that was part of the rough-and-tumble of the average boy's life. He also disliked games but he craved the security of being one of the boys. He wanted safety and companionship without any danger. He began to learn to be one of the boys, and he acquired a hunger to be macho himself.

David and George belonged to the Bromley Cub Scouts. David took his ukelele and bass with him when the scouts headed out for summer camp on the Isle of Wight; George brought along his guitar. The boys were urged to play. David was terrified; he didn't know how to play. But there was no way out. He and George sang "Hang Down Your Head, Tom Dooley." While they sang, they acted the roles of musicians so convincingly they got a rousing reception. Acting had been more than enough.

In the fall of 1958 eleven-year-old David entered the all-male, 650-student Bromley Technical High School, a two-story building replete with elegant marble staircases. On the first day of school John Jones walked his son to school.

The first two years of a student's five-year stay at Bromley Tech comprised a basic curriculum. Each boy then spent three years in a specialized program to prepare him for college or a profession in the trades. In England's class-oriented, stratified society, such schools as Bromley Tech were designed to seal a young man's fate before he ever had a chance to investigate the world.

Bromley Tech stressed conformity, and the students were required to wear uniforms. During his first two years David was bland and ordinary; the school was just as dreary as his home.

Then the family moved to another small house in Bromley. Now twelve, David had taken to sleeping over at the houses of classmates. He was drawn to households where there was love and a sense of family. As an adult he would create "families" around himself, families in which the impotent child of his youth was replaced by a man who demanded total control—a man very much like his father.

By now he was aware of the tragedy that haunted Peggy's side of the family. Her mother, Margaret Burns, was a weak woman who, as she grew older, had turned her dissatisfaction with life against herself. Three of her five daughters seemed to have inherited their mother's disposition toward mental illness. Even though she believed she was one of life's great victims, thick-skinned Peggy, who had a survivor's instinct, would keep her sanity. She passed her narcissism on to her son.

David often played the victim, suffering endlessly because his feelings were so easily hurt. Yet he would move on, refusing to stop, no matter how long it took, until he got exactly where he wanted to go. Projecting the illusion of fragility, he would prove that his skin was even thicker than his mother's as he alternated the roles of victim and survivor.

At the end of 1959, in the middle of David's second year at Bromley Tech, just before he turned thirteen, Terry returned home from his tour of duty. David hung on his every word.

Peggy would have none of it. She told Terry that there was no room for him in the house as his bedroom had been given to David. Nor did she want to upset John Jones. Terry would have to go.

Terry and David were shocked by her abrupt dismissal of her son. David watched and said nothing while Terry went to live with an aunt. The past had made his parents uncomfortable, and they had seen fit to erase it.

Then Christine's mother died and Christine was shunted around among nine foster homes. Again David watched in silence. If he allowed his feelings to pour out, he thought, he could never stop them. The force of his emotions was powerful enough to drive him mad, and in a family in which real madness lurked, the danger of letting go was compounded. An impenetrable mask had to be clamped over feelings, clamped there forever.

In the fall of 1960, David was one of thirty boys to enter the Bromley Tech Art Form, where he was instructed in the basics of painting, drawing, typography, and graphic design. David's master was Owen Frampton, whose son Peter, the future rock star, would enter Bromley Tech the following year. Frampton was the kind of male figure David adored; the teacher wholeheartedly supported the students' quests for individuality: he had no qualms about violating the dress code for Bromley Tech masters. Here was a surrogate father who had the imagination David's own father lacked and stood at odds with conformity.

George Underwood, who had been in the Cub Scouts with David, was also in the Art Form, and the boys resumed their friendship. They became friendly with a third boy, Michael Todd, whom they called Sweeney after the Demon Barber of Fleet Street. The trio developed a reputation for rebelliousness; they were caught smoking behind the bicycle shed and buying pints of ale at lunchtime.

The first assignment given the boys after they learned to set hot-metal type was to make themselves a business card. On his card David named himself LUTHER J. The fact that David had given himself an alias fascinated the other boys; their interest excited him, and the excitement propelled him forward. From that moment on he gave himself a succession of imaginative names.

Even though Terry was living with an aunt, he often visited David. He introduced David to an American phenomenon: the beatnik writers and their passion for jazz. David eagerly read Jack Kerouac's *On the Road*. He marveled at the beatniks, who were rebellious, flouted authority, and had declared war against society, conventional jobs, and family. One of the great enemies in beatnik literature was the image of the mother, the symbol of routine and everything that one ought to hate. Mother sapped one's energy and kept one tied down. By eliminating mother, at least one had a chance of survival.

Sometimes Terry took David to London to hang out at the Soho jazz clubs. Terry's favorite performer was a saxophonist named Ronnie Ross.

A few days later David spotted a white plastic saxophone in a music store window. No one at Bromley Tech had ever seen an instrument like that; he knew the boys would go wild when they saw it. He told his father about it, and John bought it for him. David found Ronnie Ross's phone number in the telephone book, called him up, and arranged for lessons.

David took a lesson a week for four months—enough to learn the fundamentals. He did not want to become a great saxophone virtuoso, he just wanted to know enough to wow the other boys. After sixteen lessons, he packed up his instrument and went home to wait for the appropriate moment with which to surprise his classmates with his newfound musicianship.

The boys never knew what to expect from David. Other boys wore the same white shirt to school two or three days in a row; David insisted on a freshly laundered and pressed white shirt every day—his shirt had to be the whitest of all. When the style in footwear changed from round-toed shoes to pointed-toed shoes, he came to school with his fingernails filed to points to match the points on his shoes. One day he appeared with an orange streak in his hair. Later, complaining that he was not blond enough, he came to school with his hair cut into a brush cut, an imitation of an American crew cut, and colored bright yellow.

Obsessed with America, David played with children of servicemen in order to dazzle his schoolmates with the latest information about the exotic American teenager. Even though the boy hated games, he learned all about American football on the radio. He even wrote to the U.S. Embassy to gather more information.

An invitation arrived summoning him to the embassy. There he was dressed in an American football uniform and given a football. A picture was taken and circulated to American and English newspapers with the caption "Limey kid digs American football." He loved being dressed up and having his picture taken.

The next day he showed up in school in his new costume. The boys were suitably awestruck.

As soon as they discovered girls, Sweeney and David spent hours in the Bromley North Wimpy Bar ogling any female who walked by. Sweeney would spend weekends at David's house, and on Saturday nights the young teenagers would sneak out, take the train to London, try to pick up girls, and then catch the milk train home at four in the morning.

Reed-thin, fragile, somewhat feminine in appearance, David could also be extremely cocky and arrogant. The combination of masculine and feminine elements in his personality and appearance gave him an edge over his classmates. Girls were curious about him, and soon one after the other began to succumb to his charms.

His many girl friends were the prettiest as well as the oldest. "The women he went out with were beyond my reach," recalls former classmate Michael Todd. "I think a lot had to do with his presence. He always went out with older women. When you're fifteen and she's eighteen, it's a big deal. David was a great womanizer in high school."

Sexual conquests made David feel irresistible, and in control. His need for these feelings propelled him toward the promiscuous social and sexual pattern that would dominate his private life as an adult.

His attempt to steal George Underwood's girl friend led to a fistfight that landed David in the hospital with a terribly wounded eye. When he recovered, one of his pupils had become enlarged and turned gray, giving his face a mysterious quality he would learn to use to his advantage.

Peggy Jones disapproved of her highly sexed teenaged son. Yet she had taught him to be seductive by telling him constantly how much prettier he was than all the other boys. Her prettiness had been the only tool available to her as she made her way in the world, but it had not gotten her what she wanted. Now she objected strenuously to David, who seemed in his own way to be following her pattern. He had to do better than his mother; he had to be respectable.

In 1962 the London music scene was undergoing a dramatic change. Intrigued by American blues and R-and-B music, young English musicians like Mick Jagger, John Mayall, Long John Baldrey, Ginger Baker, and Jack Bruce had begun to gather in a few select underground cellar clubs to emulate this music. Intense guitar licks, shrill harmonica riffs, and raw vocals dominated the sound.

During that summer, when David was fifteen, the Rolling Stones made their debut. By the beginning of 1963 they were a national sensation.

Long-haired, dirty-looking, and angry, the Stones, with their Chicago-style blues and soul-sound combinations, were England's answer to America's beatniks, a real slap in the face to the middle-class backgrounds that had spawned them.

George Underwood played guitar in a group called George and the Dragons, named after the local Bromley pub. At school during recesses David and George sang together. They loved Buddy Holly songs and the ultrafashionable American blues. Then George invited David to join his band. The boys wanted to model themselves after the first generation of American rock-and-roll guitar heros. They were stunned by David's white plastic saxophone; soon a rumor spread through the school that David had been taking lessons for the past three years. He *had* found the way to be different. The group head-lined a PTA show at Christmas and brought down the house.

At sixteen, David had already begun to spin larger-than-life myths about himself.

Then George and David formed another band, the five-piece Kon-rads. David often fell asleep in class because he had been up the night before playing in the band.

With his friend Sweeney Todd he went to the Bromley Court Hotel for its Sunday-night jazz club. They also went to the Chistel Hearth Caves, a series of caves in which jazz bands played. It seemed very beatniklike there.

In the middle of his last year at Bromley Tech the Beatles released "Love Me Do." David was the first person in his class to have a copy. Fascinated by John Lennon's harmonica part, he immediately learned it. By copying Lennon's playing he felt as if he were a Beatle.

David wore his hair like a Teddy Boy, which alarmed the other members of the Kon-rads. He asked the other boys to dress up like Teds, but they refused. To supplement his allowance and small income David had been working on Saturdays in the local record store. He and George Underwood studied all the blues records they could find. They abandoned the Kon-rads and formed a trio called the Hooker Brothers (named for the blues artist John Lee Hooker) and played wherever they could.

Under aliases such as Dave's Reds and Blues, they got other jobs. Each group played a different style, depending on what the name of the group was. David was not married to any musical style; the attention and the excitement were what kept him focused.

By now Terry had begun to drink. The mental illness that would eventually drive him to suicide in 1985 had begun to surface. Whenever David saw him he rambled on about his misery and the fate of the world. David told Terry about his bands, and Terry turned against him, accusing him of violating the musical purity of jazz, and being "as bad as the rest of them." David was shocked and hurt by his brother's anger. He had idealized Terry, and now his brother had failed him. Rather than express his rage, David ignored his brother. Terry would be replaced by "brothers" who would never turn against David, brothers he could replace.

"Mr. Jones," called the headmaster. David Jones stood up.

The headmaster faced the first graduating class of Bromley Technical High School. A Bromley Tech tradition was being instituted that morning. As the headmaster called the roll, each boy was to stand and state his future occupation.

"Mr. Jones," repeated the headmaster. He peered at David.

At sixteen the public theatrical gesture had already become part of David's personality. There was an unmistakable glint in those odd, hypnotic, unmatched eyes.

"I want to be a pop idol," he announced, and slowly took his seat.

A ripple of shock ran through the room. The silence was stunning. This was not the occupation for which the Bromley masters had trained their students.

In a few seconds' time the shock turned to scorn. How presumptuous was this bland, ordinary boy! Out of the corners of their eyes the other boys stared contemptuously at him.

David stared straight ahead, a faint smile on his lips. He knew the entire room was focused on him. He had wanted their attention, and he had known how to get it. He had spoken those seven words with startling intensity, as if the intensity could convince the others that his was a dream that would come true.

After telling his career officer that he wanted to be a jazz saxophonist, David was offered a job manufacturing harps in a Bromley factory. He refused.

Like all the other Art Form graduates who did not want to go to art college, he looked up the London advertising agencies in the phone book, took his portfolio from one to the other, and searched for a job.

He landed a job as a junior commercial artist at the Design Group Ltd, and worked as a messenger and tea-boy, occasionally doing the odd layout or preliminary sketches for a new campaign.

He wasn't happy.

CHAPTER 2

The Next
Mick Jagger

L es Conn, described by some as "a young hustler running with
the London avant-garde," worked as a talent scout for the
Beatles' music publisher, Dick James. A letter had been forwarded
to him by a friend, John Bloom, a young, bearded tycoon who made
his money selling washing machines and who was also one of London's most publicized party-givers.

"With your money you could do for us what Brian Epstein did
for the Beatles, and you could make another million for yourself,"
David wrote to Bloom in a letter that had been engineered and
supervised by John Jones. He asked for several hundred pounds to
buy new equipment for his band, Davie Jones and the King Bees.

John Jones had watched for four months as his son and his band
struggled to make ends meet. He kept David's accounts, handled his
bank account, and did his correspondence. Jones was exceptionally
tidy and prided himself on his organization of domestic matters. By
helping David he thought he was doing the right thing and never
realized he was teaching his son to expect others always to take care
of his business for him. David never developed an understanding of
what money really means and why it is so important.

In the spring of 1964 that letter was right on target. To the
amazement of English music-business entrepreneurs, four Beatles
singles—"From Me to You," "She Loves You," "I Want to Hold
Your Hand," and "Can't Buy Me Love"—had gone to the top of
the charts. For the first time in English cultural history, working-class youths were being presented as free spirits, a phenomenon that
eluded the businessmen. They were obsessed by Brian Epstein. It

seemed to them that the Beatles' manager had conquered the world by taking four raggedy Liverpudlians, giving them a cute mop-top image, and teaching them how to make the meaningless fun that is commonly known as entertainment.

Each manager fantasized being the next Brian Epstein. Before the Beatles it had been virtually impossible for a group outside London to receive a recording contract from one of London's four major record labels. Now, eager to become the next Beatles or Rolling Stones, blues-playing groups poured into London from all over. The record companies and the businessmen had never been in a situation like this, and they were overwhelmed. There was plenty of money to be made, but they did not have the imagination to know who to sign to management deals and recording contracts. Young people would have to tell them what other young people might like.

David's letter was exactly the kind of directive they were waiting for.

The band was summoned to audition for Les Conn. Meeting the talent scout for the Beatles' publisher filled David with the kind of excitement he hungered for. He would have to be really "on" to convince Conn that his destiny depended upon David's.

David's eyes gleamed. His answers to Conn's questions were articulate and good-humored. David had funny teeth and his face was too long, and there was also an awkward look about him, but on occasions like these the awkwardness melted away and he projected a quality of fragile beauty. The businessmen believed that pop success depended on capturing the imaginations of girl fans; Conn's thinking was no different. David was angelic-looking but also extremely ambitious, the perfect combination.

The band ran through its R-and-B repertoire. Conn liked what he heard. There was nothing original about either the group or its music, but he convinced John Bloom to hire them to play at an anniversary party given by the mogul.

The King Bees had played only two numbers when John Bloom stepped forward to stop the show. The washing machine magnate hated the band. His displeasure did not deter Les Conn; adults always hate the music young people like. Overcome by the magical thinking of the moment, he appointed himself manager of Davie Jones and the King Bees. He would make David a star.

The next day an audition was arranged at Decca, the Rolling Stones's label. Conn had told Decca this group would be the next Stones. The King Bees passed the audition. In a hit-or-miss atmosphere twenty new groups were recorded each week by the major recording companies in the hope that one of them would be the next Beatles or Stones.

Suddenly, less than a year after his high school graduation, David had the opportunity to be the next Mick Jagger.

Convinced of his talent, David quit his job at the advertising agency. Sixteen and jobless, he was forced to live at home.

Peggy was furious; John, although he was nervous and confused, supported his son's decision.

To Peggy it appeared that David, a promiscuous boy who slept with every girl he met, had inherited the worst parts of her family tree. He was as doomed as the rest of the Burns family.

David was incapable of tolerating criticism—he found it threatening. His mother's behavior unnerved him. But he had become expert at masking his feelings.

Whenever he needed money, David turned to Les Conn. Conn had the idea of getting money from Dick James. The plan was to have James sign David to a publishing deal and give him an advance against royalties. Like Les Conn, Dick James wanted to become the next Brian Epstein. Nothing less then the next Beatles would do, and David was summarily dismissed.

Next Conn hauled the King Bees to the offices of Mickie Most, the independent record producer/entrepreneur who was soon to have the first of a string of hits with the Animals. Most didn't care for David, but he liked George Underwood, whom he thought had more sex appeal and would make a greater impression on the girls. Underwood, with his sensitive blue eyes, pale complexion, and completely masculine personality, was more conventionally sensual than David. He was given the stage name Calvin Jones, and a date was set for him to cut his first solo single.

David and George would never again be in a group together.

Three weekly tabloids, *Melody Maker*, *New Musical Express*, and *Disc Weekly*, published national music business news and features as well as the chart positions of the Top Fifty hits. They were almost as important as radio in supporting a new artist.

David read them faithfully. More than anything he wanted to see his name in the Top Ten. The newspapers also kept him abreast of the latest pop-music trends. In order to get his imagination flowing he needed stimulation, which came from knowing what was bright and new.

Bob Dylan's first English concert that May had received enormous coverage in the music press. Hundreds of curious fans had ringed the Royal Festival Hall and slept overnight in front of the building to get an opportunity to hear the American folksinger. Their reaction had been tumultuous.

David had never heard Dylan; after reading about him, a friend gave David *Bob Dylan* and *Freewheelin' Bob Dylan*. David listened to them carefully; the attention received by Dylan demanded that he discover what Dylan was all about. Perhaps he could find the way to turn himself into Bob Dylan.

The Decca recording session took less than an hour; in those days that was all the time a new group was given in which to cut two sides. The King Bees recorded its reworking of "Liza Jane," a black folk song. It was an overwrought and uninspiring performance, but also a demonstration of how carefully David had studied what was popular. The rawness and harsh rhythmic pulse of the record echoed the Rolling Stones; the lead instrumental lines copied the Beatles.

But the record bombed.

Failing caused David such pain that the truth had to be rewritten. What *really* happened, he told himself, was that the King Bees had failed him. They were at art college and were only playing at becoming pop stars. This became David's rationale for erasing them from his life.

Les Conn was still David's only real contact in the music business. David continued to go to the talent scout's office whenever he needed money, and Conn and he began their search for a new group. David's mop-top had grown out and he looked like a carbon copy of Brian Jones of the Rolling Stones. A group called the Manish Boys was looking for a lead singer. They played R and B and took their names from a Muddy Waters lyric, just as the Stones had. A lead singer who looked like Brian Jones seemed ideal.

Conn escorted David to the audition, and David got the job.

Soon after David joined the Manish Boys, Conn, explaining that the expenses were just too great, resigned as his manager.

David mustered all his energies and made the rounds of the music agencies on Denmark Street, looking for work for the Manish Boys. In November, three months after he joined the group, the Arthur Howes Agency got the struggling group six dates on the bottom of a bill headed by Gene Pitney and Gerry and the Pacemakers.

A fourteen-year-old girl sat in the front row of the London Club, watching the Manish Boys. She couldn't take her eyes off the lead singer. He was gorgeous. His dyed yellow hair tumbled to his waist. It was the same length as her peroxide-blond hair.

After the set the girl made her way to the back of the club. She stood in front of a mirror brushing her long hair. She was exceptionally beautiful; she had often been told she looked like an angel. She had huge breasts, of which she was very proud.

A hand reached over and took the brush from her. She watched in the mirror as David stood behind her and brushed her hair. He was even better in close-up.

His touch was gentle. The way he brushed her hair seemed an act of worship. Their eyes met in the mirror, and he smiled. There was something about those odd eyes—she was mesmerized. She was used to boys making passes at her, but David's sensuality was incredible.

"Could I walk you home tonight?" he asked.

She couldn't wait.

Her name was Dana Gillespie. She was a baroness, the daughter of Austrian royalty. Later on, she would be England's water-ski champion, and her pictures would appear in all the newspapers. As a child Dana had gone to upper-class schools, but now she was attending a stage school where she met girls from entirely different social classes from her own.

Because they both lived at home Dana had to sneak David past her parents' bedroom into her bedroom on the third floor of their London townhouse late at night. After they made love David showed her chords on an old Spanish guitar and encouraged her songwriting ambitions.

He was a lover and a friend. He would disappear and then turn up weeks later, resuming their affair as if they had never been apart. He didn't feel trapped—nor did he allow real feelings to intrude. He confided in her that there were other girls, making it seem as if they were brother and sister even though they were sleeping together. It was a way of guaranteeing that no real closeness would develop. David had reached her through her vanity and fantasies. He had an innate sense of what he had to do to enthrall everyone he met.

The Manish Boys weren't getting enough work, and they desperately needed money. David was the son of a press agent. What would such a son do? Such a stunt would get the group's name into the newspapers and on television; it would also impress John Jones and prove that his investment was worthwhile.

David formed the "International League for the Preservation of Animal Filament" to defend the rights of long-haired musicians. He hoped this would get him media attention, and then job offers would begin to pour in from those who wanted to see this defender of musician's rights.

Despite some small mentions, no one cared very much about the problems a local, unknown musician endured simply because he had long hair.

The Arthur Howes Agency also represented the Kinks, who had recently landed on the charts with "You Really Got Me." Their first single had been produced by Shel Talmy. Talmy, like Les Conn and Dick James, also wanted to build a music business empire. A relatively unknown American producer, he had become a Decca house producer in London.

Interested in getting in on the ground floor, he signed up unknowns whom he would turn into stars by giving them hits. He and these soon-to-be-stars would become partners. The Manish Boys were unknown enough to fulfill his requirements; besides, their leader was an intense Brian Jones look-alike.

Talmy listened to the band's choices, a blues tune called "I Pity the Fool" and an original composition, "Take My Tip." A decision was made instantly. The lead guitar would be played by Jimmy Page, already a legendary figure in English music-business circles. Talmy used Page whenever a group's guitarist didn't make it. Rumor had it Page had played on the Kinks' early records.

At first, David was mortified. But then he realized that in order for him to look his best he needed the best musicians, superior players devoted to supporting his personal quest. The Manish Boys were not those players.

Talmy brought the record to Decca, already burned once by David Jones. Decca didn't want him or the record. While Talmy hunted for a deal for the single, he also prepared to go into the studio with another group about to cut its first single under its new name. The group was the Who.

It took considerable time for Shel Talmy to place the Manish Boys' record; it was finally released on March 5, 1965, on Parlaphone.

It was also a failure. And David had not received the star billing on the disk. The curtain was rung down on the Manish Boys. David erased the past and became a brand-new entity ready to start again.

CHAPTER 3

Bowie Is Born

The Gioconda Coffee Bar on Denmark Street was a hangout usually jammed with pop groups, publishers, agents, and recording studio personnel. There David played the role of the star. His charm enabled him to make friends with such musicians as Ray Davies and Donovan.

But there were times when he couldn't bear to walk into the Gioconda. Everywhere he looked he saw success, reminding him of his own failure. Wearing the mask of success every time he stepped outside the house exhausted him. On those days he was without ambition or focus. All he wanted to do was sleep and have someone take care of him.

In March 1965, two months after he turned eighteen and within a month after the collapse of the Manish Boys, David met a band at the Gioconda who called themselves the Lower Third. Billing themselves as "South-East Kent's Best Rhythm-and-Blues Group," they worked as a dance band and played cover versions of James Brown tunes. They hoped that adding a vocalist to the group would let them escape from the world of discothèques and become a legitimate recording and performing group.

They mistook David for Keith Relf, lead singer of the Yardbirds. With his striking good looks, David had "lead singer" written all over him. The fact that he had made two records was another thing in his favor. The only thing to do was ask him to join the group.

After an audition in which he competed against Steve Marriott (who would eventually join Small Faces), the Lower Third became Davy Jones and the Lower Third. There would be no mistakes this time. The band knew from the beginning that it was David's band

and that it would be his stardust that would rescue them from oblivion.

David immediately issued a press release announcing that he had joined the Lower Third. Lead guitarist Dennis Taylor was given the name Tea-Cup, while bass player Graham Rivens was called Death. Rivens drove the group's van; the dual roles of bass player and driver gave him the look of death warmed over. David announced the imminent release of a record, "Born of the Night." After all, he had worked with Shel Talmy; Talmy was bound to produce his new group. The producer was still in the market for unknowns but passed when he heard the song.

No one could ignore the impact the Who was having at the Marquee Club. At the beginning of April, just after David joined the Lower Third, the Who's first single, "I Can't Explain," entered the Top Ten. The thing to do was to copy the Who.

The Lower Third grew louder and louder, coating its sound with earsplitting Who-style feedback. David insisted that the show build to a devastating climax, and it ended with a crashing version of "Mars" from *The Planet Suite*. There were even odder choices of material, including a thunderous version of "Chim-Chim-Cherie" from *Mary Poppins*. Not really a rock-and-roller at heart, David surprised the group on stage by interrupting the set to perform solo acoustic numbers.

David was most comfortable singing and strumming an acoustic guitar. Without the discipline really to master an instrument, he, like so many other writers who really were folksingers, had no difficulty learning a handful of chords. Unlike typical English folksingers, he was not interested in using the American folk vocabulary to create songs of protest. He wanted a hit single.

During rehearsals David strummed his guitar and scribbled fragments of lyrics. The group would work together until a song emerged. Replacement drummer Phil Lancaster also sat at the piano, playing odd and peculiar chords at random.

"What's that? Hold that!" David exclaimed when he heard a chord structure that might make a song. The songs composed around these random chords proved hard to learn because David's unlikely choices followed no standard progressions.

The Lower Third was broke and grateful for even small sums of money earned from radio commercials for such American products as Youthquake Clothing. American sponsors were eager to co-opt the Mod sound in order to move American merchandise. Luckily David's press release got them a handful of jobs, the first at a South Coast club in Birmingham.

During their rehearsal, the Who, headliners at the club, walked into the room. After listening for a few minutes, Pete Townshend approached the stage.

"Whose stuff are you doing?" he asked.

"Ours," David replied.

Townshend stared at David. "That's a bit of cheeseoff," he snapped. "It sounds a lot like mine."

The band traveled around in an old ambulance, in which they would drive around Piccadilly Circus searching for girls. The van was ideal for sex because it had no windows. They would also pick up girls after gigs, bringing them back to the ambulance.

David, their leader and their brother, helped the group pack up their equipment and stack it into the ambulance. When it was too late to drive David back to Bromley, he slept beside them on the mattresses in the rear of the vehicle. They could have been brothers.

It was an unspoken fact that gay men controlled large segments of the English music publishing and management businesses. Homosexual Brian Epstein had created the all-powerful image of the Beatles, and homosexuals had created the image of many other top groups.

They all knew one another. They frequented the same bars and restaurants, where they showed off their latest pretty young boyfriends; they seduced the teenage musicians who came to London in search of fame. Often they were attracted to the macho heterosexual musicians they managed; their efforts on behalf of these musicians were, among other things, acts of love. The amount of money they had begun to make had taken them completely by surprise, as had their ability to challenge the stranglehold England's four major record companies, each with its own all-powerful in-house A&R man—a talent scout with the power to make deals—had on the record industry.

Among them they began to promulgate their own myth. The

fact they were attracted to boys, they felt, gave them a real advantage over music business heterosexuals. They, and only they, really understood how to create an image sexually attractive to young girls.

Young musicians took the power and myth of the homosexuals in their stride. Most of them had played or hung out in the Soho music clubs, where there was a lot of teenage male prostitution. Mod boys, stoned on pills and in need of endless supplies of cash to buy the latest clothes, often found prostitution the easiest and quickest way to earn enough pocket money to finance their extravagant investment in style. Homosexuality was an intrinsic part of the music-business scene.

One of the men David met as he prowled Denmark Street looking for work for the Lower Third was Ralph Horton. An owlish-looking man in his late twenties, Horton worked as an agent at the King's Agency.

David stared Horton straight in the eye. It was as if Horton was the only man in the world who could help the teenager. The intensity was startling; heterosexual men never approached other men with this much intensity. Yet David's narcissism cut across the conventional boundaries of sex. He flirted by suggesting intimacy, and anyone—male or female—was subjected to this unusual brand of seductiveness.

Horton set out to impress the boy by telling him about his friendship with the Moody Blues; their first single, "Go Now!," had been a Top Ten hit at the beginning of the year. Horton also knew the Moody Blues' first producer, Tony Hatch; Hatch was Pye Records' head of A&R as well as the producer/writer of Petula Clark's international hit, "Downtown."

It was a moment in which image seemed as important as music, if not more important. David Jones needed an up-to-date image, and Horton wanted to give him one. His hair was too long. Mod was "in," and this boy could be transformed into a Mod beauty, one who could magnetize the world.

Horton sensed that he could capitalize on David's narcissism. David craved being looked at, and he had no inhibitions about changing his appearance. He liked being everybody's sexual fantasy.

With the help of two dancer friends, Horton got to work. David was given a carefully sculptured Mod haircut. His face seemed rounder and his features softer, giving him a new sensuality. He looked even younger than his eighteen years. Dressed in the dapper, well-tailored jackets, shirts, and floral-patterned ties that epitomized the Mod look, he was now a Mod sensation. David Jones seemed to have found *his* homosexual, the one who would give him an image.

Finally, at the beginning of the summer, almost four months after David had joined the Lower Third, he was able to present Shel Talmy with two songs Talmy thought were worth recording. The Who's "I Can't Explain" had run its course, and Talmy was ready to attempt to duplicate its success.

The new record was an example of the offhanded sound of live performance that Talmy loved; it sounded like an elaborate demo. "You've Got the Habit of Leaving" was a blatant Who rip-off, with David doing his best to copy Who lead singer Roger Daltrey. The B-side, "Baby Loves That Way," sounded like Herman's Hermits, but the melody was listenable and coherent. That was a real improvement and an important musical development for David.

Released on Parlaphone on August 20, 1965, it was Talmy's second and last failure with David.

Horton knew that he had to keep tantalizing David in order to hold his interest. David was lovely, bright, and hardworking but he was also promiscuous. As long as they shared the same dream and Horton worked on making that dream come true, he felt assured of David's loyalty. Horton was a go-getter; he supplied the excitement David craved. He had to keep things exciting by whetting David's fantasies about his own future.

Horton had two connections, the Moody Blues and hit-making record producer Tony Hatch. First he called in his favors with the Moody Blues and co-promoted three summer weekend concerts headlined by the Moody Blues with Davie Jones and the Lower Third fourth on the bill. He also began to entice Tony Hatch into signing a record deal with David. In the middle of September Hatch gave David a six-month contract.

Horton took David to Sparta Music Publishing Company, which gave David a one-year contract guaranteeing him a ten-pound advance for each song it published. But twenty-five dollars was not going to do either of them any good. Horton needed someone with cash, and lots of it. In order to keep David's interest he had to materialize such a person.

Ken Pitt managed Manfred Mann as well as the successful singer Crispian St. Peters; he had also promoted Bob Dylan's English tour. Pitt was a successful press agent. Horton hoped that perhaps he and Pitt could co-manage David, with Pitt supplying the financing. Horton called Pitt and arranged for a meeting. Horton proudly displayed the results of a photo session of Davie Jones and the Lower Third.

In the pictures David stood center stage at all times; the band members were there to support him. In their Mod gear they looked like ordinary young men, but David effortlessly carried the style. He was a natural actor and had easily assumed the role Horton had created for him.

Pitt listened to Horton's hard sell and sensed his personal involvement with David, but was too much of a gentleman to say anything. Instead he made polite excuses. A "Davey Jones" was playing the Artful Dodger in the New York production of Lionel Bart's musical *Oliver!*. Pitt also said he wanted a performer who would be a long-term proposition and could do theatre and films.

Horton replied that David had the same dream. At that time David had never seen a musical play.

Pitt ended the meeting by saying he was too busy to consider a client until after the New Year; Horton would have to continue his search for money elsewhere.

Horton told David he needed a new last name. David decided that it ought to begin with the letter "B," as in Beatles. On his first record, he wanted to be both John Lennon and Mick Jagger. Jagger had said that in Old English, "jagger" meant "knife." David's new last name would begin with "B" and be the name of a knife. He came up with Bowie. The Bowie knife had been named after Jim Bowie, a nineteenth-century American soldier and adventurer. "Bowie" was perfect: it combined the Beatles and Rolling Stones and was also American. David Bowie erased the past. Davie Jones, his failures and family life, no longer existed.

Whenever he was asked about his change of name, all he said was, "I was someone else before that."

The Lower Third felt that Ralph Horton was separating David from them. David was dedicated, hardworking, and creative. But as soon as a gig was over, he and Horton disappeared. It was not a family any more. Horton had even made them sign an agreement giving up any record royalties the group might earn.

David's onstage behavior had also begun to puzzle them. As he grew more involved with Horton and his image grew increasingly Mod, he became more effeminate during performances. Why would anyone want to be so "queer" in public? They did not understand that it was a demand for attention as well as an attempt to translate his offstage performance of queerness into an onstage statement.

He also wanted them to follow his lead. They used women's hair spray to make their hairdos more baroque. Then David suggested they also wear makeup.

"We don't want to be queers," they announced.

Unsophisticated and good-natured, they didn't catch on that they were being replaced by Horton and his offer of excitement and a dream for the future—David's future. The band was there merely to help make the dream come true.

By mid-November Tony Hatch still had not set a date to record the Lower Third. The little money the band earned was spent as quickly as it came in. Horton needed money, so he and David went off to see Ray Cook, a director of a heating company.

Horton was quite persuasive, and by the time he was done pitching, Cook, convinced he would become even richer, had donated 1,500 pounds to the cause. A contract was quickly drawn up giving Cook 10 percent of David's earnings for the next three years, with the vague provision that Cook would continue to supply an unspecified amount of "financial investment."

David and Horton were jubilant. They finally had their backer. And when the 1,500 pounds evaporated with amazing speed, the only thing to do was hit Cook up again. Horton told David to go it alone; it would not seem like business. David would have to convince Cook that he was rescuing a helpless boy. It was an acting job.

David was breathlessly sincere with Cook. He spoke with total conviction. At the end of the meeting, check in hand, he smiled sweetly at his patron. Then he quickly headed out the door.

David needed someone else to copy. His intuition led him to Anthony Newley. More an actor than a singer, Newley had been the first to sing in a modern Cockney accent, acting the part of a member of the working-class revolution led by the Beatles. By copying

Newley's approach, David hoped that he, too, would appear to be what he most definitely was not—a passionate, rebellious, music-making member of the pop upheaval that had been sweeping England for the past four years.

That Newley's voice did not belong in rock and roll was something David did not realize. Yet by imitating Newley he had stumbled on a fruitful contradiction. Years would pass before he discovered the contradictions that would define his career and make him a rock-and-roll original.

As 1965 was coming to an end and David was about to turn nineteen, Tony Hatch finally took the Lower Third into the studio. "Can't Help Thinking About Me" was an example of pure teen melodrama and no different from the horde of teen-angst records being released on both sides of the Atlantic. A boy has committed an unnamable but presumably heinous crime; his family is in disgrace; he's on the run. But there was a twist—Bowie's boy didn't care.

The record was scheduled to be released on January 14, 1966. Horton thought it needed a send-off. He wangled ninety-five pounds out of Ray Cook for a press party and a press agent to publicize the record. It made no difference. David suffered his fourth failure.

At the end of the month they were scheduled to play at the Bromel Club in David's hometown of Bromley. It was a benefit for Bromley Technical High School and David's chance to become a local pop idol. He would show those who had found him ordinary and bland how much of a Mod peacock he had become.

Just before the performance Horton told the band that they would be working for nothing; he needed all of their money to pay his rent. The band refused to go on and headed for a pub to debate the issue. When they returned they had not changed their minds.

David burst into tears. Didn't they realize how important this was to him? Didn't they realize that he had to prove that he was a hero? The needs of the band made no sense to him.

He watched as the band walked out on him. He determined that this would *never* happen again, and the Lower Third was erased.

Within a week a new band was pulled together. They were called the Buzz and by mid-February they had begun to play dates. At the end of the month, in Chelmsford, David collapsed on stage. Exhaustion was given as the reason. The Chelmsford newspapers ignored the incident. Great stars fainted from exhaustion, and they got reams of publicity. He had begun to act like a great star, but he wasn't getting results.

Then Ralph Horton persuaded Ray Cook to give him 250 pounds to buy David's recorded imitation of the Who onto the charts. Cook, still entranced, forked over the money. The record appeared on the *Melody Maker* chart in position 45. Over the next three weeks it climbed to 26. Horton asked for another 250 pounds. This time Cook turned him down. The next week the record had disappeared.

Still, being on the charts had had an effect. After being refused earlier by "Ready! Steady! Go!," he was now allowed to appear. Steve Marriott, also on the show, watched as the awkward David lip-synched to his semihit.

Tony Hatch also decided to try again with David. The Buzz recorded "Do Anything You Say" and "Good Morning Girl," both dreadful songs. Each band member received a flat 9 pounds for playing on the sessions, with no royalties. The record, released on April Fool's Day, met sudden death. Hatch's company, Pye Records, were no-nonsense hit-makers. They quickly lost interest in an artist who had failed five times.

Ray Cook had spent close to 3,090 pounds in four months. All he had to show for it was a flop record. He suddenly demanded the return of all his money. Horton's finances were so bad the electricity in his basement had been shut off. Bill collectors hounded him.

That spring the Buzz was hired to participate in a series of Sunday afternoon concerts at the Marquee Club, the scene of the Who's Thursday night triumphs. David decided to call these performances the Bowie Showboat. The audience would be made up of a hundred parents and children; it was family entertainment. It was also David's biggest break and his first chance to build an all-important London club audience.

A week before the Bowie Showboat series was to begin, Horton, desperately broke, again approached Ken Pitt. Pitt seemed ideal. Crispian St. Peters, whom Pitt managed, had a record zooming up the charts, and Bob Dylan had recently completed another staggeringly successful tour of England, which had been promoted by Pitt. Horton did not know it, but Pitt had also just been offered the management of Marc Bolan.

This time Pitt agreed to go to the Marquee Club. David knew that he had to give his best show ever. Then he had to meet Pitt and be at his most entrancing. The entire afternoon was to be a spectacular act of seduction.

Ken Pitt stood at the back of the Marquee watching Bowie. In his early forties, he was unlike the other, far younger, businessmen that Bowie had met. He was a professional; his sensibilities were not those of a young entrepreneur. He believed in old-fashioned craft; the traditions of show business and professionalism meant more to him than making a killing. There was no tradition of rebellion in British show business, and there was no rebellion in Ken Pitt. Unlike the Beatles and Rolling Stones and their managers, he didn't think that old-fashioned show business was corny.

Pitt watched from the back of the room. David had an actor's intensity. Pitt loved the theater; he loved actors. He did not like anyone who dared to be just plain folks on stage. The theater was a place for magic, not a duplication of a working-class living room. David Bowie was magic.

When the set was over, David stepped forward. A spotlight hit him, and he looked beautiful and assured. Then he sang Rodgers and Hammerstein's "You'll Never Walk Alone." Gerry and the Pacemakers had had a Number One hit with it when David was in his last year in high school, and he was copying their success. But Pitt didn't think of Gerry and the Pacemakers. The song belonged to Judy Garland. Ralph Horton's boy *understood*. He was no working-class rebel; he respected show-business tradition. He knew that rock would come and go but artists like Judy Garland would endure forever. He lived in 1966 but was not really a part of it. David Bowie could be the electrified Judy Garland.

Pitt had a fantasy. He wanted to create a star who would be timeless, for all ages. This beautiful boy could be it. Pitt envisioned himself the general to this boy's foot soldier. Together they would march into a war against the messy rebellion that was the sixties. Pitt felt a rush of excitement as he saw his fantasy becoming reality.

A new play was about to begin, one in which Pitt would eagerly cast himself in a pivotal role. Pitt couldn't wait to meet David Bowie. He smiled expectantly as Ralph Horton proudly led the boy to the back of the room.

David was smiling too.

CHAPTER 4

A Man of Taste

After the show, David, Ralph, and Ken went to Ralph's apartment. Ken told David, "I've spent many hours at the Marquee Club and I've never seen anybody walk onto the stage and display so much potential."

After three years of failure, David's fantasies were being confirmed—by a manager with two artists in the Top Ten. He explained to Pitt his intention to create a hit single that would take him to the top of the pops.

The older man smiled tolerantly.

"There is nothing more tragic than the life of a guitar cowboy," he said firmly. "You play your guitar indifferently in a London club and then spend your time tearing up and down the M-1 [the highway between London and Birmingham] doing your act at stops along the way. You live on garbage food from motorway pubs and are lucky if you're paid thirty pounds a night for your trouble. Is that the kind of life you envision for yourself?"

This litany was Pitt's standard warning to aspiring pop artists. An experienced public relations man, Pitt knew how to persuade as well as inspire confidence. Pitt was suddenly overcome by the need to rescue this boy, who could see only a foot in front of his face. He felt an urge to expand David's horizons. "You have a tremendous amount of potential, potential of which you're not even aware." Pop music, he explained to David, was merely David's stepping stone to a full show-business career.

Unlike the other promoters and managers David had met in and around the music business, people like Les Conn, Dick James, Shel Talmy, Tony Hatch, and Ray Cook, Pitt did not seem to view him as a potential money-making machine—a means to his personal ends.

32

He offered a new and irresistible fantasy: David's destiny was to transcend mere pop stardom. He would be a pop idol/stage star/TV host/movie star, which would set David far above the run-of-the-mill musicians who roamed London.

David liked Pitt. He was a gentleman, exactly the kind of man Peggy Jones always wanted David to be. Instinctively he grasped that by mimicking Pitt he might finally quash Peggy Jones's relentless criticism. Pitt was also very much like John Jones; he intimated that David was the center of his universe, the sun around whom the other planets revolved.

David still desperately craved that elusive hit single. It was all well and good that he would someday be a star, but it was 1966 and he was nineteen and pop stardom seemed at that moment the only thing that mattered. Pitt's acts, Manfred Mann and Crispian St. Peters, had hits. The manager had to have the right record company connections to get his singles the promotion necessary to take them to the Top Ten. He also seemed to have the money required to fuel the hit-making operation. David had already seen how cash could buy one onto the pop charts.

The exchange seemed a fair one: Pitt would make him a pop idol, and he would become Pitt's paragon of versatility. That afternoon he had set out to seduce this one very special man. When he set his mind to an act of seduction he never failed.

David announced that he wanted Pitt to be his manager.

It was agreed that Pitt and Horton would co-manage David, with Pitt taking over such administrative responsibilities as the paperwork, contracts, and accounts. Ken would join Ralph in the search for work for David.

It wasn't long before the bills accumulated by David and Ralph began to pour steadily into Pitt's office. Pitt dutifully paid them, keeping accurate records so that he could deduct these loans from David's future fees. As he had done with Les Conn, David soon began to turn up in Pitt's office to ask for pocket money. Viewing all of these expenditures as investments in the glorious future he and David would share, he did not refuse.

Things looked somewhat promising. The group were weekly headliners at the prominent club that had spawned the Who; their co-manager represented two stars; they had a record deal with a hit-making label. The illusion was enough to carry them. But while they continued to build a nucleus of fans, their act wasn't strong enough to engender the kind of excitement that made London's radio stations play a group's latest record. Their records were not great, and their manager was preoccupied creating David Bowie as a show business icon, and not creating a hit-making English rock-and-roll band.

Suddenly Buzz guitarist John Hutchinson announced he was getting married. David was violently opposed. On the one hand, David existed to please those he thought could help him. On the other hand, he had real determination, and he refused to attend Hutch's wedding. After his marriage Hutch decided that he could not afford to be broke anymore, and left the band to take a job as an Air Canada maintenance engineer.

Then the Buzz created a new act featuring prerecorded tapes. It overreached itself and proved disastrous. Even though he had already been on the show, David was turned down by "Ready! Steady! Go!" By now, when things should have been getting easier, they were getting harder.

Soon after they met, David began to visit Pitt's London apartment. The agenda was to discuss David's career, but the meetings soon evolved into cultural tutorials. Pitt prided himself on being a man of taste; he was interested in literature, art, poetry, and music. His intellectual appetites kept him abreast of what was currently going on in the arts. He was up on current American literary sensations and the pop art movement. Pitt was related to Aubrey Beardsley and collected Oscar Wilde first editions and Victorian books and memorabilia. David was fascinated.

Pitt believed that David was a diamond in the rough. He was well read, and proved intensely curious about subjects that were new to him. Boys who played in groups never asked questions about Wilde or Beardsley. Pitt enjoyed being David's teacher and mentor; he was flattered that this young person showed sincere interest in the things he held so dear. David's concentration and fascination made Pitt feel as if he presided at the center of David's universe, which made him even more eager to help.

Pitt was glad to lend David his books. One of the first to which David was drawn was Oscar Wilde's *The Picture of Dorian Gray*, a classic portrayal of the narcissistic personality. Someone with David's vivid imagination could not fail to see the similarities between Dorian Gray and himself. Both were beautiful young men who appeared to be considerate and concerned. Dorian Gray attracted the dilettante Lord Henry, who endeavored to teach him the ways of the sophisticated world; David had Ken Pitt. As Lord Henry convinced Dorian that by preserving his good looks he would always remain special, Pitt attempted to convince David to become a great entertainer for essentially the same reason. Both David and Dorian seduced people and then abandoned them without feeling the slightest pain. The only difference was that David had no intention of ending up like Dorian Gray.

In his own way Ken tried to make David face everyday realities, something that made David's deeply repressed anger rise to the surface. But Pitt had also allowed himself to be seduced, and that affected his ability to view his relationship objectively. Being David's mentor, parent, and savior became his obsession. The obsession fed on itself, and the more deeply he got involved, the more he was setting himself up for inevitable abandonment.

In April Pitt suggested that David write a film score. David wrote seven songs in four days. Pitt was pleased. But the film was a minor effort that could not attract financing. It was the first of a long series of straws in the wind.

In the early part of the summer, after the failure of David's third Pye single, "I Dig Everything," Pye lost all interest in David. David complained to Pitt that he didn't like working with producer Tony Hatch; it was as if Hatch were to blame for these failures.

David threw himself into preparations for a return series of Sunday afternoon performances at the Marquee Club during August. Ads for the Bowie Showboat began appearing in the music papers. He was a headliner at a major London club. Didn't that mean stardom was imminent?

The Marquee audiences at this season consisted of French and German students on summer holiday in London. As usual, whenever David did something of importance, Peggy and John Jones were in the audience. Wearing her best dress, a fashionable straw hat perched jauntily on her head, Peggy sat in a conspicuous front seat and waved hello to David's friends and neighbors from Bromley. Pitt had already been to Bromley to meet the Joneses. He found Peggy narcissistic and overbearing. John Jones, on the other hand, was a quiet man who was really anxious about his son.

John and Pitt proved they were in agreement on the basic issue: David had to earn a living.

"Terry came home today." David announced happily.

He never discussed his family life, and Ken did not even know David had a brother. David said that Terry had returned from a tour of duty in the Merchant Marine. It was not true, but David did not want to deal with the truth. Terry had, in fact, suffered a dramatic hallucination. He believed that Christ had appeared before him to inform him that he had been chosen to do the Lord's work on earth. The police found him wandering in the woods and talking gibberish. When they brought him to Bromley, Peggy was appalled and embarrassed. She lashed out at Terry and again expelled him from the house.

When the Marquee engagement ended in early fall, Pitt had to devise a new way to keep David hopeful and busy. He financed a recording session. After the failure of seven singles on three different labels it was almost impossible to get another recording deal. Pitt called in some more favors. Hugh Mendel, an old friend and head of albums promotion at Decca, came to the rescue. Despite its stellar attraction, the Rolling Stones, Decca was an exceedingly straitlaced company. The Stones never recorded in Decca's studio—the sound equipment was too old-fashioned, and the good-old-boy staff made them edgy. Throughout the late 1960s the label survived because of three cabaret artists—Tom Jones, Engelbert Humperdinck, and Gilbert O'Sullivan.

In 1966 Decca formed a subsidiary, Deram, to record unknown rock artists. Pitt thought the new label would be an ideal place for David. There was a deal to be made there. Mendel had promoted Anthony Newley's recordings, and David seemed to be the new Anthony Newley. By signing David, Mendel entertained the fantasy of re-creating a success from his past. David and Cat Stevens were among Deram's first signings. David's advance for his first album came to 100 pounds, with Decca agreeing to reimburse Pitt seventy-one pounds for the two tracks he had already financed, which they would release as a single. David and Pitt were thrilled.

Then Pitt went to Essex Music to negotiate a new publishing deal. The company offered 1,000 pounds, which Pitt felt was too low. He told David to sit tight while he thought about the offer. Pitt was scheduled to fly to New York in early November to meet Crispian St. Peters, whom he would accompany on a month-long Australian tour. During Pitt's absence Ralph Horton would supervise the Deram recording, and on his return Pitt would sort out the Essex deal.

Pitt had a special mission in New York. He planned to meet with Andy Warhol and get permission to promote an English tour of Warhol's house band, the Velvet Underground.

By this time Britain and America were beginning to be inundated by pop art's comic-strip vision of a world dominated by Madison Avenue hucksters with their ads, packages, and neon signs. Artists, students, and young people generally were taken with pop's artifice as well as its innate sense of camp and jokiness. The Who had already gone from being the group of the Mods to calling themselves "the first pop-art band." Treating the flag as if it were pop art and the logo of a group of advertising hucksters known as government, they had draped flags over their amplifiers, and bassist John Entwistle had taken to wearing a jacket made of flag cloth.

Warhol had created himself as the first artist-as-star. His view was that *everyone* was in show business—even religion was show business.

At a college show of his work, Warhol had been mobbed by four thousand fans. The artist had skillfully used publicity and marketing principles to orchestrate the reaction; four months of planning had preceded the show. Warhol's point was that he could be manufactured like a product. He, not his art, became the real exhibit. As applied to rock and roll, it was the successful manufacture of a singer's image, not his music, that made a genuine pop phenomenon.

On his arrival in New York, Pitt went directly to London Records, Decca's American subsidiary. London had passed on Crispian St. Peters's last release, thus losing "The Pied Piper," Crispian St. Peters's Top Ten English hit, to another American pop label. In their eagerness not to miss out on another hit from one of Pitt's artists, they agreed to release David's first Deram single in America.

In America Pitt received a generous offer of a $30,000 advance for David's music publishing. David's money problems were over, and Pitt was overjoyed. Rather than call or write David with the good news, he decided to wait until the documents were on his desk and the deal was official. He wanted to tell David in person; he wanted to be a hero.

After a wonderful lunch, Andy Warhol agreed to let Pitt promote the Velvet Underground in London. Pitt was introduced to the Velvets' composer/guitarist Lou Reed and was given a copy of the Velvets' new album, which he was sure David would love.

Pitt set sail for Australia a happy man. He had rescued his beloved David and was going to be the English promoter of the Velvet Underground. Pitt did not realize that it was pop to be taken to lunch and have your check picked up; Warhol would have had lunch with anyone. It was also pop to accept someone's offer to promote a series of concerts; Warhol would have accepted anyone's offer. The most pop thing was to find someone to fly you and your friends to England, all expenses paid, and then take you all over the country.

David's surrogate father was away, and now he could have his own way. He hated playing ballrooms. The kids who came there wanted to drink and dance; they did not come to see *him*. Ken wanted him to earn a living, so David was forced to play these dates when the right thing for Ken to do was to subsidize him while he "created." Worst of all, the audiences hated him. They wanted rhythm and blues, but he gave them the opposite. It was a love test, and they had failed it by refusing to accept the music they really did not want. They had turned their backs on his pop-rock tales of Mod despair. He hated these kids. From now on he would devote his energies to his original dream. He would retire from performing to write the hit single that would make him a pop idol.

David decided to disband the Buzz. He passed the word to Ralph, who spoke for him. He could not bear committing an unpleasant act in public. When Ralph gave them the news, they, unlike the Lower Third, agreed to continue playing for no money. David burst into tears. This was the kind of devotion he knew he deserved. But he was not as devoted to them as they were to him. He could not subject himself to further public humiliation, and the backup band was let go.

Without live performances, there was no cash flow at all. The

only way to get money was to go to Essex Music and close the deal
that Pitt had begun to negotiate. The music publishers had promised
Pitt 1,000 pounds, but without Pitt in the room, and sensing Ralph
Horton's desperation, they halved their original offer. David told
John Jones that Pitt had authorized the deal, and Jones signed the
agreement on behalf of his son, a minor. Horton was given 500
pounds. He gave David 300 and kept the rest for himself. Even
though Pitt had invested 1,525 pounds of his own money in David
over the past eight months, no provision was made to pay him back.

Then Deram released David's new single, "Rubber Band." Radio
London did not like the record. At the same time Deram's first Cat
Stevens single, "Matthew and Son," climbed to the top of the English
pop charts. Stevens, not Bowie, was the man to go with.

When Pitt returned to London he was appalled by the shambles
that awaited him. Horton's rash actions had lost David his $30,000
American publishing deal, and Pitt still had to continue footing the
bills. Now there was no money and no band to work with, so David
couldn't take any more ballroom jobs. Nor was there any solo work
available to him.

When Pitt and John Jones next met, Pitt related the story of the
lost Essex advance. Jones suggested they not tell David about the
American deal. They were joined in a conspiracy to spare their fragile
David. Each loved him so much he could not believe Horton was
merely acting on David's wishes, doing for him the things David
did not want to appear to be doing for himself. Instead they saw
Horton as the villain; David remained the innocent.

CHAPTER 5

Love You
Till Tuesday

David turned twenty on January 8, 1967. Nine days later he was ready to eliminate Ralph Horton. He met with Pitt and explained that he thought Ralph's inability to deal with money was jeopardizing his future. He believed Ralph's devotion was so great that he would release David from their management agreement if it was in David's best interests. But David never eliminated anyone from his sphere until he had a replacement.

Pitt, too, wanted Horton gone, and David smiled happily.

The next day Pitt appeared at Ralph's door to tell him that he was no longer David's manager. Horton did not seem the least bit upset. David had known exactly how Ralph would respond to the news.

Pitt waited for David to ask him officially to be his manager; appropriate documents would accompany the request. A gentleman first and an entrepreneur second, he was not the kind of man to refuse to work just because he didn't have a contract.

Two weeks later David made the request. A contract was forwarded to John Jones early in April, and Pitt journeyed to Bromley to discuss it with Peggy and John. It took another two weeks before John Jones signed it on behalf of his son, who was still a minor. The term of the agreement was a year, and it provided five one-year options. According to their agreement, Pitt would be David's manager from April 25, 1967, until April 25, 1973.

Pitt charged ahead with his plan to educate David and make him "England's greatest pop music star."

David, still eager for a pop hit, had written "Over the Wall," a

40

song capitalizing on a series of prison breaks that were dominating the headlines. Pitt rushed the tune to Robert Stigwood, who assigned it to one of his management clients, Paul Nicholas. The record failed but the search for a quick hit continued, and David created another novelty tune, "The Laughing Gnome." The gnomes were sung by David, Pitt, and Les Conn. By speeding up their voices, they became the English equivalent of Alvin and the Chipmunks.

The top record in England the week "The Laughing Gnome" was released on April 14, 1967, was a Deram record, Procol Harum's "A Whiter Shade of Pale." It had come close on the heels of another Deram hit, the Move's "I Can Hear the Grass Grow." David's single sank instantly, his ninth failure in a row. It was clear to Deram's parent company, Decca, that unlike Cat Stevens, the Move, and Procol Harum, David was not a hit-maker.

Pitt's other preoccupation at this time was his commitment to bring the Velvet Underground to London. David had been intrigued with Pitt's description of his afternoon with Warhol, who seemed the epitome of the myth and glamour of New York. Pitt described Warhol as a silent major domo, his eyes hidden behind sunglasses, his face frozen into an inscrutable mask. David realized instantly that Warhol had created a human theater around him, a theater that garnered sensational publicity, which helped enhance the Warhol myth. Warhol seemed to have assembled a family that existed solely to convince the world that he was fascinating. A series of accidents and chance meetings would allow David to follow Warhol's example with a vengeance.

David had never heard of Lou Reed. He listened to the Velvets' disk Ken had brought from New York. Cynicism, despair, and hate pervaded every groove. Reed was taking his listeners on a trip through a living hell on earth. David especially liked "Waiting for the Man," a harrowing portrait of a junkie waiting restlessly for his connection; "Venus in Furs," a gleeful paean to sadomasochistic sex, and "Heroin," in which Reed sang about the power of heroin to make one feel like a man.

David was impressed by the songs' authenticity. It was one thing to take drugs, but quite another to make a theatrical statement out of the experience and then live your shocking persona. The private and public Lou Reed seemed to David to merge into one stunning image that gave Reed his authenticity. There had to be a way, David thought, to manufacture an image more emphatically brilliant than anything Reed or Warhol ever dreamed of.

Pitt had a new fantasy. Lou Reed and Andy Warhol could promote David in America, while David promoted them in London. But Pitt discovered he did not have the power to bring the Velvets to London.

Meanwhile, David and Ken waited expectantly for Deram to release *David Bowie*, his first album, and Ken continued the desperate search for a job—any job—for David. Nothing led anywhere.

In June, ten long months after the deal was made, Deram was ready to release David's LP. As soon as the albums were in stock Pitt bought a half-page advertisement in London's most important music trade paper, and purchased a hundred albums for his own promotional purposes. The album received a few reviews, which David and Ken doted over, one in particular describing Bowie as "a Cockney singer who reminds me of Anthony Newley and Tommy Steele." But there were very few sales.

Decca's Hugh Mendel and Essex's David Platz both liked David and wanted to help. Franco Zeffirelli was about to direct a film version of *Romeo and Juliet*. Mendel suggested that David might be the man to give Shakespeare's songs a contemporary setting. Dutifully David went to work making pop rock of Shakespeare. But the job went to Donovan, whose "Sunshine Superman" had gone to the top of the charts.

Still Ken adored having David around. He was fun, and he bristled with enthusiasm. He filled up page after page with scribbled lyrics, then bashed them out at the typewriter. Late at night after Ken had climbed into bed, David often knocked at his door. All smiles and youthful energy, he would burst into the room, guitar in hand, to serenade Ken with his latest songs.

Encouragement poured from Ken. David craved the approval. He needed to hear repeatedly that he was going to become a star. But in the part of himself that he hid from the world, he knew that Ken was merely telling him what he already knew was true. He *would* be a star. That belief enabled him to survive.

Things were wonderful in Ken's Manchester Street apartment, but David didn't really live there; he lived at home with his parents.

Going home made him miserable. The thought of facing Peggy and her relentless criticism turned David into a wounded bird that inflamed Pitt's rescuer fantasies. He was compelled to help David, thus making their shared dreams come true. He invited David to move in.

It was precisely what David wanted. Again he had engineered someone into doing as he wished without having to risk rejection by asking directly. The invitation served as added proof that it was he, and not Pitt, who was in charge of his destiny.

In all of David's relationships was the illusion of instant intimacy. Man or woman, lover, business associate, or friend—David had the uncanny ability to make all feel interesting, intelligent, beautiful, and sexy. David could sense who someone thought he was or who someone wanted him to be, and then he became that person. Time and again, people have said that being with David is like looking in a mirror.

In order to get what he wanted, he offered the reflection of what they wanted most. He was the ultimate seducer, and sex was just one of the tools at his disposal; his seduction ultimately was more figurative than literal. He was no one's lover in the classic sense of the word—but that didn't make the seduction any less real.

Actor/director Michael Armstrong stared at the album in the store window. What a beautiful boy! He had to have the record. It was a time when many who worked in the theater wished to synthesize theater and rock and roll, and Armstrong was no exception. He had written a musical version of the Orpheus legend, and he needed a composer. In his musical, Orpheus was a pop singer literally torn to pieces by his fans. He wanted to meet David.

David was at his most entrancing during the meeting with Armstrong, even jumping up to deliver a devastating impression of Elvis Presley. For Armstrong, David was the perfect Orpheus. As for David, he loved the idea of playing a rock-and-roll martyr.

He would appear on stage naked and play a love scene with another man. The play reeked of homosexual camp overtones, with David center stage not because he was special or destined to be "the greatest thing that ever happened to pop music," but because he had the boyish, frail good looks older homosexuals craved—the personification of a gay sexual fantasy.

That night Ken took him to a music business press party. David got drunk and picked up a teenage girl. Back home David erupted and accused Pitt of being "bloody possessive." It was the first scene in a script that would create the myth that he was the victim of Pitt's possessiveness. When the time was right, just as Pitt had rescued him from Peggy, someone would come along who would respond to his dilemma by rescuing him from Pitt.

London was undergoing a drastic change. Swinging London, a city of pop dandies frugging the night away in the trendiest disco-thèques, was gone. The San Francisco hippie revolution had been imported to London with a vengeance, with flower power replacing Mod style. Now concerts incorporated elaborate light shows, and flowers were tossed to the audience at the end. A machine sent cascades of bubbles soaring over the heads of its tripping, long-haired audience at the conclusion of a Pink Floyd show. During the four-teen-hour-long Technicolor Dream, a happening at the Alexandra Palace, lights and films were projected on the walls and the music was played at a deafening volume. People rolled around naked in a fifty-six-gallon tank of jelly. It was a time in which rock musicians began to costume themselves like hallucinatory acid visions. It was not unusual to see a musician wearing a crown of flash fire, a miner's helmet, or a black cowboy hat adorned by giant model-plane wings.

The themes of the day were the hippie themes of love, peace, and brotherhood, and they were reflected in the music as well as in drastic changes of image. Donovan, David's friend from the Gio-conda Bar, had been a folksinger attempting to copy Bob Dylan. Suddenly he appeared in flowing robes behind a cloud of incense. He was the King of the Summer of Love and had scored two huge hits, "Sunshine Superman" and "Mellow Yellow." The Move had dressed in gangster suits and had done the Who one better by using axes to chop up TV sets, cars, and dummies of political figures onstage. Suddenly they climbed out of their gangster suits and into caftans and beads and began having big hits singing about "Flowers in the Rain."

Ever the follower, David had found Mod an appealing brand of bohemianism. Hippiedom was not so easy. Dropping out was in-conceivable; he was actually struggling to find a way to drop in. The hippies wanted to turn the straight world on to beauty, love, honesty, and fun. He wanted to turn the world on to *him*.

It was a desperate, confusing moment, one in which he sensed that he had to change his image or be left behind. As David Bowie, he was half John Lennon and half Mick Jagger. So he turned to them for clues.

At the beginning of the year John Lennon had announced that he considered himself a Buddhist. At the Tibetan Society Shop, David encountered a Tibetan monk, Chimi Youngdong Rimpoche. Suddenly he too was a Buddhist and began to decorate his room with Buddhist paraphernalia. Pitt watched with amusement. David could wrap himself around anything that interested him; in a moment a fiction would be created out of those ingredients that seemed perfectly real to him.

Pitt was usually too busy to eat. David seemed to exist solely on coffee and cigarettes. When Pitt went to the office in the mornings, David was still asleep, and the two men communicated by leaving notes on the kitchen table. In the afternoon, they spoke on the phone and planned their evening. Sometimes David cooked Pitt dinner. When he wanted to he could be a very good cook, but now the only thing he put on Pitt's plate was Buddhist cuisine, brown rice and steamed vegetables, Pitt good-naturedly accepted it as just part of David's growing pains.

Then David began to embellish the role. He decided to play the part of a Buddhist Bob Dylan, an unwashed ragamuffin who wore only black.

Desperate for David to earn some money, Pitt thought he'd make a stab at getting him modeling jobs. He excused the scruffiness that he abhorred as merely another example of David's misplaced creativity. In many ways David was a self-indulgent child who could not take criticism, and Pitt indulged him further. Despite David's current appearance, Pitt sent him out on modeling jobs.

No one would hire David. The thought that he could be a model was more wishful thinking, but wishful thinking was what kept them both going.

At the end of August, John Lennon, along with Paul McCartney and George Harrison, attended a lecture given by the Maharishi Mahesh Yogi. The next day they left for Wales with the Maharishi to study transcendental meditation. David kept telling everyone that he was an even more committed Buddhist.

Throughout the Summer of Love Pitt did his best to hunt down some newspaper interviews for his Buddhist-in-residence.

He was not surprised when David began to spin the myth of his

Buddhism to reporters: he had first learned of Buddhism when he was in high school and had seen newsreels on television of the Communist invasion of Tibet; he had helped establish a Buddhist monastery in Scotland; he was considering becoming a Buddhist monk himself as well as journeying to Tibet.

Pitt excused his fabrications. "He used to make up little stories. They had a reality for him," he says.

While he tried to find a way to belong to the Summer of Love, David watched as "Love You Till Tuesday," another single from his first album, failed. It brought the total number of failures up to eleven. Pitt sent him up for a film called *The Touchables*, but he didn't get the part. Essex's David Platz kept him busy by asking him to write English lyrics to two French songs. A set of Israeli songs followed; Platz hoped to get the Israeli actor Topol to record an English-language album.

David told Pitt he had to write a Top Ten hit. He needed a producer who could make hits. Pitt wisely turned to Denny Cordell, who had a production deal with Deram and had supplied them with hits by the Move and Procol Harum. Cordell liked David and wanted to help, but hated his new songs. He suggested that David meet with his assistant, Tony Visconti.

A musical prodigy and a New Yorker by birth, Visconti had studied classical guitar and had gone to a high school for the musically gifted. He was thirteen when he began cutting demo records with bands he had formed. After high school he became the house producer for the American arm of Essex Music. One night he took charge of one of Denny Cordell's recording sessions. Cordell watched in astonishment as Tony wrote quick arrangements and directed musicians. The boy was rushed to England.

In 1967, at the age of twenty, Visconti was infected with the spirit of the sixties that compelled young people to seek out the new and different.

To a conventional, establishment music publisher like David Platz, David was definitely new and different. He didn't have one writing style; he had every writing style. Platz urged Visconti to work with Bowie.

Visconti immediately felt the zap of David's intensity. Craving a hit as well as a producer who could create one for him, David concentrated all of his considerable attention on Tony. Tony was his instant new best friend; once again this seductive dose of attention had its payoff. In no time at all they agreed to work with each other.

Now David had a producer, but he still had no cash. Ken jumped when Michael Armstrong offered David three days work in *The Image*, an artsy half-hour silent film he had written and planned to direct.

In the film an artist stands at an easel painting the face of someone who has died. Suddenly the face—David risen from the dead—appears at the window. For the first day's shoot David had to hang from a windowsill while buckets of water were poured over him to simulate rain. By the time the filming was over, he had lost his appetite for acting. Instead he'd be a playwright. He sat at Pitt's typewriter banging out a script, a parody of the flower children from whom he was so alienated. Pitt, ever the supportive surrogate parent, rushed the play to the BBC, who rejected it with equal speed.

Even though he knew David didn't stand a chance, Pitt could not resist submitting David's name for a Broadway musical. He did not get a reply. Nor did the show get to Broadway.

Pitt wanted Decca to release another single from the album, but the company refused. The company also turned down Tony Visconti's first two sides with David, "Let Me Sleep Beside You" and "Karma Man." The album and its two singles had also failed in America, but London Records indicated a willingness to attempt to promote further releases. The New York radio station WOR-FM had played David's records, an indication that a small cult audience existed that would form around any music that was novel and English.

Pitt was in a terrible bind. His artist was signed to a company that refused to release his records. If David left Decca he knew full well David's track record would make it impossible to secure a deal elsewhere. David and Tony Visconti were having a wonderful time together, but Tony knew that David's new material was mediocre. David's ability to create the illusion of vulnerability was so strong and his refusal to tolerate discipline so great that no one stepped in and took charge. One just didn't criticize someone who had such an enormous investment in seeming perfect.

Pitt tried to bluff Decca by threatening to terminate the agreement. There was no response. Finally Pitt learned that the company was not going to release a record unless they were convinced they had a hit. David was trapped. Unless he came through, nothing was going to happen.

Someone who expected everything to be done for him now had to do it for himself. But the pressure was too great. One day he had agonizing stomach cramps. He went to the doctor, who diagnosed nervous tension.

Pitt tried to peddle David's songs to other artists and continued to attempt to corral journalists and radio and TV producers on David's behalf. A TV shot was set up for a Christmas Eve pop show. Ken flew him to Amsterdam to appear on a local TV pop program. Then Michael Armstrong engineered a ten-minute charity appearance for the Catholic Stage Guild. During David's set, Pitt spotted Danny LaRue in the audience. LaRue, England's most beloved female impersonator, was riveted to the young man on stage.

CHAPTER 6

Pierrot in Turquoise

Lindsay Kemp, a mime teacher and performer, was playing David's records as accompaniment during performances at the Floral Street Dance Centre. David headed for the Dance Centre to meet his fan.

He smiled radiantly at Lindsay as he introduced himself. The mime peered at him, surprised to find David so attractive. Before forming his tiny mime company, he had lived a checkered existence as a ballet dancer, male stripper, chorus boy, and actor. At thirty-five, Kemp looked like a great diva in desperate need of dental work. Kemp, who fell in love with every pretty boy who passed by, repeatedly enjoyed the drama of having his heart broken. David's admirers were inevitably rejected. They were perfect for each other.

Lindsay stroked David's hungry ego by telling him he looked like an angel. At that desperate point in his life he especially needed a "family" that offered total devotion. Lindsay's troupe could be it. An arrangement was worked out. David would take a class from Lindsay; in exchange he would compose songs for the mime's shows. Then Lindsay asked David to appear with him in his new production, pretentiously—and appropriately—named *Pierrot in Turquoise*. One performance would be given in a small theater in Oxford, followed by three in the Lake Country. The angel-faced David would be "Cloud," and would perform his new songs.

During David's four weeks with Lindsay, he rarely took a class, instead charming the girls who floated through the Dance Centre. But, an expert mimic, he did master the essentials of mime by quickly memorizing and then imitating the movements of others.

Like Ralph Horton before him, Lindsay, looking at his reflection

in the mirror of David's wonderment, set out to play Dr. Franken-
stein. His "monster" would be a male goddess, the quintessence of
androgyny. Makeup and hair dye were his tools.

Kemp's movements and gestures were large and extravagant, as
were those of his mime partner, Jack Birkett. Birkett, an ex–ballet
dancer and male stripper, a half-blind, shaven-headed giant of a man,
lived with the mime. Lindsay and he insisted they were not lovers
but "sisters." The gnome and the giant acted out an ongoing gay
Laurel and Hardy routine. While others hid their homosexuality
behind a veil of middle-class respectability, Kemp demanded attention and, rebelling against society's conservative attitudes, demanded
to be perceived as outrageously homosexual.

David loved this world in which everyone was so dramatic onstage and off. A keen observer, he found Lindsay's style an infor-
mation-filled textbook. Lindsay's very being was a work of art, with
the world revolving exclusively around him. When he entered a room
he stood in the middle of it, devouring it with his eyes until he
decided whether *he* belonged in the room. He encouraged Birkett to
keep guests waiting a half hour to build suspense until he made a
really grand entrance.

Kemp said his art had an hallucinatory component and brought
him to the brink of madness.

David could not help wondering whether the insanity that ran
through his family would blossom when he achieved stardom, a
romantic—and frightening—thought.

Lindsay insisted that the fantasies of his youth were the source
of his art. He was an unattractive and puny child with ears far too
large for his head. His solution was to wear his mother's dresses and
makeup. He even went to school with his face brightly painted. As
someone else he could be mesmerizing. In elementary school he
pretended he was Marie Antoinette and also wished to be transformed into Jeanette MacDonald. He became Scheherazade. Each
exaggerated new tale guaranteed that the spotlight would never leave
him. He had to keep inventing new stories or face oblivion. David
intuitively understood all this. It seemed like a drag version of his
own childhood.

David listened avidly as Lindsay worshiped at the shrines of those
who inspired him: Picasso, Shakespeare, Isadora Duncan, Piaf, Marlene Dietrich, Billie Holiday, Genet, Cocteau, Bach, Mozart, the

Rolling Stones. He paid continual homage to the "vulgar" schools of theater: Kabuki, ancient Greek and Roman theater, Jacobean drama, the *commedia dell'arte.*

Pierrot in Turquoise utilized traditional *commedia dell'arte* characters—Columbine, Pierrot, and Scaramouche—but also included interpolations from Jean Genet, Oscar Wilde, and James Joyce. Kemp's sensibility was wildly eclectic, much of it a reflection of an anything-goes gay cabaret mentality. Songs like "Bye Bye Blackbird," "Chattanooga Choo Choo," and "Over the Rainbow" worked their way into his pieces, as well as music of Billie Holiday, Al Jolson, Glenn Miller, and the unknown David Bowie. He mercilessly ransacked the works of others, including bits lifted from Marcel Marceau, Federico Fellini, silent movies, and choreographers Sir Frederick Ashton, John Cranko, and Roland Petit. He took bits and pieces from the best; it was not lost on David, who worked much the same way.

Pitt was delighted to see David occupied and happy during this difficult time. It pleased him that David was allowing himself to get some basic instruction in mime, dance, stage movement, and reacting to an audience. At home he regaled Ken with imitations of Lindsay's antics. He painted his face with clown white and then climbed into his mime costume. He looked gorgeous, and Ken took adoring photographs.

But it was no way to make a living. Nineteen sixty-seven was at an end and David had earned a mere 322 pounds that year. Ken did his best, negotiating a renewal of David's contract with Essex Music. He demanded 2,000 pounds but settled for 1,500.

There was only one solution: David would have to do a cabaret act.

Lindsay's set designer was a large-boned, hefty woman named Natasha Kornilof. She had designed a production of *Volpone* in which Kemp had played the Dwarf brilliantly. After encountering the mime, she decided to devote her considerable talents to his mission. Together she and David painted the backdrop for *Pierrot in Turquoise.* By the time they were finished Natasha was entranced by David. His wretched mother needed him, he told Lindsay, when he had a rendezvous with Natasha; his wretched mother needed him, he told

Natasha, when he had an assignation with Lindsay. He was rehearsing, he told Pitt, while he carried on the two simultaneous affairs. He believed he had control over them all.

After their *Pierrot in Turquoise* performance in Oxford, Lindsay and his troupe climbed into a rented Volkswagen bus to make the trip to cold, damp Cumberland. En route Kemp discovered that David had cast him in the role of Ken Pitt. He needed someone to put his coat around his freezing shoulders. He was dreadfully shy and self-conscious offstage; the cold got to him, and he became a needy little lamb. Unless the child was taken care of, he might die.

The lamb turned out to be a stud. That night, after he went to bed with Lindsay and Kemp began to drift off to sleep, David excused himself. A little while later Kemp heard passionate moans emanating from the room next door. He tiptoed into the hall. There he learned the truth: David was in bed with Natasha. It was the moment predestined from the time he had first glimpsed David. His heart was broken, and his response was rage, dramatic rage, *very* dramatic rage. The ensuing outburst was so severe that the Kemp troupe was evicted from the country farmhouse in which they were staying.

It was a scene out of an old movie. The mist swirled around them as the gnomelike mime, the half-blind giant, the bulky peasantlike set designer, and the radiant young David slunk from the farmhouse, climbed into the Volkswagen bus and disappeared into the night.

Ken Pitt had enlisted John Jones in his mission to persuade David to do a cabaret act. In cabaret David could earn 100 pounds a week, a large sum for those times. But David was quietly resistant. Cabaret was old-fashioned show business, brash and phony. It was the last place he wanted to play. Did John Lennon or Mick Jagger have to play cabaret? And why did he have to work to earn a living? Didn't Ken know that he could never be consigned to such ordinariness? David smiled but couldn't be budged.

His first album was ten months old in April 1968 and had long been a dead issue for everyone but Pitt, who was still determined to bring his music to the world. Then Decca passed on "In the Heat of the Morning," the new single Tony Visconti and David had recorded. It had been hoped that the record would not only become a pop hit but also the centerpiece of a hit second album.

It was clear Deram wanted David to go.

It was awful news, the moment Pitt had tried to ignore and wish away for more than a year and a half. David had accumulated ten singles failures as well as an album failure and had been on four different labels. There seemed no place left for him.

It was at that moment that David declared that he wanted to join the sixties. He did not want to be on an old-fashioned label like Decca even if it did have the Number One record at the time, Tom Jones's "Delilah." He was not a cabaret artist like Tom Jones. He wanted to be on Apple, the Beatles' label.

Apple was a psychedelic madhouse. A resident astrologer guided John Lennon's moves; policy decisions were based on readings from the *I Ching*. Tapes, novels, plays, poems, film script treatments, art, and architectural blueprints—their creators all eager for the Beatles' financial support—poured into the company. Even though he knew it was hopeless, Pitt, ever the pacifier, launched an assault on Apple. Four months would pass before there was a reply.

David was torn between the world of Ken Pitt, which seemed to make the unreasonable demand that he do practical, artistically offensive things in order to survive, and the world of his buddy Tony Visconti, the Brave New World of the 1960s, replete with musician/prophets, radical social change, and hordes of flower children from whom he felt alienated, yet felt compelled to woo.

David now watched as Tony Visconti became wildly enthusiastic about an artist whom he announced was going to own the world. He had seen the future, and the future was Marc Bolan.

David had first met Marc Bolan, who was then called Marc Feld, four years before, in 1964 when they were both sixteen. Marc had also been a client of Les Conn and had experienced a similar rejection by Dick James. At the time, the baby-faced Feld had done his best to look like Cliff Richard, one of England's slicked-over Elvis clones.

David had studied the competition. While he was always "on" in public situations, his performance was no match for Marc's. By far the greater fantasist, Marc alternately imagined himself Audie Murphy, Mighty Joe Young, and the Phantom of the Opera.

In November 1965, seventeen months after David's album debut, Bolan's first single, "The Wizard," was released. He had gone to Paris for a month and spent a weekend with a magician. Bolan returned to England transformed from a baby-faced folksinger into a baby-faced Sorcerer's Apprentice. Decca signed him to a singles deal on the basis of his new image. The record failed, but Bolan and his group, Tyrannosaurus Rex, managed to generate some press attention. David read the few lines of print, and felt a bond with Bolan, who was also an actor in search of the right role.

As he had previously with David, Tony became Marc's new best friend and began work immediately on Tyrannosaurus Rex's first LP. Bolan supplanted David as the object of Tony's attention, and Visconti announced his decision to dedicate his life to Bolan—exactly the kind of devotion David craved.

Tony and Marc got David the opening spot, a short one-man mime play, when the band headlined at Royal Festival Hall. An appearance at Middle Earth, London's latest club, would precede the concert.

As the engagements approached Ken bought advertisements in the music papers and invited Jonathan King to the Festival Hall opening. King had a TV pop show, and Pitt expected him to book David after seeing him work. Again he was in for disappointment. Bolan, not Bowie, was the attention-grabber.

John Jones and Pitt had one of their rare, soft-spoken conversations. Jones was concerned about David's finances, his usual preoccupation. Pitt explained that David had failed his screen test for a speaking part in the film *The Virgin Soldiers*, and had been lucky to be hired as an extra. There was no place left for him to play except cabarets. He had been hammering away at this theme for seven months. Jones listened quietly.

The next day David seriously buckled down to work. His father wanted him to be a cabaret artist, and he would not fail him.

Pitt could not have been happier. The act they planned together featured songs David interspersed with familiar Beatles tunes. David would use life-sized Beatles cutouts as well as a gnome-shaped hand puppet. Between each song he would make bright, breezy chatter. That proved the hardest of all. When he had to speak his mind went blank, and he became tongue-tied.

Pitt suggested that he think of the entire act as a scene in a play. Together they would invent a likeable cabaret personality for David, with David speaking lines Pitt wrote.

As the act took shape Pitt became enthusiastic. He loved teaching his boy. Focusing on the job at hand, David was being taught a method of working. This act would have a structure as well as a dramatic sense of pace. A big opening would be followed by two or three numbers that sustained the bigness. Soft songs would provide contrast. A big number would lift the act again, and then David would leave the audience with a number that spoke to them personally and emotionally.

The summer of 1968, the summer after the Summer of Love, was turning out to be a far happier one. "Those were warm summer days," Pitt wrote of the experience, "and David derived comfort from leaving off his clothes, sometimes sitting cross-legged on the floor encircled by blaring hi-fi speakers, sometimes loping around the flat, naked, his long weighty penis swaying from side to side like the pendulum of a grandfather clock. . . ."

One moment David and Pitt shared the illusion that the world would be theirs, and the next moment it was gone. The debut of the fledgling cabaret artist's act occurred at the Astor Club. After David showcased his twenty-seven-minute act for two prominent cabaret agents, the verdict was swift.

They liked the act but thought it was "too good" for cabaret. "Good" meant uncommercial. Cabaret audiences craved show business, not a pop-style folksinger performing original songs they had never heard before and Beatles songs they had heard too many times accompanied by cutouts and hand puppets. The fantasy that David would be in the money if he did this act turned out to be exactly that: another fantasy.

David announced to Pitt that he was moving out. He was going to share a tiny one-room apartment with his current girlfriend, Hermione Farthingale, a ballet dancer who studied at Lindsay Kemp's school. David had attempted to fulfill Hermione's fantasies by telling her he would become a ballet dancer. Instead she had seen him fail more than once and prove incapable of generating anything resembling an income. A hectic pace and spurious enthusiasm substituted for the rigorous discipline needed for dance. But David wanted her support while he hid out with her and licked his wounds.

Pitt's departure from London on business gave David an ideal opportunity to rebel against Ken and also involve Hermione in a project that could earn some money. The last time Pitt left, David, in his passive-aggressive way, had eliminated the Buzz; this time he created a cabaret act for hippies. Buzz guitarist John Hutchinson had returned to London from Canada and was working as a draftsman. Hutch had become taken with Gordon Lightfoot and other Canadian folksingers. David decided to become a Canadian folksinger himself, with Hutch acting as his guitarist.

David named the new act Turquoise after Lindsay Kemp's *Pierrot in Turquoise*, then later changed the name to Feathers. David performed his own songs, two songs by Jacques Brel, and a short mime called "The Mask." Hermione danced and mimed with David, and all three read short poems.

During the fall Turquoise got an occasional booking, including one at the London Arts Lab, where the small audience sat on mattresses and a hat was passed around at the end of the show. The group was lucky if it collected a pound.

David was enormously enthusiastic about the act but Ken Pitt saw clearly it was no way to earn a living. It was "really rather terrible," says Lindsay Kemp.

Despite the fact that David had no record successes and was doing this pallid little act, Pitt tried to get one of America's most powerful booking agents, Frank Barselona, to take him on. He approached more TV networks, independent television producers, and record companies. There was no response to any of these overtures.

When Apple finally passed on him David told Pitt to go to Mickie Most, who had passed on him when he led the King Bees. A pop star-maker, Most had just turned Lulu into the most successful foreign female artist in America's history with his production of "To Sir With Love." The producer did not believe that David was going to be the next Lulu and once again passed.

As soon as David arrived on the set of *The Virgin Soldiers* his hair was chopped off, and he was issued green army fatigues. He looked like a little boy in his soldier's costume, and at first he loved it. But the six days were unendurable. They dragged by while he waited around with almost nothing to do. Pitt could not stand David's misery. He would have to do something bigger and better than anything he had done before.

His new fantasy was a concert in the Purcell Room, an intimate 350-seat theater in the Royal Festival Hall. He'd fill the audience with music-business, motion-picture, and theater power brokers. Finally David's genius would shine. The Purcell Room was booked a year in advance and was usually used to promote a new album or single. Pitt reached for his checkbook and reserved three dates. Somehow there would be a record to promote when one of them rolled around. He was also buying another year's time.

Then he came up with an even bolder plan. He would make a movie of David's album. He hadn't liked the way David looked on German television. In those early color broadcasts David had been washed out by the backgrounds. Now David would look beautiful. Now they would have a wonderful movie to show. To promote singles, three-minute promotional films had been shown on TV pop shows for the past three years. But no one had ever made a film of a failed album.

That didn't matter. Pitt reached for his checkbook again and commissioned a script.

Nineteen sixty-eight, the second full year of Pitt's term as David's manager, was coming to an end. In 1969 there would be no new Essex publishing advance because David's songs had not generated enough income to balance out the monies Essex had already paid him: his income for the year had come to 905 pounds. At Christmas he was offered 50 pounds to do two shows at a countryside magician's workshop. He couldn't afford the train fare.

Ken was undaunted. In 1969 his boy would shine.

David began his twenty-second year as a dancing extra in a BBC-TV drama; he began 1969, his twenty-third, as a star in *Love You Till Tuesday*, a TV film devoted to his songs. Pitt paid for classes at the Dance Centre to tune up David's body for the eight days of shooting scheduled to begin on January 26. Fresh from his appearance in *Virgin Soldiers*, David still looked like a bald eagle, and Leonard of Wig Specialists was hired to create a wig to cover his severe army haircut. His teeth looked terrible, and Pitt also picked up the dentist's bill. Thousands of dollars would be spent before the project was completed. Gratefully, just before shooting began, David got a job as an extra in a television commercial in which he came to radiant life after eating a new ice cream, named, in the style of the 1960s, LUV.

Love You Till Tuesday consisted of eight musical sequences and David's mime, "The Mask." Four songs were plucked from his first album. Pitt demanded that the movie have a smashing new song, and David set about writing it.

He and Hermione had just seen Stanley Kubrick's *2001: A Space Odyssey*. The images were overwhelming, especially the monolith doomed to float eternally in space. There was a song in David's mind and he had to get it out.

Hutch and David worked together to create chords for lyrics that David drew from himself. A story began to emerge, that of Major Tom, an astronaut doomed to float eternally in space. Plundering the past was intrinsic to his style, and David lifted a chord arrangement left behind by the Lower Third. "He knew what he wanted but didn't know how to play it or what it was called," said Hutch. The guitarist worked diligently, assuming he'd be credited as co-author.

Kubrick's *Space Odyssey* became Bowie's "Space Oddity." The song was brilliant, and everyone knew it.

For eight days David was up before dawn and worked all day making the film. When he was off camera he quickly mastered German phonetically so that three numbers could be shot in German for German TV. On camera he acted the part of a fidgety little boy during "When I'm Five," he pretended he was anguished and upset during "Rubber Band," and he juggled a fake guitar during "Let Me Sleep Beside You." During "Space Oddity" he was filmed both at the ground controls and strapped into a remarkably unconvincing-looking cheap prop spaceship.

After he climbed down, a stagehand saluted him and addressed him as Major Tom. He liked that a lot. Just by using a cheap prop, he had created a character other than himself. It was as if he had thoroughly mastered everything Lindsay Kemp had taught. Pitt had urged him to be an actor, and now he was one. And it had been so easy.

The only thing that marred the filming were bitter arguments with Hermione. Everyone looked the other way, but Hutch believed that she had fallen in love with someone else. Her thirteen-month-long affair with David was over, and Hermione seemed to be there merely as a last favor to David before she bid him a permanent farewell.

No girl had ever walked away from David before. To compound the agony of a broken heart, he had no place to live, and he returned to his parents' house.

Love You Till Tuesday was the culmination of Pitt's obsessive three-year campaign on David's behalf. It was supposed to boost David's morale, yet David had never been more miserable. Although David and Ken refused to see it, the film told the devastating truth about David—he seemed to have neither personality nor focus and gave an innocuous performance, just another nondescript middle-of-the-road pop rocker in a series of pastel, smokey, faded, amateur commercials.

At twenty-two he was an actor who was still far away from giving a finished performance. Unlike Pitt's fantasy of greatness, *Love You Till Tuesday* was cute and empty, with David going through a lot of motions.

David changed again. He permed his hair in the style of Marc Bolan and transformed himself into a swishing queen. The character David brought to life was an attention-craving, outrageous homosexual, not at all what Pitt expected. Once again Pitt was forced to face a brutal truth—David was an actor who was always acting something, but his timing and instincts were terrible. He still hadn't turned himself into the persona that could drive his career forward.

With Hutch as his partner he began to intersperse his songs with stand-up comedy. Behind his gay mask he had found a public speaking voice. As a campy gay he could prattle on and be very funny. Nonetheless, the tiny audience that came to see "David Bowie and Hutch" were left unmoved and unamused by Hutch's deadpan straight Laurel and David's swishy gay Hardy.

David believed that Pitt was going to secure a record deal for them. They were going to be the English Simon and Garfunkel. The American duo's "The Boxer" was climbing the English charts, and David had taken to copying their songs. But now that, too, seemed just another fantasy. There was no money, and once again

Hutch left to take a job, leaving the queenly David behind.

When Michael Armstrong reappeared with an offer for David to appear in a revue, he was greeted by a brazen, flirtatious man who could have passed for an effeminate male prostitute.

No one imagined that David was about to meet the woman he would marry.

PART II

TWIN SOULS

The Cypriot Terrorist

Born on Cyprus during the fall of 1950, Mary Angela Barnet was five when guerrilla warfare broke out on the Mediterranean island. Her parents, both Americans, had settled there when her father, George, a mining engineer, became head of a mining company mill.

Growing up on Cyprus provided Mary Angela with a series of disquieting thrills. She was six when a wave of terrorism gripped the island. Two years later, terrorism struck again.

A jet plane strafed her home; then a submarine exploded in the harbor, killing many members of her father's staff. One night, as George Barnet drove along a quiet road, a sniper shattered the windshield of the car. Barnet escaped death by a hairbreadth.

The danger, fear, and especially the excitement of those early years implanted themselves firmly in Mary Angela's consciousness. As she grew older her own life would be a perpetual war zone. She would feel terror and would become either a whimpering child or, in a rapid-fire switch of roles, the terrorist tossing bombs at those who strayed into her path.

Though middle class, the Barnets educated Mary Angela as if she were European nobility. She attended St. George's, a small, exclusive, all-girls Swiss boarding school and was educated in both French and English. Her classmates were the sophisticated daughters of ultrawealthy internationals, and Mary Angela became an American instilled with classic old-world values. It was assumed that Mary Angela as well as the other St. George's students would take their places in society as the wives of ambassadors or similarly distinguished men.

Mary Angela returned to Cyprus an exceptionally striking young woman. She had dark honey-blond hair, piercing blue eyes, and high, polished cheekbones. Her fine features gave her an aristocratic look, with only the small bump on her nose disturbing her classical beauty. But her breasts were very tiny, which gave her a boyish quality. She could have passed for a flat-chested young Grace Kelly.

George Barnet had raised Mary Angela as a strict Roman Catholic, and when she entered puberty he extracted a pledge from her: she would remain a virgin until she married. Intensely devoted to her father, an ex–U.S. army man whom she viewed as a military hero who bore a striking resemblance to Lawrence of Arabia, she had to obey his every wish.

The pressures on her were already extreme. She was a middle-class American girl with an upper-class European education who lived on a sultry Mediterranean island filled with dark-skinned boys attracted to her blond boyishness.

They all wanted to sleep with her. But she wanted to be true to her daddy. Mary Angela watched from a distance as every imaginable ploy was tried to land her in bed, and she enjoyed watching the boys fail. She couldn't understand why she was abiding by such an unnatural, unreasonable commitment, but the thought of breaking her agreement filled her with uncontrollable guilt. Most of all she hated the fact that she was allowing herself to be controlled. A point would come when absolutely no one would be able to control her.

From Cyprus she was sent to another small exclusive all-girls school, Connecticut College for Women, where she now called herself Angie or Angela. Suddenly she was in love with another student, a girl. The affair enabled Angela to give vent to her sexual urges while maintaining the technical virginity. After a three-month affair, the scandalized, conservative school authorities moved in to break it up. When confronted by the administration, Angela turned terrorist. She dashed to an open window, and leaped dramatically from it. Remarkably, even though she fell four stories, she was not hurt. She picked herself up and began to run. She was not the kind of person to get caught.

Her parents persuaded her to move to London to attend the Oxford Street Secretarial School College. Then she went to Kingston Polytechnic to study economics.

She really wanted to be an actress but George Barnet disapproved and would not allow his daughter to enroll in a theater school. Instead, swept away by the flamboyance of the late 1960s, she began to view the world as her stage.

"The planet is a large playground for maniacs, which is what the human species really is," she announced as she began to develop a series of dramatic personalities that she alternated with breathtaking speed.

Tough Cockney dock worker, American debutante, and dowager empress were some of the many Angelas. But the real Angela was a tremulous, lost little girl. The slightest hint of criticism inspired a hysterical outburst, unstoppable until it had run its devastating course.

In London, her attitude about sex drew attention to her. An aggressive male seemed also to live in the nineteen-year-old girl, and she liked to act the part of a brazen, oversexed stud. The performance gave her the air of a male homosexual, always cruising for new prey. The blunt fist of authority had forced her to be a virgin and had punished her when she had fallen in love for the first time. She fought back by acting the role of sexual huntress on the prowl. Whenever her Catholic guilt overcame her, she drowned the bad feelings by returning to the hunt.

Privately she was in torment. Everyone seemed so stupid; she couldn't buckle down to a job that pleased her; she didn't have a work permit; her education seemed useless. Her frustration became a public entertainment, and her unpredictability made her enormous fun.

In 1969, when she was nineteen, she met thirty-three-year-old Chinese-American Calvin Mark Lee. Slim, with shiny, shoulder-length black hair, Lee wore a red love jewel on his forehead and looked like a Chinese girl. Lee was a doctor of pharmacy, and everyone called him Doctor. He seemed to have hordes of exotic friends. Angela had never been to bed with an Oriental before, and the novelty of an affair with this beautiful androgynous man fascinated her.

Most of all, Calvin also viewed the world as theater; his casual disregard of convention drew Angela to him.

When they went out they wore matching clothes, usually brightly colored three-piece velvet suits. The couple suggested two exhibitionistic gay boys capable of picking up either men or women. "We looked like a pair of *fagelas*. Calvin only liked me because I looked like a boy," she recalls.

Calvin decorated his bedroom with photographs of his friends. Angela lay on his bed trying to figure out which of the men and women Calvin had slept with. Among the pictures were some of David Bowie, a folksinger Calvin liked enormously.

At the beginning of the year Calvin had taken her to hear Feathers. It was the first time she had been to any kind of pop or rock show, and she had had a wonderful time. But she had not paid much attention to David. He seemed too soft, too pretty, much too feminine; she was sexually attracted to rougher, tougher men. Besides, he had a girl friend, the exquisite dancer, Hermione. She put Bowie out of her mind.

One day Calvin told Angela that his best friend David was depressed. It had been five months since Hermione had walked out on him, but his heart refused to mend. He needed a shot of adrenalin, and Angela would be the perfect fix.

Angela loved the idea. Prepared to put on a raucous, rowdy display that would bowl David over and take his mind off his troubles, she dressed in an especially flamboyant costume, a deep-purple velvet suit, a wildly colored fuchsia silk shirt, and a purple silk tie.

The trio met for dinner in Chinatown. Angela sat across from David. He looked eagerly and knowingly into her eyes. She was taken aback, and her boisterousness immediately vanished. In his face she saw her face. They were the same height and weight, and there was a feline quality about both of them. It was as if twin animals of the same species had met by accident and were compelled to stalk each other. They had the same milky-textured skin, high cheekbones, and deeply hollowed cheeks; each even had a flaw in the nose that marred otherwise almost perfect features. Her fingers were long and somewhat masculine, his were expressive and feminine. They could have had the same hands. Later, when they danced together, each mimicked the other's body language. Each was an actor who acted out by mimicking someone else.

"I realized then and there what narcissism really is," says Angela. "I was looking at myself."

David overwhelmed Angela with his enthusiasms. She had no doubt that she was in the presence of someone who was going to be a great star. She wanted him immediately, and she became effusive. Everything he said was met with overwhelming praise. He loved it. The more Angela praised him the more intrigued he became with this woman who was part American and part European, masculine as well as feminine, a coaxing little girl who suddenly let go with a loud booming bellow.

David's ability to suggest intimacy turned every contemporary he met into a surrogate brother or sister. Angela could be both. They talked about sex, and she subjected him to the test by telling him about her undergraduate lesbian experience.

David understood. He was the first man she could really level with.

Then David confessed that he sometimes slept with men. She understood.

They discovered they both had slept with Calvin, and it made them feel deliciously wicked. It was as if they belonged to an elite club for special, unconventional people who stood apart from all the others. That night they went their separate ways but thought about the other.

The next night David took Angela to dinner and then to bed. That was the place where he gave his greatest performances, and that night he was at his most spectacularly ardent. Despite his feminine qualities, he was always a sexual superman.

In her inimitable way, Angela says of David, "He was a right stud. A stallion. He could poke a hole in the wall."

In the early morning, despite her protests, he left. But the next night they went to bed again. They loved the sex and also enjoyed each other's quick wit. Angela had come to conclusions about David, which she told him. He was a wonderful lover and exceptionally well endowed. He was handsome and talented and was part masculine and part feminine. All this was proof that he really was an alien being.

When Angela was fourteen, she had written a thesis called "The Light People." It stated that the prophets, messiahs, and great historical characters were actually aliens or the offspring of alien beings.

David was most definitely a Light Person. He listened knowingly. She had stumbled on the truth. When he got up to leave, Angela followed. She did not want him to go, and she hurled herself down the stairs, landing in a crumpled heap at his feet.

Laughing, he stepped over her. "You'll get less bruises if you don't act that way," he said merrily. And then the Light Person was out the door. He had enjoyed being with a woman so taken with him she would resort to violent outbursts. Her histrionics had found an audience but would get her nowhere. She knew it, which made her desperate.

A week went by, and Angela was frantic. Then he called and said he was sick. She came to the rescue, a soothing mother who nursed him back to health. Mary Finnegan, the writer David was now living with, was away, and David couldn't stand being alone. As Mary had asked him to move in, he asked Angela to move in.

Angela admitted to herself that she had fallen desperately in love. She would do anything, she told herself, to make this Light Person her own.

Angela had to have him. She realized that the only way to deal with David was as an indulgent, all-accepting mother. She showered him with praise. In her universe he was never wrong, never failed, never made a bad decision. She never stopped telling him, "Darling, you're going to be such a great star!" He couldn't hear it often enough.

Money meant nothing to her, and she loved to shop. She'd arrive home with her arms laden with parcels. Delightedly, she and David unwrapped the packages. Although they played mother and son most of the time, when it came to clothes they became sisters. They were the same size and liked to switch clothes while chattering about styles and designs.

David was attracted to Angela's finishing-school vocabulary. It was not the vocabulary of a guitar cowboy's girl friend and was another thing that set him apart from the rock-and-roll mainstream that so far had rewarded him only with failure. "Quality," "style," "taste," and "excellence" were among Angela's favorite words. David had acquired Pitt's sense of taste; now Angela provided him with a set of standards with which to judge the entire world. He loved the elitism.

When he became depressed, he refused to wash or change his clothes. Angela would lay out clean clothes for him and coax him out of one pair of jeans into a freshly washed pair. She would also coax him into the bathtub.

"I treated him like a baby, like a very precious spoiled child," she says. "His whole infatuation with our relationship was that it was totally unreal and had nothing to do with the real world."

In the evenings she was "one of the boys" and continued to go out drinking with David and Calvin. David was amused by the fact that Angela, mother/sister/lover by day, could become mother/sister/brother/lover by night. After a few glasses of barley wine he became relaxed and turned funny. Angela stared lovingly at him, her eyes bursting with admiration.

David used his sexuality indiscriminately to convert both men and women to his cause. Sex and his gift for seduction gave him a sense of self-worth. Angela's flamboyant lesbian routines were a habitual act of rebellion. Because each used sex for more deeply seated reasons than pleasure or love, neither dared make judgments about the other's behavior. Neither could tolerate the slightest bit of criticism, and so they didn't dare think critical thoughts about each other, traveling instead under a cloud of positive energy of their own making.

They imagined themselves the ideal couple of the future, and they lived life by acting. Each was the other's best audience. As they got to know each other, the performances grew in intensity. Angela's love for David drove her to greater heights; he gave her something to do. She was too afraid of failure and too hyperemotional to do anything to help herself, and David's neediness kept her happily distracted.

David kept in touch with Pitt by letter, phone, and an occasional visit, using his key to enter Pitt's apartment when the latch wasn't on, a sign that Pitt was not entertaining and did not mind a visitor. David bubbled with enthusiasm about his life in Beckenham. He was especially proud of his Arts Lab, a venture initiated by his friend and roommate Mary Finnegan, to earn some money. The Arts Lab met in the back room of a small bar in Beckenham, and was run, according to the hippie manifestos of the day, with everyone having the opportunity to participate and share in the profits—when there were any. The Arts Lab turned out to be a showcase for David. At first intimidated by the hippie revolution, he had made a complete reversal. Now, he was the hippie, an actor playing the on- and offstage role of coffee house folksinger. It was David's version of the early Bob Dylan and the Gordon Lightfoot-type Canadian folkies.

David told Pitt he wanted to be simultaneously an under- and overground star, and the author of folk-pop hits and West End musicals. Pitt recognized that David's unrestrained enthusiasm masked real confusion about his future. David had only enough money to last a few days, and none of his ideas seemed capable of earning him a penny.

Pitt didn't blame him. David's inability to cope with and learn from failure always caused him to hide out in a safe retreat where there was no competition, no danger of new failure, and, unfortunately, no opportunity to make any money. The life of a starving artist had become one of his great rationalizations ever since he had met Lindsay Kemp. Poverty was equated with safety, and nothing could be safer or more poverty-stricken than the back room of a local Beckenham bar.

What worried Pitt most of all was that David had fallen under the influence of two dreadful people, Calvin Mark Lee and Angela Barnett.

Lee had met David by writing a series of fan letters to David, in care of Pitt. They might have been love letters, and David reveled in the fact that the mere image of him on a record jacket was enough to make people fall in love with him. David introduced Calvin to Pitt.

One day David brought Angela to Pitt's office. She shyly took a seat, but was never introduced. Her face was one big, eager smile. Angela and Pitt said nothing to each other, but beneath Pitt's neutral expression and Angela's mask of devotional radiance, each surveyed the other. Angela had costumed herself for the occasion as an all-American coed who had just escaped from a Seven Sisters campus. She was even wearing white bobby sox. Pitt saw David being swept off his feet by a girl who gave the illusion that she was the prototypical American. "David mistook precociousness for intelligence," he says.

Soon David began repeating Angela's ideas. Pitt was offended. He sensed that she was jealous of him because David still spent a substantial amount of time with him. It seemed that even though she was all smiles and kisses and always greeted him with a booming "Hello, darling," she seemed to be waging a war against him. The only thing to do was forge on. The reality was simple: David lived with her and not with him, and she not only had David's ear but also the power to bend it substantially out of shape. "She was a storm trooper who yakked at him twenty-four hours a day," he recalls.

David was dissatisfied with Pitt, but he could neither complain nor take direct action. At all times he wanted to be above the human fray. Someone else had to say the things he thought. "He was just such a superb manipulator; he got me to say the things he wanted me to say. I said what he wanted to hear, but he never wanted those ideas to appear as if they were coming from him. So he subtly set up ways to make other people say what he wanted to hear, and the ideas never looked like he had originated them," Angela says.

The result was a year-long drama with David at the center. His quest would become the quest of everyone who knew and loved him. When it had become all-consuming, then he would be ready to act. But even then it would look as if someone else had made his decision for him, and that he had allowed himself to be influenced by those around him. Held unaccountable for his behavior, he had also set up a situation in which he would suffer no guilt when Pitt's head rolled.

Angela sensed David's unhappiness. "Nama-nama [her pet name for David], I'm sure if Ken could only get 'Space Oddity' released it will be a hit," she said soothingly. "It's such a wonderful song. We just have to get Ken to do a deal for us." That was not enough. A brainstorm was called for. Rising to the occasion, she said the one thing David really wanted to hear. "Let's see if Calvin can help." Lee worked at Mercury Records.

To those in David's inner circle, it appeared that Lee had become David's new manager. Then David tantalized Pitt with the information that Mercury Records wanted to sign him. The hitless Chicago-based company was the bottom of the heap, the last place to sign any artist. But David wanted a deal—any deal.

Pitt sighed philosophically. Every other label had turned David down. But despite David's information, even Mercury was not eager to acquire David. Pitt pitched the fact that "Space Oddity" was the real novelty record to release simultaneously with America's Apollo II moon walk, scheduled for July 20, 1969.

Mercury liked that. But David's track record was appalling, and the company demanded that a top-notch producer make the record. It wanted Beatles producer George Martin. That was totally unrealistic, but Pitt doggedly set out to persuade Martin to come aboard. None of his phone calls was returned. A month of waiting went by before Martin's secretary finally called to say the producer did not like the song.

Eventually it was agreed that Tony Visconti would produce "Space Oddity," and a deal was finally struck with Mercury agreeing to release three singles and an album. David would be signed for a year with two one-year options. Pitt negotiated an advance of 750 pounds, which he subsequently had increased to 1,250 pounds. But Philips Records released Mercury's products in England and had the option to pass on records they considered uncommercial. Pitt's deal did not guarantee an English release.

June 20 was the date set to record "Space Oddity," and it would be rush-released on July 11, a week before the moon walk. But then another problem cropped up. Visconti hated the song and did not want to produce it. Infused with the idealism of the 1960s, Visconti refused to do anything in which he did not believe. He did not like the fact that David was writing copies of Simon and Garfunkel songs and repeated what he had said to David many times before: He had to write in a unified style in which he really believed. Visconti believed "Space Oddity" was "a spectacular cheap shot, cashing in on the moon landing."

David was not pleased with Visconti's reaction but was encouraged that Tony thought the song was going to be a hit. Visconti's next-door neighbor at Essex Music was Gus Dudgeon, who had engineered David's first album. Dudgeon loved the song and agreed to produce it, a real stroke of luck for David. Dudgeon's production, complemented by Paul Buckmaster's arrangements, proved masterful, deftly blending strings, horns, synthesizers, and rhythm section. It was a brilliant example of the orchestrated chaos school of production first launched by Phil Spector in the early 1960s. Built from seemingly incoherent washes of sound, the song grew from a dark, distant 2001-aura into a full-blown orchestral rock masterpiece. The awesome, surreal mindscape of cold, vast, deep space had been captured perfectly.

Pitt wanted a hit. Once again he reached for his checkbook and took a half-page ad in the important English music trade paper *Record*

Retailer. The ad featured David as Major Tom in a still from *Love You Till Tuesday.* Pitt had always believed David's success would come when he began to play musical characters of his own creation. Still, the pop radio stations had no desire to play the haunting but morbid record. Pitt called in a favor from a friend at London Weekend Television, guaranteeing that the record would be played as background accompaniment during the coverage of the moon walk.

In America the record was sent to a mailing list of over a thousand pop music journalists. But radio stations appeared reticent about playing it. Their reluctance was justified as "censorship." America did not want its moon walk portrayed negatively.

Just before the moon shot, a man approached Pitt. For 100 pounds he could get the record onto the charts. More money would move the record higher. Enough money would guarantee that the record would break the Top Ten. After some thought Pitt accepted the fact that he was in the music business. Three years had gone by since Ralph Horton had used Ray Cook's money to buy David a Top Forty hit, and still they were nowhere. Hoping that he was not involved in a scam, he wrote out yet another check on David's behalf.

"Space Oddity" was played on television during astronaut Neil Armstrong's moon walk. Angela sat beside Mary watching the screen; when the song came on she screamed with joy. But David was nowhere to be found. Rather than risk the failure of something not happening, he ignored the event that most concerned him.

He had good reason to hide out. His record had received airplay only as a novelty accompanying a one-shot public event. When the event was over the record died. No matter what Pitt paid the chart riggers, another failure loomed. Still, there was some hope. Mercury had given word that David could start his album.

The time had come for Pitt to renew David's publishing deal with Essex, but Essex refused to advance any more money. David had been given 2,000 pounds and had earned back a mere 122 pounds. Ken suggested that David become a director of his music publishing company, receiving both writer's and publisher's royalties without having to pay Pitt any commissions.

It was a suggestion that motivated a major brainstorming session between Angela and David. David and Angela both had enormous investments in appearing perfect to the outside world. But Angela was pulling off a fast one, and David loved watching her mind go to work on outwitting the system. Angela knew that David wanted new equipment. She suggested that David give Essex some new songs, in exchange for new equipment. That would solve Ken's negotiating problems.

It was a wonderful idea. David could get what he wanted, and would even be doing Pitt a favor.

Then Pitt discovered that Essex was giving David equipment. That was the moment a less self-preoccupied man would have gotten out. As David had known that Ralph Horton, before Pitt, would go if asked, he also knew that no matter what he did, Pitt was determined to stay, and he had carte blanche to do as he wished. Pitt, a gentleman, believed that David was one too. They had an agreement and he was determined to do his part of it. Besides, they had shared so much. Somehow, someday, David was going to fulfill his dream, and the persuasiveness of that fantasy continued to enable Pitt to put up with anything.

Believing he was acting in David's best interests, Pitt sought to reexert his influence over David by separating him from the hippies, rebels, and nonprofessionals with whom he now lived and hung out. He did not realize that David was oscillating between three mutually exclusive dramatic canvases: the suburban hippie-ridden world of Angela, Mary, Calvin, and the Arts Lab; the world of Tony Visconti and Marc Bolan, in which music was a revolutionary act; and the urban, sophisticated London world of Ken Pitt and his friends. Ken soon learned that he would never again be alone with David. Either Angela or Calvin was always on his trail.

Pitt was the U.K. delegate to an international folk-song competition, the Maltese Song Festival, held at the end of July. From Malta David and he would travel to the Italian town of Monsummano, where the festival would be repeated. A stopover was planned in Rome. It was a nonsensical event, and no place for anyone trying to become a pop idol. But it was a holiday in the sun, and Pitt used his influence to get David a spot on the bill.

Angela told David he would love Malta. She would go to Cyprus to visit her parents, then join him in Rome en route to Monsummano.

David was relieved. Angela would rescue him from the parent who had promised to make him a great star and had failed.

In their hotel room in Monsummano, Angela and David dressed

for the festival. Angela held her dress in front of her, rose on her toes, and leaned forward. She stared at her reflection in the mirror. She was able to imagine the complete transformation that would occur when she got dressed and made up. Tonight she was going to be queen of the festival. To her a queen was someone who dared to look more outrageous than anyone else and then had the innate dignity to act as if she were to the manor born. David watched Angela, studying the art of transforming oneself into another persona.

David and Angela left the room and walked to the marble staircase that led to the lobby. David was wearing an elaborate antique shirt Angela had found for him. His golden hair was tied back with an elegant black-velvet bow. They positioned themselves for their theatrical entrance down the staircase. They arched their backs and held up their heads, and sailed slowly, majestically, down the staircase, through the lobby, and into the street. Everyone stopped and stared. The townspeople lining the festival route were flabbergasted. No woman had ever worn a see-through dress in this conservative Roman Catholic town before. Women averted their eyes while astonished boys dashed up to Angela to ogle her breasts. David and Angela ignored it all. They could have been royal monarchs touring a backward country. It was Angela's crash course not only in acting like a star but acting like the greatest of all stars. David was thrilled to have a partner in getting him the attention he craved.

David won a best-produced record award.

After the festival Angela continued on to Cyprus, and David and Pitt went back to London, with David heading straight for Beckenham to sing at the Arts Lab. During his performance a call arrived from Peggy. John Jones was dying.

After the set David was driven to Bromley. Carrying his festival trophy, he dashed into the house and up the stairs to his father's room. When he came down there was a slight suggestion of tears in his eyes. He looked at his mother and asked why it had taken her so long to get a doctor.

The next day John Jones was dead of pneumonia. With him died David's token allegiance to respectability, as well as to the conventional middle-class values espoused by his father.

Ken Pitt's values were next. The way to deal with the past was to erase it.

It was as if he had just been born.

CHAPTER 8

Everyone's Best Friend

Throughout the summer Angela had acted the role of everyone's best friend. She was effusively warm to Mary and Mary's children and equally affectionate to all of David's friends. Everyone who crossed her path was greeted with a booming "darling" and a big hug.

Raised from childhood to be the mistress of a house, she was not the mistress of Mary's house. Inevitably, Angela knew, they would have to move somewhere where she could be the official mistress.

The way to start David in this direction without making it appear that she was manipulating him—something he would resent—was to suggest they move into Peggy's house to look after the widow. After a few weeks the tension between Peggy and David would be so great that David would be only too eager to get his own apartment.

It wasn't all manipulation, however. Angela was generous and good-hearted; she believed in families and family rituals. Angela was also concerned about what would happen to David's half-brother Terry now that John was dead. After leaving Canehill Hospital Terry, with nowhere to go, had returned to Bromley, where John had experienced a change of heart. Acknowledging that his treatment of Terry had been a pivotal reason for his stepson's madness, he had gone out of his way to display the kindness toward Terry that he had never shown him as a child. Now Peggy was saying that she could not take care of Terry on her own. She seemed content to have the thirty-year-old man put back into the mental hospital.

Angela adored Terry. He was so handsome—even better-looking

than David—and had such bright blue eyes, jet black hair, and gorgeous, masculine features.

"I never thought for a minute I was good-looking because I had a brother who looked like James Dean," David told her.

David had already confessed to Mary Finnegan that he measured his sanity by his brother's insanity. The reality of the genetic madness that lurked in his family was a theme to which he turned whenever his life seemed out of control or he made mistakes that he did not wish to acknowledge. It could be used to explain anything.

From the minute David and Angela arrived in Peggy's house, Angela revved herself up to be the most wonderful Angela imaginable. It did no good. Peggy hated her, and hypocritical moral objections poured nonstop from her. Her son was taking a course in sin, and this young woman was his teacher-in-residence. Peggy didn't mince words about her objections, and the war raged in the living room, bedroom, and kitchen—her kitchen, from which Angela was banished.

It became clear that David and Angela could not stay.

On September 8, seven long weeks after its release, five weeks after his father's death, "Space Oddity" made an appearance at the bottom of the pop charts. Everyone's heart jumped. The next week, it fell off. The sensation of hope was replaced with gigantic despair. Again David pretended to be uncaring. Then it jumped back on in thirty-ninth position. The record traveled slowly, seeming to take forever to wend its way toward the Top Ten.

One day David's former guitarist John Hutchinson heard the record on the radio. He had assumed that when the song was recorded it would be recorded by Bowie and Hutch with him getting co-authorship credit. Then a Beckenham local came forward to announce that he had told David the story of Major Tom and that David had made a record of *his* story.

On November 5 "Space Oddity" crested at Number Eight. At last David had the pop hit that had been his goal for six years.

A new illusion settled over everyone: David had become a star. Pitt set up a stream of interviews and photo sessions. One radio interviewer went so far as to say, "With his fanatical following, he reminds me of a prophet." But there was no fanatical following; there was almost no following at all.

In America "Space Oddity" had died a miserable death. But a Mercury Records publicist loved the record and kept hammering away at the American press, especially the all-important *Rolling Stone* magazine. One letter to *Rolling Stone* editor Jann Wenner read: "I sincerely believe David Bowie is going to be a major force on the pop music scene. . . . I know *Rolling Stone* likes to be ahead of what's going on in the music scene." David was being positioned in America as an English trend-setter.

Because of the record's English success, Mercury reserviced the single. Every reviewer, programmer, and major disk jockey received a second package of information. Again there was no air play, but the message that David Bowie was a comer was reinforced.

Among the few requests for David's services to arrive at Ken's office was one to judge a drag contest featuring a popular female impersonator named Pussy. "That he was a frustrated drag act," David quipped.

Everyone expected that the hit would bring offers of more work at increased fees, but "Space Oddity" was viewed as a novelty record, and no one cared to hear the artist who wrote it. It was also an orchestral record, and David was doing the one thing that was most natural and comfortable. He was a folksinger, not someone who fronted a band.

Finally David was offered a twelve-minute mime spot, opening for the first nine-day Humble Pie tour. When his tapes failed before his first show, he performed the acoustical set he had done at the Arts Lab. The Humble Pie audience were not suburban Arts Lab hippies; nor did they expect the author of "Space Oddity" to come on in a guise that was dated by two years. They had already lived through Donovan in the role of the English Bob Dylan, and David's well-worn "I'm-here-to-change-the-world-with-my-acoustic-guitar-routine" was no way to win new fans.

At the end of the tour he and Ken flew to West Berlin to do a pop TV show. This was the city of *Cabaret* (David had loved the play's expressionistic lighting and set designs), and David and Ken celebrated by touring the decadent bars. Pitt had primed every club to play a Bowie record as soon as David walked in. In the Berlin nightlife, unlike London, he seemed to be a star. Eight years later he would settle in West Berlin close to the Berlin Wall, which he saw for the first time that night.

Though he had no interest in politics and no real social consciousness, he would make the following pronouncement in England at the year's end. "The country is crying out for a leader. God knows what it is looking for, but if it is not careful it's going to end up with a Hitler."

Their next stop was Zurich. "Space Oddity" had become a hit in Switzerland, and David had been invited to do a Swiss pop show. The Swiss division of Philips Records was represented by a dignified, elderly man, and David became upset when some hippie Swiss journalists made fun of the man behind his back. It was bad for David's image. He didn't like being represented by an old man. Marc Bolan and Tony Visconti were right. He had to free himself from the old men and their values.

Meanwhile no music publisher in London wanted the songs that were about to be released on his debut album for Mercury. The great irony was that a pop hit had meant nothing.

David needed a refuge and he needed someone totally devoted to look after him. He had escaped from the house in Bromley when he was nineteen; at twenty-two the time had come to escape from it again—to somewhere really safe.

Angela knew this was the moment to make her move. Marshaling all her forces, she set out to find them a home of their own. She quickly found the place.

"It's called Haddon Hall and it's divine!" she exclaimed. "It's got its own charm and elegance. You'll adore it."

David made one thing clear to Angela. He would live with her but he did not love her. Angela smiled sweetly. She liked the challenge of making him love her, and was inspired to be an even more wonderful mommy.

Haddon Hall, originally an Edwardian mansion, had been converted into apartments. David and Angela's parlor-floor apartment had a large, wide, grand entrance hall with an imposing curved staircase at its end. It was like something out of an MGM costume musical starring Nelson Eddy and Jeanette MacDonald. A beautiful stained-glass window had been mounted in the wall halfway up the staircase on the first landing. At the top of the staircase was a small gallery that overlooked the entrance hall. The gallery had the once-upon-a-time feel of a place where minstrels sat and played. It was where David's band would sleep when they had no place to go.

Most of the apartment was to the right of the entrance hall. There were a bathroom, a small kitchen, a living room (which David and Angela called the sitting room), and the room David used as his studio. These rooms faced the front and had imposing bay windows that overlooked the garden. On the left side of the hall was the bedroom.

David hired some out-of-work musician friends to paint the apartment. The walls of the sitting room were painted a neutral beige with the ceiling a sparkly silver that stood in sharp contrast to the plush dark-blue Oriental rug. Both the carpet and walls of the bedroom were pink; that ceiling too was painted silver. A seven-foot-wide Regency bed dominated the room. Jokingly, David described it to a journalist as "a huge coffin with a canopy."

David was now a man of taste like Pitt. He had started to collect fine objects. His desire to emulate his mentor inspired Angela to create an Art Nouveau setting. David's bits and pieces of Lalique and Galle glassware were displayed alongside books of Victorian prints. A twelve-foot teak sideboard made in Burma became the centerpiece of the sitting room, and a growing collection of Art Nouveau vases, jugs, bottles, ashtrays, and paperweights rested on top of it.

The walls were decorated with Victorian paintings, designs, and storybook illustrations. The result was a cozy stage setting that hardly looked like the home of a musician, even though David's studio was littered with guitars, tape recorders, and electronic equipment.

Haddon Hall had been designed as a place in which Angela could give a noisy, perpetual party, with people coming and going day and night. Connections were never made; it was an ongoing stream. But it guaranteed that David would never be alone and would never become bored. There would always be someone for him to play with.

While Angela roamed around stirring everyone up, David, who felt safe and in control only when he dealt with someone on an intense one-to-one basis, elicited information that he thought might prove helpful by zeroing in on somebody in a corner, going from person to person to discuss his career, and playing his new songs.

The drama of what to do about David's career was the topic of prime concern. Ken had gotten him nine dates in Scottish ballrooms (three would be canceled because of lack of business). Those were exactly the kinds of engagements that had made him abandon performing behind Ken's back at the end of 1967. Nothing seemed to have changed.

David left for several dates in Scotland.

On his return his second LP, which in England was called *David Bowie*, like his first, was released. The reviews reinforced what had already been sensed: David was still woefully out of touch. The Beatles had become cynical, Bob Dylan had renounced his savior role and gone country, heavy-metal music was sprouting roots all over England, but there was David playing the role of earnest folksinger in a hodgepodge of leftover pop-rock and moody Dylan copies. His vocal style neither grabbed a listener's attention nor had the finesse to upgrade pedestrian lyrics. Visconti's production, especially when placed beside Dudgeon's "Space Oddity," the high point of the LP, emphasized the worst.

In America, however, one track seemed to fascinate the small cult of fanatics who turned to England to spot the new trends. A mention or two even appeared in print suggesting that England was spawning its own homegrown Bob Dylan.

This track was the nine-and-a-half-minute-long "Cygnet Committee," which introduced a Superman character who "gave them life, gave them all," only to have them "drain [his] very soul dry." David's lyric reeked of metaphor when the song demanded a stark set of brilliantly engraved images.

Three years later a character would appear with the necessary starkness to engrave him permanently in rock lore. This time David would name the character Ziggy Stardust.

A firm believer in appearances, Angela wrestled with David until he agreed to visit Ken. At all costs she and David had to be loved by everyone, with no hard feelings ever directed at them.

The conversation turned to the new LP. Pitt suggested that David was trying to get his old attachment to Dylan out of his system.

David turned white. He caught his breath and burst into tears. He fled from the room, Angela following after him.

"Don't worry, Nama-nama," she roared, "don't worry. He didn't mean it. It's all going to be fine."

When he returned, David acted as if nothing had been said. It was impossible to guess from his manner that he was deeply wounded.

The childlike part of him could not stand criticism from any parental figure.

It was November 20, 1969. The performance at the Purcell Room, which Pitt had reserved a year before, went splendidly. Gus Dudgeon was in charge of the expert musicians. David glowed with authority. Then midway through the set, much to everyone's dismay, he performed "Space Oddity" as a folk song, accompanied only by his guitar. The one song everyone knew and expected to hear with a musical backing was perversely performed another way. David was making a statement: He was not a singles artist; this was no mere pop single. He was a folk singer who happened to be working with musicians. While the audience loved the show, there wasn't one person there who could help David. Calvin, acting as David's manager, had not known who to invite.

David was furious. The event had received no press coverage because he had let Calvin run things. He had worked harder than he had ever worked before to stage a media event at which there had been no media.

Angela and Calvin had fought a subtle war for David's affections. Angela sensed Calvin's jealousy and it made her nervous. "Perhaps Calvin is not the one to help you," she said. "Perhaps he doesn't understand what you need. Perhaps he's too emotionally involved to think clearly and rationally."

It was the permission David needed to erase Calvin, who had failed him. He would not reappear until three years later, when David was a star.

Pitt was fascinated by female stars like Judy Garland and Marlene Dietrich, who cultivated huge gay audiences. Thus he hit on an inspired fantasy: suppose David were to become a gay cult hero? He would automatically receive the hysterical devotion of at least 5 percent, maybe 10 percent, of all the men in the Western world.

It was delicious. The first thing was to have David interviewed by *Jeremy*, the one London gay newspaper. David could play cat and mouse. Was he or wasn't he? David agreed. It was impossible for him ever to say no directly.

Angela was hurt and angry. A conspiracy had formed suddenly to make her the lover of a man the world saw as homosexual. She told David it was a silly idea. Judy Garland wasn't homosexual, and so why should he be? Judy Garland had qualities that homosexuals identify with. She was fragile, strong, and touching. Those were the qualities David ought to be aiming for. She thought Pitt's plan would destroy David's career.

There was obviously a generation gap between Ken and them. Ken's plan would sell records only to well-heeled, middle-class aunties. That would severely limit David's box office appeal.

"Your cause is sexual freedom, which interests everyone," she told David. "Your image should be sexual freedom. You could be the kind of sex symbol the world has never seen before."

Later the phone rang. It was Pitt with the news that "Space Oddity" had won the Songwriters Guild of Great Britain's Ivor Novello Award.

David was upset. He told Angela he believed that the award was controlled by English gay power brokers, and that the prize had been rigged so that he would win. He also said that Pitt had told him he didn't want Angela at the awards ceremony.

Angela had been patient and supportive from the time she had thrown herself down the staircase on their second date, but this insult was too much.

Overcome by fury, she screamed loudly enough to be heard in the other apartments. She went on and on, and suddenly, exhausted, she collapsed into a stupor.

David went to dinner with Ken. That made him even more upset. Everything—absolutely everything—was wrong, and he was very quiet.

Angela took his hand. This was the end of the world—two abandoned children surrounded by snipers and grenades. They were in danger, but somehow both knew that it was inevitable that not only would they be rescued but also would triumph no matter how the cards were stacked against them.

Angela and David were both talkers. Talk seemed like action to them. David's judgment was usually terrible, and Angela was too manic to be very practical. Day after day they pretended to be scientists, analyzing the pop moment and determining how to conquer it. Their gracious manners and articulateness drew people to them who wanted to help. Acting the roles of visionaries, they supplied the illusion of purpose to those who fell into their orbit, with the promise that, in the spirit of the 1960s, the fruits of their success would be shared by everyone.

Helping David enveloped everyone who came to Haddon Hall.

Tony Visconti, Marc Bolan, and Bolan's girl friend/manager June Child believed that all managers should be done away with. They could manage themselves because only they understood the changing world and how their music was changing it. Bolan had abandoned Tyrannosaurus Rex and had formed T. Rex with the startlingly handsome artist/musician Mickey Finn. Angela loathed the arrogant Bolan but craved Finn's masculine good looks. Bolan spoke intensely about UFO's, Fellini films, and fifties rock and roll. He had gone electric and was moving beyond hippiedom to create a new stage persona. David watched his every move.

One night a long bull session went on with photographer Ray Stevenson. He too sensed that there was a step beyond flower power. "What if one went in entirely the opposite direction," Ray pontificated. "Suppose a band announced that it was in it only for the money. Suppose a musician said it was all a hype. Suppose a band called itself the Hype."

David listened carefully. In his mind, he was already rehearsing his next interview as the leader of that as-yet-unformed band.

Pitt couldn't be stopped, and David couldn't say no. *Sunday, Bloody Sunday*, John Schlesinger's new film, concerned a bisexual triangle. Peter Finch was scheduled to play a middle-aged doctor and Glenda Jackson a divorced business consultant. Both characters were simultaneously involved with a beautiful young male artist who deserts them. Ken thought David would make an ideal bisexual heartbreaker. Pitt knew that David couldn't pull his weight against Finch and Jackson, but he hoped the director might find him attractive. David went to the audition and failed it.

To soften the blow Pitt got David a spot on a benefit at the London Palladium for the Invalid Children's Aid Association. David was presented to Princess Margaret along with all the other entertainers. The Beatles had been presented to the royal family, and such moments made him feel important.

Meanwhile, the rest of the news was bad. The English album reviews for David's first Mercury LP (released in England on Philips) were terrible. After the success of "Space Oddity," Essex Music had offered a new advance of 5,000 pounds, but the money would be stretched over three years. There would be no immediate cash, and so no publishing deal was concluded. A release date for the Mercury album had not yet been scheduled for America, and Pitt thought David should go to America to promote the album. But he could not get the president of Mercury Records on the phone. NEMS, the booking agency founded by Brian Epstein, was hired to book David. The agency turned up precious little suitable work. England loved Major Tom but no one wanted to see David Bowie, Dylanesque folksinger.

As Christmas approached Angela announced that she planned to return to Cyprus for the Christmas holidays. David would be alone during the holiday season as well as on his twenty-third birthday on January 8. Before Angela went she gave David a vital piece of information: she believed she was pregnant. Nothing was said directly but it was clear to David that the right and noble thing to do was to marry her. In case that wasn't enough, she reminded him that she did not have English citizenship and had to keep leaving and reentering the country in order to maintain her visa. As a single woman she could not get a work permit and could do nothing official on his behalf.

After she left quiet descended on Haddon Hall. David couldn't stand it. He knew there were many reasons why he should marry Angela. She was pregnant. She was an ideal caretaker. She knew he didn't love her and didn't expect him to behave like a conventional husband. Their relationship would remain "experimental," and they would continue to sleep with whomever they wished, confiding in each other as if they were sisters. Marrying Angela would also infuriate Peggy, who deserved to be punished. Angela would help him fight and then erase Ken. And Marc Bolan was about to marry June. June was Marc's eagle scout, protecting him and running interference while he moved ahead. Now he would have exactly what Marc had.

The idea of marriage was defiant, funny, scary, and very entertaining, and it guaranteed that he would be worshiped, looked after, and never left alone. At the end of the Christmas holidays, he sent a postcard to Cyprus. It read: "Merry Christmas. There's a postal strike. Sorry about this. P.S.: This year we will marry."

Angela thought he might be in love with her but was too over-controlled to say it. She thought even the promise of being in love was enough to make him think she was cramping his style. Her own narcissism led her to believe that if he didn't love her, he would.

The postcard arrived in Cyprus on January 8, David's twenty-third birthday. That night David was booked to do a late-night set at London's premier rock hangout, the Speakeasy. Afterward he would record a new single, "The Prettiest Star," a song he had written for Angela.

The Speakeasy was filled with guitar cowboys dressed in tight velvet pants. Surrounding them were clusters of groupies eagerly giving them the eye. There was no more macho club in London, and this was the epitome of London's rock culture.

Occupying a good table near the playing area were Ken Pitt and a journalist for *Jeremy*. As if it weren't hard enough to invade this authentic rock-and-roll world, it was even harder when the only press covering you is trying to determine if you are gay. Pitt was in an especially good mood. Another of his fantasies about David seemed to be coming true. An offer had turned up for David to score and star in a musical version of Sir Walter Scott's *The Fair Lady of Perth*. David was trying to reenter the world of rock, the antithesis of writing and performing Scottish-style ballads on the West End stage.

England was going Simon-and-Garfunkel-crazy, but that fervor didn't help David. The audience talked during his Dylanesque folk songs, Jacques Brel selections, and recitations of Mason Williams poems. The Speakeasy exuded rock and sex; it ignored wimpiness. There was almost no applause between numbers and even less at the end. They didn't care.

David was flabbergasted and humiliated. It was all wrong. He had to be rescued.

He headed for Trident Studios. Marc Bolan had been invited to play on "The Prettiest Star." He stomped into the studio and ignored David. The success of "Space Oddity" had infuriated him, and he was terribly jealous. David, who demanded to be loved, was stricken by the disapproval.

In the control booth Pitt and June Bolan met for the first time. June lashed out at him.

When Bolan's guitar solo was over, he stormed from the studio without saying good night. But the cloud of anger he left behind refused to dissipate.

At dawn David was alone again. There had been no sexual conquests to prove he was special. There had only been disapproval and failure on his birthday. He felt physically ill. He needed help.

He called Angela. Had she gotten the postcard? It had come that morning, and their conversation turned to his proposal.

"Can you deal with the fact that I don't love you?" he asked.

"Yes, yes. I can deal with anything. But you'll love me before the year is out."

He told her about Bolan's behavior at the recording studio.

"You'll get your own guitarist," she said. "Then you won't ever have to deal with Bolan again."

He played her a tape of "The Prettiest Star." The Prettiest Star listened to yet another of his auditions and showered him with yet another dose of praise. The song was a weak one, no follow-up to "Space Oddity." But at all costs David and Angela had to pretend that a new and even greater hit was in the offing.

"I'm so happy," said Angela. "I can't wait to see you. I'll be there as soon as I can."

She was on the next plane back to London. There the Prettiest Star fell into the arms of her Light Person. It was the only way she knew of becoming a Light Person herself.

Angela throbbed with renewed energy and devotion, exactly what was expected of the future Mrs. David Bowie.

David and Angela settled into the public role of lovebirds, holding hands and billing and cooing at each other wherever they went. Then Tony Visconti and his girl friend Liz moved into Haddon Hall. So did a homeless boy whom they called Roger the Lodger, who would be David's roadie, as well as musician John Cambridge.

Angela, the matriarch, and the entire "family" were especially supportive when David received a copy of the American release of his first Mercury album. It had been retitled *Man of Words/Man of Music* and it bore a different cover from the English pressing. The liner notes were also wrong. It was more proof that neither David nor Pitt had the slightest control over the all-important American market. David became despondent.

But then a call came from Lindsay Kemp inviting David to come to Scotland to appear on a television show.

"You'll adore Lindsay!" David exclaimed.

Angela did adore him. Much to David's delight Kemp gave a great performance for his bride-to-be. He made ultradramatic entrances and exits, swirled his cape to emphasize a point, and used his full repertoire of emphatic gestures to demonstrate that acting life was far superior to living it.

For almost a week Angela and David slept side by side on the floor with the other members of Lindsay's acting family. They loved this family of poor but noble artists joined together in the special mission of demonstrating their art for the enrichment of others. This was Bohemia, and even though people acted such emotions as love and jealousy, it was distinctly bad form to experience real feelings. It was dramatic, and it was safe.

"You simply go and see everything, and you nick the good ideas," Lindsay said of his art. "You nick a touch of this; you nick a touch of that. Then you do it better simply by using scotch tape, sawdust, and a little imagination. And everyone will do it for you because they love you." It was the mime's crash course in how to be an artist.

The night after his return to London David was booked at the Marquee Club. It was another disaster. Even with his hit, which had been off the chart less than two months, only 129 people came. He had attracted more attention at the Marquee four years earlier when he led the Lower Third.

John Cambridge had been telling David about a guitarist friend, Mick Ronson, whom he wanted him to meet. Ronno supported himself by wheeling a machine across rugby fields to mark out the playing lines. A muscular, handsome young man with a beautiful pink English complexion, he had a North Country accent so thick he could hardly be understood even by other Englishmen. By nature he was shy and self-conscious, reluctant to leave Hull for London to audition for someone who had had a Top Ten record. Finally Cambridge had his way, and David and Ronson met for the first time at the Marquee Club gig.

Two days later Ronno was invited to Haddon Hall. David needed a guitarist to tape a radio program that day.

David gently told Ronno what to play. John Jones had been a Yorkshireman, and David had an instinctive rapport with anyone from the North Country. Ronno liked his manner. David seemed like a real London gentleman.

The men played together. David's music seemed too hard for him; it did not have enough melody. But Ronno assumed that was his fault and not David's, and anyway he was a man whose insecurities expressed themselves as passivity. He was very controllable, and now, suddenly, he was on the radio. The shy, gentle musician was very happy; it was the perfect mix of passivity, enthusiasm, and talent.

Ronno had nowhere to stay, and Angela and David invited him to join the Haddon Hall family and sleep in a sleeping bag on the minstrel's gallery.

The next day a fever settled over Haddon Hall. It would last nineteen days. During that time the Hype would be created. Angela was the sergeant-at-arms. She made lists, organized activities, told people what to do, and kept everyone on the run. The Hype would be unlike any other group; it would present a theatrical experience of the kind created by Lindsay Kemp, not mere rock and roll.

Angela became David's interpreter. David didn't tell anyone what he wanted, and Angela stared anxiously into his face, divining his desires. Then she barked orders. As things progressed David indicated by a gesture, a nod, or a comment whether Angela had correctly perceived his wishes. In the midst of her volcanic bursts of activity David held quiet private conversations with the other members of his rock trio.

As Angela served as his organizer/interpreter, Ronno fell easily into the role of band leader, interpreting David's musical ideas for him. Ronno was a versatile musician, wrote arrangements, and could hear the musical sounds in David's head. David's creativity and permissiveness impressed him even if he had to do all the nuts-and-bolts work. He felt lucky to be working with such a talented, nice man.

David enjoyed playing Ken Pitt to Ronno's Davie Jones while they set about making a band that would demonstrate the Lindsay Kemp "scotch tape-sawdust-imagination-nip-a-little-of-this-nip-a-little-of-that" school of theater. If luck was with them, they would sell this new image with the panache of suburban English Andy Warhols.

Angela had a job to do and had no patience with stuttering guitar cowboys. Ronno had to be lectured about the fact he was an actor and nothing as pedestrian as a blues musician. He had to look a part and then play that part on stage and off. He would have to maintain an image, but what would Ronno's new image be?

Angela stared at Ronno. "What are your fantasies?" she bellowed. "What would you like to be?" The guitarist had no fantasies. It was hard enough drifting along being himself.

"What are fantasies? Tell me your fantasies," she urged. Ronno was tongue-tied.

"You must have a fantasy."

Finally he stuttered, "I'd . . . I'd like to be . . . I'd to be a gangster."

"Gangster Man!" she exclaimed. "You're going to be a bloody gangster."

David did not object. It was as if he had wanted all along for Ronno to be Gangster Man.

Choosing to humor Angela, Ronno did as he was told. She was lovable and funny, but he also thought she was crazy. It was beyond him to fathom that she, like David, craved unconditional love and that the man she loved survived by being good-humored but ironically detached. David avoided any semblance of routine that would make him feel frighteningly ordinary. His energy was saved for romance, the romance of himself. Angela, whom he mimicked and trusted, represented the key player of the moment in his theater of everyday life.

David called Pitt. He enthusiastically described his new rock trio. By the time the call was over, Pitt was convinced he had named the group the Hype. During the call David suggested that Pitt hunt down jobs for the group.

Pitt eagerly set about getting jobs for the group he believed he had just named. At the end of the month the Hype would make its debut—on February 22, 1970, at the Round House, the theater in which Ken had fantasized presenting the Velvet Underground three years before.

At the Round House David, dressed in a glittery white jacket, a huge metal necklace, and lots of flowing scarves tied around his neck, was resplendent as Rainbow Man; Visconti in a Superman cape with a big H on his sweater made a hilarious-looking Hype Man; and Ronno, in a pinstriped suit, did his good-humored best as Gangster Man. This "theater of image" was dress-up, and they had dressed up nicely. But one major element was beyond their grasp. They were doing David's old songs, songs that did not work as folk songs and seemed even more ludicrously wimpish when blasted at the audience by three men in homemade Marvel Comics outfits. The guitars were so loud that David could hardly be heard, and the set made almost no impact at all. They may have been "actors," but actors need a good script.

A few days after the performance, "The Prettiest Star" was released. The radio stations didn't like the record, and the reviews were mixed. *New Musical Express* labeled it "quiet," "inoffensive," and *Record Mirror* said David was "near to croaking in his emotionless voice."

As Tony Visconti had predicted, the spectacular success of "Space Oddity" was being followed by a dud.

After a benefit appearance at the Royal Albert Hall, David turned to Pitt and said, "Well, we're going to get married."

Pitt viewed Angela as the enemy, someone who was marrying his boy merely to obtain British citizenship.

By now David knew that Angela wasn't pregnant, but he always liked playing new roles, and the role of husband and father had intrigued him. That made it seem to Angela that he could—and would—love her. They were getting married, and at the core of the marriage was the simple fact that each had tricked the other, Angela with her suspected pregnancy, David with his imitation of real feelings.

March 20, 1970, was set as the date. Neither Angela's family nor Peggy was told, but Peggy got wind of it anyway. She hated Angela. She called Pitt. He told her he didn't know a thing about it, but that he doubted it would really happen.

When David and Angela were sure that Peggy had learned of their plans, David called his mother. Peggy immediately called Pitt and said that she was going to the wedding. She was not going to miss this opportunity. She never missed any of her son's performances.

Pitt made it clear he would not go.

The marriage was conceived on a theoretical basis. Infidelity was acceptable; jealousy and possessiveness were impermissible; each would tell the other about his or her extramarital affairs; and they would stay together forever because of the extraordinary trust and understanding they shared.

David assured Angela that she would always be the most important figure in his life. At the time he believed what he was saying; so did she.

The day before the wedding David and Angela went shopping for Angela's antique wedding dress and then paid a visit to a girl friend. She invited them to stay for dinner, and a long conversation followed. David was remarkably intense and his intensity created the seductive illusion of intimacy that so many found so beguiling. Angela sensed that David wanted sex. She was the more brazen, and even though she had never participated in a threesome before, she grew more openly bawdy.

The next day everyone overslept and was an hour and a half late for the wedding. The guests, kept waiting at the Bromley Register Office, were few in number. Tony Visconti was recording the Strawbs, but his girl friend, Liz Hartley, was there, along with John Cambridge and another musician buddy, Roger Fry.

As best man, John Cambridge had to sign the register. Suddenly Peggy stepped forward, took the pen, and signed it herself. If David was to be given away, she would be the one to do it.

Meanwhile, Angela had gotten exactly what she wanted. The Light Person was officially hers.

CHAPTER 9

Control

As usual, things were in a shambles. "The Prettiest Star" had sold fewer than a thousand copies, and Mercury had gone so far as to instruct Tony Visconti on how to give David's new single, "Memory of a Free Festival," a hit format and sound.

David and Olav Wyper, the general manager of Philips Records, had become friendly, and David told him about his problems with Pitt. Management contracts were virtually impossible to break in England, and Wyper suggested he see a lawyer. He gave David three names, including that of his own lawyer, Tony Defries.

To eliminate Pitt was to commit an act of patricide. David had done his best to play wonderful son with Ken. Now Pitt had to be erased. The process was a simple one: David took no action, but shunted him out of his mind.

"Nama-nama," said Angela, "we must do something for you. You must go see the man Olav says can help." David agreed but did nothing.

Then Pitt received an extension on David's Mercury contract. David would be a Mercury artist at least until June 1972. A small amount of money was released for a new album, which David would have to record quickly.

Ken wanted Mercury to commit to bringing David to the United States on the American release of the LP. Mercury refused. Pitt told David that he would pay for the trip himself, as well as for the services of a major publicity firm. Now another fantasy took shape: David would be the contemporary Oscar Wilde. Wilde had gone to the United States to publicize Gilbert and Sullivan's *Patience*. Dressed outrageously in a velvet coat, breeches, buckle shoes, and a large green tie, he had traveled by sea, and when the boat docked the press was brought to inspect him. David would duplicate Wilde's stunt.

"Wilde was a Victorian literary sensation," said Angela. "That's why *that* worked. You must go see the man Olav told you about."

Again David agreed but did nothing. It was hard for him to deal realistically with any situation. Instead he played the lost child while everyone told him what to do, and he appeared to be their pawn. Then he would move swiftly and directly. The process brought those who cared to their breaking points. Then, when they were on the brink of exhaustion, his speedy decisiveness gave the illusion that he was all action and business while everyone else was a victim of emotional burnout.

Pitt had gotten David a booking on the same day he was scheduled to record. David erupted when Pitt said he had to keep the date. Didn't Ken know that a recording date was far more important than one of those hideous ballroom bookings?

"You must see the man Olav told you about," moaned Angela. "You *must!*"

A meeting was finally arranged with Tony Defries. David did not shave and looked exhausted and racked with pain. He had transformed himself into the irresistible orphan-waif who screamed out to be adopted. It was a pose that almost never failed, and he believed every second of it.

He waited nervously in Defries's waiting room. Alternately he chain-smoked, paced, and chewed his nails. It was not easy erasing a father whose fantasy he had promised to fulfill and who had spent so much money on him in the pursuit of that fantasy.

The wait was a long one. David kept everyone waiting, but being kept waiting was new to him. Finally a man appeared in the doorway, and greeted him softly. Defries's tone rang of familiarity. They could have been old friends. David quickly took in the lawyer. Defries looked like a chubby, baby-faced teddy bear. His face was dominated by blue eyes and a huge nose and was framed by a halo of thick brown, medium-length curly hair. It sat on a round-shouldered, paunchy body. Even though he was only a year older than David, he loped instead of walked, and his slowness made him seem much older.

Defries walked toward David, staring deeply into David's eyes. It seemed as if he was taking David in while reading his mind at the same time. David became more nervous. Defries's initial reaction was that David was a pathetic little fellow in some terrible mess. It was his job to straighten out the lives and affairs of all the pathetic people who passed through his doors and were just not smart enough to keep themselves out of trouble.

Defries led David to his office and ushered him into a seat. He calmly took his place behind his desk, slowly picked up his phone, and ordered tea. Then he seemed to fall into deep thought. He picked up the phone again and in a soft, soothing voice began to discuss another matter with his secretary.

David demanded attention. But here he would get none until this man was good and ready. David knew that he had stumbled onto another one of life's stage sets and had come face-to-face with another actor.

Defries turned to the papers on his desk, thumbing through and rearranging them. He made another call. Then tea arrived.

David had not expected to be brought to his breaking point. Defries's manner indicated that he was totally in charge. That meant that David was the child who had to impress him. David would impress him with the life-and-death nature of his dilemma.

Defries took out a cigar, methodically clipped its ends, and lit up. He asked David to describe his problem.

David explained that Pitt had taken a "long-term view" of his career, which seemed to him one long frustrating series of failed experiments that supposedly were to lead to David's becoming "the greatest entertainer of the century." David was especially upset about the status of his recording career. "It isn't happening," he said sadly. "Not a thing is happening."

The lawyer seemed hardly to be listening. He thumbed through books, occasionally making notes on a yellow legal pad in front of him. David paused. Defries picked up the phone and made calls about other business. David resumed talking and Defries got up and looked out the window. Occasionally he looked at David, seeming to read his mind.

When David was done, Defries said nothing, as if there were nothing worth saying. The silence was not even interrupted by a sympathetic comment.

"You do have a problem," Defries finally said. But David's problem was not his contract with Ken. In the long term a contract was merely a piece of paper, and had value only when both parties agree to it. Contracts had nothing to do with becoming the greatest entertainer of the century.

It was said with an air of total self-confidence. So many people had told David that the agreement couldn't be broken. This man not only said that it could be dissolved, but also indicated that he could dissolve it with no problem at all. Defries, like David, took ideas he heard and incorporated them into his thinking. Defries would spin Pitt's "long-term view" of David and his vision of David as "the greatest entertainer of the century" further than Pitt had ever dared.

He explained that David's real problem was the fact that he recorded for Mercury. Record companies existed to do what you wanted them to do. It was apparent that David had given away control over his recording when the whole point was to gain control over his work. The more control he had, the more say-so he would have over how his product was presented and sold.

Defries loved to expound on his philosophy of how the music business should be run. Anyone, including the office boy, who stepped into that office was subjected to his soft-spoken endless discursiveness. Defries was driven to win approval by demonstrating that he was the most intelligent and superior of all.

David sat back and listened. Defries's demonstration made him feel special. It was entertaining; it also made sense.

Defries told him that record company people were all fools and idiots. To trust them to do anything was lunacy, absolute lunacy. They were all a bunch of nonstarters. If they weren't nonstarters they wouldn't be in the business in the first place. They wouldn't be working for a record company. They'd be doing something real, something productive.

What David was experiencing was a group of second-level people taking orders from someone above them who were only concerned about collecting their paychecks at the end of the week. They couldn't be expected to look after David's interests. To think that was more lunacy. The only way around that was to have all the control.

Upon hearing the word "control," David leaned forward. Defries rose to the occasion.

Defries believed that Pitt had given too much control to Mercury, and that David had to get the control back. That was to be the priority they shared together. After all, he said, Mercury was a lackluster record company, the biggest nonstarters of all.

David nodded in agreement.

Epstein was a terrible manager, expounded Defries. He just happened to be lucky. He happened to have the Beatles. But he didn't know what he was doing. Defries said that an inspection of Brian Epstein's contracts would reveal that Epstein had created a terrible mess. He gave lots away. He had no real control and got into serious trouble. Such mistakes could be avoided, especially if one looked at those made by Epstein.

Then Defries spoke the words David had been longing to hear. David did not have to do anything he did not wish to do. He was an artist, and his only job was to create. His manager was supposed to do whatever was necessary to enable him to be creative. His manager was supposed to take away the worries of living so that he felt free. His manager should pay his rent and pay all the bills. In return all he needed to do was be creative.

The roughest outlines of a plan were emerging. Defries could solve his problem with Ken Pitt. He could retrieve David's albums from Mercury. David could have control. And this man would pay the rent without ever forcing him to risk public humiliation by making him audition for films and commercials that he was bound not to get. It was exactly the way someone creative should be treated.

David left Defries's office in a state of euphoria. He was so happy tears streamed down his cheeks. This man was strong the way a child expected an ideal father to be. Defries was the smartest and most powerful manager of all, and David was not at all bothered by the fact that Defries had never managed a single act.

David brought Angela to meet his new friend. Defries stared at them. They did not seem like man and wife, but rather like two three-year-olds who were best friends. The lawyer quickly surmised that David used his sexuality to exert control over Angela. As long as David tantalized her she would behave obediently. By surrendering his sexuality, David had already lost much of the control. Defries enjoyed that. No one exerted sexual control over him. He was above such flaws in the human character.

During the meeting the subject of David's doing a promotional tour of America came up.

Defries explained that it was all a question of supply and demand. There had to be a demand for David's services, and at that point there was no demand for David in America. That was why it was so difficult to obtain any kind of record-company backing.

The first thing to do was get David off Mercury. Why try to move a record company to do something when they're not very interested in doing it? That was a waste of time and energy. They had to create a demand for David in America and then book a tour designed for the greatest entertainer of the twentieth century.

Angela was as enthralled as David. This man knew how to create a demand for David in America, and David and Angela were happy and hopeful.

After the wedding Angela's parents gave the couple a wedding present of $1,000. Angela, cash in hand, David trailing behind her, marched from Haddon Hall to practice her one great art: shopping. All of the money was spent on furnishings for the apartment. By the end of the day they were broke. The subject of cash flow provoked a long brainstorming session.

Angela said what David wanted to hear. "You've already learned so much from Tony," said Angela. "Why don't you manage yourself? Ken might even give you an advance to get you started."

David met Pitt, told him he wanted to manage himself, and asked for an advance of 200 pounds. Again, Pitt took out his checkbook.

Angela's instinct was to turn their next meeting with Defries into a social occasion at which she could demonstrate what she had been trained to do: cook elegant meals and be a gracious hostess. It was exactly what David wanted her to do. Angela's job included being David's eagle scout. She was to use her finishing-school charms to entice Defries further into their orbit. Then when he was thoroughly disarmed David would take over.

The lawyer accepted the children's invitation to Sunday lunch at Haddon Hall with no hesitation. It was the first of many long afternoons spent eating and talking together. In many ways David and Tony were similar. David never spoke about his family background, and neither did Tony. And neither bothered to ask the other any personal questions.

Defries's childhood had rivaled that of Oliver Twist's. Sickly and asthmatic, he spent a great deal of time in hospitals. He believed that he survived only by developing control over each of his breaths; he had proved that he had enough control to subjugate his body to his will. Gaining total control became the means to ensure his survival.

Defries's parents were peddlers, and as a child Defries had been a market boy in Petticoat Lane. It was his job to run from peddler to peddler memorizing the merchandise and the prices and then report back to his father, who lowered his prices to undercut the competition. Wise to the trick, the other peddlers beat him with sticks whenever he approached their stalls; if he gave his father faulty or incomplete information, his father beat him.

The scars of childhood created a man who refused to admit to human feelings and transcended a world in which such brutalities occurred by dismissing it with an attitude of overwhelming superiority. Defries also needed to create ideal families around him, families he could totally control.

David and Tony were both narcissistic personalities, each in search of the ideal family, each determined to control the family he created. Meanwhile, Defries viewed Angela and David as ideal children. They were "the little ones," and they happily accepted him in the role of ideal father. No clash would occur unless either man became bored or unhappy in his part.

At these get-togethers Defries did not really think about becoming David's manager. The reality of the moment was always too small for Tony, and he was concerned with the glorious future two or three years down the road. These fantasies were spoken with so much conviction that everyone believed them. Defries's authority and self-confidence enabled him to spin myths as if they were truths.

It had been eight years since the Beatles had had their first hit, and Defries had studied the management, music publishing, and taxation problems of the major music groups. He was interested in making a killing in the music business, but only to demonstrate that he knew where all the loopholes were and was the only one who knew how to close them. He wanted to be a manager but refused to search for an act. To secure his services an act would have to come to him.

A mating dance went on at Haddon Hall. David and Angela

wanted Tony's help, so they listened to and believed everything he said. Tony brought such an air of authority to any topic. He seemed to know everything.

David mentioned how he disliked his ballroom engagements. Tony didn't see the point of David's appearing in ballrooms when his music wasn't danceable. If Tony was his manager, David would never have to play a ballroom again.

David brought up the failed movie and theater auditions. Tony said that auditions had nothing to do with selling records and building a career. Why should one try to make a movie until someone wants to put you in a movie? To Tony, that seemed like a waste of time.

David would never have to audition again—never have to face anyone who didn't want him.

At the end of the month a letter from David arrived at Ken Pitt's office. It attempted to be confusing and complicated, but the gist was that Pitt was no longer to consider himself David's manager.

Ken was willing to give David a six-month grace period in which he managed himself, and then release him if he wished; administer David's career while he managed himself; or let him go on the spot if that was what he really wanted. The last thing he expected was a secretary to call and make an appointment for a meeting with him, David, and David's lawyer, Tony Defries.

David and Tony arrived promptly at Ken Pitt's office. Defries wore a business suit and was neatly groomed, and David was dressed in satin pants that Angela had chosen for him. There was a vacant expression on David's face, and he seemed so distant he could hardly say hello.

Both Ken and Tony were gentlemen. The brief meeting was conducted at almost whisper level. Defries stared at Pitt. Immediately he surmised that the manager was another of those held captive by David, but nothing registered on his face or in the neutral tone of his voice.

Defries explained that he was a lawyer who worked with people in the music business. Pitt stared at him. This litigation clerk was pretending he was a lawyer. A surge of condescension ran through him.

David looked straight ahead. He could have been a zombie. Pitt tried to catch his eye. He had to warn the boy, protect him. He

focused on sending David a psychic message: "Don't be taken in . . .
you have a brilliant future ahead of you . . . we've been together
four years . . . it's beginning to work . . . it will work . . . this man
wants to steal you for himself. . . ."

Defries and Pitt politely parried back and forth. Pitt used buzz
words he was sure David could understand, language they alone
shared, but no matter how hard he tried he could not break through.

It was over and Pitt knew it. Inevitably his boy was going to be
a great star, but not with him at the helm. In his gut he knew that
his dream had been snatched by this curly-headed litigation clerk.

The conversation shifted to a discussion of the money David
owed Pitt, and the future monies Pitt would sacrifice by losing David.

Tony replied slowly and evenly. He said he would consider the
size of the settlement after he saw Pitt's figures.

Pitt feels that Defries made a great mistake by not negotiating a
settlement then and there. He had planned to be gentlemanly and
ask for a token settlement of 2,000 pounds. He did not understand
that Defries thought it ridiculous to promise a specific sum to a man
who had spent his own money on David and not reaped the long-
term profits from that investment.

The meeting drew to a conclusion, and David quietly thanked
Ken.

Four years of Pitt's life walked out the door, but he did not blame
David. David was easily influenced and never to blame.

Pitt decided never again to make a contract with another artist.
Three years would pass before David spoke another word to him.
By that time David had become a sensational star in England, had
launched a triumphant entry into America, and had completed a
vastly successful tour of Japan. With those credentials behind him,
he was able to look his ex-father straight in the eye.

But for the moment, Pitt had been erased.

Angela had no inhibitions, and that intrigued Defries. Sometimes
he was awkward around women. By instinct, Angela thought up a
next step. They both knew that the ravishing Dana Gillespie, David's
off-again on-again girl friend from the time she was fourteen, was
drawn to Jewish men, especially Jewish businessmen, whom she
perceived as having especially large noses. They would deliver a
goddess to Defries.

Dana was appearing in a West End production of *Catch My Soul*, a pop-rock musical based on Shakespeare's *Othello*. David and Angela went to the show and then visited Dana backstage.

"I really think you should go meet this guy," said David. It was the first time in their four-year friendship that David had volunteered to be of help; it was the first time he had anything tangible to offer.

A few days later David brought Dana to Defries's office. Defries inspected the eighteen-year-old. She was extraordinarily curvaceous, a really beautiful woman with a wonderful mane of golden hair that tumbled down her back. He studied the face that rested on that sensual body. She looked like an angel with dirty thoughts. Dana wore an overpowering amount of gardenia perfume. There are some people who are obviously sexual beings, and she was one of them.

Dana inspected Defries. She was attracted to him. She liked his measured, calm, analytical approach. He explained what her career needed and what he could do for her. Everything seemed so simple, clear, possible. His paternal style did not seem like effective salesmanship, but like real expertise. Defries was a great salesman. As she listened to him Dana felt as if she were three years old and listening to a very wise daddy explain how the world worked.

They began to see each other alone, and then began to doubledate with Angela and David. They would drive to Beckenham on Sundays for lunch, or Defries would take them to dinner at Mimo's, their favorite London restaurant, or they would retreat to Haddon Hall where they sat in the garden or went inside to watch television.

Dana's sharpest memories of those days were of David sitting on his bed "waiting for Angela to bring him food, waiting for a visitor to arrive, waiting for a program he wanted to see to come on the television." His favorite activity seemed to be waiting. But his inscrutability remained intact. No matter how long he waited, his talent guaranteed that he would become a star.

Defries had left his law firm and formed a partnership with an accountant friend, Laurence Myers, called the Gem Group. It was to be a combination music production, publishing, booking, and management company. Defries would sign new artists, as would Myers, with the running of the company split between them. Myers would supply financial support over and above the initial start-up income. The accountant had married well, and there was money to spend.

Soon all any of them could talk about was "the long term." In the long term, Tony would have a building in America like the Pan Am Building, a building on Park Avenue—the Gem Building, which would be the New York headquarters of an international entertainment conglomerate. They liked that.

Defries turned to one of his favorite subjects, the great Hollywood motion picture studios. He explained that the studios took care of everything. Everyone was a *family*. The studios had *total control*. David and Tony both liked the idea of families who could be controlled.

Tony said that the studios controlled every aspect of the manufacture and distribution of motion pictures. They developed the properties, made the pictures, invented and then created the images of each of their stars. They owned their chains of movie theaters and controlled the distribution. *They* controlled the industry, not the other way around. They liked that too.

In the long term, Gem would have the total control that was the hallmark of Metro-Goldwyn-Mayer—that's why it would accomplish so much more than record companies like Mercury. In the long term it was inevitable that they would wind up in the motion picture business on a studio-sized level. Everyone was very happy.

Twenty or thirty minutes were devoted by Defries to a discussion of motion picture moguls like Louis B. Mayer and his special favorite, Howard Hughes.

No one ever knew where Hughes was. He was never photographed, never seen—he was a total mystery. Was Howard Hughes dead or was he really alive? Who knew for sure? Hughes's secret was his ability to create confusion. By confusing people he was able to exert total control over them. As an invisible man he was able to be everywhere at all times without ever being seen. His very invisibility was the great secret of his success.

It was inevitable: Defries was destined to be the next Invisible Man. By following his lead, David was destined to be the Greatest Entertainer of the Twentieth Century, Angela was destined to be Mrs. Greatest Entertainer of the Twentieth Century, and Dana, who viewed the whole thing with detachment and humor, would also be a great star.

Imaginative, hungry people in their twenties often engage in fantasies like these. But there was a difference. Defries, who spun the greatest fantasies of all, could also, when he was ready, take swift and effective action. David and Angela listened while Dana described how Defries had met with her managers. By the time the meeting was over he had broken Dana's management contract and had retrieved the rights to her music publishing. By midsummer Dana had officially become a Gem artist. She was working, and her salary could be commissioned by Gem, reason enough for the speed with which Defries took over her business affairs.

Tony said that his vision of David was as an artist at home at Beckenham writing new songs. Then they would think about his future—a year or a year and a half down the line. When he was free of his Mercury commitment, Tony would make a deal with one of the majors. Until Mercury was replaced, it was all academic. David was to amuse himself.

Defries stressed the long term, because in the short term he didn't know what to do with David. David didn't complain. He had permission to stay at home and take it easy, something he was always inclined to do.

Defries then explained his master plan for his own future. Stevie Wonder was going to turn twenty-one the following May. He would be of legal age and could make his own contracts. Tony's associate Don Hunter worked at Motown and knew Wonder. His plan was to take Wonder from Motown and manage him. He was going to make his own record deal for Wonder—a deal of major proportions commensurate with Wonder's stature on the American entertainment scene.

He believed he would be Stevie Wonder's manager. It would take the failure of that dream the following May before he turned his full attention to David, who would be put on hold for most of the following year. It appeared that David would have to wait until Stevie Wonder was twenty-one before Defries could launch the process of making him the greatest entertainer of the century.

There was a very specific reason why neither David nor Angela dared contradict Defries's plans: He put his money where his mouth was. In the short term, even though he didn't have much cash, he didn't mind giving away what he had. Whenever David and Angela needed money, Defries handed Angela cash. This act of faith in the long term made the couple especially eager to support Tony's fantasies while reinforcing the fact that their fate was secured. They did not think about the fact that it was Tony's nature to keep accurate records of every cent. He believed he was advancing them their own future earnings; in the long term they, not he, were paying their own way. But not before they became dependent on him.

The Man Who Sold the World

At the end of a summer of lunches, dinners, endless conversations, and ongoing confusion, Defries struck quickly and effectively. A publishing deal was concluded with Chrysalis Music, and David received a lump sum of $12,000. David and Angela were delighted.

Then Tony set up an overdraft system at the bank. Money would go from Gem into the Bowies' account. If they overspent the sum, the amount would be made up by Defries the following month. This system allowed them to charge things and have the bills forwarded to the bank, which would pay them even when there was no actual money in the account. For the first time in their lives they had credit, and they were ecstatic.

Now Angela could do what she did best—shop.

One day at Mr. Fish's boutique Angela spotted a row of men's dresses. Mick Jagger had been photographed in one the year before.

"Oh, darling, they're beautiful," she cooed. David looked at her. Angela's eyes danced with encouragement.

"I think they would make a perfectly wonderful promotional picture. Darling, I think you should try one on. It's perfect for you."

"You don't think it's a bit much?" David asked.

"No, darling. It's beautifully designed. The color's perfect for you. After all, it is a *man's* dress. It's very medieval looking. You'll look like a medieval prince. And our good friend Mr. Fish wouldn't steer us wrong."

David's instinct was to trust Angela. When it came to a sense of style she was almost always right. By mimicking her he was learning how to create and then project different visual personifications of himself.

The photograph of him in the dress, taken at Haddon Hall, was selected as the jacket photograph for *The Man Who Sold the World*, his second album for Mercury. When the artwork reached Chicago, it was rejected. Conservative American radio stations would never give airplay to songs written by a transvestite. A Beckenham artist did a new piece of artwork, a stick-figure drawing of Terry Burns in front of Cane Hill Hospital, where he was incarcerated.

Terry had been in and out of the mental hospital and had stayed periodically at Haddon Hall at Angela's invitation. Angela did her best with him but his madness was real, unlike the ongoing swirl of chaos that marked her domestic life. In reality, he had nowhere to go, and Cane Hill was the only place that accepted him unequivocally.

Defries continued to visit the Beckenham beehive. He watched Angela proudly display all the clothes she had bought. He approved of the spending; after all, they were spending *their* money. Though he could never admit it, he was as fascinated by her spending as he was by their sexuality. As she taught David the art of visualization, she taught Defries the art of excess as a way of life. In the long term he would spend on the grandest scale of all. In that way *he* would demonstrate that he was above the human fray.

In November 1970 *The Man Who Sold the World* was released in America. David, obsessed with Angela and going through the trauma of firing Pitt, had supplied chord changes and song titles and had added lyrics after the final mix, but the album essentially belonged to Ronno and Tony Visconti, who did all of the nuts-and-bolts work.

The LP demonstrated David's growing pains to achieve songwriting authenticity, with Ronno underpinning him in the guise of Jimi Hendrix and Jeff Beck. While David's lyrics were dark and fatalistic, Ronno's contribution paid tribute to the English heavy-metal mongers of 1968 through 1970.

"The Width of a Circle," the album's epic minute lead-off, kicked in with a feedback-drenched guitar figure that would have been at home on Hendrix's *Axis: Bold as Love*. The song was a speedy collection of images. Representative of the tone of the LP was "All the Madmen," a song in which David presented a madman, foot in hand

and talking to the wall. Depressing and boorishly produced, *The Man Who Sold the World* lacked the originality, musicality, and production sheen of "Space Oddity." But it was unexpected and thoroughly different from David's first two LP's.

Eventually critics, treating David's lyrics as if they were Rorschach tests, would conclude that *The Man Who Sold the World* portrayed Terry Burns's schizophrenia and that David had accepted Terry's madness as his own. Such unconscious processes conceivably were at work, but Defries observed that Terry's illness was one of a horde of things that obsessed David for the minute. Like a fickle child, he was always finding something new to preoccupy him. The only thing about Terry's madness that seemed to be a constant was David's ability to use it as a public relations ploy, something he would refer to when he wanted to capture someone's attention or impress a reporter with "truths" about the pain of his existence.

In America *The Man Who Sold the World* was ignored. Those who reviewed it disliked it, and the album sank quickly. The relief of financial pressures softened the blow at Haddon Hall. Everyone had fallen into Defries's slow tempo. He really was the man who sold the world, and he had all the time in the world in which to sell. When he was ready he would sell David to the world. All David need do was keep himself busy, write new songs when the mood was upon him, and wait for the magical moment that was bound to arrive.

While David waited, he studied the progress of his friend Marc Bolan. At the end of 1970 Marc suddenly became a star. The first T. Rex single, "Ride a Swan," rode into the English Top Ten.

When Ray Stevenson next visited David he felt real energy emanating from David for the first time. If Bolan could do it, David finally knew he could do it too.

Haddon Hall was a family, and the family existed to serve David. No bad words were exchanged; it was not David's style ever to act aggressively. But Tony Visconti had given Marc a hit while David's album failed. Within a month after Bolan's triumph, Visconti would move out of Haddon Hall.

This time Angela really was pregnant. Parenthood was a role each seemed eager to play. While they waited for the baby, Angela sensed that her very precious child/husband had to be kept entertained. One of the few late-night places that pleased them both was the trendy gay discotheque, the Sombrero. David and Angela loved its crazy mix of cheer and decadence. They loved the homosexuals who gathered there, a collection of well-heeled, middle-aged men from all over the world, pretty young boys, outrageously dressed queens, gorgeous female models whose pictures were always turning up in London's fashion magazines, and a certain number of women who were turned on by being with gays. Most of all they loved the drag queens. The more outrageously feminine the transvestite, the more macho David felt. Being macho was always a great kick for the actor in him.

The dance floor at the Sombrero was made of translucent glass and it lit up, giving the sensation that you were not on solid ground anymore. It was like dancing on air, and David and Angela loved cavorting on it, dancing with each other, gay men, or with the drag queens or effeminate little Oriental boys who occasionally wandered by.

The atmosphere was the antithesis of the world of English rock music, reigned over at that time by bands like Led Zeppelin and Black Sabbath. To the habitués of the Sombrero, rock music was synonymous with the English hippies, creatures who were unconcerned about style and elegance and, therefore, not to be given a second thought. Rock was *never* played at the club; the music was pallid early Euro-disco and no rock aficionado—gay or straight— would be caught dead there. It was a place in which David could escape from the competitive rock world and its emphasis on authenticity. Here only style counted, and it was a relief.

There was a star system at the Sombrero. The most stylish boys, those who had the most attitude of all, were the biggest stars. Freddi Burrett was the acknowledged leader, a willowy nineteen-year-old who wore extravagant costumes and seemed to have a lot of money. He said he was a student and fashion designer. Freddi spent most of his evenings posing in the corner of the Sombrero. Though men stared at him from a distance, he looked so haughty he was rarely if ever approached. As accomplished role-players, David and Angela were amused by the role Freddi had assumed. By acting as if he were the epitome of sexual desire, the most desirable boy in the club, he lived to impress with his sense of style. Angela and David loved his every move.

"Miss Frieda looks sportive tonight," said Angela to David, "considering her tragedy." A close friend of Freddi's had just been murdered. He had been blackmailing a "pederast colonel," who had instructed two soldiers to slit his throat.

At the Sombrero Angela indulged her appetite for being lots of different people. She minced, talked tough, and played sex kitten as well as boldly aggressive sexual huntress. Her performance was outrageous and it captivated the queens.

She enjoyed herself wildly, but there was also some method to her madness. In his imagination David lived in a world of constant magic. He would spend a brief amount of time with a person and then perceive that person as magical. In David's eyes Freddi Burrett had become some magical incarnation of style. David's genius was to see people and events through magical glasses and then take that magic, which he himself had created, and use it as a source of his own creativity. In the same way a grain of sand gets into an oyster and the oyster begins to secrete a nacre around it, David used Freddi, Lindsay Kemp, Marc Bolan, Bob Dylan, Jean Genet, even Terry Burns's schizophrenia.

To keep David busy and happy, Angela networked Freddi Burrett. Soon he was coming to Haddon Hall, where he spent two or three hours dressing Angela for her nights at the club. David studied Freddi and the art of dressing up. Like Angela, he also began to mimic Freddi.

He smiled at Freddi. "You could be the new Jagger," he said. "Jagger is so old hat. You're the pop star of the future. I'd like to write some songs for you. Then I'll record you. We'll manufacture your image and it will sweep the world."

David's enthusiasm was boundless. In Freddi he saw the reflection of his fantasies about himself. Freddi was delighted. David had flattered him. No one ever thought that he could be a pop idol; by kindling such fantasies David had guaranteed that Freddi would be his adoring fan.

In the process of camping with his new playmate David enjoyed acting gay. Because he was married he could act gay without wearing the label of homosexual, without having the macho part of his personality threatened by being in a room filled with homosexuals and being considered one of them. He could get attention and yet feel superior to those he entranced. The Sombrero was another family he could enter and then make his own. It was an act, but like all his performances, for the moment it took him over.

It appeared to those around him that Freddi and David had become lovers. No one would ever know for sure whether they actually slept together. Even more confusing was the fact that Freddi also had a girl friend, Daniella Parma. What did David's and Freddi's public kisses mean? Was it true love or were they participating in an act of outrage because they were addicted to getting attention? What did Angela think of the relationship between David and Freddi? What was Daniella's reaction? David and Angela had given the queens of the Sombrero plenty to chew over, and David, like Defries, thrived on manufacturing his own brand of confusion.

This confusion made them intriguing enough for Angela to attract any oddball David might find interesting. After her initial contact, she would extend an invitation to Haddon Hall. Then in the safety of his own home David would turn on the charm and elicit information that he might find stimulating.

They were both sexual adventurers, but their bisexual shenanigans took second place to their curiosity about those they met. After a guest left, David would go to the mirror and copy the look and hairstyle of the stranger. Haddon Hall was a laboratory devoted not only to sexual experimentation but also to information-gathering and image-making. And that was what took precedence.

Nonetheless, Tony Visconti and Liz Hartley trembled in the bedroom. It appeared that David was bringing home boys, Angela was bringing home girls, both were bringing home any and every crazy they met. The noise and madness never stopped, and when everyone had had his or her way with one another, drunk, crazed, horny people were trying to invade their bedroom to have their way with them.

Angela and David were oblivious to the discomfort their socializing caused others. The only thing that was real to them was the vision of happiness and success that lay ahead for David. His search for an ideal family seemed to have come to a rest.

By 1971, not one of Mercury's singles had cracked America's Top Twenty. The young people on the staff knew they were working for an insignificant label, and they didn't like it. Eager to hold their heads high in the music business community, they craved stars to promote and publicize like all the other record companies. Then they would feel an intrinsic part of the pop music community, not like second-class citizens in the world of rock and roll.

Earnest young Ron Oberman, Mercury's head of publicity, loved "Space Oddity," as well as *The Man Who Sold the World*. Oberman knew his best—and only—bet was David. At least David had had an English hit. England was always easy to sell to America. After two "British invasions," the first led by the Beatles, Rolling Stones, and Animals, the second by Cream and Led Zeppelin, England was automatically seen as a rock-and-roll fantasy world.

It did not matter to Oberman that *The Man Who Sold the World* had flopped along with the single pulled from it, the ultradepressing "All the Madmen." An English star would lend enormous credence to the label and could be used to attract other stars. Oberman had met David twice in the London offices of Philips Records. (Philips released the album in England, Mercury in America.) Charming, intelligent, and compliant, David seemed eager to cooperate in the publicity process. Normally a record company would finance a short tour for a new artist and encourage journalists and radio promotion people to come to the performances.

It proved impossible to get David an American work permit on short notice. But that also did not matter to Oberman. He wanted David in America. Nor did it matter that David had not supplied Mercury with music suitable for radio air play. David would be sent to radio stations to meet the program directors and would be introduced to important American rock critics. It was hoped he would also "get a lot of press." These clippings would accompany his next Mercury release and would lend authenticity to Mercury's claim that David was a significant new artist. That would get him even more press, which hopefully would encourage the radio airplay that could make him a bona fide star and not just the media hype Oberman was attempting to create.

David had become Ron Oberman's fantasy. It was an earnest, naive plan, but Oberman persuaded Mercury to bring David to the United States at the end of January 1971. He had no idea that David was looking toward "the long term" and that Defries had repeatedly told him nothing would happen until Defries removed him from Mercury.

Mercury would only pay for one plane ticket, so Angela had to stay behind. She was five months pregnant, and flying did not seem like the best idea anyway. David assured her he would call every other day.

"You're not going to be able to do shows," she said, "and if you're not going to perform, at least you have to look magnificent. Ken was right about some things. You have to go in style; you have to make a splash. We've got to get the most theatrical wardrobe together for you. You can make a visual impact."

Normally David wore faded jeans and looked like a hippie. For this trip he wore a knee-length purple coat, a beret, and a bag slung provocatively over one shoulder. Eye shadow was artfully dabbed on his lids. He looked strange and beautiful. By mimicking Angela's carriage and style he suggested enormous femininity. From the moment he got on the plane, his projection of androgyny made the straight world perceive him as a full-fledged transvestite even when he wasn't wearing drag.

At approximately the same time, Defries also set off for America. Stevie Wonder's twenty-first birthday was a mere four months away; the time had come for him to make Wonder's "record deal of the century." This moment had obsessed him for almost a year, and finally it was close at hand. Neither David nor Tony really knew what to expect in America; their trips were fact-finding expeditions. They shared the same fantasy: to conquer America. America would prove more than willing to surrender.

Ron Oberman paced nervously at the gate. It had been over an hour since the plane landed in Washington, and David had not appeared. Playing the role of a make-believe English rock sensation had proved a bit too effective. At customs David had been seized and subjected to an endless search. Who knew what a transvestite was smuggling into the United States?

A shaken David finally appeared. His looks did not faze Oberman. He had lived through the shock when Mercury rejected the original David-in-a-dress album cover for *The Man Who Sold the World*.

Oberman took David to his parents' home. After they visited they would all go to dinner. The publicist's father was sales director of a local brewery. On his first night in America David found himself playing the role of adopted, bright, witty English son in a happy middle-class American family. So what if he wore eye shadow? The Obermans liked this English boy, and Mrs. Oberman took out her Polaroid camera to document the evening for her scrapbook.

The Washington press and radio promotion tour proved ordinary. David didn't have a hit; the stations didn't like his album or new single; journalists, bombarded with requests for interviews with new artists, were more likely to give their time to those with the more powerful record companies. The attempt to present David as a "significant" artist wasn't easy.

New York was next. The results approximated those in Washington. Only when a favor could be called in was any attention paid to David. But everywhere he went he made friends. His looks inspired curiosity; his interest in Andy Warhol, pop culture, avant-garde theater, and modern dance made him even more intriguing. Those he met were flattered by the intense way he focused his curiosity on them.

In New York his desire to see what was really "pop" and the most up to date encouraged his Mercury companions to take him to the city's most avant-garde hangouts.

When he called Angela, he described an encounter with an avant-garde painter. He told Angela that he had gone home with the woman. It was part of their agreement to tell each other everything.

"She was a masochist!" he exclaimed with astonishment.

They both burst out laughing.

The tour proceeded to Chicago, Texas, and then to San Francisco. Los Angeles would be the last stop.

L.A. Mercury publicist Lou Siegel was friendly with John Mendelssohn, who wrote for *Rolling Stone*. In exchange for an all-expenses-paid trip to San Francisco, a city Mendelssohn loved, Siegel extracted a promise from the critic to review *The Man Who Sold the World* and do a feature about David for *Rolling Stone*. This is not an uncommon practice. Free-lance rock writers usually augment their small incomes with free lunches, trips, receptions, and the like from record companies. In the process the writer often tacitly becomes one of the media arms of the record-company publicity process. Mendelssohn wrote that "Bowie's music offers an experience that is as intriguing as it is chilling, but only to the listener sufficiently together to withstand its schizophrenia."

The review would appear during David's West Coast stay and was perfect fodder for Mercury to give credibility to this unknown English artist they were presenting as a major new talent.

Mendelssohn was waiting for David at San Francisco Airport.

The price of his trip was to follow David around interviewing him and documenting his moves. To him David looked like a "mutant Lauren Bacall." It would become part of David's myth that he was emulating Bacall when he created the look he took on the road in America.

Besides Mercury's Lou Siegel, another Mercury employee, FM promotion man Rodney Bingenheimer, was thrilled by David's arrival. Rodney was a short, stringy-haired young man who wore glasses and had terrible teeth. He was not very articulate and spoke in a slow sing-song whine, and it was hard to tell whether he was bored or exhausted. But Bingenheimer was a charter member of the Los Angeles street culture that had grown up around the music business. L.A. was enamored with stars and the making of stars, and Bingenheimer was thrilled to play some part in the star-making process. He expressed his gratitude by displaying his Hollywood A-list credentials. He knew the in-crowd gossip, the in-crowd people to meet and places to go. He knew how to get people like David whatever they wanted and was anxious to please.

In San Francisco it seemed that every gay man who saw David was attracted to him. Many of the passes were brazen. David seemed to enjoy them, but expressed no interest in taking up any of them. Then Rodney called from L.A. to announce that he could get David a date with a nymphet who loved famous men. David loved the idea.

That night the girl had dinner with David, Mendelssohn, and Siegel. The men talked among themselves, with no one paying much attention to her. Finally she got up and started to leave.

David invited the girl up to his room. His tone was so firm she seemed to have no choice.

David's mixture of butch and femininity startled the other two men at the table.

The next morning, the nymphet confessed that she had learned a few chords she had never played before.

In San Francisco, David really got the hang of utilizing the American media. He wore his male dress. During an interview he made an outrageously witty remark with sexual overtones. The interviewer loved it. He made another, which was met with even more approval. Word spread throughout the press that this Englishman in a dress was "outrageous." It appeared that the secret to "getting press" was outrageousness. He set out to become a media sensation.

"He was doing this act for effect and was aware of the effect he was producing," observes Lou Siegel, who was at his side. "He was smart, determined to make it, worked hard, and did whatever was necessary."

David was to go to a local San Jose radio station to play guest DJ. As they left the suite Mendelssohn automatically held the door open for him. David's projection of femininity was so overpowering that Mendelssohn found himself treating David as if he were a woman. The experience unnerved the rock critic.

During the drive they sang a parody of a then current hit, Edwin Starr's "War." The word "war" became "tits." "Tits," they sang lustily, "What are they good for? / Absolutely nothing."

At the radio station David sashayed in, adjusted his hemline, and smiled a vampire smile at the radio host.

"What do you want to play?" he was asked.

"*Loaded.*" The Lou Reed album was the most hip album he could think of.

"The Stooges," whispered Mendelssohn.

Later David learned that the most progressive rock critics were all supporters of the Detroit-based band Iggy and the Stooges. Iggy Pop was described as a performer who knew no limits. On stage he broke bottles, jammed the cracked glass into his bare flesh, and drew his own blood; he imitated a wild dog and whipped himself; he risked his life by hurling himself into the crowd and allowing them to do whatever they wanted to him. Iggy had vomited on the daughter of a local mayor during a performance; and he and his band had driven a fourteen-foot truck filled with equipment under a twelve-foot bridge. The bridge and truck had both been destroyed, and the group was being sued by the truck owner, the equipment rental company, and the city of Ann Arbor.

It seemed that more than anything else, outrage captured the American media.

On his first night in L.A., when Siegel took David to dinner, the maitre d' at first refused to seat them because he thought David was a transvestite. Siegel was surprised. The straight world automatically perceived David as transvestite even though he was no drag queen; the media was willing to promote his outrageousness

◊ David playing with the Kon-Rads under the name of Dave Jay, 1963 (*Kevin Cann collection*).

◊ Ad for Davy Jones and the Lower Third, 1965 (*Kevin Cann collection*).

◇ ABOVE: Performing with the Lower Third, 1965 (*Kevin Cann collection*).

◇ RIGHT: Clare Shenstone and Calvin Lee at the Free Festival in Beckenham, England, in 1970 (*Ray Stephenson*).

◇ Rodney Bingenheimer, Andy Warhol superstar Ultra Violet, and David, who was wearing his famous dress, Hollywood, 1970 (*Rodney Bingenheimer collection*).

◊ TOP LEFT: Listening to the playback of his *Hunky Dory* album at Trident recording studios, 1971 (*Rodney Bingenheimer*).

◊ TOP RIGHT: From left, Mick Ronson, David, and Trevor Bolder rehearsing in 1971 (*Rodney Bingenheimer*).

◊ David at a party in Hollywood in 1970 for his Mercury promotional tour (*Rodney Bingenheimer collection*).

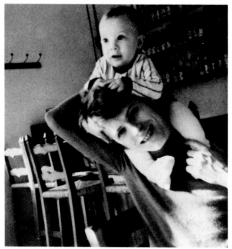

◊ David and son Zowie in Angela's parents' house in Cyprus, Christmas, 1971 (*Angela Bowie*).

◊ "Pork" cast members Wayne County, Tony Zanetta, and Via Valentina, 1971 (*James J. C. Andrews*).

◊ David and Mick Ronson in Dennis Katz's RCA office at the signing of his first RCA contract, September 1971 (*B. W. Wilkinson collection*).

◊ ABOVE: At press conference in New York after the first American tour, December 1972 (*James J. C. Andrews collection*).

◊ OPPOSITE: At the Rainbow concert in London, 1972 (© *Mick Rock*).

◊ Performing his notorious stage move with Mick Ronson's guitar, London, 1972 (© *Mick Rock*).

◊ Ziggy and his Spiders from Mars: from left, Mick Ronson, David, Mick Woodmansey, and Trevor Bolder, 1972 (© *Mick Rock*).

◊ David, an impish Iggy Pop, and an enameled-nailed Lou Reed; Tony Defries looking over their shoulders, Dorchester Hotel, London, 1972 (© *Mick Rock*).

◇ Cyrinda Foxe, left, and Angela Bowie at the Plaza Hotel after Ziggy's Carnegie Hall debut, 1972 (© *Mick Rock*).

◇ On a train during the first American tour in 1972. From left, Birgit Underwood, Bowie's childhood friend George Underwood, and fellow traveler (© *Mick Rock*).

◇ Angela Bowie in the guise of Jipp Jones, Hollywood starlet, Hollywood, 1973 (*Richard Creamer*).

◇ David in one of his futuristic Kansai outfits, Hollywood Palladium, 1973 (*Richard Creamer*).

◇ David and Angela, *the* celebrated couple of 1973 (*James J. C. Andrews collection*).

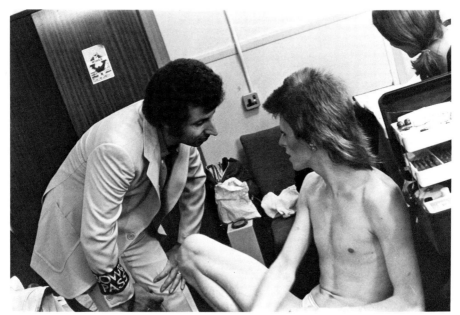

◇ Tony Defries and David discussing strategy at the "retirement" concert at the Hammersmith Odeon, London, July 1973 (© *Mick Rock*).

◇ Lou Reed, Mick Jagger, and Bowie at a party at the Cafe Royal to celebrate Ziggy's retirement (© *Mick Rock*).

◇ MainMan staff, New York, Christmas, 1973. Tony Zanetta is third from left, Cherry Vanilla fourth from left in the center row; Jaime Andrews is third from left, Leee Black Childers is fourth from left in the top row (*Tony Zanetta collection*).

because it made good copy; and those in the hip rock-and-roll world knew drag queens far more flamboyant than David but were also willing to promote him as outrageous because they liked the idea of star-making and were delighted by anyone's attempt to become a star.

The opportunity to escort David to L.A.'s rock radio stations thrilled Rodney Bingenheimer. He loved chaperoning an Englishman who had the potential to be a star. David told Rodney he was tired of Holiday Inns and hated staying in hotels. Rodney immediately found him a house to stay in. It was no ordinary house but a legendary Hollywood mansion that had belonged to Dorothy and Lillian Gish, two of the great silent-film stars.

The current occupant of the house was Rodney's friend Tom Ayers, an RCA Records staff producer. The house was a huge three-story affair with an Olympic-sized swimming pool.

David quickly caught on to Hollywood. Billboards of stars adorned Sunset Boulevard; stars were engraved in the sidewalk on Hollywood Boulevard. The talk and gossip dealt mainly with star-making. A good-natured cynicism pervaded the conversation. This was a town of deals, promotion, and publicity. It was a company town where stars were manufactured, and every day the people who lived there saw them being churned out by the machine.

David enjoyed his instant new family. He had four new loving brothers: Rodney, who was his tour guide; Mendelssohn, who was documenting his moves; Siegel, who was his publicist; and Ayers, who encouraged him musically.

Ayers had a beautiful young girl friend, who had been lured to Hollywood from the Midwest by the dream of meeting stars. She especially wanted to meet Neil Young. (Rodney's girl friend, Melanie, had a similar dream: she wanted to meet the Monkees.) After David told the record producer he liked her, Ayers turned the girl over to David.

As his tour guide, Rodney took David to the Whiskey-à-Go-Go and Hollywood High School and to meet such friends as record producer Kim Fowley. David told him that Andy Warhol was his idol and that he wanted to meet Lou Reed and Iggy Pop. RCA had shipped recording equipment to the house, and Ayers was producing a demo tape with Andy Warhol superstar Ultra Violet. The mysterious Ultra came to the house to do her work, but seemed unapproachable. She liked being a mystery. David confessed that he worshiped her. Ayers was also producing Gene Vincent and delightedly asked David to jam with the fifties rock star. Unlike Ultra Violet Vincent was very friendly.

Ayers watched while David scribbled lyrics on a batch of Holiday Inn stationery that he had gathered while tramping across America. David explained that he was writing about an imaginary character, Ziggy Stardust. "Ziggy," emblematic of Iggy Pop and the Stooges, would be even more outrageous than Iggy; "Stardust" was a tribute to the preoccupation with stars that permeated the dizzy, sunbaked atmosphere of Los Angeles.

Reality reared its head during David's L.A. stay. A Valentine's Day press party had been arranged at the home of Paul Feigen, an attorney and well-known party-giver; David would perform a set at it. Ultra Violet was to be feted on the same night at the home of another well-known Los Angeles party-giver, Dianne Bennett. It had been arranged that each would visit the other's party. David liked the arrangement; it was as if he, too, were a Warhol superstar.

Feigen's house crawled with scene-makers. A horde of music-business secretaries dressed in hot pants, their hair brushed into tight beehive hairdos, their eyes adorned with huge false eyelashes, roamed the house.

At the appropriate hour David climbed onto a waterbed in a corner of the living room and began his set. But no one listened. With each number the talk grew louder. In the middle of the set he quit.

Both Rodney and Ayers adored David and were concerned about his recording career. They believed he could be a great star, loved the fact that they might be able to make him one, and knew his career was doomed if he stayed with Mercury.

Rodney was close to Eli Bird, an A&R man at United Artists Records. He brought David to meet Bird and made the introduction. Bird was impressed.

Then Ayers had a heart-to-heart with David. "I think you should be on RCA," he said. "I love it there. They allow me to do exactly what I want to do. They don't interfere at all. The only thing they've got is Elvis, and Elvis can't last forever. Look at what RCA's done for Elvis. You'll get worldwide coverage, tour support, and a lot of money."

To have total control of his work and to be the next Elvis Presley sounded too good to be true.

Before David left L.A., Ayers arranged a meeting with Greylun Landon, RCA's West Coast head of publicity. Landon was an older gentleman who had been instrumental in publicizing Elvis.

He smiled graciously at the young man in the dress, taking note that each of his eyes was a different color. An open-minded man, Landon responded favorably to David's graciousness, intensity, and fine manners.

"He's very bizarre," Landon told Ayers, "but I think he's going to be the Bob Dylan of the seventies."

"Friend, you have a real shot at RCA," Ayers told David before his friend left for his trip home to London.

Rodney Bingenheimer's desire to please had led David to Ayers, who had led him to RCA. It was a chain of events that would culminate in David's stardom. Those were the chance occurrences that would erase seven years of failure.

In New York, Defries established an office at the Gotham Hotel. It was here that record company presidents would come to hear the Stevie Wonder tapes. Even though no one had ever heard of Tony Defries, everyone had heard of Stevie Wonder, and he had no trouble getting top executives on the phone.

Through the suite traipsed New York City's legendary music moguls. Each had a chance to meet Defries and be subjected to his long, calm discourses. As the days went on, it became clear to Defries that what he had suspected about America was true. He could bring the country to his feet.

Then a small problem occurred: Stevie Wonder stopped responding to Defries. Defries had finally made the move to sign a major act to an American record company, but now he needed an act to sign. He had only two choices: David and Dana Gillespie.

On their return to England David and Defries discussed their trips to New York. David told Tony about the interest expressed by RCA and United Artists. "The only thing RCA's got is Elvis," said David, "and Elvis can't last forever. Look at what RCA's done for Elvis. We'll get worldwide coverage, tour support, and a lot of money."

Just as David had listened to Ayers, Defries listened carefully to

David. To have total control of one's work and to be the next Colonel Tom Parker sounded very amusing.

Defries replied that what they were striving for was to make David the greatest entertainer in the world, an entertainer at least on a par with if not superior to Presley. But even though Parker did a lot of good things, he also made his share of mistakes. They had to make sure to take only Parker's proper moves while rectifying the mistakes he made.

They were both happy. The Elvis–Colonel Parker fantasy was exactly the thing that both men found the most entertaining.

Defries told David to start preparing his new material. Then they would make an acetate to take to the record companies.

David called Ronno in Hull. "What are you doing?" he asked. "Why don't you come back down to London?"

Desperate, Ronno couldn't wait. He was playing in a band called the Rats and felt he had no future. He wanted a way out of Hull and craved an opportunity to make something of his life. One by one the members of the Rats would follow him until one day the Rats' lead singer awoke to find his entire band had disappeared. David would rename the Rats the Spiders, and they would be his band.

A feverish amount of musical activity was launched. David began to write the songs that would become *Hunky Dory* and continued to write Ziggy Stardust songs. They were earmarked for Freddi Burrett, whom David was going to turn into the new Mick Jagger. Freddi Burrett would be Rudi Valentino, and his band would be called Arnold Corns. In the studio, Freddi's vocals were not up to par, and David mixed his own on top of Freddi's. In hindsight, it was as if Freddi were playing Ziggy Stardust while David directed him in the part, ready to step in when the proper moment came for him to assume the role.

Turning back to Ken Pitt's concept for him, David thought that Ziggy Stardust would be the proper vehicle for a one-man West End show. The album would be his rock opera, a score for a stage presentation. He would open in it and eventually would be replaced by other singing actors. *Sgt. Pepper's Lonely Hearts Club Band* was a song cycle presented in the guise of a mythical band, the Lonely Hearts Club Band, and a mythical lead singer, Billy Shears. Ziggy Stardust would be his Billy and the Spiders from Mars, the Lonely Hearts

Club Band. The year of *Sgt. Pepper* was also the year of the Stones' *Her Satanic Majesties Request*, with its emphasis on science fiction. *The Rise and Fall of Ziggy Stardust and the Spiders from Mars* would mate the two as the name "Bowie" had combined Lennon and Jagger.

Only one unpleasant moment occurred during these days. Philips, after a six-month wait, decided to release *The Man Who Sold the World*. The company was convinced that the album would not sell, and their prediction was accurate. Nonetheless, David's new music publisher, Chrysalis, hosted a reception for David.

At a promotional interview David said, "I'm going to become more theatrical, more outrageous—much more outrageous than Iggy Pop and the Stooges have ever been."

On this occasion he was telling the press the blunt truth.

It was May, and Stevie Wonder was twenty-one, and Defries did not have a deal. So he turned his attention to David.

Defries had told David he was destined to be the greatest entertainer in the world. He called David and Angela "my little ones" or "children." They *were* his children.

He kept his private views about David to himself. Defries could be harshly accurate and considered David a failed folk artist. After seven years in the music business, David was always being left out. He had never done the right thing in the right place at the right time.

Defries had seen David play with Ronno. They were a poor Simon and Garfunkel making social statements no one was interested in. David wasn't good at the moment, but was all Defries had to work with. Besides, David was willing, talented, and "could be molded, manufactured, and sold like an item. He would do anything."

Defries believed the formula for success depended upon 10 percent of talent backed by 90 percent of promotion. Anyone and everyone who came to that office was told the same thing, and it turned those who feared failure into Defries worshippers.

On May 28, 1971, a son was born to David and Angela. He was named Duncan Zowie Haywood Bowie, and David and Angela called him Zowie.

The delivery was exceedingly difficult, and during it Angela cracked her pelvis. At the time David was at home listening to a

Neil Young album. He had become very curious about Young ever since his affair in Hollywood with Tom Ayers's girl friend.

Angela had complained endlessly during her pregnancy. Motherhood proved even more stressful. She was afraid she didn't know how to cope with the baby.

They moved Peggy into an apartment near them in Beckenham. Now the overly critical grandmother had even more reason to criticize Angela. Peggy was sent to Cyprus to visit Angela's parents. On her return, Peggy could not be appeased. John Jones had betrayed her by dying, and she was unbearable. David wasn't very helpful. He ignored it all, too busy with his music. Angela had hoped the baby would win him over. She was giving him a *real* family; perhaps it was too real.

Angela panicked. In desperation, she called Dana, who was about to leave for an Italian holiday. Dana, hearing her upset, invited her to come along. David had no objections, and Angela fled. She hoped that leaving him on his own would make him love her.

While she was in Italy, David began calling. He missed her; he wanted her back; he needed her. That was all she needed. She was on the next plane home.

When she arrived, it was business as usual. She had to escape from a situation that frustrated and bored her; once away, she couldn't wait to get back. She couldn't face the fact that David's fantasy of getting her back was far more dramatic and intriguing to him than the reality that accompanied it.

On occasion, they had begun to fight. One day Angela locked herself in the bedroom. David hurled himself against the door and smashed it open. For someone who seemed so frail, real anger made him surprisingly strong. It seemed clear why real feelings scared him so.

One of the things David expected from Angela was a performance of English housewife to his macho English husband. She was to have babies and keep the house. It was a role she would play only when she was in the mood to humor him. But it was not the role she wanted, so she ignored his signals. Zowie was deposited with a nanny downstairs. Angela explained that babies were better off brought up by nannies. In that way they wouldn't mimic and then assimilate their parents' neuroses.

David understood. He did not object.

An acetate was finally made so that Defries would have something to sell when he visited the record companies. One side consisted of songs by David; the other, songs by Dana Gillespie. Defries was going to try to sell either or both. Soon he discovered that no English label, including RCA London, would sign David. His one single hit did not offset three album failures and fourteen failed singles. Defries knew he would have to go to the United States.

He did not discuss the English situation with David. What he said was that an American major had to be found. Unless he made it in America there was no sense doing it at all.

On August 1, 1971, a recording agreement was drawn up between Defries's Gem and David. It would run for six years. On August 12, 1971, Defries and David signed a management agreement. It was dated April 1970. Its term was *timeless*.

David will always regret having signed that agreement.

PART III

YOU'RE MY MAIN MAN

Enter Zanetta

In August 1971, after a successful run at the La Mama Experimental Theatre, Tony Zanetta and six other young New York actors flew to London to re-create their roles in *Andy Warhol's Pork*, a play Warhol had "written." Zanetta and his colleagues were not actors in any conventional sense of the word; they had no training and wanted to work neither on Broadway nor in Hollywood. But then again *Pork* had not been written in any conventional sense of the word. From 1965 on, Warhol had taken to tape recording his dialogues and phone conversations with his friends. The tapes contained the most salacious gossip about their sex lives, drug habits, love affairs, and familial and personal relationships. The two hundred worst were transcribed and then edited into a play. Zanetta, who had appeared in a number of experimental theater productions, had been asked by *Pork*'s director, a 400-pound *wunderkind* named Anthony Ingrassia, to play the part of Andy Warhol.

Zanetta proceeded to become a Warhol clone. First he bleached the top, front, and sides of his hair white and kept the back brown, duplicating Warhol's current hairstyle. Like Warhol, he also bleached one of his eyebrows white. After listening to the artist at rehearsals, he practiced until he could exactly duplicate Warhol's nasal, sing-songy *Boys in the Band* speech pattern.

Warhol did not seem to mind. In 1967, after allowing a lecturer to pretend that he was Warhol on the college lecture circuit, he remarked that the fake Andy Warhol was better than the real one because the fake was much younger and handsomer.

People began to treat Zanetta as if he were Warhol, even though they knew he wasn't. Zanetta discovered that he could get attention not because of who he was but because he was being someone else.

Now Zanetta was flying across the Atlantic with six other flamboyant people who, like him, had come from irreproachably narrow, lower-middle-class backgrounds. One cast member, Wayne County, who had been brought up as an evangelical Pentecostal, was now a bizarre-looking actor who worked in drag.

When *Pork* arrived in London, the city had already become a battleground between the establishment and the underground culture spawned in the mid-1960s. The name Andy Warhol was enough to enrage the censors, who were having their sensibilities offended every day. Warhol's film *Trash*, a graphic depiction of an East Village junkie who supports his drug habit by hustling, had been banned by the censors and could be seen only in London's private cinema clubs.

Then *Pork* came along with its simulated masturbation, onstage douching, and sex—hetero and homo, oral, anal, and genital—to settle down to a sellout run at the Round House. To avoid action by the censors, the theater placed advance ads in the newspapers that read: "Warning. This play has explicit sexual content and offensive language. If you are likely to be disturbed, do not attend."

No one could be kept away. *Pork* fascinated and unnerved English audiences. It represented the sensibility of both Warhol and the New York underground. The play oozed contempt and hatred for everyone and everything while mocking all concepts of middle-class morality.

A few days after its opening, the cast was interviewed for an English scandal sheet, *The News of the World*. The interview portrayed them as American sex fiends. A house called Langham Mansion had been rented for them in Earls Court Square; the scandal sheet dubbed it Pig Mansion. The English incorrectly perceived them as true Warhol superstars. They decided to live all the lies.

One day one of the *Pork* cast members saw a small ad announcing that David Bowie would be performing that night in a place called the Country Club. "Here's that guy in a dress!" he exclaimed. Even though Bowie was virtually unknown to a mass audience, everyone in *Pork* knew who he was. A long profile of Warhol's assistant Paul Morrissey had appeared in the issue of *Rolling Stone* that included John Mendelssohn's short article about David, written while David was in Los Angeles.

The fact that a transvestite English composer/performer was flaunting his effeminacy in the face of the macho, straight rock-and-roll mainstream tickled the actors, many of whom were flamboyantly homosexual. They perceived David as a kindred soul who could easily have belonged to the school of Andy Warhol. It never occurred to any of them that he might not be gay. Their belief in media publicity had created an undeniable reality for them.

That night after their show three members of the cast went to the Country Club, among them Cherry Vanilla, an ex–Roman Catholic who played *Pork*'s title character, Amanda Pork. Vanilla, whose real name was Kathy Dorritie, called herself a groupie and had adopted Amanda Pork's endearing habit of opening her blouse and displaying a bare breast whenever she saw a musician she found attractive. Also present were Leee Black Childers, who wore mascara and bleached his DA blond, and the company's drag "actress," Wayne County.

The Country Club was a tiny garagelike building behind a shopping center at the north end of London. The club held seventy people but there were only twenty in the audience, all of them sitting in a semicircle on the floor while David played against one wall of the room. At the end of his performance, David asked the visiting American "celebrities" to stand up and take a bow. Vanilla jumped up and waved a bare breast at him; Wayne County bowed demurely in his best Southern belle fashion.

When they returned to Pig Mansion, everyone wanted to know what had happened.

"Was he wearing a dress?"

"No dress," snorted Wayne County. "He was wearing floppy pants and a brocade jacket. He had stringy hair, much too little blue eye-shadow, and didn't look at all like Lauren Bacall." County was disappointed that David had not turned out to be the English drag-queen sister of his dreams. "He was just a folkie," sneered Wayne. "Just another folkie."

The thing that had fascinated them most was the fact that David had a wife. Angela had plunked herself down in the middle of the semicircle where David and everyone else could see her. The consensus was that, of the two Bowies, Angela was definitely the more masculine.

"They're really lovely, friendly people," said Leee Black Childers. "I've invited them all to the show."

A week later, at the end of a performance, while the cast was busily changing into street clothes in their single tiny dressing room, the dressing room door suddenly flew open. A woman stood there, and behind her stood a man, and behind him hovered three other people.

"Angela! David!" shrieked Dorritie, always the noisiest of the lot. "How nice to see you."

Dorritie began to make introductions. As soon as she was done, Angela took Kathy's hands in hers and said earnestly, "Oh, darlings, it was just such a wonderful play. You were all so good! Every second fascinated us. It was so-o-o New York. It was just too, too good." When Angela was nervous she sometimes used her dowager empress voice, a sign that she desperately wanted to be liked.

David had often said that he wanted to meet Andy Warhol, and Angela thought the actors could help David get closer to him.

As Wayne County reported, David didn't look at all like his glamorous picture in *Rolling Stone*. He was dressed in a turtleneck sweater, floppy pants, and cape, and his long hair was messy; he looked like an undernourished hippie. But his face was beautiful—his features were delicate and his eyes were alive and sparkling. And when he smiled, his smile was unexpectedly shy and sweet.

Tony Defries, Dana Gillespie, and Mick Ronson remained silent.

Dorritie immediately assumed the role of hostess and began to bombard the guests with small talk. David remained silent, but it was a relaxed silence. He looked around the room, taking everything in. His attention was extremely focused, and the odd result was that the actors rather enjoyed being inspected by him. After a few minutes the visitors left. The cast finished changing and dashed out without giving them a second thought.

The kids from Pig Mansion loved the Sombrero. A few nights later, after a couple of dances on the Sombrero's lit-up dance floor, the group decided to have a drink. As they stood at the bar they spotted Angela, David, and Ronno sitting at a corner table. Beside Angela sat Freddi Burrett. They naturally couldn't distinguish Angela's voice through the hubbub but her face looked angry, and she was gesticulating wildly as she described something to Freddi. They pushed their way through the crowd until they were standing directly behind Angela.

"Well, dear, the dyke was supposed to meet me here!" Angela ranted. She noticed that Freddi's eyes had drifted away from her and that he was staring imperiously at the people behind her. She turned. When she saw the actors her expression changed abruptly, and she burst into a radiant smile. "Oh, darlings," she trilled, "it was a wonderful performance. You were so good. The play was just divine. It's so nice to see you."

David smiled and nodded but said nothing. His eyes drifted to an attractive Oriental boy in his early twenties. Suddenly, he got up and asked the boy to dance. Meanwhile, Vanilla headed straight for Ronno.

"Hi," spat Vanilla, imitating Amanda Pork's speed-freak voice. "Remember me, Pork from New York?"

Angela always made it a point to be the most outrageous person in the room. At the Sombrero she played at being tough and crude, and now she was challenged by Vanilla. She jumped up, grabbed Vanilla by the shoulder, pulled her away from Ronno, and spun her around. "I want to see if you're as luscious as your name."

The actors plopped themselves down at the table. After his dance David returned to the table but stayed for only a minute or two. He didn't want the Oriental boy he favored to be swallowed up by the crowd in his absence.

At the table Freddi commented endlessly on the men who passed by while Ronno sat quietly drinking beer after beer, saying very little. It was as if he had landed unexpectedly on Mars—strange, but not as terrifying as he had imagined.

Angela had invited Zanetta to Haddon Hall. As promised, at precisely one the following afternoon a short, middle-aged woman dressed in a pale gray uniform appeared at Pig Mansion.

"I'm Mrs. Rutherford from the car service," she announced. "Please follow me."

A half hour later the car pulled into Haddon Hall's semicircular driveway. The moment it stopped, Angela and David appeared at the front door.

"Hello, darling," Angela said softly. "Thank you so much for coming." David flashed his disarming smile and shook Zanetta's hand briskly.

"Come see the house," said Angela, leading the way.

"When we get a little bit of money we're going to do the whole place," said David at the end of the tour. His tone was slightly expectant as well as apologetic, as if he wanted his guest to know that the future held better things for him.

In the sitting room, David turned to Angela. "Darling, would you bring us some tea?"

"Of course, dear." She disappeared into the kitchen. David plopped down on the beautiful carpet, beckoning Zanetta to join him. A few minutes later Angela returned with the tea.

This was Zanetta's first exposure to David's social technique, which was to make his conversational partners feel very important, like the most interesting people he had ever met. David didn't ask many questions, but by a smile or an inquiring gesture he kept the conversation flowing. Naturally, with such an attentive audience, David's guests remembered things and became eager to tell more, and in the most amusing fashion. It was David's way of building an enormous fund of information about what he thought might be useful.

His curiosity spurred Zanetta on. "It all began with the Playhouse of the Ridiculous. In New York we call it 'underground theater' or 'experimental theater' or 'Off-Off Broadway'; you'd call it 'fringe theater.' The plays ridicule the conventions of society. The actors play freaks, cripples, perverts, and degenerates. There is a lot of nudity and simulated sex. The actors wear huge wigs, sequins, netting, and tiaras. They sprinkle glitter on their eyelids and dust it all over their bodies. There are always drag queens in the plays, but they're not conventional show-business transvestites. They don't want to transform themselves into beautiful women. Some have beards, some show their genitals. They make fun of men, women, homosexuals. They hate everybody." David laughed appreciatively.

"Our director, Tony Ingrassia, was a member of the Playhouse of the Ridiculous. That's where Andy Warhol discovered him. Warhol loved Ingrassia. He had such a vicious sense of humor. He was the essence of 'ridiculous.' Ingrassia became Warhol's playwright. Then Ingrassia got the idea of turning Warhol's tapes into a play, and that's how *Pork* was born."

David and Angela wanted to hear stories about Andy Warhol himself.

"Andy appeared to get a little nervous during rehearsals, and I became more Warholian in my appearance and gestures. We had some wonderful Warhol–like exchanges. I always let him initiate the encounters, and then I would try to repeat his words. 'Hi' he'd say

to me. 'Hi' I'd reply, echoing his cadence exactly. 'How are you?'
he'd ask. 'How are you?' I'd reply. He'd pause, searching for another
purposely boring, trivial question. Finally he'd ask, 'How's it going?'
I'd reply, 'How's it going with you?' We'd stare at each other. I used
these moments to look for any detail that I could add to my performance. Meanwhile he'd study me studying him. At that moment
we were each other's mirrors. Two wonderfully boring people. . . .
Even his friends treat me like I'm Andy."

"How wonderful!" exclaimed David. Angela and he exchanged
smiles of delight.

David pumped Zanetta for stories about Warhol's studio, the
Factory, until finally it was David's turn to impress.

"I'm going to play a character called Ziggy Stardust. We're going
to do it as a stage show. We may even do it on the West End. When
I'm tired of playing Ziggy I can step out, and someone else can take
over for me."

David put on a tape. "I write songs about people and experiences," he commented. "I've written songs on this album for Bob
Dylan and Lou Reed, and a song for Andy Warhol."

Zanetta didn't know much about rock and roll and was pleased
that the songs had an engaging pop flavor.

David played selections from his Ziggy Stardust project. As soon
as the music was over David said suddenly, "He hasn't seen the
baby."

Angela jumped up. Until then Zanetta didn't even know they
had a baby. No part of the apartment had been converted into a
nursery, and there had been no sign of a baby anywhere.

She returned holding Zowie in her arms. He was three months
old. Everyone admired him. Angela explained that Zowie spent
much of his time in the downstairs apartment with his new nanny,
a neighbor, Sue Frost. She kissed the baby and then said, "Zows,
it's time to go back to Sue's."

"Hurry back, Nama darling," said David.

Just then a woman in her late fifties came into the room. "Dinner's
almost ready," she announced.

"Hello, Mum," said David. "Meet our friend Tony."

Zanetta was introduced to Peggy Jones, who apparently had been
tucked away in the Bowies' cramped kitchen. The resemblance between Peggy and her son was startling.

After dinner David picked up exactly where he left off. There were more pictures, more music, more stories, more of his dreams for the future. David made his conversation sound as if it concerned another person. It seemed that he had to be at a distance from himself to give the appearance of objectivity about his self-involvement. As a result, even though he was enormously ego-involved, David did not seem egotistical.

Zanetta sneaked a look at his watch; it was past ten. By this time he had the illusion that he was one of David's best friends and had known him all his life. He was experiencing an overdose of the Bowie charm and intensity. Like a spider from Mars, David spun his web around everyone to whom he granted an audience.

By now David was able to complete Zanetta's sentences, one of his tried and true seduction techniques.

During the ride home the visit replayed itself in Zanetta's head. It had been extraordinary. Under David's gentle but persuasive questioning he had told him everything he knew about the New York scene. But information had flowed in only one direction. When Zanetta asked him about his records, David had pulled back, quickly changing the subject. The past and its failures were not allowed to be discussed; it appeared that at Haddon Hall they did not even exist.

CHAPTER 12

New York,
New York

I n 1971, forty percent of the profits of the RCA Corporation came from the manufacture of electronics equipment. Its record division, RCA Records, was a poor sister to its electronic divisions.

During the 1960s RCA Records had labored under the thumb of Elvis Presley's manager, Col. Tom Parker, who made sure that the label would not sign an act that would compete against Presley. The result was a record company that missed the entire rock revolution of the 1960s.

In the early 1970s the RCA Corporation had a reputation for poor financial restraint, bad management, and insufficient planning. It threw money around and seemed to hire anyone whether or not he was qualified. Its record division was run by middle-aged corporate men with no feel for or interest in rock music. Like its parent organization, RCA Records was mismanaged and confused, with no new stars to feed the young promotion people who headed its two hundred branch offices.

It needed acts, and it needed them fast. Lou Reed was signed. He didn't sell many records, but could give the stodgy company a hip credibility. The Kinks were signed to demonstrate that RCA had finally become interested in classic rock and roll. But the answer was a totally new star, preferably British.

At precisely this moment Tony Defries knocked on RCA's door.

The deal, made with remarkable ease, took less than two weeks to complete. Defries's partner, Laurence Myers, simply contacted the New York legal firm that represented Gem in America. The lawyers called RCA Records A&R head Dennis Katz and requested that he listen to two Gem artists, David Bowie and Dana Gillespie. Katz and his assistants were part of a new record company regime that was supposed to be attuned to all the new acts.

"Who's David Bowie?" Katz asked an assistant, Bob Ringe.

Ringe knew David's Mercury albums and said Bowie might be worth a listen.

A meeting was arranged between Defries and Katz, and Defries arrived, acetate in hand. There was not much to discuss; Katz had to listen to the music and make a decision.

Katz listened. He didn't like Gillespie but he loved Bowie's *Hunky Dory* selections. Whatever rock-and-roll sensibility David possessed had been submerged by Ronno and Ken Scott's production and arranging skills. More melody, less meaningless metaphor in the lyrics, and an emphasis on keyboards and strings sweetened the music enough to give the songs the veneer of potential pop-rock hits.

Katz played the selections for other RCA staff members and then for his friends. They responded positively. Then he played it for his wife. She loved it. That was all he needed to know.

The deal was a generous one for 1971, though not extravagant. It was a two-year contract, with David required to deliver three albums. He would receive a $37,500 advance for each LP. In addition RCA had either a one-year two-album option (with a $37,500 advance per album) or a two-year four-album option (with a $56,250 advance per album). The company also had the right to release two "Greatest Hits" albums. David's royalty was a straight, fair 11 percent.

Defries's strategy was to get the deal, and then improve it. This deal would be improved mightily as time went on.

In Los Angeles Rodney Bingenheimer and his group gossiped about the deal. The word spread through the underground music-business grapevine that United Artists had offered a million-dollar advance and had been topped by RCA. It was the sort of gigantic hype that L.A. loved. To tell the story made Bingenheimer and his group part of a myth they had a hand in creating. Unknown to David this L.A. "in-crowd" had become his personal media promoters. By the time they were done David would have a huge audience in Los

Angeles even though he didn't have any hits and had never given a single show there.

Ron Oberman had led David to Rodney Bingenheimer, who led David to Tom Ayers, who then led him to RCA; and Laurence Myers had led Defries to RCA's Dennis Katz. In Haddon Hall, the triumph belonged to Tony.

"Tony's doing such a good job of taking care of us," Angela announced happily. "Tony really understands business. He's into contracts. He's such a genius."

David concurred. Then Tony told them that RCA was flying them and Ronno to New York for the formal signing of the contract. They were beside themselves.

Angela said, "You have to look magnificent. You have to go in style. You have to make a splash, a visual impact. We'll give the old so-and-so's at RCA something to think about when they go home to their wives and kiddies in the countryside."

David, Angela, and Freddi went to work. They hit the stores, and Angela shopped and shopped and then shopped some more. By the time they were done an adorable new David had emerged. His costume consisted of a full-sleeved paisley shirt, very wide cream-colored bell-bottomed trousers, a short imitation leopard jacket, a hat and cape, and yellow Mary Jane shoes from Italy.

When his shoulder-length hair was shaped and parted to the side so that the locks fell over one eye, he suddenly took on the peek-a-boo look of a pop-art Veronica Lake. This would be the look featured in the *Hunky Dory* artwork, and the press would label it the Hunky Dory look.

"Darling, you're going to be a great, great star," trilled Angela.

In September, just two weeks after *Pork* closed in London, they flew to New York where David, Angela, Ronno, Defries, and Defries's associate Don Hunter checked into the Warwick Hotel.

Defries chose the same suite the Beatles stayed in during their 1965 tour, the perfect suite for his "little ones."

Zanetta arrived at the Warwick to find Defries sitting shirtless and sockless at a room service table in the living room while David, Ronno, and Hunter sat on the couch facing him. He looked first at David, who, in less than two weeks' time, had transformed himself from a scraggly hippie into a glorious Veronica Lake clone. Then he looked at Defries, who was slowly eating breakfast; it would take him almost two hours to eat two fried eggs.

David reintroduced Zanetta to Defries by saying, "Here's Tony Zanetta, the actor who played Andy Warhol." Defries peered at Zanetta, studying him for what seemed an interminable length of time.

Defries observed that there were a great many z's around: Ziggy . . . Zowie . . . Zanetta. There were also a great many Tonys. He was Tony; Zanetta was Tony. They couldn't have a second Tony. Zowie would be their small z, and Zanetta would be their big Z. From that moment on Zanetta would be called Z. He had been anointed with a stage name in the play that was the life of David Bowie.

Defries told Z that Andy Warhol was working in the dark and should be much richer than he is. His films were not being handled properly. There was no reason why Warhol shouldn't be making Hollywood films, said Defries. Warhol should be enormous. His films should be mass marketed throughout the world with enormous promotional campaigns. It's not enough to have the hip audience. Proper distribution could put Warhol into the mainstream.

Z was instantly appointed New York liaison with Warhol. He was told to get Warhol on the phone and arrange a meeting.

Defries's imperiousness gave him an enormous amount of conviction, and almost no one ever turned him down. There was also a hint of a job in this particular request, and the unemployed actor went to the phone, called Warhol, and arranged an appointment for the following afternoon.

They were due at RCA in a half hour and Defries was preparing David for the meeting. David did not have to do anything, he was told. He just had to sit there. RCA needed David to save them.

Dennis Katz was young and bright, but the others were old— old washing-machine salesmen, Defries said. RCA was an antiquated company. It had missed the 1960s and was quite desperate to catch up.

David excused himself and went into the bedroom. This was an especially dramatic moment in his life, and he wanted to look just right. A perfect visual presentation would enable him to have a sense of control over the imminent public event.

He stared into the mirror and began to concentrate. Slowly he applied a thin layer of royal blue eye shadow, lined his eyes, and then beaded his lashes with mascara. It was actor's work, and he was an actor preparing for the role of David Bowie.

He looked beautiful. From that moment on, he would never appear on the streets of New York without makeup.

A cold institutional feel permeated the ninth floor of the RCA Building. A maze of tiny offices occupied the center of the floor. Surrounding them were forty more cubbyhole offices. Because they ringed the building, each had a window, and had been assigned to an executive. Because Dennis Katz headed a department he occupied a corner office and had two windows.

Defries automatically sat down on the windowsill. It gave him the tallest position in the room. Everyone else sat on the couch facing Dennis.

The meeting was mainly small talk. Following Defries's instructions David sat perfectly still and said nothing. He seemed shy but studious, a keen observer who was taking in the whole situation. His silence obligated Katz to explain thoroughly the company's plans. People who are being watched usually want to be observed in the most favorable light.

David's style provided him with a wonderful way to gather information, keep everyone on their toes, and dominate a situation without having visibly to take control.

Katz's two assistants, Richard Robinson and Bob Ringe, came in to pay their respects. So did a steady stream of middle-aged executives. Most were friendly, but a few seemed wary and stared nervously at David. This company was the home of Perry Como, not some Englishman who had been known to wear a dress. Theirs would be the position that a "fag" could never sell records in the Midwest.

David relaxed and began to enjoy himself. He liked the attention, and he had begun to feel safe. RCA's young people were on his side; Defries would teach the old people how to behave. This was what he had always wanted.

At the end of the meeting Katz invited everyone to a celebration dinner at the Ginger Man. Then he offered a special treat. "I know how you love Lou Reed," he told David. "I'll invite him, too."

"That would be wonderful," David replied, pleased.

Katz then explained that Richard Robinson would also be coming, along with his wife, Lisa.

"She's a journalist," Katz explained, "and she's very important. She knows everybody, and once she puts her mind to something she can really turn out the press."

In the elevator going down Defries said, that Lou Reed was "cult." He just had the hip audience. He could be enormous if his image were exploited on an international basis. Reed needed to be mass-marketed if he was to sell large numbers of records.

Everyone nodded sympathetically, and a single thought hung in the air: Defries might be the one to rescue Lou Reed from cult status and turn him into an international pop draw.

By nature Lou Reed was caustic and smart-alecky. He was "very New York" in style and tone. A graduate of Syracuse University, he had been a protégé of the poet Delmore Schwartz. Schwartz, an alcoholic, had been addicted to speed and tranquilizers; Reed also drank on occasion and used speed.

Though he was a member of Andy Warhol's court, he was more than Andy Warhol surface. Beneath his surface lurked a menacing quality.

Reed's defensiveness expressed itself in a stream of witty talk laced with snappy, snide one-liners. While he held forth, his wife, Betty, a blond stewardess, looked at him adoringly.

Throughout the meal, David and Lou checked each other out, one using talkativeness, the other silence as his mask. While their styles were dissimilar, both were hungry for attention, and as the dinner progressed, David trotted out his full arsenal of responses.

Lou said something sharp. David was ultrapolite. After Reed told an odd anecdote, David, who was not half the raconteur Reed was, masked the deficiency by turning shy and coy. When Lou stopped for breath, David leaned forward, looked into his eyes, and stared at him flirtatiously.

Once again, by being the perfect English gentleman, all charm and perfect manners, but at the same time somewhat aloof and distant, David encouraged others to treat him solicitously. Yet his eyes never left Lou. He seemed to be drinking him in. David could not help noticing that Lisa Robinson and Reed were enjoying a running private dialogue. They seemed to know everybody and had a secret to share about each of their mutual friends.

At the end of the dinner someone suggested that they take David to Max's Kansas City. Reed did not want to go.

"I hope we see each other again," David said to him. "This has been such a thrill for me." They shook hands warmly.

Max's Kansas City had its own status symbols. The small back room was the place to see and be seen; the big round corner table was the preferred table.

After David was seated at the right table in the right room, he sat back. Slowly he looked around, taking the pulse of the underground power brokers who gathered there. Suddenly a friendly looking man came bounding over to say hello to Lisa Robinson.

"This is Danny Fields," she said. "He manages Iggy Pop."

Fields smiled warmly at David. "Thank you for mentioning Iggy's name in your English interviews. It's the only time Iggy has ever been mentioned in England."

"I love Iggy," David replied.

Pop, whose real name was Jimmy Osterberg, was staying at Fields's loft. Danny went to the phone. Iggy was engrossed in *Mr. Smith Goes to Washington* on TV, and it took a couple of phone calls before he pulled himself away. He didn't know why these people wanted him to make an appearance.

He bounded into Max's back room, a bundle of hyperkinetic energy. Despite his onstage ferocity, off stage he seemed an irresistible Peck's Bad Boy. Pop had a deep foghorn speaking voice and spat his words out.

He circled the table, performing for the group. Iggy described life in a Detroit trailer park, then turned to the subject of his heroin addiction and his current enrollment in a methadone program.

In Hollywood, during the *The Man Who Sold the World* publicity tour, David had been fascinated by "pop" America—the sleazy underbelly of the country. He and Defries both loved this encounter with a slice of American life they had never seen before.

"Methadone is long-lasting," Iggy croaked. "It lasts a day or two. Heroin is short-acting. It gets you real high, but it only lasts four to eight hours. You can substitute one to do battle with the other. Heroin was my main man, but now I'm getting my shit together. Man, I'm on my way to being clean."

David and Defries were so much in synch that all David had to do was throw Defries a look, and Defries was able to speak for David. Iggy was *theater*, American theater, and they wanted more of it.

Defries invited Iggy to come to the Warwick Hotel around noon the next day and join them for breakfast.

"That'd be cool, man," Iggy replied. "I'll come by on the way to the methadone clinic."

"Wasn't Iggy a gas!" exclaimed David to Zanetta at the end of the evening.

Angela had returned from visiting her college girl friend in Connecticut, and she sat at David's side as they watched Iggy wolf down two complete breakfasts. He wiped his lips with his napkin and then was off and running, paying for his breakfast by keeping everyone amused.

Iggy launched into a description of the harrowing incidents that comprised his life.

David was incredibly sympathetic and fascinated. He had never before met anyone with a life like this one—someone who was so spunky and yet so much the classic victim and in need of so much help. It was like having a crazy brother you could help make sane. Defries was also riveted by Iggy's desperate circumstances. He wanted to know what could be done for young James. What did he need?

"Everything," Iggy replied. He was a helpless, charming, playful wraith.

Defries went on to give a very long speech about the glorious future that awaited Iggy. He told Iggy to conclude his methadone program. Then Defries would send for Iggy.

"Sounds terrific," said Iggy. "You can be my main man." He gobbled down another roll and headed off to the methadone clinic.

When he was in the mood Defries moved swiftly. No doubts entered his mind about the wisdom of any decision he made. David liked Iggy, and they were both entertained by him. That was enough. With the proper publicity and promotion, Iggy, like everyone else, stood a chance of becoming an international name. Five-year-long management, music publishing, and recording agreements were drawn up between Pop and the appropriate Gem companies, and Iggy joined Bowie and Dana Gillespie as Gem artists.

The Factory was deserted when the group arrived that afternoon for their appointment with Andy Warhol. They stared at the huge stuffed dog in the reception area, the receptionist's desk that was missing a receptionist, and the large prints of Warhol superstar Viva and *Lonesome Cowboys* star Tom Hompertz that adorned the bare white walls.

Paul Morrissey appeared and ushered the group into the back room. They all shook hands with Warhol. Then Defries began to talk softly to Morrissey.

"Distribution," intoned Defries.

"Distribution?" whined Morrissey.

Meanwhile everyone else stared at Warhol, and he stared at them. David was not a talker, and Angela, overwhelmed by nerves, also turned quiet. The silence was agonizing and embarrassing.

Warhol smiled. It was part of the human carnival, and he was enjoying it. But he maintained his silence.

"Distribution . . . mass marketing . . . promotional campaigns . . . ," said Defries.

David looked at Tony with an agonized expression on his face —he needed to be rescued—but Tony was too busy talking to Morrissey to notice.

"Oh, what pretty shoes," said Warhol. David politely told Warhol the story of how he had obtained the shoes while Angela stood there in a state bordering on paralysis.

Warhol reached for his Polaroid camera and began photographing David's feet. After a few minutes David couldn't stand it anymore. He wanted the attention off his shoes and on him.

"I've written a song called 'Andy Warhol,' " he said. "It's on my new album." He had brought the acetate and played Warhol the track. Warhol didn't know what to say, so he said nothing.

David threw Defries another pained look. Defries was telling Morrissey that Andy's movies were being distributed haphazardly in Europe, and that they had to change the way the business was done.

Finally Defries turned to David, signaling that they should leave. Everyone sweetly thanked Warhol.

"Goodbye," Andy replied. "You have such nice shoes."

In the elevator, David burst into laughter. For four years he had wanted to view this man in close-up, and now he had. He found the experience very, very funny.

The rest of the day was spent sightseeing and included a visit to Radio City Music Hall.

"It's absolutely fabulous!" David exclaimed. Turning to Tony, he said, "This is where I want to play." A rock act had never played the Music Hall, and at that time it seemed inconceivable that one ever would. Defries agreed that Radio City would be the perfect spot for David.

It was said with the usual definitiveness, and as usual, Defries was left unchallenged. Yet it seemed a preposterous notion.

A few nights later Zanetta joined David and Angela at the hotel. They were all tired and wanted to spend the night in. The suite was cluttered with Angela's purchases. As explorer scout for a reclusive man, she had made forays into the world and returned with magazines, newspapers, clothes, and makeup with which to amuse themselves. They ate dinner and watched television, and Angela became sleepy.

"Good night, Nama," she said as she kissed David's cheek. "I love you."

"Good night, Ang."

Bowie and Zanetta talked until dawn. They stretched out on the floor and looked out at the brightly lit New York skyline. David again recapitulated the magic of finding someone like Tony Defries, who could put his fantasies into motion. "You know, Z, it's bigger than a new album or tour or anything like that. I want to do everything and I feel that I can. I'm going to be huge, and it's a little scary."

They looked down at the glittering Manhattan lights. David's happiness was infectious, and each seemed to believe that the city was at his feet, the lights shining just for him.

CHAPTER 13

Ziggy Comes Out

Fueled by the triumph of the RCA deal, David, Angela, and Tony returned to England and resumed in earnest their Haddon Hall brainstorming sessions. The talks went on day and night.

Marc Bolan failed in the States because there was no demand for him, Defries said. It was merely a question of the right promotion. It was really quite simple: To be a star one must act like a star. When David went to America, he had to go first class. After all when one travels by limousine, people take do notice. That's what an American tour is really all about: to create the illusion of stardom.

David was relieved and enthusiastic. He liked reducing stardom to a question of proper promotion and enjoyed the idea that it was his task to act like a star. It made it easier to set out creating a star vehicle for himself that, in the long term, would lead to his domination of the American music scene.

He turned to his past. Now he would finally set about creating the stage show that Ken Pitt had repeatedly told him would catapult him to fame.

Hunky Dory and the Hunky Dory look were instantly forgotten. Haddon Hall suddenly became its own version of a Judy Garland– Mickey Rooney movie as David set out to become Ziggy Stardust, the title character of his new album.

Every stage show needs a cast. As David would be Ziggy, Ronno would lead Ziggy's band, the Spiders from Mars. David named the two other Spiders Weird and Gilley, and Ronno cast his fellow mates from Hull, former Rats Woody Woodmansey and Trevor Bolder, in the parts.

Woody and Trevor were quiet and gentle, with no drug or alcohol problems. Like Ronno they were North Country provincials, and the relative sophistication of David and Angela seemed exotic and somewhat intimidating. It was essential that they be on their best manners with people as knowledgeable as these.

Ronno had an inexhaustible supply of friends from Hull who were available to lend a helping hand. Rats roadie Peter Hunsley came next. Bright and somewhat sarcastic, he loved the former Rats, whom he treated like the naive children they were. Stuie George, a muscular black man who was a nonstop laugher and joker, followed.

"He has a shady past," Ronno told David and Angela.

"Thank fuckin' God!" exclaimed Angela. "I like a man with a past. It shows he has character."

Stuie was eagerly welcomed to the fold. He had a tiny girl friend, Maggie. Despite her petite size, when she lost her temper she lashed out mercilessly against Stuie. He lashed back, and Maggie usually had one or two black eyes.

Space was booked at the Underhill Rehearsal Studios in southeast London. Another wide-eyed innocent, Willie Palin, worked there. Palin had left a sheep farm to spend six weeks in London earning enough money to buy a stash of hashish and had wound up at the studio.

One day Willie learned that "Bo" had booked rehearsal time; he thought it was Marc Bolan and became excited and nervous about the arrival of such a great star. "Bo" turned out to be Bowie, but David and his band were having so much fun that Palin allowed himself to be scooped up as roadie. Another team member, sound man Robin Mayhew, also joined the contingent.

The rehearsals of David's new act—the stage show—went on throughout the late fall with everyone having a terrific time.

When they weren't rehearsing, they and their friends swarmed in and out of Haddon Hall, where a family atmosphere always prevailed. This loving family also included George Underwood, who made sketches of the Ziggy Stardust character, and neighbor Geoffrey MacCormack, with whom David liked to pal around. To add to the mayhem Angela moved Freddi Burrett and Daniella Parma into the apartment.

The activity and the hanging out seemed to go on twenty-four hours a day. Haddon Hall had never been noisier or more confused, but everyone seemed to dote on the good-natured chaos.

Following after Freddi were his fluttering collection of Sombrero queens, including Freddi's special favorites, Silly Billy and Darryl. The mixture of chattering young gays and tongue-tied, macho North Country musicians exemplified the startling contradiction that David was unwittingly synthesizing in his new act.

Soon everyone was accustomed to the sexual theater that was part and parcel of David and Angela's lives. The Haddon Hall bathroom was littered with girlie magazines featuring naked black women with huge pendulous breasts. Angela insisted that the magazines were hers. Or were they really David's? Or were they there just to shock the others? It was part of the mystery David and Angela found so delicious.

In this household David played daddy. Like his own father, he was aloof, yet perfectly willing to discuss his ideas with anyone who approached him as well as listen to and incorporate the others' suggestions.

On the other hand, Angela was as outspoken as Peggy. She never stopped spinning her wheels. Her energy was fearsome, and her ideas ranged from brilliant to crazy. It was apparent that she was pushing David, pushing him further than he had dared go before. She wanted him to be brilliant and dazzling. It was the only way she seemed to have to display her own brilliance.

When there were problems, Tony Defries reached into his pocket and peeled off some bills. A man who put his money where his mouth was was a man everyone at Haddon Hall could believe in.

In his one-to-one conversations David became his own version of Defries's plans for him by acting the part of the greatest star of the century. That was his destiny, he assured everybody. With total self-assurance Defries, in his ultrasoft-spoken way, let everyone know that as David had a destiny, so did they. Defries had to be everyone's father, and all of his children were destined for greatness.

Finally into these directionless lives had come a real sense of purpose.

After convincing RCA to sign David, it became Dennis Katz's mission to make David *happen* in the United States.

In November 1971 RCA released *Hunky Dory* along with a single, "Changes." It would take another two months before the U.K. division of the company released the record in England. RCA U.K. did not like *Hunky Dory* and was convinced that David was destined to repeat his pattern of failure. Pressured by Dennis Katz, RCA president Rocco Laginestra had to intervene personally and force the English division to accept David as an English artist.

On *Hunky Dory*, producer/remixer Ken Scott gave David his first really professional-sounding LP. For starters Scott turned down the hard rock and buried Ronno's wailing guitar in the mix, turning instead to Rick Wakeman's piano for the disk's lead instrumental role.

David still had difficulties crafting a lyric, but the record had real charm and a likable sound. In "Oh! You Pretty Things," he refers to "homo sapiens," a foreshadowing of the "Homo Superior" that would dominate a portion of his later work. There were also three homages on the album: "Andy Warhol," "Queen Bitch" (an ode to Lou Reed and the Velvet Underground), and "Song for Bob Dylan." David seemed to be boosting his personal heroes like a cheerleader.

More important was the delightful song "Changes" which indicated that David was at a crossroads and went on to announce that he was going to change his position in the world. It concluded with an admonition to Earth's elders to lay off the kids. He told the rock and rollers to face the "strange changes" as authenticity was replaced by style.

The time was coming for him to make some strange changes of his own.

The most important thing was the packaging of the disc. David was sublimely androgynous on the record jacket. His look represented a strange change, a strikingly new and exotic brand of stylishness.

No one knew it then but the pop David Bowie had acquired a small cult of fans, as had the Dylanesque folksinger David Bowie. The-man-in-a-dress David had also stimulated a nerve. And then there were the children of the seventies who wanted their own pop gods, their own icons, in a brand new style they could call their own. This was the David of *Hunky Dory*.

John Mendelsohn, David's old friend from Los Angeles, had not forgotten the two weeks they had spent together, and he rushed into print with a *Rolling Stone* review that could be used as record company propaganda without saying anything too committal. It was David's "most easily accessible, and thus, most readily enjoyable album since *Man of Words/Man of Music*," wrote the rock critic. "With his affection for using intriguing and unusual themes in musical settings that most rock 'artists' would dismiss with a quick fart as old-fashioned and uncool, he's definitely an original. . . ."

Traditionally, at the time of release RCA would have had David in the United States on a promotional tour either headlining in small rock clubs or as the opening act for an established star à la Marc Bolan. The appearance would be used to generate publicity, stimulate radio air play, and give radio promotion people a chance to see the act in person.

RCA had no real plan for promoting the record; neither did Defries. The only thing he knew was that David had to come to the United States draped in the illusion of stardom, or he wouldn't come at all. The record company and the manager were in a holding pattern.

Defries arrived in New York in December. He roamed RCA, dropping into offices and talking endlessly about David's impending English tour at the beginning of 1972. He made it sound like the tour of the century. He discussed the fact that David would then come to the United States. *Hunky Dory* sales were only fair and RCA was eager to have David tour, and Defries teased them and whetted their appetite.

It was his job to lead them on, and he enjoyed doing it. Though he never got visibly excited, he had a real flair for playing the game of coquette. His manner was such that no executive sensed that he lacked a strategy. Instead they looked to him for concrete details about David's future, and he gleefully left them dangling.

At that time Tony Zanetta was drafted, along with his buddy, Kathy "Pork from New York" Dorritie (temporarily retired from the Cherry Vanilla persona), to begin a local promotion of their own. Boxes of *Hunky Dory* were given to them to distribute to their friends.

As Rodney Bingenheimer and his group talked David up on the West Coast, Zanetta and Dorritie promoted him to a small corps of young New York queens. Suddenly David became the pinup of a New York gay cult that wanted a rock star who was not macho and, therefore, threatening to them, but who might be gay as they were.

Suzy Fussey and all the other girls in the Beckenham hair parlor knew David by sight. He was the man in the dress with the long, flowing blond hair who walked beside the mannish woman in slacks with close-cropped hair as she wheeled a baby carriage down the street.

One day the mannish woman came in and sat in Suzy's chair. "My name is Angie," she cooed as she studied her reflection in the mirror. "Oh, honey, do you know what I'd like?"

"No," said Suzy. "What would you like?"

"I'd like a white stripe and a red stripe and a blue stripe on the side of my head. How about that?"

When the job was done, they were both thrilled.

"Oh, honey," Angela shouted, "you're a genius. An artist. This is just wonderful. You've made me so happy I could just fall over and die!"

Angela kissed Suzy on the cheek and dashed out. Suzy loved having the stultifying suburban routine shattered by this enthusiastic and daring woman.

Then Angela called and invited her to Haddon Hall. As David's test pilot she had auditioned Suzy, and the hairdresser had passed the test.

Suzy walked around David studying him carefully.

"Do you like the way my hair's been cut?" asked David.

Suzy didn't mince words. "It's a bit boring," she replied. "Everybody's got a long shag."

"What would you do?" he asked.

"I'd have short hair because no one has short hair."

Angela erupted in glee. "You're fuckin' right," she screamed.

David resisted by saying, "I don't want an ordinary short cut."

"Don't you worry, Nama," coaxed Angela. She reached for a huge stack of *Vogue* magazines. "All right, sweetie," she said to Suzy, "the search is on." Three different *Vogues* became the source of the haircut. A French *Vogue* would contribute the pointy front; two German *Vogues* the sides and back. There would be two long points down either side of David's face but the hair would be cut very short above the ears.

When it was finished, they studied it carefully. No one had ever seen anything quite like it before.

David looked warily at Angela.

"Lovely," she pronounced. "Truly, truly lovely."

There was a moment of silence. Angela's eyes never left David. She was imagining a next step, a step that would take this exotic new look even further.

"Let's dye it red," she suddenly announced.

"Red?" asked David. He needed another push.

"Red is such a beautiful color," said Angela. "It's so stylish. You'll be so pleased with your new red, red hair."

The next morning David woke up and looked in the mirror. His new red hair lay limply on his head. A few wispy strands stuck up in front; the side pieces lay dankly on his face. It was a mess. He stared at Angela in panic. His panic panicked her.

"Oh, darling," she screamed, "we'll fix it. You'll see." She phoned Suzy. "We have to do something. He's going crazy. He hates it."

Like everyone else Suzy didn't know what to do; like everyone else that wasn't going to stop her. Suzy dyed his hair again.

Angela studied the result. "Let's make it luminous," she said. "Darling, you're going to be such a great star, and you need a star's hair color. Your hair should glow."

Suzy knew of a German hair dye called Red Hot Red. An enormous amount of peroxide was used to give the red a hot cast.

Then she used a setting lotion to give a cast-iron quality to the spikes of orangy red-hot-red hair on David's forehead. The mission was accomplished, and Angela and she were delighted, but David was still wary.

That night they went to the Sombrero to try the haircut out on Freddi and his gang. The first queen who spotted David went berserk. "That's super," he shrieked.

Queens stood around his table staring enviously at him. His rooster-cut luminous red hair was a sensation. He was ecstatic.

Angela and David clasped hands. It had taken eight long years, but he finally had an image that was ahead of and not behind the times. Finally, he had become a leader and not a follower.

Defries was pleased with the haircut. "It's very marketable," he announced. A great deal of money could be made simply by owning and then exploiting an image. He envisioned a line of Ziggy Stardust dolls with bright red hair. They loved that.

Defries turned to Suzy and told her to leave her job immediately and work for them.

It didn't make any sense for her to give up a salary to work for someone who had once had one hit record. But soon she would also be swept up on a full-time basis by the adventure that was about to take place.

Christmas was approaching and Angela looked forward to going to Cyprus with David and Zowie to visit her parents. She loved the ritual of Christmas, something that seemed to have no meaning for David, who had successfully separated himself from anything that reminded him of childhood.

Defries watched from a distance. He had seen the pained look on David's face when Angela annoyed him. Angela's energy and loudness seemed to have become a little too much for him to take.

Defries knew that David did not want to go to Cyprus with Angela, but wanted to stay behind with Freddi. But he couldn't say no to Angela. It was impossible for him to refuse a direct request from anybody.

On the flight back from Cyprus at the end of the holiday, David became very upset.

"My father came to me in a dream," he confessed. "He told me that I must never fly again. I've only got five years to live, and I must never get in an airplane again."

After he said it, he began believing it, and he reinforced the belief system by telling variations of the story to anyone who would listen. By inventing this ruse he would never again have to fly to Cyprus with Angela. He would also never be able to get into an airplane while he was a married man. The story would have terribly inconvenient ramifications.

David sat perfectly still while Angela did the talking for him. It was as if he was too upset to speak.

"Tony, how will we tour America if David can't fly?" She looked stricken. Was the dream over before it had begun?

A faint smile appeared on Defries's lips. He said they would charter their own private train. It would start when they wanted it to start, stop when they wanted it to stop, and go wherever they wanted it to go. It was a wonderful solution. It was all promotion, Defries said. They could promote the fact that their little spaceman refuses to fly.

David smiled faintly. The noise was a little too much for him.

A series of interviews was set up in mid-January 1972, ostensibly to publicize *Hunky Dory*. Fourteen dates were being lined up for David's stage show during February and March. Without a hit record there was no guarantee that David, even though he was acting like a star and was creating a star's act, would do the business of a star.

The press had to be used in a sensational way if David was to do business during these "rehearsals" for the American conquest, and the forthcoming *Melody Maker* interview was especially important.

Once again Haddon Hall buzzed with talk about image and how outrageousness was the answer.

Angela wanted to push the new and improved David further than he wanted to be pushed. She knew she would have to plant the seed carefully. David couldn't be told what to do, but he could be motivated to do as she wished by thinking her ideas were really his.

"We are representatives of the gay community," she said, "which doesn't mean that we're political creatures. We don't have a cause. We simply represent the wave of the future.

"Nama," she continued, "if someone would just speak out on behalf of the gay community the result would be extraordinary. Think of the attention that person would receive. It would be so brave, and command so much attention. We'd finally hear the voice of the future."

She kept returning to these points until her message became clear. If David told the press he was gay, then he would receive the attention he craved.

David costumed himself with great care for the interview. He wore a combat suit with the shirt unbuttoned halfway down the chest. His trousers were turned up at the cuffs, and he wore thick-soled red plastic boots.

He took the offensive, something Marc Bolan always did with the press, and Defries did with everybody. His songs were ten years ahead of their time, he declared, adding that "I'm going to be huge, and it's quite frightening in a way."

Then he trilled the words that would guarantee him instant international media stardom: "I'm gay and always have been, even when I was David Jones."

A day or two before the story broke, David gave another interview, again delivering his hard sell. His new act was "outrageous, quite outrageous, but very theatrical . . . quite different from anything anyone else has tried to do before. . . ."

David's admission of homosexuality was front-page news, and Defries was especially delighted. *Any* publicity was good publicity.

At RCA the old guard was taken aback, while the young honchos viewed it as a really promotable angle. The challenge became one of promoting David without condoning homosexuality. A company that made washing machines and television sets was in no position to appear to support a self-declared sexual deviate.

Peggy Jones seemed the most flabbergasted of all by the admission. She loathed the musicians who haunted Haddon Hall, but not so much as she loathed the young gays who hung out there. She couldn't bear Angela and was especially chagrined that her grandson was being raised by a downstairs neighbor. Now her son was a homosexual. Her whole life had been based on creating the illusion of respectability, and David kept shattering that illusion.

Never one to mince words, she picked up the phone and called her son to say how upset she was.

Meanwhile David was becoming uncomfortable. He had no qualms about his behavior, and he didn't mind it becoming public. But he didn't like the label "homosexual." Labels made him feel mortal and ordinary. Ordinary lives end in inevitable death, the ultimate revenge on a narcissistic personality. He began to hallucinate his own death. He was going to be assassinated on stage because he had said he was homosexual.

That was no problem as far as Defries was concerned. David was to be surrounded with bodyguards. All great stars have bodyguards. It would be a marvelous promotional touch.

David liked the idea of bodyguards. But he began to lose weight and feel ill. Suddenly he had to be taken to the doctor. It was reminiscent of the time Ken Pitt had had to have him checked out after he had experienced a number of career failures.

He was about to enact Ziggy Stardust, a character doomed to self-destruct. He was beginning to develop Ziggy-like paranoid symptoms, as if watching his own performance from afar.

He really was afraid. And the fear had begun before a single show had even been given.

Backstage in Aylesbury, England, the first Ziggy preview at the end of January, David finishes dressing and making up, and sits perfectly still. He is nervous. His hair is perfectly coiffed, and he sports a gleaming makeup job. His costume consists of a bomber jacket and Freddi's version of the designer pants of the moment.

Angela likes the line of these pants because they feature a codpiece effect that makes the crotch bulge. Ziggy Stardust may be an alien creature, but he is hung like an Earth bull. David's trousers are rolled up to display his flaming red plastic boots. It is an odd, exotic look.

The lights finally dim and the *alla marcia* from Beethoven's Ninth is played loudly over the sound system while a strobe light flickers ominously on the stage and David and the Spiders take their places in the eerie light. The music has been nicked from the sound track of *A Clockwork Orange*.

Suddenly, the footlights, each a furious red, come up. "Hello, Aylesbury, I'm David Bowie and these are the Spiders from Mars," shouts David as the band hurls into a loud, pounding opening number. The Spiders are wearing gold Ziggy-style suits, and they shimmer under the lights, but only Ronno's hair is dyed a brazen gold. Woody and Trevor, the other Spiders, have thus far resisted the "tarting up," and their hair remains its normal long hippie length and dull brown color.

Two shows seem to be happening on that stage. David's Flash Gordon has become the lead singer in Ronno's version of Jimi Hendrix's band.

In the center of the action a gleaming, enameled, perfectly cool David sings his leads. He is the perfect pop androgyne, a chimera who bridges the unbridgeable gap between masculine and feminine. His ability to project Angela's and Freddi's mix of butch and fem without any offensive effeminacy is uncanny.

David stands at the microphone and sings, his hand resting languidly on his hip. A green spotlight hits his face, and he looks like a future-world artist's model. Significant words are accompanied by elementary gestures. When he sings the word "head" he touches his head; the singing of "heart" is accompanied by a tap on the heart.

The audience senses the intriguing tension between the familiarity of a band like the Spiders, highlighted by Ronno's good-natured, macho, natural sex appeal, and the novelty of David, who seems as if he does not—could not—ever sweat the way normal people do. He is otherworldly.

The studied nature of the performance and David's icy, distanced vocals seem perfect in this alien guise. Mere mortals were never this self-possessed.

It is a new kind of passion—the passion of artifice.

Meanwhile Ronno and Trevor, in contrast, wheel around the stage like demented tops. A wall of fast, hard rock and roll pours from either side of David as he sings "Space Oddity" and several more tunes.

Then, during "The Width of a Circle," David disappears into the wings. Ronno suddenly crashes into a series of crunching guitar chords, performing a brazen Cream-style guitar solo. The guitarist asks the first row to caress his guitar. Hands reach up to pluck the strings. For a second, all the audience members vicariously become Spiders from Mars.

When David reappears, he is wearing another of Freddi Burrett's bomber jacket/designer trousers mix-and-match creations. The band goes into Lou Reed's "Waiting for the Man," followed by a rousing version of Reed's "White Light, White Heat," topped by a frenetic "Suffragette City," from the forthcoming Ziggy Stardust album.

The encore, "Rock 'n' Roll Suicide," is performed while posters are tossed over the heads of the audience, an homage to the Alice Cooper show.

The response is not wild enthusiasm, but everyone seems to like David. He is beautiful to look at, very sexy in a *different* kind of way. He also projects an upper-middle-class patrician quality and seems impressively elegant, with far more "class" than the macho rockers who normally play at the Borough Hall. And he has beautifully tailored flamboyant clothes.

Backstage after the show, everyone is euphoric. After seven and a half years of failure, it is clear that David is on to something new—something that can work—something that everyone believes must work. There is no other choice.

Headliner was a new role for David. On stage throughout the tune-up tour of some fourteen dates in England and Scotland, he would study the audience. The girls seemed equally sexually attracted to Ronno and him. Stars did not have to do anything to attract girls. Their fame was aphrodisiac enough. A star never suffered rejection. To prove he had become a star, he needed to work his magic on a different girl after every show.

This was impossible to accomplish with Angela around. Instead of sexual conquest after the shows, there was talk. For hours David, Angela, and Tony went over every detail of the performance. They also talked endlessly about Defries's merchandising fantasies. There would be mechanical Ziggy Stardust dolls that said, "Wham! Bam! Thank you, ma'am," Ziggy jumpsuits, and Ziggy boots. The world was going to look like Ziggy Stardust.

David loved this concentrated dose of attention, but he wanted to act like a star, and stars fooled around.

The tensions between David and Angela flared in bits and pieces during this first series of shows. As usual Defries watched from a distance. It seemed to him that the marriage was over.

Everyone knew the show was new and different, but it was up to the press to tell them exactly what they had. *Melody Maker* did not fail them. It declaimed: "Bowie and his band are nothing if not superb parodists." David loved the review. At last he was being acknowledged for maintaining an ironic distance. Hype had been a parody, and Ziggy was the ultimate parody of the 1960s.

The battle would be waged in the press. The more press David got the more famous he would become. David and Angela were thrilled when they learned that Mick Rock, a *Rolling Stone* photojournalist, was coming to Birmingham to see the seventh show of the tour.

Rock was immediately invited into the Haddon Hall family and became David's new instant best friend. An Oxford graduate, Rock loved Lou Reed and was very interested in the mythology of rock stardom. So was David, and they talked for hours while David established his astonishing brand of intimacy.

David explained that Ziggy Stardust was a "cartoon," and told Rock that he was gay although he wasn't a queen. Those who pretended they were homosexual, like Alice Cooper, distressed him.

The conviction David projected enabled him to win Rock to his side. He began to photograph David on stage and off. He "didn't know what he was doing but was just doing it anyway." The pictures were stunning.

Defries gave Rock the exclusive right to photograph David. It was clear, though, that no one else wanted to photograph David at that point in his career. Of course Rock was drawn into the sexual playacting that was part and parcel of Haddon Hall.

Rock's wife Sheila was a beautiful Japanese woman, and Angela good-naturedly propositioned her.

Everyone loved Angela's performance as Mrs. Outrageous.

CHAPTER 14

Starman

I n March of 1972 Defries returned to New York. At RCA he delivered *The Rise and Fall of Ziggy Stardust and the Spiders from Mars*. David and the Spiders were earning around $200 a night on the road. They were broke, and everyone desperately needed the $37,500 advance Defries would receive for the album.

Defries commandeered Dennis Katz's secretary, Barbara Fulk, and made her his secretary. Katz's office was suddenly his office. He was so charming and persuasive that no one questioned him. He made his way from office to office showing everyone the *Ziggy Stardust* artwork, David's rave reviews, and Rock's gorgeous pictures.

There were long descriptions of the stage show and the success that David was having, as well as talk of the merchandising that was going to result.

David's ability to photograph well made people irresistibly curious about him; the thing to do was get as many pictures as possible into print. It did not matter what people wrote. The right pictures in the right places would make him the greatest star of the century.

During a meeting with Katz, Defries learned that the A&R man was distressed with Lou Reed's first RCA album. It was news Defries would bring back to David in England.

While in New York, he also had dinner with David's cousin Christine, who worked in New York as a literary agent. Among the things they talked about were the Jones family and Terry Burns's mental problems. They searched for reasons for David's seeming indifference about his half-brother.

Early in April, "Starman," the first Ziggy Stardust single, was released in England. It was the missing element, and with its release a flash fire of excitement began to envelop David. The increasing amount of publicity encouraged radio air play, which won David new fans. He was quickly becoming a star.

Three shows were scheduled in April, followed by eight in May. Thirteen more dates would comprise a June tour. As the dates wore on, the real innovation of the show was becoming clear. It was the first time a rock star and his band were from beginning to end playing a *fictional* rock star and band. It was also becoming clear that an even more effective promotional tool would be David's offstage performance as Ziggy whenever he encountered the press. The press would meet him only when he was in full regalia and acting the role of Ziggy. David adored the idea.

In England the release of *The Rise and Fall of Ziggy Stardust and the Spiders from Mars* demonstrated that David had become a star. A substantial 8,000 copies were sold during the first week it was in the stores.

While songs like "Space Oddity" hinted at David's interest in otherworldly happenings and "Oh! You Pretty Things" brought the extraterrestrial theme back to earth, neither had prepared the listener for the polished brilliance of the *Ziggy Stardust* LP. The musical sophistication achieved on *Hunky Dory* and the solid rock drive of *The Man Who Sold the World* had come together to produce a lyrically inspired, musically cogent rock concept album as well as a paralyzing analysis of rock's star-making—and star-breaking—process.

Finally, David had used his gift for imagery sparingly; the result was a literate story line. By writing in the third person, he was no longer constrained by the limited poetic license and shallow image-making that accompanied his role of singer/songwriter. Ziggy's complexity was explored from many different angles, giving the album unprecedented depth and scope.

It was a context that made his vocal limitations inconsequential. By assuming the guise of Ziggy Stardust, he transcended the roles of pop singer and folksinger. He was an actor acting a singing role. With no precedents before him, he had created a framework in which his lack of vocal and emotional color was indicative of who and what Ziggy was. This was Ziggy's deadpan vocal style, Ziggy's pop operatic outpourings.

Additionally, Ronno was gifted enough to make the Spiders sound like a working musical unit, not a sundry collection of studio musicians. For the most part the guitarist laid back, expertly adding subtle colors and textures around David's voice.

The disk was launched by "Five Years," with David playing dispassionate correspondent as he chronicled the reactions to the news that the world had five years left to exist. Panicked images balanced against a skillful arrangement create a bleak, harrowing vision of a world in crisis. "Starman" presents David as a child seeing a UFO who tells his friends about it and then contacts the Starman. David's spoken vocal fits were ingenious, and the straightforwardness of the lyric served to create an engaging fantasy.

Three songs, "Ziggy Stardust," "Suffragette City," and "Rock 'n' Roll Suicide," form the centerpiece of the album. Here Ziggy is accepted, venerated, and ultimately destroyed by the same societal mechanism that created him in the first place. Intrigued by pop manufacture, David's inspiration led to a rock-and-roll metaphor for a society that churns out pop stars who inevitably self-destruct and wind up on the dung heap. It was a trenchant comment, a powerful fantasy, and unwittingly the mechanism that would put him in the position of facing not only his metaphoric rise, but, conceivably, his inevitable fall.

During a conversation with Dennis Katz, an invitation was extended to bring David, Angela, and Ronno to New York in June to see Elvis Presley at Madison Square Garden. There would probably be a reception, and David was promised a chance to meet Elvis.

David jumped at the invitation. The purpose of the trip, he said with a grin, was to give the king of rock and roll the opportunity to meet the queen of rock and roll.

"I must look younger," he said. "It's very important that I'm the younger-looking one."

They had to fly, and by the time they arrived in New York City on Friday afternoon David was close to collapse because of his fear of flying.

Dennis Katz's secretary, Barbara Fulk, got a message that the Bowies had checked into the Park Lane Hotel and that David needed a hairdrier. After five months of phone calls between Haddon Hall and Katz's office, Barbara couldn't wait to meet them, and she rushed to the hotel.

"Come in, darling," said Angela. "It's such a thrill to meet you. David's asleep."

Angela walked Barbara into the bedroom. A nude David was sprawled on top of the bed. His orange hair made a stunning contrast against the white sheets.

Angela propositioned Barbara, and they both had a good laugh.

While Angela took a bath, David awoke. Barbara introduced herself, and David, Mr. Outrageous, immediately began to flirt. Moving quickly, he stole a kiss. He was a wonderful kisser. Somehow it all seemed so good-natured and so much fun she wasn't the least bit intimidated or embarrassed.

Angela came out of the bathroom, and Barbara watched as the two partially undressed Bowies pranced around the suite trying to decide what to wear to the concert.

At Madison Square Garden the seats had been arranged by Defries so that David would sit next to RCA Records president Rocco Laginestra. The sight of David in full Ziggy drag greeting the middle-aged executive in his neatly pressed suit and conservative tie while Elvis crooned "Don't Be Cruel" had exactly the visual impact Defries was aiming for.

By the time the show was over, each RCA executive had had the opportunity to inspect David for himself. They were not disappointed. They didn't know what an English pop phenomenon was supposed to look like, so they figured this had to be the real thing.

Barbara Fulk had brought a date to the show, a good-looking young man who was introduced to David. David looked at him imploringly, and invited him back to the hotel. Everyone enjoyed that. David and Angela were *so* outrageous.

Dennis Katz did his best to apologize for the fact that RCA had not been able to engineer a way for David to meet Elvis. David was extremely disappointed; it was a fantasy that he had desperately wanted to convert into reality.

Back at the hotel David was scheduled for a late-night interview with Lillian Roxon of the *Daily News*. There was much talk about how important she was because the *News* had the largest circulation in New York City.

Roxon, Angela, and David had a long chat about merchandising, and David showed the journalist his sketches for a series of Ziggy Stardust decals. The writer liked them and liked to use her column to encourage artists whom she thought kids might like. In her heated way she would write that the *Ziggy* album "is probably the best album to come out this year."

It was the sort of thing that made RCA drool. It seemed extremely easy to get press for David, unlike their other artists, and no one had ever complimented RCA's albums so extravagantly.

Just before he checked out of the Park Lane at the end of the Elvis weekend, Defries received a phone call from a young promoter, Rick Green. Green wanted to book David as an opening act for Dave Mason. The most enterprising American promoters were on the lookout for acts they could become involved with on the ground floor.

Green thought Defries would be grateful and was in for a surprise. Defries said that David was no opening act, but one of the major headliners of the age.

The phone call signified that a demand for David's services was beginning in America, and it made Defries even more eager to intimidate RCA into offering even greater support. He moved into an apartment on East 58th Street so that he could start making plans to launch David in the United States. He met with America's most powerful booking agent, Frank Barselona, and flabbergasted him by stating that David should be booked as a headliner in America's largest venues.

Barselona had already turned down Ken Pitt, and was not interested in creating the illusion of David's stardom. The William Morris Agency was hired instead. Defries informed them that he wanted 90 percent of the gross, with local promoters receiving 10 percent. It was the kind of deal commanded by only the greatest stars and unheard of in the case of someone who had never played America and had never had an American hit. But it was part of the illusion that Defries believed would eventually make David a real star.

RCA was ripe to play right into Defries's hands. Corporately, the company had sunk millions of dollars into manufacturing black-and-white home video games, only to discover that their competitors had manufactured theirs in color. They were also trapped in enormous expenditures for the manufacture of ill-fated video disks. To make up their huge losses the record division was given a mandate to meet a series of financial projections, an impossible task considering they had few artists worthy of promotion.

Defries was repeatedly urged to allow David to tour the United States. The young people in the company were convinced they could promote him. Each request was rebuffed. He said that without a huge demand, he would not supply his artist.

RCA had to manufacture the demand, and they did not know how to do it. The frustration spilled over during an endless series of internal meetings.

One day as they were banging their heads against the walls, Stu Ginsberg, a young press officer, said, "If he won't come here, why don't we take the press to London to see him? Let's create an enormous media event." Ginsberg had never been to England and wanted a trip.

The idea delighted the company. The American press would be used to create Defries's "demand."

Martin Last, a young press-release writer, insisted that David could—and should—be sold to the intelligentsia. As Dennis and Barbara Katz had been attracted to *Hunky Dory* because of its middle-of-the-road feel, Last loved David's music because it seemed so intellectual. It was music for smart people, not mindless hippies. There were those who felt excluded by the raw energy of 1960s rock and roll. Their pleasure came from style, not an explosion of feelings, and they all seemed to be at RCA.

Conservative RCA didn't much care for rock and roll, and liked the idea of inviting the straight press to England. They needed hits, but in their confusion they seemed willing to target David for an audience that did not buy many pop records. As unlikely as it sounds, representatives of *The New Yorker* as well as *New York* magazine's classical music critic were among the first invited on the trip.

RCA A&R man Richard Robinson told Lisa about the impending junket. Lisa got on the phone and soon everyone knew. Lisa's writer friends hardly knew who David was. They played *Hunky Dory* and didn't like it; it was "too cute." But hoping to convince RCA that they were Bowie fans and deserving of the London trip, some of them rushed into print with rave reviews of the album six months after its release. An American press hype had begun in earnest before the trip was even planned.

The wave of print reinforced RCA's thinking. The print had to mean that David was promotable. More promotion would result in a major record seller. No one addressed the issue that conservative American radio was not about to play records by a man who wore dresses and was bisexual.

Defries's move to New York City distressed his partner, Laurence Myers. Myers believed in a traditional, businesslike approach. It made no sense to him to take David to the United States as a headliner after a mere four months of English dates, nor did it seem logical to build up a roster of artists based on chance meetings like Defries's encounter with Iggy Pop. And David's admission of homosexuality continued to embarrass him. Logic and financial prudence seemed to be missing from Defries's grand plan.

Myers and Defries agreed to end their association, and Defries formed a new company, MainMan. He was Iggy's main man; now he would be everyone's main man.

The artists contracted to Defries at Gem were assigned to MainMan, and Myers, who liked Tony and would remain his friend, made a loan of around $40,000 so that Defries could begin his company with solid financial footing.

One night Defries and Barbara Fulk drove down the West Side Highway, and Defries spotted the RCA Building. The letters RCA glowed a fiery red against the skyline.

Defries told her he saw a building on Park Avenue like the Pan Am Building. On top of it would be the word *MainMan*—the seat of an international entertainment conglomerate.

The words were spoken softly and with incredible conviction. To her amazement Barbara believed Defries. He was impossible to doubt.

David's third trip to the United States had exactly the same effect as the first two. The smell of success invigorated him.

As soon as he and Angela returned to England from the Elvis weekend, Freddi was assigned the task of copying Elvis's onstage white costume. He did a spectacular job, down to Elvis's white scarves. David would change into it before the finale of his set.

Woody Woodmansey allowed his hair to be dyed platinum blond and cut into a DA, and Trevor Bolder submitted to a rooster cut that featured blue sideboards.

The tour resumed, and with it another round of discussions about how to be even more outrageous and make an even greater visual statement. Something had to be done that would make a spectacular photograph that every newspaper would feel compelled to print.

They were playing the Oxford Town Hall, and during a number David suddenly grabbed Ronno's buttocks and slid between his legs so that his crotch bulged between Ronno's legs. Then David began to perform fellatio on Ronson's extended guitar.

"Did you get it? Did you get the picture?" David excitedly asked Mick Rock as he came off stage. The photographer had captured it perfectly.

Defries was back from New York, and he loved the promotional possibilities of the picture. At the beginning of the week, the photograph of Ziggy going down on Ronno's guitar was splashed across two pages in *Melody Maker*.

It was precisely the outrageousness for which they had been striving. David looked at it. The Ziggy Stardust part of his personality took over. He had gone too far, and his doom was sealed. His face became a mask of terror.

"Oh, my God? What are we going to do?" Angela asked Defries.

Defries replied that the solution was quite simple. If David's being gay has been such a superb promotional vehicle, then imagine the publicity they would get when Ronno said he was gay too.

David liked the idea of having a gay brother. It would take the heat off him, and it would make the girls in the audience less vulnerable to Ronno's powerful sexual pull. Ronno hated the idea.

Tony was ready to summon the press.

Unlike David, Ronno kept in close touch with his mother and his friends from Hull. They were all shocked by the fellatio photograph.

Pressure was applied to him, but he balked. He was not going to be embarrassed in front of his family and friends. His real family meant more to him than the David/Defries family. A few days later, at the end of the tour, he quit.

Offers were pouring into Defries's office. David was going to headline the Royal Festival Hall, and a week later the American press was arriving to see him at the Borough Assembly Hall in Aylesbury, where it had all begun five months before. This was no moment to attempt to replace the band leader.

Ronno was talked into returning with the promise that he could remain his straight self. Yet he had demonstrated that he was a deserter. It was inevitable that when he was not needed anymore, he, like the deserters before him, was destined to be erased.

The William Morris office was struggling to get any kind of American tour together for David, whom most people had never heard of. New York's leading concert promoter, Ron Delsener, was approached. He studied the photographs, which were spectacular. "This is the man who is bringing theatrics to rock and roll," he was told.

Delsener liked the idea of being an impresario, a creator of major theatrical events. He thought for a second, then announced, "If he's this theatrical he should play Carnegie Hall."

Barbara Fulk belonged to a network of music business secretaries who worked for the top honchos across America. She had told them all about her new best friends, David, Angela, Defries, and Ronno.

Often their bosses turned to these secretaries to get the most up-to-date information.

"What about Bowie at Carnegie Hall?" Delsener asked the girls in the know. The reply was always the same: What a great idea!

Delsener turned to his friends who were rock journalists and asked the same question. They were all worked up about the impending London junket; it seemed the most elaborate promotion in the history of the record business. Obviously, Bowie was the next great rock star to be produced by England. They, too, responded affirmatively.

With no hits to speak of and only fair record sales in the United States, David was penciled in to make his New York debut the following fall as a headliner at Carnegie Hall. It was audacious and risky, but Delsener had a hunch that David was going to make it. If it worked, he would have the star's loyalty and could count on promoting Bowie whenever he played the East Coast.

The twenty-two American journalists heading for London represented the straight, rock, and underground presses, as well as the wire services. From the moment they arrived at the airport, they were plunged into RCA's illusion of enormous affluence. Flown first class on BOAC, they were not told that the tickets were free in exchange for a commitment from RCA to use photographs of BOAC planes on eight album covers.

In London the group was checked into the plush Inn on the Park Hotel. They did not know that the rooms had been rented at a huge discount in return for the publicity they would give the hotel.

Food and drink flowed lavishly, and room service was worn to the bone.

An entire floor of the even more chic Dorchester Hotel was given over for interviews with David. The journalists were assigned a suite and told precisely when to appear for their fifteen-minute audience with David. The thought of giving twenty-two interviews in a single day filled David with dread, and the times for the meetings were changed repeatedly throughout the day to suit his mood.

A journalist waited patiently for him. Finally, David swept into the room, artfully made up and wearing one of his Elvis Presley suits.

"Everything in his pants is absolutely real, sweetie," Angela thundered from another part of the room.

During the interview David was every inch Ziggy Stardust. "It's a brave new world, and we either join it or we become living relics," he said. "There are people who are aware of this, and there are people who are spearheading the future on one level or another. . . . Alice Cooper, Marc Bolan, myself, Iggy Pop, Lou Reed—we all anticipated it almost a few years too early. Now we're all starting to emerge at the same time, which is interesting."

The journalist pointed out that Marc Bolan and Alice Cooper were huge stars, and that almost no one knew who David was. David smiled sweetly and forged on. "There is a wave of the future and the kids have begun to discover that wave. They have begun to discover us. They may not know what to make of us but they are eager to reach out anyway."

Angela announced that a press agent was arranging an interview with her and all the gay women in New York. She was going to lecture them on life with a bisexual pop star. Later her sense of merriment would carry her away, when she bit a female rock critic on the breast.

As the writer got up to go, David said, "Call me Ziggy! Call me Ziggy Stardust."

The press watched it all. They saw Angela embracing MainMan "artiste" Dana Gillespie; MainMan "artiste" Iggy Pop, dressed in a Mark Bolan T-shirt, threatening to jump out a window; and Lou Reed staring contemptuously at everyone who walked by. They had divided feelings about David. Some found the show amateurish and thought that David's overcontrolled performance lacked power and did not fill the stage with the electricity great rock stars usually generate. It seemed an illusion, more an exercise in pretending something outrageous was going on than being a really new, really outrageous kind of star.

But it could not be denied that David was a hero to his audience. His new look and style represented the classic theme of shocking the establishment. David would upset parents while being beautiful enough to be young people's personal pinup. Ziggy Stardust symbolized liberation from society's constraints, and David's audience loved him.

The music press, harbingers of all that was new, did not want to be left out of the wave of the future. Despite their personal objections they were primed to write, write favorably, and write reams. After all, David did have an English Top Ten album and single; a self-proclaimed married bisexual certainly made good copy; and the trip had been an enormous amount of fun.

It became their game to think up new names for the phenomenon, and each name inspired detailed analysis. Articles would soon appear about "camp rock," "glam rock," "freak rock," "glitter rock," "mascara rock," and "rock 'n' rouge." Pictures of David would appear with each, and after people saw those pictures they wanted to see David.

There were those, however, who remained unimpressed by the whole thing. "I went to England and saw the queen," classical music critic Alan Rich scoffed in his *New York* magazine column.

Throughout the summer of 1972, David and the Spiders toured England. The series of concerts gave them a chance to work on the act in preparation for their eight-city U.S. tour in the fall.

Tony Defries and his girl friend, Melanie McDonald, whom Tony had met when she came to England as Rodney Bingenheimer's escort, arrived in New York on September 12, and David and Angela arrived on September 17. The tour would begin in Cleveland five days later, on September 22, 1972.

Absolutely no preparations had been made for the tour, and not a cent was left after the extravagance of the London junket.

Angela wanted to sail to New York on the *Queen Elizabeth II*. Nervous about the forthcoming American reception, David wanted to surround himself with family, the safest of all possible families. He wanted to take his childhood friend George Underwood and Underwood's wife, Birgit, with him.

Defries agreed. He had great difficulty saying no to members of his surrogate family. First-class passage was booked on the ocean liner for the two couples.

It was decided that the entire group would be booked into the Plaza Hotel because it would look right. In a similar situation, another band and its staff might have stayed at a Holiday Inn or a budget hotel. Not this group. The Plaza would play host not only to David and Angela and George and Birgit, but also to the Ziggy Stardust retinue, personal hairdresser Suzy Fussey, personal photographer Mick Rock, the Spiders from Mars, the roadies, and David's three bodyguards, Stuie George, Tony Frost, and Anton Jones. Because there was no money everything was to be charged.

On September 3, a little more than a week before Defries was scheduled to go to New York, he held a postperformance production meeting at the Excelsior Airport Hotel in Manchester. Defries sat at one end of the long table, David at the other.

Tony explained that in two weeks' time they would be in the United States, and as far as RCA was concerned, David was the biggest thing to come out of England since and possibly before the Beatles. Each and every member of that group had to look like a million dollars. They had to act like stars so that they would be treated like stars. They had to learn to spend money, and spend it in the right way. They were to go out and buy everything they needed for America. They were to buy all the new clothes they needed, all the necessary equipment—two of everything because they might need spares. They had to learn to spend.

No one dared challenge Defries. They charged $50,000 worth of new equipment for the eight American shows. Spending was part of their mission, and they were cushioned by the unreality that was at the core of the entire experience.

In direct contrast to the divine illogic that Defries applied to everything else, he was obsessed with writing meticulous, complicated, iron-clad contracts. MainMan Ltd. already existed in England, and just before the American expedition he established two new companies: an American company, MainMan Ltd., and an English company, MainMan Artistes Ltd.

MainMan Artistes Ltd. would be the employer of MainMan artists who lived in England for work outside the U.K. It would own the worldwide rights, services, products, and income arising from their services, and would be both licensor and licensee of those services.

The American company would be the employer/contractor of MainMan artists who lived in the United States, and would own the worldwide rights, services, products, and income arising from those services as well as being the licensor/licensee of those services.

An employment agreement with David was drawn up to run ten years. Until March 31, 1983, it appeared that Tony Defries owned everything that David would do.

All MainMan companies could lease one another the rights they controlled and also be the .ecipients of those rights from one another. The licensee was empowered to collect income arising in the licensed territory and retain 10 percent of the gross income, together with all production costs, artists' advances, artists' royalties, marketing costs, and other monies expended in exploitation or protection of the rights of the licensor.

Defries had guaranteed himself 10 percent of the worldwide grosses as well as repayment of all of MainMan's expenses.

A MainMan document drawn up in 1974 summarizes the basic nature of the business relationship Defries had with his "artistes." In its own language, it states:

> Scrutiny of the existing agreements will show that there is no obligation to pay the artists any fixed or actual proportion of income arising from services beyond basic salaries set out in those agreements, however, the practice, intention, and understanding of all the artists employed is MainMan will arrange and finance such activities as it is mutually agreed that the artist should undertake from time to time and will meanwhile provide all necessary financial and other support for the artist to live and work without the normal commercial pressures. This means that MainMan provide all the artists' expenses including:
> a) supporting them, their families
> b) necessary personal staff

c) necessary special personnel (musicians, make-up artists, stage director, sound engineers, costume designers, etc.) . . .

MainMan charges all monies expended in such exploitation, protection and dealing in the rights and product against the entire income. The result is a profit or a loss in respect of that particular asset. Assuming a loss it is carried to the artist i.e. to other assets arising from the same source assuming a profit. That profit is then split 50–50 (50% to MainMan and 50% to the artist). Insofar as the artist may have received advances or expenditures of a personal sort those advances or expenditures will be deducted from the artist's share of profit.

MainMan may at its discretion account on this basis currently or at the expiry of the employment. Insofar as MainMan may account during the employment it may nevertheless not make any remittance but simply act as investment manager for artists' funds meanwhile.

The overall effect of these arrangements is that all income arising is MainMan income until such time as they choose to distribute same and all of the artists are investing in all of the other artists and or the growth of MainMan.

Care will have to be taken to determine which expenses are those in which MainMan should participate i.e. which expenses should be deducted from the gross before profits are determined. On the face of it, items such as production costs, recording costs, marketing costs, promotional and publicity costs should well be shared expenses any form of personal advance rent payment automobile purchase [sic].

Defries appeared to be responsible for supporting David for the ten-year term of the employment agreement, but had to pay him only his salary, around $75 a week. But that didn't matter. Tony wouldn't deny him anything. If Defries so chose, he need not give an accounting until the ten years had elapsed. David had also given Defries the right to use his money as he saw fit to develop the company.

David and Tony were equal partners, but partners only in any profits that resulted after all of the expenses were deducted. This was a typical arrangement between English managers and clients, enabling managers to own and control their clients' music publishing and master recordings. It also made manager and artist the watchdog of each other. Normally, each would try to minimize expenses in order to increase profits. But neither David nor Tony was typical in this respect.

Traveling on a cloud of unreality, David prepared to go to America. As far as he was concerned, he and Tony were equal partners in every aspect of their shared great adventure, and they were both going to live happily ever after.

CHAPTER 15

The Illusion
of Perfection

Defries and Melanie moved into the master bedroom of the Upper East Side MainMan duplex Defries had rented, installing Tony Zanetta in the second bedroom. Zanetta was urged to dye his hair red and get a Ziggy Stardust cut. He refused.

Then Zanetta was instructed to convert the first floor of the apartment into an office so that preparations could commence for the eight-city tour Defries labeled U.S. Tour One.

"But there's no money," he said.

Defries assumed that people would be delighted to advance credit to someone who was bringing the major artist of the nineteen seventies to the United States.

Zanetta set out to create a New York "family" for Defries by going to his own "family," the exhibitionistic underground "celebrities" who haunted the back room of Max's Kansas City.

First there was Cyrinda Foxe, the underground Marilyn Monroe lookalike who was dating David Johansen of the New York Dolls. She would be the MainMan receptionist.

Defries was amused by Cyrinda's flamboyant look; for him the more flamboyant the better. Defries cordially welcomed her to the family. He insisted that she immediately dye her hair acrylic red and give it a Ziggy Stardust cut, but she turned him down.

The duplex impressed Leee Black Childers, who had stage managed *Pork*. Childers now worked as a messenger at the teen fanzine *Sixteen*. He wore eye makeup, and his bleached platinum blond hair was cut into DA. At dinner he eagerly sold himself to the manager, and Defries invited him to join the family. Leee accepted, but refused to get a Ziggy Stardust haircut.

Then an English PR man, Dy Davies, arrived from London. Defries had casually invited him to serve as "advance man" on the tour before he even knew what an advance man did. Advance men are troubleshooters who make sure every technical aspect of a concert is perfectly in place before a star arrives.

Tony quickly realized that an American and not an Englishman should advance an American tour and Leee was sent along with Dy.

The fact that Childers knew nothing about the technical aspects of touring meant nothing to Defries. Leee could *act* the role of advance man.

The ex-messenger was given a bill of particulars concerning each concert. The list had evolved during the English dates. Among other things, Defries demanded that the promoters agree that no cameras be allowed into the auditorium, and that each promoter supply a concert grand piano over six feet in length.

If there was the slightest deviation from this list, the date was to be canceled. That decision was left up to Leee.

He was dispatched to Cleveland with more authority than he had ever had in his life. Dressed in black leather, leopard-print scarfs, with colorful butterfly decals sewn all over his clothes, he would be David's official representative and a display of theatricalized androgyny that would more than pave the way for the arrival of the Queen of Rock and Roll.

Answering the phones baffled Cyrinda Foxe, and she left at the end of the first day. Her replacement was Kathy "Pork from New York" Dorritie, who had had a successful Madison Avenue advertising career before she succumbed to the lure of rock and roll. She, too, did not want a Ziggy Stardust haircut.

In less than two weeks the MainMan family had to pull together the organizational details of the completely disorganized U.S. Tour One. The Morris office had never booked an artist who did not fly and had no idea how much driving time to allow David to get from one concert to the next. As the tour progressed it would not be a tour at all, but a collection of oddly spaced dates that would leave David stranded for weeks on end in oddly chosen cities—Phoenix, for one.

Suddenly the MainMan duplex became a carbon copy of Defries's chaotic Gunter Grove home. But the New York family was wildly enthusiastic and willing to work very hard, both at doing the job and at catering to Defries's obsessive concern about small details.

Whole afternoons were devoted to the Ziggy Stardust slide show, hundreds of slides that Defries projected against the wall. Anyone who wandered into the office was corraled into watching and also urged to cut his or her hair Ziggy Stardust–style. The manager wanted everyone to be a walking advertisement for David, the living legend.

Instilled in everyone was the belief that Bowie had been created by Defries in the same way that film stars had been created by the studio moguls.

In their eagerness the family felt compelled to prove to Defries that they shared his quest. Fascinated by the notion of a star-making machine, everyone secretly hoped that Defries would turn his attention to them and also manufacture them as stars.

Defries's ability to appear unruffled by anything convinced them he could do anything, and his narcissism stimulated theirs. MainMan was fast becoming a religious tabernacle and its staff a collection of zealots.

One of RCA's problems was that they did not have an available executive to send on the road with David. Then someone thought of Gustl Breuer, vice president of RCA's classical music label, Red Seal. The opera aficionado was summoned to the conference room.

"Congratulations," everyone called out when Breuer stepped into the room. "You're going to tour with David Bowie." Breuer knew nothing about rock and roll, and his friends were all important opera stars. "What is a 'David Bowie?' " he asked imperiously.

He would soon find out.

Ken Pitt had wanted David to sail to New York dressed in all his finery as if he were a contemporary Oscar Wilde. According to Pitt's fantasy the American press would descend on the boat in a frenzy. Before David touched foot on American soil, the press would have made him a star.

David's fourth trip to America was no star's entrance. The Bowies and the Underwoods stepped off the boat looking like two young English couples on a sight-seeing tour of the New World.

Nor was the reception at the gangplank starlike either. The welcoming party consisted of Gustl Breuer and one or two other RCA representatives, as well as Barbara Fulk, Tony Zanetta, and Kathy Dorritie.

Breuer stepped forward. "I'm the RCA man," he said, "who will accompany you on your tour."

David fixed Breuer with his most disarming smile. "Any relation to Josef Breuer?" Josef Breuer had been Freud's teacher.

"Grandson."

"That's very nice. We must talk."

The aristocratic record company executive was instantly charmed.

Limousines took the group to the stately Plaza Hotel. At the entranceway, David and Angela stopped suddenly to focus their energies. Then they entered the lobby. Except for his odd hair coloring, this time there was nothing unusual about David's appearance, and his face was virtually unrecognizable at that time. But heads turned anyway. David and Angela projected star quality.

They went to the Oak Room, where Defries was hosting a welcoming brunch.

"You must go," said Defries to Barbara Fulk. "This is only for family." Barbara left the table. Barbara had served as Defries's New York personal secretary for a year and had also spoken by telephone two or three times a week to David and Angela. She thought she was family. But she had a fling with Ronno and the solution was to eliminate her. It was a family in which anyone could be erased in an instant with no remorse shown by anyone.

Essential to the success of the Ziggy Stardust dates was the illusion of perfection that David projected from the stage. Yet with only three days to go no lighting designer had been hired, and the Spiders were without a keyboardist.

No one at MainMan knew what to do. Finally, Kathy Dorritie placed a call to Joshua White, creator of the Joshua Light Show. He recommended Bob See, a former Fillmore East employee who ran a lighting business. See was hired sight unseen and told to get to Cleveland to begin preparations for opening night.

The day before everyone was to leave for Cleveland, auditions were held at RCA for a keyboardist. An RCA artist who played avant-garde music suggested jazz pianist Mike Garson. Garson had never played rock music before. He played jazz piano in a tiny New

York jazz club called Poopy's Pub. Garson came to the audition and played "Changes," making it sound like the cocktail lounge accompaniment for Tony Bennett.

David adored it. Then and there, Garson was hired. He didn't know any of the music, but that didn't seem to matter. A cassette was handed to him, and he was told to learn the music overnight. Garson, married and with a young child, was told to pack his bags. He would leave his Brooklyn home the next day to get on the tour bus that would transport him to Cleveland and the opening of U.S. Tour One.

Garson asked for a weekly salary of $800 and Defries instantly agreed. Garson did not know that the Spiders were working for $75 a week, and they did not know that he was getting a much larger sum.

The keyboard player was a practicing Scientologist and brought his faith with him. It would have a devastating effect on the Spiders from Mars.

In Cleveland, Leee Black Childers was in a panic. The piano wasn't big enough. Should he or shouldn't he cancel the opening night?

He called Defries, who took the phone and spoke to the promoters of the Cleveland date.

Defries said that if the piano was not more than six feet in length, then at least it must be the biggest piano in Cleveland.

The biggest piano in Cleveland belonged to the Cleveland Symphony Orchestra. Defries allowed the date to proceed because it was opening night. But he assured everyone that he would cancel from here on in if he didn't get precisely what he wanted.

On the day before the tour was to begin Defries turned to Zanetta and said that because he was an American, he ought to go on the bus to look after David and the lads. He would be the road manager.

Defries didn't know what a road manager did, and neither did Zanetta.

Defries told him to look after everyone, and make sure they found Cleveland.

U.S. Tour One was being advanced by an ex-messenger; now its road manager would be an unemployed underground actor.

Everyone thought it was a wonderful idea. That, after all, was the MainMan way.

At 2:30 in the afternoon on Wednesday September 20, 1972, David was led from the hotel to the bus that would take him to Cleveland for his first American performance two days later. An old Greyhound that had not been customized for touring, it was driven by a middle-aged black man with a resigned expression on his face. Throughout the journey, the expression would never change.

During the nine-hour ride, all of David's many personalities manifested themselves.

There was the invisible David. When he wasn't on, he seemed not to be there and was ignored by everyone.

The studious David perused American comic books. He was especially interested in science-fiction adventure comics, as well as any comic book that featured a mythical hero or heroine, such as Wonder Woman. He also scribbled lyrics and looked out the bus window, fascinated by anything that suggested what he considered to be the real America.

The princely David held court in isolation from the back of the bus, receiving those court members who chose to venture back to talk to him.

There was also the one-of-the-boys David who would come to life and throw in a one-liner that made everyone roar with laughter. He dominated any conversation he interrupted.

Then there was the quiet, nervous David. Except for him, the bus ride soon became a party led by bodyguards Stuie George and Tony Frost, who had brought a bottle of scotch with them. They told dirty jokes about "knockers," a word that made them scream with laughter, and also mercilessly teased Suzy Fussey with a string of dirty jokes.

Embarrassed by their crassness, Spiders Woody and Trevor, simple North Country boys, chose to act the roles of the Beatles in *A Hard Day's Night* by pretending they were witty, bright English rock stars on the road. The bizarre-looking duo was touching in its innocence.

In this context David's silence proved intimidating. By nature the bodyguards were wild men and inclined to violence. But with only one distressed look from David, they turned meek, folding their hands on their laps like schoolboys. The entire group had been conditioned to David's complete control without his having to utter a single word.

Angela played ambassador's wife. "Are you all right, darling?" she asked graciously as she strolled down the aisle. "Can I get you anything? . . . Want a coffee, darling? . . . Thirsty? . . . Why don't you take a good nap, sweetie . . ." Then she exclaimed, "Isn't it wonderful that we're all here!"

When she discovered a stash of vitamins, she became Florence Nightingale. "Everyone, line up for your vitamins," she coaxed, "so we won't have any sickness on this tour."

When Angela approached, David played mommy's little boy. "Ang, may I have a glass of milk?" he asked plaintively.

When it became dark, Angela snuggled next to Anton Jones. They seemed to playing a game of feel-me touch-me while David lay immobile in the back of the bus.

Suddenly Angela would jump up, make the rounds of the bus, check on David and give him a few words of encouragement, then return to Anton.

It was midnight when they arrived at the motel in Erie, Pennsylvania. Everyone was hungry, and Stuie and Zanetta went into the city to hunt for food.

David was sitting alone in his room when Zanetta returned with hamburgers.

"Where's Angie? I want Angie," he whispered.

"I'll get her for you," replied the actor.

Angela was skinny-dipping in the motel pool with Anton.

Cleveland is often considered the indicator of an act's potential. Success there usually means success across America. The fact that Cleveland had gone Bowie-mad became clear when David stepped off the bus. Groupies, hard-core fans, glitter kids, journalists, freaks, and idle curiosity-seekers jammed the hotel lobby. The 3,500-seat Cleveland Music Hall was sold out, and U.S. Tour One was about to begin in a burst of triumph.

Because of his fear of heights, David's suite could be no higher than the eighth floor. He stayed in seclusion, venturing out only when necessary, until the show the following evening.

At the end of the concert, as the audience cheered, in a burst of real feeling he began to cry. Tears tumbled down his cheeks, and he wept like a baby.

Certain rituals began that night that would continue for the entire tour. Suzy Fussey was in charge of David's dressing room, and she discovered that he had to be left alone before showtime. He also needed constant reassurance and had to be told that the show was sold out. When there were good reviews, he had also to be reminded of them. Her job included a lot of basic coddling. At the end of the first portion of the show, he wanted her waiting for him in the wings with a lit cigarette and a glass of wine.

Zanetta discovered that the audience would follow him at the end of the show if he ran down to the stage. David loved the idea of the kids rushing the stage. He liked to tantalize them and reach out to them, tempting them to pull him off the stage and into the audience.

It became a piece of choreography. When it didn't happen, David's mood would turn dark, so the ends of the shows would be greeted by a frantic "spontaneous" uproar from the MainMan staff. Their wild outburst was all the audience needed to go wild itself.

A sold-out concert in Memphis preceded David's Carnegie Hall appearance. In Cleveland and Memphis, David wanted the press kept away. *Rolling Stone* was doing a cover story, but David had to be jollied into seeing the reporter. MainMan had agreed to allow small promotion parties to be given after the concerts, and the hotels inevitably swarmed with kids and freaks who wanted to get to David. He did not want to go to the parties. After enormous persuasion he would make an entrance, brilliantly work the room, say witty, bright things to anyone of importance, and then disappear.

There were also flashes of the Ziggy Stardust paranoia. En route to Memphis, the tour stopped overnight at a Nashville Ramada Inn. The marquee read: WELCOME DAVID BOWIE. It had to come down. David was too panicked.

He never wanted to be alone, yet wanted only one or two worshipers with him. After Memphis and before Carnegie Hall, Defries and Angela sat with him for hours, soothing him while he expressed his nervousness about his New York debut.

Defries remained concerned primarily about the cash advances spinning off the tour. They desperately needed the money to go on. After the Cleveland sellout, he launched negotiations to bring David back to Cleveland for a two-night stand in the 10,000-seat house that was part of the city's entertainment complex. In Memphis, the evening's take was spread over the floor of his hotel room, and people marched around the room, ankle deep in cash.

Ziggy Stardust had arrived in America.

CHAPTER 16

Running Riot

Throughout the tour David had not wanted to give interviews. But in New York, the press was far too important, and there was no way for David to ignore it. A dinner interview was scheduled with the *New York Post*'s Al Aronowitz, one of the early supporters of Bob Dylan. Then David and Angela met for drinks with *Newsweek*'s music editor.

The press unnerved David, especially when it tried to label him a homosexual. It was a subject that obsessed this particular *Newsweek* journalist.

"It is *bi*sexual, not *homo*sexual," said David.

"I can't figure out how your marriage works," replied the writer. "I can't get over this. How do your parents deal with this?"

"May we please discuss my music?" David asked.

The journalist turned to Angela. "I understand you have a child. Isn't being married to a gay man difficult for you? How will your son feel when he grows up and discovers his father is a homosexual?"

Angela pulled herself up to her full height. She had never looked more regal. Pursing her lips, she said calmly but firmly, "In our marriage David and I have found the way least to hurt each other."

The writer became embarrassed. Angela seemed so dignified, so devoted, so much in love. Within the week a full-page rave entitled "The Stardust Kid" would appear in *Newsweek*.

The media outburst reached further than anyone could have rightfully expected. In the Colombian jungles, a cocaine smuggler read about the impending Carnegie Hall concert in a copy of *The New York Times*. He had gone to Bromley Technical High School and had been a best buddy of David's. He had to see the show. His pockets bulging with cocaine, he hopped in his plane and headed it in the direction of Carnegie Hall.

A klieg light played against the facade of the venerable concert hall. Inside, the aisles were clogged with boys with silver-painted faces and girls dressed in see-through tops. Boy and girl Ziggy Stardust look-alikes were everywhere. Often it was difficult to tell the gender of the army of androgynous teenagers who turned out for the show.

Every important person in New York seemed to be sitting in one of the choicest seats. Reporters roamed the aisles cornering Anthony Perkins, Alan Bates, Lee Radziwill, and Andy Warhol to ask their opinions of the new rock music.

David was suffering from the flu, and the New York performance paled in comparison to the earlier part of the tour. But the audience still loved him.

Some of the critics reviewed David unfavorably, but had trouble locating their anger. They were confronting a new conservatism in rock and roll disguised as something progressive and avant garde. Music that once had political connotations and was emblematic of a belief in social change was being transformed into entertainment specifically geared for youthful audiences.

Worst was Al Aronowitz's *New York Post* column. After dining with David, Aronowitz had not even gone to the show. In his place he had sent his scout, Tattler Bob—Bob Weiner, producer of the film *Groupies* and a well-known New York gadfly.

Tattler Bob tattled: "Are they applauding the image or the musician?" and declared the show "an excuse to infuse basic theatrics to cover up a lack of dominant stage presence" with a star who "did not stand out among the band the way a star should."

David was appalled that a "tattler" should have the right to review him instead of a renowned music critic.

Defries declared that there is no bad press, but to appease David he made all other interviews off limits.

The bodyguards were restless. Then they discovered Max's Kansas City. The bar/restaurant seemed to be crawling with groupies who wanted to sleep with David. As the gay MainMan staffers used David's myth to corral young boys, the straight bodyguards utilized the same ruse to satisfy their sexual urges. The groupies believed that the bodyguards were the king's tasters. The bodyguards would have sex with them and check them out for venereal disease. If they passed the test, they would be submitted to the prince.

The word was out, and suddenly the bodyguards' suite overflowed with glitter groupies, eager to have sex with them in order to have sex with Ziggy Stardust.

"We'd spy through those huge old Plaza Hotel keyholes, and we'd watch the bodyguards giving it to some groupie," says Cyrinda Foxe. "After they were through David would occasionally take over, and I would sit in a chair sometimes and talk to him while he was having sex. I'd watch television and sit in a chair, because he wanted somebody to talk to, so I was good for that."

Janis Cavasso, the girl friend of Dolls' head guitarist Johnny Thunder, frequently came to visit. She observed the "hordes of girls" waiting to be tested and then submitted for David's pleasure. She also observed Angela's anger. "Slut!" she would shriek at her husband. David burst into laughter.

While David was exceptionally warm and tender to Cyrinda Foxe, he never seemed tender to Angela. But Angela bit the bullet, and Cyrinda, Janis, and she became a trio, shopping and gossiping together.

Angela discussed her marriage freely with Janis. "I adore him," she said. "I'll do anything to keep the marriage together. I do whatever I think he wants me to do—any outrageous thing."

Cyrinda had never met anyone who seemed so obsessed with boys. She called Janis from the Plaza to whisper, "Angie's sex starved. What do I do about it?"

David was due in Boston, but Angela decided to stay behind at the Plaza, where she was having so much fun hanging out with Cyrinda.

Boston is one of the great college towns, and the undergraduate academic crowd came out in full force for David's performance.

David read every word printed about him. The press always offered clues to what he needed to say and do in order to fulfill the expectations of his audience. The press focused on the Ziggy Stardust image, which they wrote was as much a work of art as his songs. The press wrote that rock and roll was the ultimate expression of our society, hinting that a new messiah could be only a rock star—

the ultimate rock star—an actor playing the role of ultimate rock star.

As David saw it, that meant he was the new messiah.

During his finale David sang, "You're not alone . . . gimme your hands." Every hand in the place reached up to him.

Photographs of the moment exactly duplicated the finale of a Judy Garland concert, and the Boston papers called him "the Judy Garland of rock and roll."

David had done as Ken Pitt wished him to do, but he had done it his way.

While the Boston young sat up late in their dorms discussing the new messiah, David was full of energy and good cheer. This was the first time Angela was not with him on the road, and he wanted to make the most of it.

Still wearing his makeup, he headed for the Other Side, a Boston gay bar. He danced the twist with a bodyguard. People said hello and asked for autographs. The man dancing beside him gave him a wet kiss on the lips.

He loved it all. It was fun being a star.

Then the bodyguards took charge. "It's too dangerous," they growled.

David didn't want to leave, but he was hustled out anyway. It was for his own good, he was told, and he couldn't object to that.

During David's absence, Angela was having a ball in New York.

She was also going to do something for David. He seemed to want to be the King of Glitter Rock. She would become Queen. It was the only way she seemed to have of giving him what he wanted.

Cyrinda Foxe was her model. She bleached her hair the same platinum color as Cyrinda's and cut it into Cyrinda's style. She painted her lips with "Love That Red" lipstick and ordered Pelican shoes from Cyrinda's friend in the Village who made them.

While David was in Boston, the cocaine dealer who had been a Bromley Tech mate, hung out with those who remained behind. Cocaine was still an underground drug at that time, and it had an aura of excitement.

On his return David discovered that cocaine was floating around his kingdom, and he panicked. Defries hated drugs, and, therefore, so did he. He ignored his high school friend.

David was fascinated by Angela, who seemed to be transforming herself into Cyrinda. That meant that it was almost time for him to make the transformation himself.

A few days before the resumption of the tour he concluded his *Rolling Stone* interview. "I'm a . . . very cold person," he said. "I can't feel strongly. I get so numb. I find I'm walking around numb. I'm a bit of an iceman."

Two days later the Iceman was on a train for Chicago.

Cyrinda One and Cyrinda Two stood before David in Chicago. He smiled warmly at the genuine article and was distant and withdrawn, the paranoid/vulnerable Ziggy Stardust–David, with Angela.

To complete her transformation she had shaved off her eyebrows. David continued to ignore her, and Angela had a tantrum, then collapsed into a deep sleep before the concert.

At the concert, when it came time for the MainMan staffers to lead the audience toward the stage, they were viciously attacked by the Chicago Auditorium bouncers, with some of them even being dragged forcibly from the theater. The closing effect was ruined, and David sank into despair.

It was the beginning of a very difficult series of dates, dates during which David would show his best and worst traits.

In Detroit David had a chance to renew his friendship with Iggy Pop, whom Defries was now managing. Iggy was experiencing Tony Defries's star treatment. Defries had flown him from London to Detroit with the tapes of *Raw Power*, the album Iggy had recorded in London while Iggy's band, the Stooges, "mere sidemen," were left behind.

Leee Black Childers was sent to Detroit to make sure Iggy got to visit his mother in the Ann Arbor trailer park in which she lived, and then make it back to Detroit to see David's show. Pop would go from Detroit to L.A.

After a successful date in Detroit, disaster loomed in St. Louis. David had been booked into a 10,000-seat hall, and less then one thousand tickets had been sold.

Everyone set out to plaster pictures of David in men's and women's bathrooms across the city, and the MainMan staff roamed through the streets giving away free pictures, singles, albums, and posters.

It was to no avail, but that didn't stop David. He invited everyone to cluster closely around him and gave an especially impassioned show. An embarrassing failure became a personal triumph.

By now the tour was bankrupt. The idea that David could sell 10,000 tickets in the Midwest had been a preposterous one. Defries's 90/10 deal made him responsible for all expenses, and the losses were spectacular.

The group traveled to Kansas City without a cent to spare. Business in Kansas City was even worse. Then David learned that Cat Stevens was selling out in the Midwest. It had been Stevens and not he who had scored a commercial triumph on the Deram label, and he was especially distressed.

The truth was clear. David was a sensation in some cities and almost totally unknown in others. It was a truth he didn't like. It was Tony's fault for booking him in cities in which he was playing to empty seats. Empty seats destroyed the illusion of stardom. But he could not give himself permission to get angry at Tony; instead he went on stage drunk.

He was so upset he got very drunk, and during the show he fell off the stage into the house. But he didn't miss a note. It was a *graceful* fall. Even in his despair, he seemed to be always watching himself. His ironic distance from himself would always save him no matter how much he misbehaved.

The next stop was Los Angeles. Everyone couldn't wait to get out of Kansas City. David loved Los Angeles. It was the city where images were manufactured as a way of life—a city in which he really felt understood.

Publicity was their god, and the press could always tell them what to do.

"You've got to stay at the Beverly Hills Hotel," rock critic Lisa Robinson told Leee Black Childers. "You're supposed to be promoting a big star. David and Tony must each have his own private bungalow; the others can stay in suites. Make sure to reserve poolside cabanas; that means you're really important. When you're poolside have yourself paged continually. That's the Hollywood way. And if you want the house specialty, chocolate soufflé, make sure you order it at breakfast."

"*Lisa Robinson* says we must all stay at the Beverly Hills Hotel," Childers demanded of RCA's L.A. promotion department. RCA gulped, but Childers was insistent. A professional would have balked at such monumental extravagance, but Defries's amateurs did not know any better and would not take no for an answer.

For two weeks, every single person on U.S. Tour One bedded down at the pink plaster hotel set in twelve acres of tropical foliage.

No one had any money, so everything had to be charged to room service. Because no one had taxi fare, limousines had to be ordered whenever anyone left the hotel. The limousines were also put on the room service bill, which would mount to $20,000 by the time their stay was over.

For the most part, with the exception of David, the group traveled en masse. Every night at six the exclusive Polo Lounge was turned into Max's Kansas City's back room. The Polo Lounge was Ziggy Stardust's mess hall.

Andy Warhol and Paul Morrissey were staying in the hotel.

"How did that trash get in here?" Morrissey whined as the group passed by.

So they spent their days sitting at the pool drinking Scorpions and Tequila Sunrises, soaking up the sun, and being paged. Suzy Fussey dyed Iggy Pop's hair silver, but the chlorine in the pool turned it emerald green. The combination of the sun and chlorine turned Ronno's hair green also, and the color almost matched the color of the leaves on the Beverly Hills Hotel banana-tree wallpaper.

Whenever a roadie needed extra cash, he'd find a tourist, and sell him a Polo Lounge bargain meal. The roadie pocketed the cash while RCA paid for the dinners.

Unreality had became a way of life.

David's old friend Rodney Bingenheimer had taken David's advice and opened Rodney's English Disco on Sunset Strip. The crowd at the club ranged in age from twelve to fifteen. They were the "stargirls," "foxy ladies" in search of "superfox" boys. Some were "evil she-foxes," girls who thought nothing of stealing a superfox from another foxy lady.

These nymphet groupies were stars in their tight little world. Some dressed like Shirley Temple; others wore dominatrix outfits or "Hollywood underwear," a knee-length shirt, nylon stockings, and garter belts. The star girls streaked their hair chartreuse and liked to lift their skirts to display their bare crotches. As they danced they mimed fellatio and cunnilingus in tribute to David's onstage act of fellatio on Ronno's guitar.

The club was a shrine to David, and his records were played

nonstop. Bingenheimer, a fanatical fan, had inspired a cult, and the cult had become large enough to sell out the Santa Monica Civic Auditorium concert. A second night sellout was added.

It was kiddy decadence, and the decadent kiddies eagerly awaited their demigod Ziggy Stardust.

When David arrived, they descended on the hotel. Their presence enraged the hotel security force, and the army of prepubescent trollops camped out in the lobby was repeatedly evicted from the premises. Finally, four of them checked into the hotel and rented the bungalow next to David's, where they spent their days and nights lying in wait for him.

The star-girls were so tenacious they wound up having their way with the Spiders, roadies, and bodyguards. It offended Defries's puritanical nature, and he issued an imperial order: Groupies must be gone by breakfast.

It was Hollywood, and David could play James Dean. He could *be* James Dean. All he needed was a legendary co-star, and he asked Defries to send for Marilyn Monroe look-alike Cyrinda Foxe. Cyrinda, who had returned from Chicago to New York with Angela, was flown to Los Angeles immediately and took up residence in David's bungalow.

When they awoke at around two in the afternoon, Cyrinda fed David croissants in bed. They went to a party at Wolfman Jack's house, as well as to Rodney's English Disco, and had some people in to listen to David's new favorite, the most *American* comedian of all, Lenny Bruce.

Elton John was staying in one of the bungalows and also came to visit. David had commented that John's "Rocket Man" was a rip off of his "Space Oddity," but the opinion was overlooked, and the two Englishmen bantered wittily with each other.

With time on their hands, the Spiders listened to Mike Garson extoll the virtues of Scientology. The keyboardist also approached David and began to talk to him about it. David stiffened. The last thing a new messiah wanted to hear about was this peculiar-sounding religion.

Accompanied by bodyguard Tony Frost, Garson and the Spiders attended a one-week communications course at the Los Angeles

Scientology Celebrity Center. They came back changed men. The groupie action had begun to peel away their innocence, and Scientology had encouraged them to speak up and stop being good children. At the completion of the course Frost turned against Stuie and they had a violent altercation. The bodyguards had to be separated and would not speak again.

David watched in consternation. He hated anything that disturbed the illusion of smoothness in his family. He had dealt with Terry Burns's madness by ignoring it. These troublesome brothers would also have to be eliminated.

He did not realize that being in Los Angeles with time on your hands easily led to madness.

A young secretary in Bill Graham's office had badgered Graham into booking David in San Francisco. But the two-night stint in Winterland was not moving many tickets and loomed as a potential disaster.

Defries ambled into Winterland and surveyed the scene. He was unconcerned about the lack of business, but the layout of the theater displeased him. David would have to make his entrance through the audience. Stars stood above their audiences and never rubbed shoulders with them.

He told Graham to build a wall along the side of the theater. It should run seventy-five feet and stretch from the back of the house to the stage. David could pass behind the wall, and the audience would not see him until he was on stage, and making the entrance of a grand star.

Graham was flabbergasted. The greatest entertainer of the age had racked up a sale of a mere eight hundred tickets for his opening-night show.

Defries calmly stated that he planned to cancel the shows. Nothing the promoter could say made him change his mind. It was clear that he would not let David go on unless he got his way, without regard to the cost consequences of his actions.

The wall was built, and Defries's soft-spoken bravura reassured everyone. While audiences and critics were treating David with the fervor appropriate to a god, Defries seemed to be the real god, a man who insisted and then demonstrated that the world was going to run on his terms, and his terms alone.

David and Tony continued to have long discussions, and Defries spoke at length about another of his favorite subjects, the Japanese system of management.

He said that he planned to buy Sony, and no one doubted it.

Wall or no wall, the two Los Angeles sellouts were followed in San Francisco by two nights of half houses. Again, the 90/10 deal turned against Defries, and RCA lost another large chunk of money. The entourage checked out of the Beverly Hills Hotel with so little loose change they couldn't afford to buy cigarettes.

While they were in San Francisco, Mick Rock filmed the promotional film for "Jean Genie," a song David had written on the tour. Defries sensed that David was about to lose interest in Cyrinda Foxe. He summoned her and told her to pack her bags because he was sending her home to New York.

David was regretful, but the regret seemed to pass quickly. A half-hour or so after she left, he became preoccupied with something else.

During David's West Coast stay Miss Christine of Frank Zappa's singing groupies, the G.T.O.'s, introduced Michael Lippman to Iggy Pop. Lippman was a young lawyer who worked for the talent agency CMA, and Iggy told him that David was planning to leave the William Morris Agency. Lippman wanted David as a client. His calls to MainMan remained unanswered until he said he knew Miss Christine. Suddenly he was able to get through.

Later, Miss Christine called Lippman and made him promise to look after David even though David and he had never met.

The next day Miss Christine died of a drug overdose. The promise that Lippman made hung over his head. It seemed imperative that he find a way to represent David. When Defries replaced the Morris office with CMA, he would suddenly find himself thrust into a position that would enable him eventually to achieve that goal. He would also discover that his promise to Miss Christine would demand of him far more than he had bargained for.

At the end of the two-week stay in L.A. and just before the group left for Seattle, Defries instructed Leee Black Childers to remain behind and establish MainMan West. He was to rent a house and move Iggy Pop into it. They were to wait there until there was a demand from the public to see Iggy. The wait could be days or years—it did not matter. Pop was not to perform in public until the public clamored to see him.

Even though there was no money to pay the rent on a Los Angeles house, it was clear that Defries would find the way.

Now there was MainMan U.K., MainMan New York, and MainMan L.A. The illusion of an international entertainment conglomerate seemed about to become reality.

CHAPTER 17

The Feeling of Triumph

Angela especially galled Defries. Of the entire entourage, she was the only one he could not control. She spent whatever she liked whenever she liked and flew anywhere on a moment's notice. She had returned to London, where she decided to rescue those mere sidemen, the Stooges, and take them home to Detroit. Without consulting Defries she charged the airfare to the company and was hanging out with the Stooges in Ann Arbor.

Defries hated the fact that Angela had acted on her own. He ordered a stop to Angela's check-writing privileges and rescinded her ability to charge airline tickets and hotel reservations to the company.

But she would not be stopped. He knew it and hated it. His manner seemed to indicate that David would be better off without her, but David bridled. When David and Angela were together, Angela insisted that he play "Nama-nama" with her, a role that he now had lost all interest in. But Angela had urged him to abandon Ken Pitt, sign with Tony Defries, and become Ziggy Stardust. David did not love her, but he trusted her judgment and did not yet trust himself enough to do without her.

Defries watched. In the long term he was sure she would be erased.

On November 26, two months after his American debut in Cleveland, David returned to this first stop on the tour. The *Rolling Stone* cover story was on every newsstand in the country, and it had an amazing effect. Publicity proved capable of turning out audiences

by the thousands. David played two sellout shows to 10,000 people
each night. After each performance the roaring audience rose in
unison and lit matches. David and the Spiders looked out at a sea
of fire. This tribute was new to them, and the sight amazed them.
It was the kind of success that transcended even the most fantastical
dreams.

At that moment Angela made her triumphant return to U.S.
Tour One.

"Nama, you were wonderful," she boomed after the show.

She was in high spirits. She had a new boyfriend, Scott Richardson, whom she had met in Ann Arbor. He was young, good-
looking, charming, and smart. Angela was very pleased.

In Cleveland that night there was a small party in David's suite.
At the end of it Angela took Scott to her room. A tenacious black
groupie had corralled David, and she seemed to have ordered him
into his bedroom. David could never say no to anyone and did
precisely what he was told.

David made his own choice in Pittsburgh, an attractive black
boy. At the end of the tour David summoned the boy to New York
to be his lover; on his arrival, he lost all interest in him. The boy
had no money, so MainMan had to pay his way back to Pittsburgh
and also give him a few dollars for his time and trouble.

The next night, Philadelphia proved to have the most fanatical
fans of all, many of them Main Line preppies who thought it daring
to give their allegiance to as rebellious a figure as Ziggy Stardust.
Among those fans was Pat Gibbons, an assistant to Philadelphia
promoter Rick Green. Gibbons would eventually maneuver himself
into becoming David's personal assistant.

Angela made her next appearance in Philadelphia. She was ele-
gantly dressed and at her most reserved. Her escort was another
story. The boy was dressed in green from head to toe and wore
green eyeshadow, green lipstick, and green nail polish.

"Nama, nama," said Angela, "this is for you." She took David's
hand, pressed it against the boy's, and clasped them together. The
Green Genie was a present to David; David was appalled.

To add to his upset, Calvin Mark Lee, of all people, began to
call. They had not seen each other in three years, and David, dread-
ing a reminder of past failures, refused to come to the phone.

Despite the mammoth security surrounding David, Lee found an open window at the Tower Theatre. He climbed through the window, landed backstage, and marched into David's dressing room.

David was exceptionally cordial. But his eyes kept darting around the room, begging someone to rescue him.

The Philadelphia shows went brilliantly, and when they were over, U.S. Tour One seemed like an explosive triumph. Everyone headed back to New York floating on air.

The amount of publicity generated by the tour was astounding, but the publicity hadn't sold that many records.

Always in need of cash, Defries had purchased David's two albums from Mercury and marched into RCA, masters in hand.

He explained that RCA could start building a catalog of Bowie albums. In the future the recordings would be extremely valuable. Now RCA would have four recordings instead of two. An advertisement featuring two LPs could now feature four, and it wouldn't cost a dollar more in advertising.

Defries had paid $20,000 apiece for the albums and leased them to RCA for $37,500 apiece.

At the outset of the tour the company had issued a four-cut promotional EP that was used as a giveaway by radio stores and radio stations. The single "Jean Genie" had been issued midway into the tour, and RCA was about to reissue the two Mercury LPs, with *Man of Words, Man of Music* retitled *Space Oddity*.

"Space Oddity" would also be re-released as a single, its third appearance in the United States in three years. Spurred by the fantasy that publicity would translate into record sales, the market was flooded with product in defiance of the fact that conservative radio programmers were not inclined to play the records.

U.S. Tour One had stretched on for seventy-one days. But David had given only twenty-one shows in only sixteen cities. The tour had grossed $114,000, but the seventy-one day extravaganza had cost RCA over $400,000. RCA lost about $20,000 each time David stepped on stage.

In the MainMan New York offices, Defries conducted meetings late into the night to plan the next move. RCA's loss of nearly $300,000 meant nothing to him. It was mere pocket money.

He announced that U.S. Tour One was merely a rehearsal. If

one looked beyond the publicity, it was clear that David was not selling records. The momentum had to be kept going until record sales caught up to the publicity.

At RCA Defries met a Japanese promoter; Japan was the second-largest record market in the world. By the time they were done talking, Defries had scored a very good deal. The promoter would finance a Japanese tour, paying all air fare and expenses, and guaranteeing MainMan $6,000 a show. The illusion of superstardom that had been created in America could now be duplicated in Japan.

An even larger plan evolved. U.S. Tour Two would be followed by the Japanese tour. After Japan, David would stage a triumphant return-to-England tour and then travel again to America in a coast-to-coast tour. But for the moment U.S. Tour Two would take him only to those cities where there was real demand, and he automatically would sell out. It would cement the markets in which David was already a star. But MainMan was penniless, and U.S. Tour Two could be accomplished only with the financial support of RCA.

The RCA executives were kept waiting for hours before Defries made his entrance. By now they were used to it.

Defries told RCA that he was giving them the opportunity to share in the profits that would be generated by touring. By financing David's touring activity they would share in the future profits that would accrue as his influence and importance was realized.

Feedback was coming from RCA's branch promotional offices to continue supporting David. The young RCA promotion men liked him, and wherever the young staff supported David, he did sellout business.

RCA loved the publicity and wanted more. At that time the RCA Corporation was spending untold millions to develop a home video system they called Selectavision. Among their problems was the fact that they, like their record division, had no product. David seemed ideal as a home video attraction, and the corporate heads also pressured the record division on David's behalf.

The record company agreed to share in future tour profits. To make sure there would be profits, an RCA corporation accountant was assigned to supervise the spending as well as control the costs.

CMA did a masterful, efficient job of setting up a twenty-three day tour that would take David to eleven cities. Defries demanded that David play only in theaters because he was a theatrical and not a conventional rock attraction. David had said he wanted to play Radio City Music Hall; Defries passed on the word to the agency. It was conveyed to promoter Ron Delsener, who mustered enormous powers of persuasion to convince the conservative Music Hall officials to book David.

The tour would open Valentine's Day, 1973, at the Music Hall, with David returning to the United States just ten weeks after his first tour had ended.

RCA's tour accountant and Defries invented elaborate book-keeping systems, which Defries loved. The illusions of control and order gave him real pleasure. Mid-priced hotels were booked instead of four-star hotels; only David would be allowed room service and twenty-four-hour use of a limousine. Everyone else would get a per diem and pay his own expenses.

As soon as David returned to England in December, he went back on the road. Unlike in America, here his single release, "Jean Genie," had climbed easily into the Top Twenty and seemed to be heading all the way to the top. A triumphant two-night return was made at the Rainbow Theatre. Five concerts would follow before his return to New York in early February.

When Cherry Vanilla's friend, a luscious black backup singer, visited London, Cherry arranged a meeting with David.

David and she began seeing each other.

Meanwhile Angela knew that something had to be done to make Ziggy shine even more brightly when David returned to America. She returned to Kansai Yamamoto's boutique, where she had purchased the outrageous costume David had worn at his first Rainbow Theatre appearance.

They both loved Kansai's "young rebel" clothes, a strange blend of Mod and Japanese Kabuki-like fashion. Kansai showed them a film of one of his fashion shows, and David carefully studied the Japanese models' formalized gestures. They bought some clothes, and Kansai made gifts of a number of outfits that could be worn on stage and at home.

Ziggy had gone Japanese designer–chic. The "wave of the future" would have a look years ahead of its time.

The feeling of triumph that accompanied David's return to America in January was not shared by the Spiders.

Terrified that either David or Defries would find out, Ronno secretly made contact with Barbara Fulk, who had left RCA. She arranged a late-night meeting for the Spiders and Dennis Katz. Katz had also left RCA and was again practicing law.

Ronno served as spokesman. They were upset about money. Even they had been fooled by appearances and assumed that David was personally earning a fortune while they earned $75 weekly. They wanted more money, but were too afraid of the godlike Defries to ask for it, and afraid also that the godlike David would find out they were acting behind his back.

Ronno was upset because he was not getting enough credit. Even though he was David's musical director and worked up all of David's songs, he had receded far into the background while David had gone on to become an instant "legend."

When the tour was over, the Spiders were determined to set out on their own. Katz was asked to begin the search for a record deal for the group.

Both outwitting and punishing the Spiders would prove especially easy for Defries.

They demanded a percentage of all income generated by the tour, with a guaranteed minimum. Defries compromised by offering them larger salaries, which they gratefully accepted. But they would have to pay their own personal expenses. They didn't know at the time that they would wind up earning even less money by accepting Defries's offer.

As for David, he would never forget the feeling of desertion that had overcome him when the Lower Third had deserted him for money. The Spiders would have to be deserted before history had a chance to repeat itself.

One night after they arrived in New York City to prepare for U.S. Tour Two, Angela and David went to Max's Kansas City. Their eyes drifted over the room and came to rest on Bebe Buell, an eighteen-year-old beauty.

As they got up to leave, David went to her table and introduced himself. Bebe thought he looked wonderful in his elegant blue suit.

His makeup was flawless, and a thin layer of lip gloss made his lips gleam.

"Angela's returning to London tomorrow, and I would really like to see a few places in New York," he said. "Would you like to come with me?"

Bebe told David her boyfriend, Todd Rundgren, was a very big fan of his, and had turned her on to David's music.

"Right, yes, Todd Rundgren. Very intelligent man," David said quickly. Now that David knew she had a boyfriend, Bebe felt safe about giving him her telephone number.

The next night Bebe and David had a romantic dinner at Nirvana, a penthouse Indian restaurant overlooking Central Park. Then they went to Radio City Music Hall; David wanted to see the stage machinery in operation with an audience in the house. As a gesture toward economy, U.S. Tour Two was using the Gramercy Park Hotel, not the Plaza, as its New York base. At the hotel Bebe played Rundgren's new album for David.

They quickly grew fond of each other. Bebe perceived David as a little boy lost. She had never met anyone so taken care of. His staff seemed to wash, feed, and dress him. He was also unlike any of the rock-and-rollers that she knew. He liked to help her do her hair and makeup. He told her how beautiful she was and gave her practical advice about how to be even more beautiful. He was sister, father, and friend.

Sometimes David turned into a little boy and began to weep. Even though Bebe was young, a maternal feeling swept over her, and she soothed him and spoke gently to him until he wasn't unhappy any more.

They went to Bloomingdale's together, and David bought her some dresses. He also gave her her first bottle of Dom Perignon.

David was so generous and really seemed to care about her. Most of all, he told her magical things. "You're special," he said repeatedly. "You're more than a model. You've got so much more to offer."

Bebe looked into his eyes and saw her own reflection in them. In his eyes she was special and beautiful and destined for greater things.

They went to Kenny's Castaways to hear the New York Dolls and necked passionately in public. Whenever they went out, they drank the best wine and always took a limousine. Bebe asked where all the money was coming from, but David just laughed. Tony took care of that.

At home she babbled to Rundgren about her new best friend and how normal, sweet, and generous he was. It drove Rundgren crazy.

Then David began to call at three or four in the morning. Rundgren watched as Bebe headed for the door. She told him that she loved him, but had to go to David because he was so upset.

Finally, Todd asked, "Are you sleeping with him?"

The answer was no. They later went to bed—only two or three times. The first time took hours and lots of champagne before Bebe was ready, and David had to chase her around the room like a virgin. They collapsed on the floor in hysterics, and Bebe explained that Rundgren was the only man she had been to bed with.

During the lovemaking, when David became too daring, Bebe laughed, jumped up and headed into the bathroom. David enjoyed her shyness. "I really love being with you. It's refreshing—different," he told her.

One night after returning from hearing Thelonius Monk, David and Bebe burst into a room that belonged to a tour member. He was in bed with a girl, and David stripped off his clothes and climbed into bed with them.

Bebe announced that she had to leave, and asked David to put her in a cab. The orgy was aborted before it even began.

A day or two before the Music Hall opening, David and Bebe went to Max's and joined Alice Cooper's table. Suddenly Todd Rundgren came into the restaurant. He was wearing tight blue jeans and a silver jacket. His hair was streaked and he was wearing makeup. He had gone glitter in order to win back his girl friend.

Then Angela returned to New York with Zowie, and David invited Bebe to lunch to meet them. Bebe stood at the door to the suite just as Angela came down the hall with Cyrinda Foxe. The door opened and a beautiful black girl left David's room.

Everyone was wonderfully cordial to each other.

In the first row at the Music Hall on David's opening night were Angela, Cyrinda, Bebe, and Todd.

A few days before the opening David had gone to the Music Hall and was provided with a long list of backdrops and special theatrical effects used in their stage shows. He chose only three. More, he believed, would weight the show against the music and alienate the record-buying rock music audience.

Yet his entrance had to be spectacular, and he'd chosen to descend from the flies on a prop decorated with moons that looked like an overgrown Christmas-tree ornament.

The height terrified him, but he was going to do it anyway. As David descended from the heavens, Angela, Bebe, and Cyrinda went wild. Todd sank back into his chair. Throughout the show, the three female worshipers were almost uncontrollable in their enthusiasm, and David responded by blowing them kisses.

The show was the same as the one on his previous American tour. But now David made twelve costume changes instead of two.

Even though the key to this Ziggy Stardust edition depended on costuming, when the Spiders' costumes arrived from England the day before the opening, none of them fit. Throughout that night and into opening day, Suzy Fussey single-handedly ripped them all apart and restitched them. It was a hideous job, but it had to be done, and she was the only one willing to do it.

On stage, though, everything was perfect. A new makeup man had painted a gold circle in the center of David's forehead, and he was a stunning, enameled, lacquered mannequin. At the end of the opening number two Kabuki-style shadowmen appeared from the darkness to rip his outer garments from him. His confidence had grown during U.S. Tour One, and now he was supremely confident, a spontaneous rock-and-roller and a futuristic fashion model whose every stylized move reflected a startling Kabuki influence.

The contradiction between the two elements gave the show an uncanny novelty value. The audience was fascinated. But the biggest surprise came at the end. Suddenly David fainted. His wonderfully dramatic, gracefully executed collapse was the last thing the audience saw as the great Music Hall curtain fell.

"Tattler" Bob Weiner's guest that night was Bette Midler, the hottest new musical star in the country. She had been launched by a gay cult and was often compared to Judy Garland, who had a reputation for fainting on stage. Midler was also being compared to David because she, too, had an on stage persona, the Divine Miss M.

The fainting seemed to panic her. "I want to go back and help David. I've got to help him," she insisted.

"But you don't even know him," "Tattler" Bob replied.

Backstage David quickly revived and explained he hadn't been eating properly. He had never seemed more fragile. But the MainMan staff had its doubts about whether he had really fainted or if it was just a stage faint. If he was so undernourished why was he overcome at exactly the end of the show?

No one knew that he had fainted once before on stage, years ago in the provinces of England. That fainting spell had been viewed as a publicity stunt.

Publicity stunt or not, David's fainting generated another burst of national attention.

Ava Cherry, eighteen, the same age as Bebe Buell, was an exotic-looking black girl who shaved her eyebrows and bleached her short cropped hair platinum blond. It was a startling effect, but even though her look was exotic Ava had an ingenuous personality. She was the kind of girl who faithfully called her mother in Chicago once a week.

She worked as a cocktail waitress at Genesis, a discotheque. On the day after David's two-night Music Hall engagement, Genesis played host to a party for Stevie Wonder. The guests, mainly black, included Aretha Franklin and Bill Cosby, but one of them was white and had orange hair.

David looked around the room and headed straight for the blond-haired black girl dressed in her waitress costume, a formal tuxedo. He asked her if she'd like to go home with him, and she refused. Then he asked her for her phone number.

Suddenly an idea came to him. He had already added two horn players to his retinue, now he wanted backup singers. Ava would be one of them.

"After my Japanese tour, I'm doing a tour of England," he told her. "You might be interested in working with me. Are you going to call me?"

A few days later he called her and invited her to dinner at the Gramercy Park Hotel. They went to hear Charlie Mingus, and Ava came back to the hotel. David played her a series of records. They were new releases, and he listened carefully as he determined which musical elements might make them successful.

David impressed Ava. He was a gentleman who opened the door for her and held her hand throughout the evening. He was far more polite than the other men who approached her. And he also wanted her to work with him. It made her feel special and gave her a sense of her future.

That night was the first time they made love. One day she came to the hotel to visit David, and Angela and Zowie were there.

"This is my wife and kid," said David.

"Oh, darling, it's so nice to meet you," said Angela.

Ava had never gone out with a married man before and didn't even know David was married. She was taken aback, but it also aroused her competitive spirit. She believed that when she hypnotized a man, another woman didn't stand a chance.

Ava was convinced she was going on the English tour that would follow Japan. She quit her job, gave up her apartment, and returned to her mother's house in Chicago, where she packed her bags and waited by the telephone.

She also kept in touch with MainMan. The MainMan staff took an immediate liking to her, but Defries didn't want David to have backup singers at that time. The news was broken to Ava, but she was philosophical. She had planned to go to Europe, and she would go anyway. She would go to Paris and work as a model there.

David had put Ava out of his mind completely. And Ava also forgot about David. Both thought they would never see each other again and never suspected that five months late they would meet in Paris.

Defries loved to talk about Elvis and Parker, and his staff lived to please him. So they invented a dramatic Elvis-like way to demonstrate that David was the new Elvis and that U.S. Tour Two was a rehearsal for the last date, his first arena performance scheduled for March 10 in Long Beach, California. In the long term it was a rehearsal for David's appearance in every American arena.

As soon as a show ended, David, in costume and full makeup, was rushed from the stage to a waiting limousine. Any musician not ready to leave the theater right after a show was left behind to face mobs of hysterical fans. Sometimes David would dawdle so that he would be caught up in the crowd. He loved the pandemonium that resulted when he was discovered on the street. It was like being in a movie, and David and Defries loved it. And it was all a rehearsal for the rewards that would be reaped in the long term.

At a party after one of David's four sold-out performances at

Philadelphia's Tower Theater, he overheard someone say that his success was merely a result of hair dye.

He looked stricken. Then he overheard someone comparing his power over his audience to that of Hitler.

His frown became a smile, and suddenly he became very happy.

In Memphis, six days later, Defries emerged from an endless meeting with David. Then Tony met with Ronno, offering him the opportunity to be a solo artist for MainMan. The MainMan star-making machine would be set to work for him, and he would be manufactured the way David was being manufactured. Ronno looked into Defries's eyes and saw the reflection of his own fame and glory.

The naive guitarist accepted Defries's offer and shifted his loyalties from the Spiders to Tony. Without a spokesman, the even more naive Spiders were stymied. Defries's manipulation of Ronno had effectively castrated them, and for the moment they had no option but to do as they were told.

It was beyond them to realize that the moment they weren't needed anymore, they would be erased, and that they didn't stand a chance in this particular battle.

In L.A., the last stop of U.S. Tour Two, David was in his Ziggy Stardust mode, and refused to go out during the day. After watching a TV newscast about UFOs, he began to act as if he really were an alien being.

"I can't go out in the sun because I'll melt," he announced.

Like Ken Pitt before him, Defries now wanted David to become a movie star, and he hired CMA agent Stevie Phillips to represent David. Phillips did not represent rock stars, but movie stars like Liza Minnelli and Robert Redford. It was Phillips's job to get David into the movies.

Defries decided to whet Hollywood's appetite by creating the illusion that a number of movie producers were interested in hiring David for the movies. He announced a nonexistent film project, David's appearance in the title role of the science-fiction classic *Stranger in a Strange Land*.

Then a legitimate offer arrived. David was asked to play the title role in a film biography of Edith Piaf. It was an idea that he found especially appealing.

Neither David nor Defries wanted Angela to come to Japan after the Long Beach date, but she came anyway. Then she tried desperately to convince them to play Australia so she could also visit there for the first time.

Her presence made David tense, and the tension did not lighten until he met a beautiful Japanese dancer. He was infatuated. The boy was going to teach him Japanese movement and systems of exercise. David decided that after the tour the boy would go to England to live with Angela and him at Haddon Hall.

The three Tokyo concerts did enormous business, but the concerts in Nagoya, Hiroshima, Kobe, and Osaka were disasters for the promoter. David had been booked into halls seating between 3,000 and 5,000 people, with fewer than a thousand turning up each night.

The empty seats made David unhappy, but Defries didn't mind because he was turning a profit. He had secured a guarantee and expenses from the Japanese promoter, and, for once, none of the losses was his.

Just before they were to leave Japan, Defries delivered an ultimatum to David. David had asked for eight-millimeter film equipment. If he wanted to bring the Japanese boy back to England, he had to forgo his new toys. David chose the film equipment.

The boy was packed and ready to go when he got the news. He seemed heartbroken. So did David. But his despair passed quickly as he turned his attention to learning how to operate his new camera.

At the same time there were a number of meetings with clothing designer Kansai Yamamoto.

Defries told Kansai that he needed promotion in the United States, and Kansai agreed. Defries instantly assumed representation of Kansai and launched a Japanese division, MainMan Tokyo.

The illusion of international expansion thrilled everyone.

In the meantime, MainMan West was in a shambles. After ten weeks at the Beverly Hills Hotel, Iggy Pop had finally selected a house in which he would wait for the demand to build. The MainMan West mansion was a large, comfortable house with an Olympic-sized swimming pool high on Mulholland Drive.

Iggy was upset because David was getting all the attention, so he rebelled. Junkie groupie star-girls gathered by the pool. Drugs, burnt spoons, and broken needles lay around the house. Iggy cut himself in public with a steak knife. The sound equipment was pawned but the musicians said it was stolen.

Leee Black Childers was panicked. Unless Defries had his eye on you, you were forgotten, and MainMan West seemed to have been erased. There was no money to pay the rent, but Leee was afraid to confront Defries. Overwhelmed by Defries's grand plan, he dared not challenge it, and was dipping into his small salary to keep the forgotten operation alive.

Defries had sent Sue Fussey to California to cut hair for Iggy and the Stooges. She reported that some of them had eyes with pupils like pinpricks.

Defries quizzed her relentlessly. He knew they were doing drugs and having sex when they should be practicing, waiting for the moment when they would become stars.

Finally Leee convinced Defries to allow the group to do one show. They were booked into the Ford Auditorium in Detroit, Iggy's hometown.

During a radio show, Iggy took off his clothes and announced over the air that he was masturbating. Defries terminated his contract.

In London, MainMan U.K. hired a new secretary to answer the fan mail. Corinne Schwab was a plain girl who seemed to have only one outfit, a long denim skirt and a gray sweater. Corinne talked endlessly about her ex-boyfriend, a guitarist who looked like Ronno. She didn't have a boyfriend then, though, and filled her time by working.

Corinne Schwab was one of those bright girls who came of age in the late 1960s and had made rock and roll musicians the focus of their sexual desire. Black women and drag queens made David feel "hot"; musicians did the same for Corinne. Going to bed with a musician was the equivalent of dating a "bad boy." It had all the excitement that always accompanies sexual slumming.

She single-handedly held down the MainMan U.K. office. Remarkably efficient, she also held off the army of creditors who called every day. Everyone admired her devotion and single-mindedness, most of all Tony Defries.

Angela could finally be replaced.

CHAPTER 18

Life on Mars

Nothing prepared David for the madness that greeted his return to England. Advance orders for a hundred thousand copies greeted the release of *Aladdin Sane*, the largest advance order in English music-business history since the Beatles.

Aladdin Sane provoked enormous comment for both its music and its packaging. David appeared on the record jacket with a vivid lightning bolt slashed across his face.

The truth was that the disk represented a sophomoric slump. None of the songs have either the grace or continuity that made *Ziggy Stardust* so appealing, and the album seemed more about failed potential than successfully realized effort. It screamed out for more time and craft and a real desire to achieve perfection rather than capitalizing on the moment.

Aladdin Sane needed the conceptual webbing that held *Ziggy Stardust* together. An intriguing story line or a series of sinister mindscapes, both characteristic of David's prior work, could have held the album together. Instead, the disk represented the pressure, tension, and problems accompanying the rise of David Bowie.

The reviews ran from adoration to loathing. Inevitably *Ziggy* had persuaded some reviewers that, by nature, David wrote concept albums. On the album jacket David had listed next to its title the names of the American cities in which each song had been written. *Aladdin Sane* was inevitably declared a concept album, David's visionary tract about contemporary America.

Critics aside, to the public David could do no wrong. He *was* Ziggy Stardust, and in England Ziggy had become a new character, the Lad Insane. After eight weeks in the Number One position, it became the best-selling English album of the year. David's four other RCA album releases also landed in the Top Fifty.

He also had three Top Ten single hits, "Jean Genie," "Drive in Saturday," and "Life on Mars." Having the last laugh, Deram re-released "The Laughing Gnome," the single that had sabotaged his career on Deram, and it, too, went Top Ten.

David was England's biggest record star since the Beatles, and England was Bowie mad. The Aladdin Sane tour was scheduled to begin May 12 at the 18,000-seat Earl's Court. Forty concerts were scheduled over a period of seven weeks, the most extensive tour of England ever undertaken by an English artist. Business was so good and the sellouts happened so quickly Defries added seventeen matinees to the schedule.

But opening night at Earl's Court was a disaster. The sight lines were appalling, and almost no one could see the stage.

These difficulties compounded the misbehavior of a rowdy audience filled with drunk toughs who danced naked in the aisles when they weren't urinating in them. The bodyguards also behaved outrageously, screaming at the audience, "Get your asses back in the seats."

The press was scandalized, and the backlash hit and hit hard. The evening was called "one of the worst examples of a bad deal ever perpetrated on English rock audiences."

Worse still, another major paper declared, "The whole Bowie mystique will soon be replaced and solemnly laid to rest."

Before the show for the first time visitors were allowed backstage to meet David. David, in full Ziggy regalia, greeted Mick Jagger as if he were an old friend. They eyed each other, checking each other out, and then it was time for David to go on.

Meanwhile, at Haddon Hall David and Angela had a houseguest. Angela had brought Scott Richardson from Ann Arbor to live with them.

Scott looked at all the framed photographs of James Dean in the living room. David looked at Scott. It was as if he had a new brother who was American, macho, and a James Dean look-alike.

During the Aladdin Sane tour David called Angela at home at least once a day and sometimes as many as three times from the road. He and Scott got along nicely, and Scott liked joining him on the road. Scott loved the myth of rock stardom; he and David talked for hours about the mythic nature of rock and roll. Angela watched as her lover became David's best friend.

The workload was staggering, especially on those days when David gave two shows. He sometimes fainted in the dressing room. Often fire engines and police squad cars had to be called to get him through the crowds and back to his hotel.

But the hysteria was thrilling. In Scotland, fans surrounded the hotel. He stepped to the window, and they cheered. He loved being idolized.

As the exhausting, frenzied seven-week-long tour hurtled towards its conclusion, Defries talked repeatedly about "U.S.A. Tour Three," David's return to America at the conclusion of English Aladdin Sane tour.

By nature Tony Defries was given only to the grand statement and the extravagant gesture. His plan was to have his "artiste" return immediately to America after David's triumphant English tour came to an end on July 3, 1973. That was the date for the Hammersmith-Odeon concert scheduled to make up for the Earl's Court disaster. In America, Defries announced, David would travel coast-to-coast appearing in every one of the country's giant arenas.

Every amazing thing Defries said he would deliver he had delivered, and everyone assumed David would be returning to America as Defries planned. By following Defries's dictums David had become the biggest English star since the Beatles; if Defries said that America was about to succumb to David's magic, there was no question in anyone's mind that David's dream for America was about to come true.

Defries's grand and extravagant plan for an American tour was opposed by CMA, the agency booking David's tours; RCA and key members of Defries's own staff also objected.

Defries remained undeterred. After a two-month summer layoff, he insisted that David return to America in September with seventy arena bookings. Defries said his deal for each of these dates was non-negotiable, a 90/10 split of the gross with each American promoter receiving 10 percent. To book David these promoters had to deliver a 30 percent guarantee of the gross as soon as contracts were signed.

These were the kinds of financial terms demanded by the greatest of superstars, those whose managers were superstars in their own rights.

The demands shocked CMA. The agency's position was that publicity had made David a star in America, but David hadn't really paid his dues. Despite the size of the media build-up, there had been only two short American Ziggy Stardust tours. All told David had given a mere *thirty-two* Ziggy Stardust concerts in all of America. There was no proof he could fill seventy arenas.

RCA seemed willing to co-venture another American promotional tour, but also did not want David in arenas. David was a media star, but had played only sixteen American cities, doing sellout business in just ten of them. Despite the reams of publicity his American record sales were good but not stupendous. RCA felt David hadn't gained the mass popularity to fill arenas, and didn't want to take a beating by investing in an arena tour. The label wanted David to appear in safer territory, medium-sized concert halls.

Defries knew the truth. During 1973 David had become the most successful recording artist in England, but, to the chagrin of both David and Defries, none of his RCA Records album releases had been certified "gold" in America. (At that time the criterion for "gold" certification was $1 million in sales based on the wholesale price of an album. A "gold" album usually sold around 400,000 copies.) In America, David was a media celebrity perceived as a superstar even though he didn't do superstar-sized business either in record stores or at the box office. To send him on another tour of medium-sized concert halls was to admit the truth: that David was not really the superstar the publicity made him out to be. Defries was convinced that he could create the promotion necessary to fill America's arenas. Despite the fact that David was not selling a stupendous number of records in America, Defries remained convinced that the most important thing was to continue to create and enhance the illusion implanted in the minds of the American public that David was the most successful new superstar of the 1970s. That meant the tour of a superstar, an arena tour—nothing more and nothing less.

RCA remained adamant. Defries was not distressed; nothing ever ruffled his feathers. If there was to be no arena tour the only logical thing to do was to have no tour at all; *there would never be a tour again.*

It was Defries's belief in the law of supply and demand. By removing David from the live performance, demand would build until he would automatically be able to fill arenas.

Defries told David that he had to "retire" because he was exhausted. David had worked almost nonstop for two years, and in that time he had become a star of legendary proportions. Even though he seemed raring to go, suddenly he began to sag from exhaustion.

"Retiring" David seemed to solve two other problems for Defries. His first deal for David had been a publishing deal with Chrysalis. Defries wanted the publishing back. After David "retired" he would do an album of golden oldies. That would be the fuel Defries could use to convince Chrysalis that David was not only never going to perform again but also was never going to write original music. David's publishing would be worthless.

And by retiring David, Defries could permanently eliminate those two annoying sidemen, the Spiders.

Ronno knew of the plan to make a surprise announcement of the retirement from the stage of the Hammersmith-Odeon two weeks before the concert. But he couldn't bring himself to tell his buddies, the other two Spiders. Defries didn't tell them; nor did David. Of all the people who were going to be surprised, even though they worked side-by-side with David, they would be the most surprised of all.

David had a new artistic mission: to make an album of golden oldies. Bryan Ferry was already hard at work recording *These Foolish Things*, his album of golden oldies. David told Scott Richardson that he wanted to get the jump on Ferry, but didn't know what to record. Richardson had an encyclopedic knowledge of the history of rock and roll.

Richardson suggested he record old tunes by the Who and the Byrds. He also suggested "Where Have All the Good Times Gone," and picked two songs by the Pretty Things.

David and Scott were having a wonderful time together.

Scott told David that he wanted to call his own band Fallen Angels.

David loved the name. "You're going to be a space invader, an American guy with no history, no known facts about your life," he said as he began planning Scott's image.

Scott loved David's ideas about Scott as much as David loved Scott's song selections for the golden oldies album.

A promise was made by David that he would record with Scott.

Scott really wanted to make that record. But pressuring David about that promise was exactly the wrong thing to do.

———

Just before David left the stage near the end of the Hammersmith-Odeon concert on July 3 he signaled the band to vamp underneath him.

David stood erectly at the microphone waiting for the audience to quiet down.

"Not only is this the last show of the tour but it is the last show we'll ever do," he announced. "Bye-bye. We love you."

And then he was gone. The moment was recorded on film by Don Pennebaker, and would be released as the film *The Rise and Fall of Ziggy Stardust and the Spiders from Mars* in 1983.

As Trevor and Woody came off stage Sue Fussey rushed up to them.

"What are you going to do now?" she asked nervously.

Woody seemed stunned and confused. "What do you mean what am I going to do. I'm going to America."

Neither Spider seemed capable of realizing he'd been erased.

"You didn't hear David on stage," said Fussey.

"Yes. But he just means this tour."

"I got news for you."

Fussey recalls, "It's my worst memory of my entire experience with David. I just thought it was very cold."

On July 3, 1973, MainMan issued the following release: "David Bowie—U.S. Tour Three Has Been Canceled. The massive arenas of eighty U.S. and Canadian cities will not now, or perhaps ever again, hold within the walls the magic essence of a live Aladdin Sane."

There was no U.S. Tour Three, but that didn't mean that the press could not be used as a vehicle for canceling what did not exist. The international publicity reaped by the announcement was enormous—exactly what Defries had hoped for.

The time had come to allow demand to catch up with supply.

David was in England, Defries in America. It was Defries's tendency to forget about anyone or anything unless it was directly under his nose. David would not return to the United States for ten months. During that time Defries turned his attention to the task of building his empire.

The expansion was financed by money advanced by RCA. David's English success had made them willing participants in Defries's adventure.

It was inevitable that the "family" should now fragment along three separate lines: David's, Defries's, and the sporadic interactions between David and the "empire."

Six days after his retirement in early July, David boarded the train for Paris and the Chateau d'Herouville (Strawberry Studios) where Marc Bolan suggested he record. At the *Pin-Ups* sessions he was in good form and in control of everything. He listened to the session musicians' input, utilizing the suggestions that worked. As always, everyone endeavored to please him.

In Paris a Bowie record came over the air, and Ava Cherry told a model friend, "I was supposed to work with this man."

Her friend replied, "His buddy is staying at my house."

The friend was Geoffrey MacCormack, and he took Ava to the chateau to visit David, who was delighted to see her. Ava had a bad case of the flu that day.

"You're so warm, you know," said David. He grinned and put his arm around her waist. The affair was resumed immediately. Then David cut a demo record with Ava.

He loved the way she sang. "You could be the next Josephine Baker! You could be a star!" he exclaimed.

No one had ever said *that* to Ava before. But when she called the chateau she couldn't get through to David. She learned that he had finished recording, and had gone to Rome.

Rome was to be a holiday and David brought most of the family with him to a rented villa. Angela, Zowie, and Scott were there, along with Ronno, Suzy Fussey, and Geoffrey MacCormack. Suzy became involved with Ronno, whom she eventually married. She became Ronno's personal assistant, leaving a strategic vacancy in David's personal staff.

In a few days David became restless, and everybody returned to London. Fans were camped night and day outside Haddon Hall, and Angela set out to find them a new home. David, Scott, and she sublet Diana Rigg's apartment in Maida Vale.

At Maida Vale the phone rang off the hook. Everybody wanted to get to David, but he refused to come out of his room.

An invitation arrived from Mick Jagger to see the Rolling Stones in concert. Scott and David rented a Bentley and driver and went to Newcastle to see the show. Mick had rented them a hotel room.

Wine and flowers were waiting, along with a note that said, "Love, Mick."

David watched the show from the wings. Mick stared at him from the stage. The audience had spotted David's orange hair and was gaping into the wings. No one was paying attention to Jagger. David had to be pulled back from view in order for the audience to focus its attention on Jagger.

"David loved it," says Richardson.

Back at the hotel, David and Scott climbed under the covers with their clothes on. David was very upset. The Stones concert seemed to indicate to him that Jagger, like Ziggy Stardust, was inevitably destined to fall; his fall could be next.

At the concert Scott had snorted some heroin. But he did his best to keep up. David and he spoke about how Jagger seemed lost. They didn't like his costume, and he seemed to be doing a poor impersonation of Wilson Pickett. It was as if the day of the Rolling Stones had really passed.

There was a faint knock on the door, and Jagger stepped into the room. Scott sensed that Mick had eavesdropped on the entire conversation.

Mick and his wife, Bianca, took David and Scott to a gambling casino, and they stayed up until dawn as Mick and David competed to see who could lose the most money.

At the end of his tour Mick began to call on what seemed a daily basis. He always sounded nervous, as if he were preoccupied with the fate of the Rolling Stones.

He invited David to hang out with him at the trendy late-night disco, Tramps. David, Angela, Scott, Mick, and Bianca went to a Diana Ross concert at the Royal Albert Hall, and the boys went by themselves to the Norton-Ali fight.

At first David was nervous about this socializing. On the one hand, Mick's legendary status intimidated him; on the other, he was delighted by Mick's fascination with him. They were brothers, but competitive brothers, always eyeing each other to see what the other was wearing, what new music he was listening to.

Angela loathed the new friendship. She thought it was the kiss of death to have anything to do with the Jaggers. "So old wave," she says. "Two rock-and-roll stars, one of them a great deal older than the other, hanging out together."

It was the moment of bisexual chic, a moment that David and Angela had helped inspire, and everyone in English society was either bisexual or pretending to be. When Angela was photographed dancing with Bianca a rumor swept through the group that they were lovers. The rumor re-emerged three years later when members of Robert Stigwood's staff said they had been seen together in Cannes at a party on Stigwood's yacht after the premiere of Stigwood's film version of *Tommy*.

Angela says she hardly knows Bianca, and vehemently denies the rumor, which she finds offensive.

During this moment the boys all enjoyed acting gay. After David got off the phone with Mick, Scott and he joked about David's new best friend. "You can top him in thirty seconds," said Scott.

Their nickname for Mick was "Rubber Lips."

At the end of their nights in Tramps, groups of people were invited back to Maida Vale. The next day at around two o'clock Scott would wake up and find himself at the bottom of a pile of bodies. The entire rest of the day was spent trying on clothes to wear to Tramps that night.

During this time David also acquired two new girl friends, each befitting a star: Marianne Faithfull, who had been Jagger's old girl friend, and model Amanda Lear, whom many people believed might have had a sex change. Lear had appeared on Roxy Music's first album cover; supposedly she had had an affair with Bryan Ferry. (In reality Ferry and Lear were just close friends. Ferry was too much of a gentleman to find out whether Amanda had or had not had the sex change.)

Angela was enraged. She ignored David's attraction to black women and drag queens. But a beautiful woman like Amanda who had such an outrageous reputation was real competition.

"The Dating Game" was the name given to David and Angela's ability to materialize any famous woman Scott wanted to go out with. Fixing up Scott enabled them to play loving parents to him.

But everyone was playing the Dating Game. According to Richardson, "It was Ryan O'Neal and Bianca Jagger, Mick and Angie, David and Amanda Lear, me and Marianne Faithfull, and Marianne and David. Marianne wouldn't talk to Mick." The only time David didn't want to play was when Lou Reed came to London. David seemed genuinely frightened of him. Through it all Scott believed that David still loved Angela "because he needed her."

It seemed like an awful lot of fun and wildness.

But at home David was upset. Jagger was rich, and David was penniless. Mick acted like a stockbroker, and David was financially in the dark. Everywhere David and Angela turned there were unpaid bills and overdrawn bank accounts.

The truth overwhelmed David, and he pushed it from his mind. He was the biggest English rock star since the Beatles, but Defries's illusion of monstrous success suddenly seemed like a scam.

Tony had always taken care of him before; he had to believe that Tony would take care of him again. There was no place left to turn. But Tony was in the States and didn't seem the least bit interested in turning up.

In November, four months after David's retirement, David and Angela moved to a house that came to be known as the House on Oakley Street. The move brought them closer to the Jaggers, who lived around the corner on Cheyne Walk.

Scott moved out. During his stay with David and Angela, he had urged David to make rhythm-and-blues music, music with authenticity. At this time David summoned from Paris his own rhythm-and-blues artist, Ava Cherry.

Ava was checked into the Portobello Hotel, but Angela thought she would be more comfortable living with them.

At first David, Angela, Ava, and "a real jive black chick from Trinidad" shared the same bed. According to Ava, David and she would sometimes go to the Sombrero where David would pick up an Oriental boy and take him home.

Ava also became embroiled in David's friendship with Mick Jagger. She says it was *quite* extraordinary. "Boys will be boys will be boys." It seems as if such cavorting was merely part of the times.

One morning Angela served David and Mick breakfast. She says, "Taking orange juice and coffee up to people who were sleeping together doesn't necessarily mean they've been indulging in sexual activities. Unless you see someone on the job, it's really all surmise, isn't it?"

Meanwhile London society gossiped that the subject of the Rolling Stones' "Angie" was not Angela at all, but was actually David.

While all of this was going on, in New York, a MainMan release announced that Tony Zanetta had been appointed president of MainMan, ex-messenger Leee Black Childers executive vice president, Cherry Vanilla (Kathy Dorritie) vice president in charge of press and public relations, and Tony Ingrassia creative consultant. Ingrassia had directed *Andy Warhol's Pork*. The "international entertainment conglomerate" officially had its chief offices.

MainMan had moved to a lavish fourteen-room suite of offices located on Park Avenue and East Fifty-fourth Street. This was where most of MainMan's greatly expanded staff of twenty-six (excluding maids and chauffeurs) worked. These offices were the seat of Tony Defries's "empire." Just as England had once been the center of an expanding empire, so Defries saw himself as the center of his own ever-expanding empire. His territories included the twenty-room MainMan estate in Greenwich, Connecticut; a MainMan penthouse on the Upper East Side; the original MainMan duplex on East Fifty-eighth Street; a MainMan apartment at the Sherry Netherlands Hotel; a MainMan loft on the lower West Side; and four MainMan apartments occupied by four of MainMan's clients, whom Defries now called "artistes."

Defries began traveling by MainMan limousine, a brown customized Cadillac with brown window shades and a customized interior of cream-colored leather that had been perforated so that he would not perspire during the summer. The limousine was on call twenty-four hours a day, and Defries's driver, an enormous black man named Charles, was kept stationed in front of the office.

Defries continued to feel the need to create families around himself, families he could control by making them financially dependent on him. He created a giant-sized family of employees and "artistes," paying their rent, rewarding them with gifts, trips, and bonuses, giving them corporate titles and responsibilities no other company would have given them.

At the same time, Defries did not want his children to become too competent; then they would have no need of him. So he encouraged them to play and act out.

In this bizarre reality, all the members of "the MainMan family" considered Tony Defries—not David Bowie—to be the real star. He had *manufactured* David Bowie, who existed to generate the funds necessary to enable the MainMan machine to thrive.

To be a star, one had to act like one, and to be a star-making machine a company had to act accordingly. Believing that appearance was everything, Defries encouraged everyone to spend recklessly to create the illusion that MainMan was a company of great wealth. His chief executives had American Express cards, Bloomingdale's and Harrod's of London charge plates, and expense accounts at the Four Seasons and Max's Kansas City. Anyone could be wined and dined at those restaurants; it was all part of the illusion. MainMan also had an in-house travel agency. The company ran up staggering flower and limousine bills.

Throughout the music industry a question was beginning to be asked: Without David's talent and ability to generate money, would any of MainMan's enormous self-promotion have been possible?

For the most part MainMan used Defries's Barnum-like approach on a number of doomed projects. Ronno's solo LP, *Slaughter on Tenth Avenue*, was given a massive advertising campaign, and Ronno's face was plastered across a huge Times Square billboard. This was MainMan's "rehearsal" for David's re-emergence from "retirement." Work also began on *Fame*, a play written by Ingrassia.

From America Defries watched David and Angela. Their behavior annoyed him. Defries was busy working at organizing the cash flow of his company. He wanted budgets prepared for everything, and demanded to know everyone's cash demands in advance. He didn't really mind how David and Angela spent their money, but he didn't want any surprises.

But they were impulse buyers, and frequently there *were* surprises. David and Angela couldn't play by Defries's rules. When it came to spending they were uncontrollable. Defries was irked by children who misbehaved.

Defries believed that all children eventually rebel against their parents. He seemed prepared nonchalantly to dismiss David for such rebellious acts.

Even though Defries was living on the MainMan estate, he refused to allow David and Angela to buy a lavish country retreat of their own. It was too expensive, he said. By denying them, he was proving to himself that he could control them.

In reality he was having too much fun in New York to put up with the two English annoyances. With RCA under his thumb he was finally able to support and control a huge family. It was a gravy train, and all of New York seemed to be turning to him to have their rent paid and their teeth capped. And everyone assumed that these were David's wishes. The incredible extravagance would also become part of David's myth.

Craig Copetas, who worked for the English bureau of *Rolling Stone*, first became a writer because of William S. Burroughs. Burroughs and he thought it would be an interesting idea if Burroughs interviewed David.

Copetas called MainMan U.K. and spoke to Corinne Schwab. She seemed especially overprotective, had never heard of Burroughs, and dismissed the idea.

Corinne was working day and night at that time to please David and Angela, and they were delighted with her Herculean efforts. She fended off bill collectors and always did their bidding. She was perfect.

Yet when David finally found out about Burroughs, he was eager to meet the legendary grandfather of the beats.

An elaborate lunch centering around an elegant fish dish was prepared, and David addressed the writer as Mr. Burroughs. When lunch was served, Burroughs refused to touch a morsel because he never ate lunch. David was afraid he had embarrassed his guest by not knowing he didn't take lunch.

He and Burroughs talked for hours. David seemed to Burroughs to be one of the "wild boys" who were immortalized in the writer's work. Luckily for David, a visit to London from a new MainMan employee, Macs McCaree, had turned into a long discussion about contemporary literature, and McCaree had given David an excerpt to read from Burroughs's *Naked Lunch*.

It was enough to make him sound really knowledgeable.

David, Burroughs, and Copetas so enjoyed the afternoon that they met several more times. Corinne had wrapped a blanket of protection around David, but Copetas believed he had penetrated it.

Then Lindsay Kemp arrived in London to present *Flowers*, a mime version of Jean Genet's *Our Lady of the Flowers*. But Genet's English agent interfered, saying that Kemp had violated Genet's copyright. David was upset.

"Where's Genet?" he asked Copetas.

"He's an elusive character," Copetas replied. "No one can ever find him. He lives in a number of seedy homosexual hotels in the Algerian section of Paris."

Copetas and Corinne were delegated by David to go to Paris to find Genet and intercede on Kemp's behalf. In Paris, they visited Burroughs's friend Byron Gysin, who they hoped would tell them where to look.

Craig and Corinne scoured Paris looking for Genet. She was relentlessly determined to please David and even got into the office of Genet's French publisher to rifle through his Rolodex.

Genet was tracked to a hotel but became paranoid and bolted. Someone named David Bowie was looking for him; he didn't know who Bowie was or why Bowie's people wanted to get to him.

Copetas wound up having a meeting with Jean-Paul Sartre to explain David's problem. Sartre was of no help. He was in the midst of a bitter feud with Genet. Then the writers at *Liberation*, the French leftist newspaper, erupted. Genet as well as Sartre infuriated them, as did anyone who came close to them.

In London Genet's English agent finally relented. Seeking out Genet had had the same effect as finding him.

In September Defries had dispatched Tony Ingrassia, MainMan's creative consultant, to England to co-write and direct with David a musical production of George Orwell's *1984*, one of David's favorite books.

David loathed doing anything on assignment. The portly Ingrassia was a dictator, and immediately took charge. They worked together for a few days, then David refused to get out of bed. Moreover, Orwell's widow, appalled at the idea, refused to give MainMan the rights.

Nonetheless, David's discussions with Ingrassia had stimulated his imagination. They had conceived of a futuristic city as an urban jungle. Iggy Pop had a number, "I Wanna Be Your Dog," and David wondered about playing a dog in this urban jungle of the future. The ideas for his next album, *Diamond Dogs*, were beginning to come together.

Defries next wanted David to invade the world of films and television. At CMA, Michael Lippman convinced Burt Sugarman to give him an entire edition of the late-night TV rock concert show, "The Midnight Special." David decided to make the concert his version of the Sonny and Cher Show. Amanda Lear would be the

Marlene Dietrich of the future, and Marianne Faithfull, dressed as a nun in a backless dress, would play Cher to his Sonny. Amanda introduced David to the designs and drawings of Erte, which he loved, and he decided to wear Erte-inspired costumes and have dancers spell out the credits à la Erte.

Called "The 1980 Floor Show," it was the most elaborate, the most decadent edition of Ziggy yet seen.

The 1980 Floor Show was designed ostensibly to promote *Pin-Ups*, which was released on the day the television show was filmed. During its recording the "retired" David and his fellow musicians had been in a lighthearted mood, and their joviality found its way onto the disk. The run-throughs of songs by the Pretty Things, Them (a hilarious deadpan reading of "Here Comes the Night"), Easybeats, Yardbirds, Kinks, and the Who were merely functional, but the enthusiasm with which the projects were approached was infectious. It was an elaborate joke, the first time David seemed to be smiling on record.

The record itself was a throwaway, but it helped establish David's postmodernist bent. All pop culture could be ransacked and reinterpreted with a sense of irony and detachment. The cover portrait of him posing with Twiggy was from a photo session for *Vogue* that the magazine did not use. One of the great pop icons of the then recent 1960s, Twiggy, merely by appearing beside David, illustrated that legends of the moment inevitably would become grist for the ironic commentary of those who followed after them.

The only way David himself could avoid this fate was to find the way to establish himself for the long term.

After her appearance on The 1980 Floor Show, David sent Ava to New York. She was moved into one of the MainMan apartments and allowed to charge her clothing bills to the company; her singing and tap dancing lessons also became a MainMan expense. The company committed itself to picking up the costs of a solo LP. In addition, Ava received a weekly MainMan allowance of one hundred seventy-five dollars. MainMan sent her to premieres in limousines that matched the colors of the gowns she charged to them. She was overwhelmed by her good fortune and traveled in a cloud of amazement.

After the TV taping David said he had his own idea for a film. It involved three gods played by three New York underground performers who worked in drag, Jackie Curtis, Wayne County, and

Holly Woodlawn. The gods lived on human babies, and communicated their wishes to the world through Ziggy Stardust, whom David would play.

At the end of October Defries met with RCA. The record company was desperate. David's sales were making the English division thrive. Twenty-five percent of the American budget was diverted from English funds. The American label needed David to sell records. He accounted for 4 percent of the earnings of RCA. UK.

Defries threw the English success up to the American executives, who had to appease him. They admitted they did not know how to sell *Pin-Ups* without live appearances by David. Defries asked for an advertising commitment to support "The Midnight Special." He believed the record could be sold through a saturation campaign of television commercials.

Tony Zanetta had read an article about a prospective Alice Cooper appearance at the Palace Theatre on Broadway. The evening would be called *Alice at the Palace*. The idea was born to bring David to Broadway in an evening called *Bowie on Broadway*.

David had to be "unretired," and would be unretired as a theater and not a rock artist. To cover their tracks, it was decided to label David's eventual return a "theatour" instead of rock tour.

Obsessed with the idea of a national television campaign, Defries announced a $1-million advertising blitz and began a round of meetings with major advertising agency heads. He wanted David sold as a product and believed Madison Avenue could do it. He was also convinced that television was the sales tool to sell anything and wanted to load the airwaves with commercials for David. He spent around $400,000, billed it to RCA, and convinced them to pay for the commercials manufactured by the radio and television department of his empire.

They didn't dare refuse him.

As 1974 began David went into the studio to record *Diamond Dogs*, and as spring approached it was clear that Defries could finally have his arena tour, and dates began to be booked.

In order to sell records, U.S. Tour Four, the tour that followed the tour that never happened, the tour that would take David out of retirement, had to be the most lavish of all.

PART IV

THE FALL OF
ZIGGY STARDUST

CHAPTER 19

Diamond Dogs

The first question that confronted Defries and his staff was how to "unretire" Bowie plausibly. Defries's management practices derived from the patterns established by Colonel Tom Parker, Elvis Presley's manager, whom Defries referred to as "Parker." Colonel Parker's roots had been in The Royal American Shows, a giant-sized touring carnival. When Colonel Parker went to work for The Royal American Shows, the carnival had been run by the "King of the Carneys," Carl Sedlmeyer, who lived by a show business maxim that he had impressed upon the young Tom Parker. *"I want everything bigger 'n everybody!"* Sedlmeyer had exclaimed repeatedly. It was Tony Defries's plan to ensure *Bowie's* superstardom by being "bigger 'n everybody!"

In the tradition of such great stars as *Elvis, Piaf*, and *Judy*, Defries decreed that the little one will be known by one name and one name alone—*Bowie:* That would be his name forever.

It was then that Defries commissioned the most spectacular rock concert that had ever been given until the Jacksons' Victory Tour during the summer and fall of 1984. Its physical production weighed six tons and was made of 20,000 moveable parts. An arena tour was booked that would begin on June 14, 1974, in Montreal, and play twenty-three cities in Canada and the United States. The first half of the tour was scheduled to end on July 19 in New York City, and then resume in Los Angeles on September 2 after a five-week layoff. David's new LP, *Diamond Dogs*, would be released on June 1 two weeks before the tour began. Preceding the LP by three weeks was a single, "Rebel Rebel." The plan was to have the album and single climbing the pop charts just as the tour was launched so that the tour would promote the two new releases. This would give David, it was hoped, the hit single that had so far eluded him in America.

On *Diamond Dogs*, David felt compelled to go further than he had on *Ziggy Stardust* and *Aladdin Sane*. This disk was pervaded by literary pretensions. "Future Legend," the deadly serious spoken piece that opens the album, is derivative of William Burroughs in both language and meter; his attempt to musicalize *1984* also colors the record.

Two songs indicate, though, that David was as creatively alert as ever. Fleshed out by Tony Visconti's strings arrangement, "1984" clearly indicates the white soul direction toward which David was heading. There was also "Rebel Rebel," a masterful piece of Rolling Stones–derived hard rock with only one easy-to-learn guitar riff repeated four times. By taking "Jean Genie," speeding up its music, and supplying a punchier lyric, David had created *the* rock anthem for the 1970s glitter-rock generation.

Mick Jagger had told David that the Rolling Stones were planning to have their next album jacket painted by the Dutch artist Guy Peellaert. David didn't know Peellaert's work and attended a show by the artist in Paris. Peellaert was a photorealist whose work had grotesque surrealist overtones. A book of his paintings, *Rock Dreams*, had just been published, and the jacket painting portrayed John Lennon, Bob Dylan, Elvis Presley, Jagger, and David, with David presented as an icy, remote figure who set himself apart from the rest of the group.

That intrigued David. Peellaert seemed to understand his need to repress feelings. He did an end run and commissioned Peellaert to paint the *Diamond Dogs* jacket cover, scooping Jagger in the process.

The theme of decadence was brilliantly captured by Peellaert. David appeared as a human dog against a sideshow backdrop of two fat, grinning female human dogs. The backdrop was captioned "The Strangest Living Curiosities." It was the kind of ironic representation of himself that David adored. It also seemed to symbolize the decadence that permeated the Ziggy Stardust and Aladdin Sane performances, the outrageous overelaboration of David's "Midnight Special" appearance, the year of retirement and the endless sexual shenanigans that accompanied it.

The painting featured a huge, swollen red dog's penis, which threw RCA into an uproar. But this piece of sensationalistic packaging automatically titillated the public and increased their fascination with David.

At the same time, it was self-defeating. America was listening to Barbra Streisand sing "The Way We Were," and conservative AM stations were not about to play records by one of the world's "strangest living curiosities."

Michael Bennett and *Equus* director John Dexter were sent to meet with David. Finally Broadway lighting designer Jules Fisher was hired to create the theatrical extravaganza Defries had demanded. David's input was expressionism. He wanted his show to reflect the futuristic city in his favorite movie at the time, Fritz Lang's *Metropolis*.

Left unsupervised by Defries and his staff, the "experts" ran riot, creating a $400,000 spectacle that would take thirty men a full day to assemble.

The key MainMan staff members, all refugees from *Andy Warhol's Pork*, were devoted Warhol disciples and believed wholeheartedly, as did Warhol, that publicity was its own art form. Determined to demonstrate to their "daddy" just how artistic *they* were, they set about manufacturing David's return to America with a vengeance. The only press Defries wanted was David's picture on the cover of *Time* or *Newsweek*. As for the rest of it, he was content to watch as his "children" played. David was not consulted about this process; yet, he would not only reap the rewards of all of the publicity, but also the credit for being a master media manipulator. As always his myth absorbed the efforts of others; at the same time as he watched from the distance he continued to learn for himself the skills needed to use the media to package any image he wished to project.

To make sure no embarrassing questions were asked about the "unretirement" and in accord with Defries's belief in brand names, the staff decided that since David's new album was called *Diamond Dogs*, the year of retirement that preceded it would always be referred to as "The Year of the Diamond Dogs" whenever it was mentioned to the press. The tour would bear the same name.

The year of "The Year of the Diamond Dogs" would be sold as a year during which David had worked at a feverish pace despite the fact that he had "retired." It was also decided to portray the year as one David had devoted to the act of changing. Rock stars usually had an image that stayed with them throughout their careers, but

David would be portrayed as a human chameleon. The fact that David had abandoned his Ziggy Stardust look and was beginning to evolve the look of a chic decadent European gigolo would be sold as a prime aspect of his creativity, part of his art, the art of changing.

The publicity and promotional barrage began on April 1, ten weeks in advance of the tour. A MainMan newsletter announcing the event was sent to the MainMan mailing list of 5,000, a list about five times the size of any other small management company. No press person, opinion maker, or fan had been left off this giant-sized roster. On April 12, the list of 5,000 received a newsletter announcing the dates of the first half of the tour. Instead of sending a traditional press photo, a black and white reproduction of the shocking Paellart record jacket was included. The photograph was reproduced in music columns across the country, a clever piece of free advertising.

It was clear that among the most effective ways of promoting David was to supply the print media with an endless series of photographs. An expensive promotional looseleaf book of stills was prepared including photographs of David from the "retirement" concert, the party at the Cafe Royale after the show, and three different recording sessions. Each showed him with a different look, visual evidence that his year away had been a year of work and continual change. This book was also serviced to the national press.

After David arrived in New York, new pictures were made, and they were sent to everyone. A petition was circulated on the Brooklyn College campus with one thousand students signing their names to a statement that read: "I would like to hear more of David Bowie's music on your station." The petition was serviced to key radio stations across the country.

In the seven weeks between April 1 and May 22, the MainMan list was barraged with five elaborate mailings and seven different photographs, all different, all printable. Any other rock star would have received just one mailing, but MainMan provided the largest mailing list in rock history with the most unrelenting series of mailings in the history of pop music promotion. Anyone who counted was browbeaten into perceiving David's return as the second coming. The MainMan years would end, but the message had been engraved indelibly on the collective minds of the media: David would always be associated with creativity, hard work, and change.

The payoff was quick. Sacks of clippings poured into MainMan's offices. Stories and pictures had been printed everywhere.

The next step was to get David's face onto the covers of the nation's magazines. *Circus, Creem, Hit Parade,* and *Rock Scene* quickly agreed to print covers with *Creem* featuring a David Bowie Look-Alike Contest. *Spec* was selected for an Aladdin Sane Look-Alike contest.

To promote the *Diamond Dogs* LP, an album mailing was done along with a MainMan announcement characterizing the disk as "about the breakdown of an overmechanized society, a society that's literally gone to the dogs. It's filled with images of urban decadence and collapse." Many rock critics used MainMan's comments as the basis for their own criticism.

An extensive advertising schedule was also created with full page color advertisements featuring the *Diamond Dogs* jacket in *After Dark; Billboard; Cash Box; Circus; Creem; Record World; Interview; Rolling Stone; Phonograph Record Magazine; the Hollywood Reporter; National Lampoon; Rock Scene;* and the *Village Voice.* Billboards featuring the album cover art were planned for Times Square and Sunset Boulevard, and RCA supplied displays and posters for the nation's record stores. A schedule of local advertising was initiated with the record store chains. MainMan also manufactured a series of Diamond Dogs metal dog tags as souvenirs of the tour.

Then David made both a radio and a television commercial, and two saturation radio and television campaigns were planned, one to precede the release of *Diamond Dogs,* the other keyed city to city before each concert. The radio spots would run continually before each concert, and the television commercials would be aired in local markets during "The Midnight Special"; "In Concert"; "Don Kirschner's Rock and Roll Concert"; "The Dick Clark Show"; "The Brady Bunch"; "Mod Squad"; "Mission Impossible"; "Star Trek"; "The Partridge Family"; and "Room 222", all teenage favorites.

The blitz produced so much publicity RCA felt compelled to spend even more money to promote David, and Defries found it easier to command high fees for David's appearances.

Still, no one really knew whether David would get the necessary air play to have a Top Ten single, and whether or not the elaborate Year of the Diamond Dogs would sell out across America. It was clear David would do no interviews, and it was decided to repeat the junket staged in Aylesbury before Ziggy Stardust came to America. This time the press would be flown to Toronto to see a preview. It would be up to them to describe David's new decadent-chic image, and explain the nature of his rock-theater evening. The national coverage they would provide would tell America what to think when they saw the new-and-improved David. In that way MainMan hoped to transcend any potential backlash from those fans who missed Ziggy Stardust or wanted to see the characterization again as well as build excitement for the star and the show that was "bigger 'n everybody."

When David arrived in New York in April, his family consisted of personal assistant Corinne Schwab, who was to travel by his side, and Stuie George and limousine driver Jim James, who were there to protect him. Geoffrey MacCormack was again to play the role of brother/best friend, and Angela would do her usual on tour–off tour routine along with Zowie and his nanny Marian. Ava was on-call as chief mistress.

Defries had removed himself.

David dropped in at the new MainMan offices. This was against the rules. The army of clerical workers became nervous when they saw him; they didn't know how to act around a superstar. That interfered with orderly work. Defries wanted David to make appointments.

It was obvious to David that MainMan was no longer his family, but Defries's, and a feeling of abandonment surged through him.

The new MainMan staffers began to hang out with David, contrary to Defries's rules. The staff found David charming and fascinating, and began to prowl the city with him as he searched for soul musicians in the Latin disco Corso and Harlem's Apollo Theatre.

Defries was not pleased by their affection for his errant son.

At a meeting with the MainMan publicity staff, David found himself continually referred to as *Bowie* by his old friends. It was clear that in the eyes of the original members of Defries's staff, David the man did not exist. To his face he was treated as a commodity, the object MainMan was in business to sell.

He felt deeply hurt.

The staff reported back to Defries that David had started to snort cocaine supplied by an art dealer, Norman Fisher. Those close to him seemed to think he was experimenting with drugs because he wanted to be an authentic rock and roller. MainMan was paying for the cocaine, and that was not the way Defries wanted to spend his money.

"I won't talk to a drug," remarked Defries. David was an outcast, no longer a member of the happy MainMan family.

Two months of rehearsals were scheduled. David worked very hard before the late June opening. The show was a difficult one, two acts of production numbers that had to be staged precisely and then rehearsed until each on-stage move was mastered. A stage set was designed representing Hunger City, a decaying city of the future. The evening would feature three giant-sized props, a motorized Bridge which could be raised and lowered by remote control, a four-ton, thirty-five-foot-long "Catapult," to be lowered over the heads of the audience; and "the Diamond." Once this contraption unfurled its leaves a huge mechanical hand would extend from it. As its palm opened David would be revealed perched triumphantly on the palm.

These three numbers were gone over and over, but the props themselves would not be ready until six days before opening night. No one could have known beforehand that none of them would work properly, and the "bigger 'n' everybody" evening was going to be launched amidst total confusion.

Still he found time to go out. At Club 82 he spotted a beautiful Puerto Rican drag queen coming out of the ladies bathroom.

He began an affair with the drag queen and wanted Ava to participate in threesomes.

In some ways it was business as usual.

On Sunday towards the end of the second of the three days of full rehearsal at the Capitol Theatre in Port Chester, New York, Tony Defries, Tony Zanetta, and Jaime DeCarlo Lotts Andrews arrived at the theater. They expected to see a perfect run-through of the Year of the Diamond Dogs which was scheduled to open four days later in Montreal.

Defries strolled into the theater, and looked around grandly as if he owned the building—if not the world. He took a puff on his Cuban cigar as his eyes roamed over the pandemonium. His first response was a look of amusement. His next response was curiosity. Finally, after eight weeks he was seeing for himself where all of the money—*his* money was being spent. He glanced at the gigantic stage set; Hunger City was not only immense but also haunting and beautiful.

People began to recognize him and came over to bombard him with explanations of why the show was in such a shambles. David may have been the star but Defries signed the checks.

Defries walked slowly to the apron of the stage, and looked up at David. Sweat poured down David's face. He looked impatiently at Defries, but his impatience had no effect. Defries stared at David, one of those long awkward stares he used to make people uncomfortable. After a few forced words of small talk, Corinne, who had been watching from the audience, suddenly jumped up and came to David's rescue.

"Oh, Tony. We've saved you a seat in the middle of the house. You can have a view of the entire spectacle."

She led him to the seat.

The rehearsal turned out to be a shambles. The Bridge refused to descend, leaving David stranded on top of it, and the minute David began singing "Space Oddity" the Catapult was supposed to descend but got stuck halfway down. The sound was also terrible, and the show sounded like sludge.

Defries smelled disaster. He believed that David's concept had been taken far too literally, and that the show was out of control. He didn't know why David needed dancers, singers, dogs, and diamonds. After all, David was really a singer/songwriter, and all he really needed was a stool, his guitar, and a spotlight. Obviously, there had been no real growth since David became famous. Instead, there were insecurities, cocaine, and theatrics to make him look good. But then you couldn't tell him what to do; you couldn't tell anyone what to do. The only thing to do was let them get on with it.

Defries had not told his staff what to do, and the result was a $400,000 white elephant that looked as if it was never going to leave town. David was working at fever pitch but Defries's tone indicated that David had failed him.

No matter how hard David worked he knew he was perceived as a failure. That was what really hurt.

On Wednesday, June 12, three trailor-trucks, each normally forty feet in length, now extended five additional feet and still bulging to capacity, left the Capitol Theatre and headed for the Montreal opening night.

"The technical problems were never resolved before we left Port Chester," recalls Diamond Dogs stage manager Nick Russiyan. "David was in great danger physically, and could have gotten electrocuted or killed."

It had always been Defries's and MainMan's mission to protect David at all costs—that is, until the Year of the Diamond Dogs.

Thursday was David's moving day and because he still refused to fly he was to be driven from New York City to Montreal. It would be a nine-hour ride. The trip to Montreal had to be especially efficient, and plans had begun the night before when Corinne had told David that they would leave as soon as he had arisen. He always had to be prepared for the events of the following day; otherwise, if taken by surprise, he might balk. Next she had to anticipate his wake-up time so that she could get him moving.

David loved rituals and the solemn ritual of his waking up never changed. First Corinne prepared his orange juice and coffee, then lit a Gitanes cigarette. After she had given him his cigarette, juice, and coffee, she would hand him any music business publications and newspapers in which he had been mentioned; David liked to start his day by reading every word written about him.

Two hours later, David was ready to go. He tended to wear the same shirt and trousers for weeks in a row, eventually discarding them for another outfit. It usually took an hour to style his hair for a performance; without that styling his hair lay limply on his head and was tucked under a large black Panama hat. Strands of bleached blond hair would peek out from under the front of the hat; strands of bleached magenta hair peeked out from under the back. Off stage with no makeup on and his hair undone David looked scruffy and tired, a pale version of the glamorous public David Bowie.

Bodyguard Stuie George had checked the lobby. There was no danger. He led the way and David's driver Jim James picked up the rear while Corinne stood by David's side. They headed from the MainMan suite to the elevator, their aim to sail to the elevator, down to the lobby, and through the lobby to the waiting car as quickly as possible, without being stopped by anyone—anyone who might catch David without his behavioral or cosmetic mask on. As they waited for the elevator Stuie and Jim hovered protectively near their charge. Surrounded by the family David was led through the lobby without a hitch. Finally, he was inside the car, and safe.

David liked these long limousine rides, which gave him a chance to see the countryside. He also sensed the world wanted to get to him; in the car no one could get to him and he could drop his mask and relax; he liked that best of all. He didn't think about the wear and tear he would put himself through by driving to twenty-six different cities during a thirty-day period, especially since he was doing so much of Norman Fisher's cocaine and sleeping so little. Great stars like Marilyn, Piaf, Elvis, and Judy inevitably self-destructed; that was the story of Ziggy Stardust, and the kind of drama that turned a star into a mythic hero.

Throughout the long ride, there was a happy grin on Corinne's face. In the car, she, too, was at peace. No one could get to her in order to get to David. In the car, she had him almost all to herself, and that felt really wonderful.

In Montreal, it took thirty-six hours to get Hunger City on its feet. During the show the Bridge crashed to the ground with David on it, and the sound system was so overloaded the wires literally began to melt. The sound distortion was enormous.

But the audience loved it and cheered for twenty minutes at its conclusion. It was clear that with the kinks worked out, the evening would be a brilliant one.

As soon as it was over David quietly stated that the sound company had to be replaced. He was told that a Porsche break was going to be installed in the Bridge so that a brakes man could control its descent.

He was afraid of heights, but he gasped in mock terror, "A Porsche break? Isn't that how James Dean died?"

Then he went on stage, and fixed the stage crew with his devastating smile. "Thank you. Thank you for your help," he said gently, before disappearing into the wings.

That would be the most personal contact any of them would have with him for the duration of the tour, but the simplicity and decency of his gesture was enough to convince them that he was a prince. Though exhausted they would continue to work endlessly. Theirs was a mission: to do anything and everything to make their prince shine.

The press junket occurred two nights later, on June 16, at the O'Keefe Auditorium in Toronto with rock critics told they were attending a theatrical event and theater critics told they were attending a major rock event. The plan was to intimidate both critical factions. Included also were key English reporters. Their raves would encourage English promoters to pay Defries's huge fees.

The Toronto performance was perfect, and it was clear that David had synthesized rock and theater with stunning results. No one could have guessed that two nights before it had been a debacle. For the most part, the press wrote raves, though one or two complained again about the coldness of the evening, described as a visual tribute to decadence. It was another lament about the death of the 1960s, and the triumph of stylistics over so-called authenticity.

MainMan was thrilled. Against all odds it seemed to them that Defries had done it again; everything he wanted he got, and no matter what mistakes they made, they were always going to win.

Everyone went back to New York in a cloud of euphoria, while David set out to do twenty grueling one-night stands followed by a week at the Tower Theatre in Philadelphia, and then two nights on July 19 and 20 at Madison Square Garden. To play the Garden was a symbol to both David and Defries that their shared dream had come true. By selling out the Garden, David would prove that he had legitimately conquered America.

As the tour had progressed, the musicians caught wind that a live recording of the show was in the planning stage. But no one gave them any information about it. Whether or not such a record would be made became a constant topic of conversation among them. Playing on live recording meant extra bucks—probably a couple of thousand dollars.

Then bass player Herbie Flowers believed he had the answer. "They're going to do it on July 14 and 15, just before Madison Square Garden, at the Tower Theatre in Philadelphia," he announced one night. "How much do you think we're going to get?" They decided they should be paid $5000 apiece.

Defries believed they should be paid nothing. He wouldn't think of going to Philadelphia to negotiate with the musicians. He now lived in the clouds, and had no desire to ever operate at sea level again. Instead vice-president of production Jaime DeCarlo Lotts Andrews was dispatched. His instructions: Pay the musicians union scale (about $150 a man) and not a cent more.

After hearing the offer the musicians hemmed and hawed. Then the best sound equipment began to arrive in Philadelphia. From the beginning they had complained that the sound was inferior. The fact that the band could have whatever it wanted when a recording was to be made infuriated them. Having had little personal contact with anyone from MainMan except for their unsuccessful meetings with Andrews, they began to perceive the company as an invisible enemy: *MainMan* had scrimped on the sound equipment.

Secret meetings were held to plot strategy. One of the things that concerned them was David. Was he for Defries or for them? They liked him very much, but they didn't know where he stood and he could not be approached easily with the question. David arrived before the show, did a quick soundcheck, then disappeared into his dressing room to dress and makeup; after the performance he would dash directly from the stage to a waiting limousine. On stage, David appeared with two male singing and dancing sidekicks billed as "Dogs." One "Dog" was played by his old friend Geoffrey MacCormack. When the musicians had their meetings, MacCormack as backup vocalist went to them. His presence stimulated the paranoia of the band. Was he carrying reports of their discussions back to David, and was David repeating what he heard from MacCormack to Defries? The paranoia spread to anyone who was a stranger. After five weeks on the road, it had become a cloak-and-dagger movie in which anyone could be the enemy.

Sound technicians began to prepare the Tower Theatre's stage for the recording.

"Are you going to record the show?" asked Herbie Flowers.

"Yes," came the reply.

A half-hour before showtime, Flowers made his grandstand play. "I'm not playing a note until all that recording equipment is unplugged," he declared.

The musicians backed him up. Overcome by strike fever against Bowie, Defries, and MainMan they all refused to play. Cold, hard cash was the only answer.

Ten minutes later, twenty minutes before curtain time, Flowers was summoned to David's dressing room. The strike was the kind of situation MainMan had always kept from David, and that he had never had to deal with before. Yet this time he was the only one available to solve the problem at hand.

Twenty minutes later Flowers emerged from his meeting with a triumphant grin on his face. The musicians flocked around him.

"Bowie's guaranteed us five thousand dollars a man," Flowers told them, "even if he has to pay us out of his own pocket. We'll have a written contract before Madison Square Garden."

The musicians erupted in cheers and went straight to work.

The $45,000 that David gave away had no real meaning to him. He didn't care about the cost of anything. Like Defries he felt it imperative to suggest that he was above the human struggle; Defries existed to engage in the human struggle for him. Tony had promised that he would never have to engage in that struggle because he was an "artiste." Without the buffer of Tony Defries he was naked and vulnerable, and that made him feel really uncomfortable.

The hurt David felt touched something very deep in him. These were exactly the feelings he was determined never to experience.

It was a tour in which nothing was what it seemed. Nothing had been bigger in size or more publicized, yet there still wasn't a Top Ten single from the album. They were playing to full houses but it took enormous advertising and publicity to fill them. The illusion of lavishness and success was everywhere but David was still not the superstar he wanted to be.

On July 18, 1974, America was to celebrate the fifth anniversary of Neil Armstrong's landing on the moon. Two Soviet cosmonauts, Colonel Pavel Popovitch and Lieutenant Colonel Yuri Ardtukhiam, were completing a daring space maneuver in which they docked with an orbiting laboratory. And Bowie and his "bigger-than-everybody" spectacle were coming to New York.

At 8:00 A.M. the trucks arrived at Madison Square Garden, and the madness began. A one-way alley faces the Garden's loading dock. The trucks drove up Eighth Avenue, turned into the alley, and found themselves facing against the traffic. They had turned in the wrong way. They were too big to back out, nor could they drive through the street the wrong way because a battery of cars faced them. They were stuck, and within minutes an enormous traffic snarl had formed around the Garden, which would last into the night. All day irate drivers got out of their cars to see what was going on. They were told, "It's the Bowie show," as if that was an explanation unto itself.

For six weeks the Diamond Dogs crew had existed on only three or four hours of sleep a night. Theirs was an impossible mission, and its very impossibility inspired them to fight against their exhaustion. By surviving it, they were proving that the impossible could be accomplished, that where Bowie was concerned every conventional rule could be broken. The crew had watched David work and had come to a conclusion about him: he was a prince. To them, the only thing that mattered was that when Bowie appeared on stage he had to shine.

The teamsters who worked for Madison Square Garden didn't give a damn if Bowie shone at all. Under the direction of the Diamond Dogs two-man advance crew, it was their job to transfer the contents of the trailer-trucks to a smaller truck that would be driven to the arena's loading dock. They then had to wrestle the scenery through a pair of narrow double doors and into the elevator to the third floor, which was the stage floor. The scenery was assembled on the stage. Never before had three truckloads of scenery arrived for a two-night stand.

The Catapult was the first piece off the trucks.

"We might get a disease just from touching it," one of the Garden's carpenters remarked as he stared at a gigantic phallis.

It took a dozen men to unload the obscene-looking object. A small crowd formed to watch the bizarre maneuver. Finally the arm was at the Garden doors, a Diamond Dogs advance man leading the way. The first thing he noticed when he stepped into the building was the terrible smell.

"The circus was just here," explained a member of the Garden's staff. "The smell of elephant shit stays for months." The man didn't realize that another circus had just hit town.

At ten that morning MainMan's vice-president, Jaime DeCarlo Lotts Andrews, was playing with his favorite toy, the office's color Xerox machine. Even though there was no real need for a color Xerox at MainMan, Defries felt it essential to the company image that the staff have access to state-of-the-art technology.

The previous night, after everyone had gone home, Andrews dropped his pants and underpants, climbed on top of the Xerox machine, spread the cheeks of his buttocks, and pressed "print." He didn't stop until twenty-six copies of the picture had emerged. He dropped one on everyone's desk.

While the teamsters were busy unloading Diamond Dogs at Madison Square Garden, everyone was greeted by a three-color Xerox of vice-president Andrews's anus. Another day at MainMan had officially begun.

Tony Defries knew that his relationship with his most important artist was strained. The only reasonable way to solve the problem was to go on the road, do some hand-holding, and smooth things over. But at this point Defries had no desire to hold anybody's hand anymore—he had lost interest in playing daddy. He had graduated to a position where hand-holding could be delegated. Since Defries did not seem to acknowledge his own feelings it didn't occur to him that the machine named Bowie *did* have feelings and those feelings had been hurt by his neglect.

Defries expected David to turn on him one day. Naughty children always turn against their parents. The manager could be as childish as David. Adopting an "I'll show him" attitude, he decided to make a deal for Bowie's services so large that Bowie couldn't help realizing how powerful his daddy really was. He would also manufacture another star and produce a hit Broadway show, believing that those successes would demonstrate to David that even if he did leave MainMan, the company would survive very well indeed.

The deal that Defries was trying to close was outrageous. It concerned a nine-night stand the following May 28 to June 5, 1975, at the Empire Pool in Wembley, London. Defries had a tricky negotiating strategy: He'd create an impossible deal and then challenge a promoter to agree to it. Usually the promoter's counteroffer was much larger than normal because Defries had opened the negotiations with such excessive terms.

The deal Defries had cooked up for Wembley was a doozy, and he didn't expect any promoter to agree to it unconditionally. The Empire Pool's 7,927 seats would be scaled to a top price of $16.80 (at an exchange rate of $2.40 per English pound). A sold-out engagement would gross just under $1 million. Defries demanded 90 percent of the box office gross up to $432,000 and 100 percent above that figure. He had budgeted the promoter's expenses at a maximum of $125,000, which the promoter would *advance*, to be deducted from Defries's fee. Defries would make $750,000 and the promoter a mere $43,000, even though he had risked all of the expense monies. To secure the deal Defries had made the most outrageous demand of all: a $500,000 nonrefundable advance payable on or before August 15, 1974, nine months before the concerts. If that wasn't enough, he also demanded 50 percent of the monies earned by the promoter from such concessions as ice cream, soft drinks, juices, candy, food, alcoholic beverages, and cigarettes.

While these negotiations were going on, Defries had jacked up his staff to apply the MainMan machine to Dana Gillespie. The idea that an old girl friend of Bowie's could be manufactured and become as big as David seemed deliciously ironic.

There were other activities going on as well, all of them treated with equal if not more importance than Bowie's impending concerts at Madison Square Garden. MainMan had produced an Off-Off Broadway showcase of *Fame*, a play based on the life of Marilyn Monroe, which had been written and directed by MainMan artiste Anthony Ingrassia, co-author and director of *Andy Warhol's Pork*. The showcase had not been successful, but MainMan was bringing the play to Broadway anyway. A weak script was insignificant in the face of the company's vast promotional machine.

In the next few weeks the Wembley deal would collapse, Dana Gillespie's album would fail, and *Fame* would receive disastrous reviews and close after one night. But at the moment everyone at MainMan thought that Tony Defries was a genius. After all, he *acted* like a genius, and where the management of Bowie was concerned he had *been* a genius. In an atmosphere where $500,000 might be collected with so much ease, it was impossible to think about the problems connected with getting Diamond Dogs ready to open at Madison Square Garden.

No one worried what might be going on in David's mind. It was an agile and clever mind; David was always incubating his future. Could he be contemplating an act of patricide? Without Bowie there would be no cash flow. An act of patricide could instantly topple the empire, tossing the MainMan children onto the street even though their daddy had guaranteed they would always be safe.

The Year of the Diamond Dogs tour was the beginning of the end between Bowie and Defries.

On Thursday, as soon as Angela had checked into the MainMan apartment at the Sherry Netherland, a meeting was scheduled for her and Defries. The location of the meeting was the first issue that had to be resolved. Defries played power politics continually. He demanded that the meeting be on his home turf, the MainMan penthouse he used as his New York pied à terre. The penthouse was a Gothic fantasy. The walls were decorated with medieval tapestries, and the furniture would have been at home in the court of King Arthur. Because it had been decorated to resemble a stage setting in some sword-and-sorcery epic, it was the place people were usually brought when they were being drummed out of the MainMan "family." The penthouse had been aptly nicknamed "the Executioner's Suite."

The need for the meeting did not please Defries. Everyone was his child, and most of his children were good children. His most important child, Bowie, had become a naughty child by speaking up, questioning Defries's decisions, acting independently of Defries, and becoming involved with cocaine, all of which made Defries uncomfortable. Angie had always been naughty, and now she was out of control. During David's ten-month-long retirement she had invaded Defries's London house, painted it white, and renamed it "the MainMan Studio." Using it as her base of operations, she had begun to plan publicity and promotional campaigns for Bowie as well as for Dana Gillespie. She was also creating a MainMan television special based on the myth of the water-sprite Ondine, in which she would play the title character, and was searching for a location for a MainMan retail outlet to feature clothing designed by Bowie's costume designer Freddi Burrett. Under Defries's aegis, people could act any role that pleased them. Angela had cast herself in the role of Tony Defries.

Defries told Zanetta that Angela's spending had to stop. She was a nuisance. She was in the way and had no function in the scheme of things. She was meddling in his business, and had to be told to get out.

The scene had been set for a major confrontation. Unlike the others who surrounded Defries, Angela was an emotional woman who let her emotions show. At the slightest cue, she could become hysterical. She could grow steely and tough and begin shouting. She had a strong, resonant voice that made the simplest statement sound like a royal command. She had no place in a world run by a man who liked to pontificate slowly and softly for hours about the way the world and the entertainment industry should be run.

But Angela was also a woman of infinite surprises. On the day of this meeting, she had decided to be the dignified young matron. She was dressed in a blue-gray copy of a Chanel suit, her blond hair was pulled back, and she was wearing little makeup. She spoke softly, and there was a tremulous quality in her voice, as if she might begin to weep at any second. She was so much the vulnerable child, the little girl hungering for approval, that it was virtually impossible not to be sympathetic toward her.

Angela carried with her an eight-page mimeographed newsletter of the activities of the MainMan Studio. She handed the newsletter to Defries, looking at him expectantly. He lit a Cuban cigar and perused the memorandum. For the next four hours he would slowly and methodically pull the plug on each of her ideas.

The first page dealt with Angela's plans for an English radio and television promotional tour to promote Dana Gillespie's debut solo LP.

He explained that Dana was his artist and not Angela's. If he needed Angela's help, he would ask for it. Of course, Angela could form her own company and then might be able to sign Dana for management. But at the moment Dana was signed to him. Besides, it was Tony's money that Angela was spending to perform a job that RCA was perfectly capable of performing with its own staff and without Angela's help. He paused, and then almost as an afterthought told her that he didn't want his English house used as a place where she entertained her boyfriends.

Angela curled up on the couch. "I'm sorry, Tony," she said contritely. "I really wasn't trying to step on anybody's toes. I thought I was doing the right thing."

Angela had supplied the names of four English journalists she thought MainMan should fly to New York to attend the Madison Square Garden shows and then interview David.

Defries reminded her that MainMan had a press department, the purpose of which was to keep interviewers *away* from David. The only thing he'd settle for was the cover of *Time* or *Newsweek*. Setting up interviews with music papers like the *New Record Mirror* didn't help at all.

Angela looked even more contrite. The meeting continued, interrupted by gossipy exchanges, snacks and tea.

Defries announced that Angela's spending really had to stop once and for all. MainMan had started to do an accounting. Between airline tickets, hotel bills, and limousine bills, she had spent over one hundred thousand dollars that year on travel alone.

"Well, I thought I was only doing what I was supposed to be doing. I thought you wanted me to be here for the shows. I thought I was helping my husband. I didn't realize I was being a burden. If someone had told me earlier I never would have done all this traveling."

After a long pause Defries told her that she ought to stop fooling around. She didn't have a real marriage, and she was getting in the way.

Angela stared at him in disbelief. She looked like a prize fighter who had just taken a powerful blow to the solar plexus. Defries, a cold and calculating businessman, actually could not stand the pain of others. Often there was a soft touch behind his imperial veneer. One look at Angela's anguished face, and he began to back off. He told her that he was prepared to go on supporting her as a MainMan artist, but that everyone was caught up in Bowie's tour. Her personal projects could not be dealt with until the following year. In the interim, she could consult with Z and keep him informed of her progress.

Angela stood and smiled faintly. She knew Defries had palmed her off on his president.

"I understand, Tony. I'm glad you've spoken to me like this. I didn't realize how much my activities had upset you. I would never do anything to hurt you or Dana or David or any of the other artists. I'm so glad we had this conversation. Good-bye, Tony. Good-bye, Z."

Angela loved David madly; he knew she had only his best interests at heart, and he trusted her implicitly. Her instinct had taken them to Tony Defries in the first place, and her report of the meeting would deepen David's desire to topple the MainMan machine. Angela, through her power of suggestion, had the power to help marshal Bowie to demolish the MainMan dream.

But there were certain facts that she didn't acknowledge. David viewed her as his best friend. Part of him wanted her to be a traditional wife and mother, having babies and tending his house. This part did not approve of her compulsive restlessness—like Defries she did not want to look after him all day every day—but the Prince

Charming in him would never have a direct confrontation with her. Instead, he supported her publicly even though her presence unnerved him. Nor did Angela grasp that Defries *and* David would block her independent moves at every turn. Her behavior—indeed her mere presence—threatened Defries, and he was always ready to punish her. At one time she had been the perfect human buffer for Bowie; he was loath to see her become autonomous.

The game would grow in intensity, not ending until Angela lost entirely. She would be erased from David's life, receiving no credit whatsoever for her significant contributions.

That Friday night David arrived at Madison Square Garden at six o'clock for the first of his two shows in time for the sound check. He usually arrived just before curtain time; his presence this early indicated how important he considered the show.

At 7:30 David was in his dressing room. His current hairdresser Jac Colello was busy making up his star. It had been Colello's decision to make David's hair shorter and more conservative-looking and had given it its new blondish-burgundy color. David studied himself intently in the mirror while Colello worked on him. Corinne hovered in the background.

David slipped into his costume, an elegant pale blue suit, white shirt with an open collar, and light yellow socks. David, who had never been thinner, now looked more like an alien being than he had when he was in his Ziggy Stardust getup. Almost no one wore designer suits in 1974; David's elegance seemed the epitome of decadence, giving him the appearance of a fashion model who dressed —even existed—only to be seen. This was the ultimate version of Ziggy Stardust, Ziggy returned from the grave, an elegant, enameled, singing, dancing corpse and the ringmaster of a future Hell.

Despite all the futuristic mumbo jumbo, at its core the Year of the Diamond Dogs was really a show about energy and astonishment. The astonishment began the minute the audience took its seats. Hunger City loomed over them, and the sound of yelping, maddened dogs filled the air. There were lots of glitter kids in the audience, affecting flashy, home-grown versions of the Ziggy Stardust look that David had abandoned. A few of the real trendies wore European designer suits, extremely exotic and unfashionable at that time. It was a look David would certify as "in" before the evening was over. What bound them all together, however, was the sense that tonight would be an event, an event "bigger 'n everybody," an event for which the press had been priming them for weeks.

Of all the onstage surprises they seemed most taken with the Catapult.

The lights turned a deep blue, and David, perched in a glowing red booth, appeared at the top of the stage on the Catapult and began to sing "Space Oddity." As the lights changed from blue to deep purple he seemed to ride through space, heading directly for the audience. It was an astonishing effect. As he hovered above the first few rows of the orchestra, he was captured in a piercing red light the color of hellfire. It looked as if a god had arrived in a ball of fire. The first few rows were also bathed in the red light. For a few minutes, they were sharing *his* light with *him*! It drove them into a frenzy. They reached and jumped, trying to touch their god, or they just raised their hands in supplication, a spectacle resembling religious ecstasy.

The Year of the Diamond Dogs had been designed for Broadway-sized houses, and past the twentieth row it looked like a child's toy in the giant-sized arena. But it didn't matter. No one had ever seen anything like it before; it had been crafted as a foolproof showcase for David, and he had performed it brilliantly. Tony Defries had wanted to create the ultimate rock-and-roll media event, and *Diamond Dogs* had not let him down. Everywhere, David was once again being hailed as rock's great innovator. Shortly thereafter two Bowie albums, *The Rise and Fall of Ziggy Stardust and the Spiders from Mars* and *Diamond Dogs*, would achieve gold status. Despite the reams of publicity, Bowie had proved especially difficult to sell to the American public. It had taken six tons of scenery and the agony of mounting The Year of the Diamond Dogs. But it had been done.

The reception at the Plaza Hotel after the concert had been organized with only one thing in mind: to divert people from going to the MainMan apartment at the Sherry Netherland and invading David's privacy. Because of his discomfort in crowds, the guest list had been limited to forty people. They were an odd assortment of MainMan and tour personnel. There were also Bette Midler, Mick Jagger, and Rudolf Nureyev. Their presence in such a small group had the paradoxical effect of making the other guests nervous; they did not know how to make small talk with stars.

There was also the tension that accompanied anything having to do with David. One never knew if he was even going to arrive. While the guests waited for him, Rudolf Nureyev stood poised against a wall. He stared arrogantly into space and gave off a feeling of un-approachability. Then he went into a bedroom to wait for David expecting the star to be brought to him when he arrived.

Bodyguard Stuie George led in David with Ava on his arm. They greeted Angela, who was cordial to them both. David had a glass of champagne and moved around the room, bantering quietly with the guests. He greeted one of his buddies, who had brought the beautiful daughter of a very famous actor.

Off the bedroom was a large walk-in closet. The only people at the party who really interested David were Bette Midler and Mick Jagger. The trio stepped into the closet and closed the door. They stayed there for almost an hour. A man who craves attention at all costs, David's instincts for getting that attention have always been uncanny. Every pair of eyes in the room was riveted to the closet door.

The stars emerged from the closet an hour later. David was ready to leave the party. He suggested that the actor's daughter join him at the Sherry Netherland.

Ava Cherry was sent back to her MainMan apartment in Green-wich Village, Angie spent the night in her bedroom in the Sherry Netherland apartment, while the actor's daughter spent the rest of the evening with David. A movie star's beautiful daughter proved the ideal match for the triumphant star of the Year of the Diamond Dogs.

CHAPTER 20

"I Don't Understand"

Around noon on the Sunday following the second Diamond Dogs concert at Madison Square Garden, Tony Zanetta received a call at home from Angela. "Good morning, honey," she boomed and began chatting away about the previous night's concert. Finally, she said, "Z, why don't you come over to the hotel at the end of the afternoon."

"That would be terrific," Zanetta replied.

"Oh, good, honey." Right before she hung up she added, "David would also like to see you." Zanetta realized then that David had decreed that he be summoned to the hotel.

Zanetta was greeted at the MainMan suite by Corinne. "David's still asleep," she explained, "and Angie just left. She got a sudden urge to take Zowie and Marion Skene, Zowie's nurse, on a buggy ride through Central Park. They'll be back in an hour or so."

The suite had been converted into David's creative playroom. Everywhere lay unsheathed records, pads, drawing pencils, and magazines opened to pictures that had caught his eye. David was attracted to strong, unusual, or exaggerated visual statements. He pored over these pictures, trying to decipher a way to incorporate their elements in his work. Diane Arbus's photographs were his current obsession; a book of her pictures lay open on the dining-room table.

As usual, Corinne, clipboard in hand, sat by the telephone in the center of the debris. She looked exhausted. A month of being on the road working sixteen or more hours a day had taken its toll.

There were dark circles around her eyes, and she was slumped into the chair.

Her exhaustion had in no way affected her compulsiveness about David. "Z," she began, "Raquel is having trouble getting call-backs from the musicians David wants to play on the new album. I don't even know whether she's gotten hold of them."

Raquel Narvaez was Jaime Andrews's secretary. Tony Defries believed that the hallmark of a good executive was his ability to delegate authority and shrink his workload to next to nothing. Tasks like booking musicians fell to secretaries, who rarely had the clout to do the job properly.

"David also made a list of the Latino records he wants to listen to before he records the new album. I gave it to Raquel. It's a week later, and I still don't have the records."

Corinne looked pleadingly at Zanetta. "You know how difficult it is to get anything out of that office. David keeps asking for these records, and I'm getting nowhere. The cost of the records is probably only around thirty dollars. Maybe if I gave the list to you, you'd have better luck. You could just go to a record store without all the red tape. You could get David the records, couldn't you?"

The phone began to ring again. There was a look of anguish on Corinne's face as she answered it. When she was done with the call, she was able to resume her complaints without missing a beat.

"I can't deal with the attitude of the office," she continued. "They're sweet, but they don't understand. They seem so busy having a wonderful time, they don't have any time to do any work. Whenever I ask for a check for anything, they make me feel like a criminal."

Twenty-six people were employed by MainMan; surely someone could buy him a handful of LP's. But there were complicated systems.

It was absurd, thought Zanetta, that neither David nor Corinne had the thirty dollars to buy the records themselves. For the most part David's expenses, both on the road and in the MainMan suite, could be charged. During one week at the Sherry Netherland, David, who could be as unrealistic about money as Defries, ran up a $17,000 room service bill after allowing everyone who visited him to order whatever they wanted all night long. Corinne was allotted $200 a week for "household expenses," and David had a $500 weekly allowance. The $700 barely covered cigarettes and taxis, and David and Corinne rarely had a cent in their pockets. Dependent on the MainMan machinery for every penny, they were frustrated and infuriated by Defries's passion for systematic choke-holds.

As if all of that weren't enough, Corinne had to contend with serious problems. "David never eats anymore," she said sadly. "I'm afraid he's going to get sick." She looked really miserable.

"You know, Z, I'm so worried about the cocaine. He's using more and more of it. It's the only thing that keeps him going. It scares me. I'm in this all by myself, and there are days when I don't know what to do."

Telling David that cocaine was a destructive habit meant banishment from the prince's court. Corinne was trapped between her desire to be wonderful to David, and being a party to his self-destructiveness.

Suddenly, she looked up and smiled girlishly. "Oh, Z, I really do love him! I love him so very much!"

There was a pause. Then her tone changed abruptly, and she was all business again. "I really do need those records for him," she implored. "You will get them for me, won't you?"

She got up, and headed for David's bedroom. She returned and said, "As soon as he wakes up, I'll let you see him." It was Zanetta's reward for agreeing to get her the records.

Twenty minutes later, as if responding to a sixth sense, Corinne knew that David was about to wake up. She took his orange juice, coffee, and cigarettes into the bedroom, along with a copy of *The New York Times*, which she had opened to a review of the show. When she came out, she said, "Soon."

After another twenty minutes Corinne said, "He's ready to see you now," and Zanetta was ushered into the bedroom.

As soon as David saw Zanetta, he began to act. "Is it morning already?" he camped flirtatiously. "Hi, Z. Want to sit down on my bed?"

"By all means." Zanetta plunked himself on the edge of the bed.

Suddenly, Angela's booming voice could be heard in the living room.

"I'll be right along," David told Zanetta. "Why don't you go say hello to Ang and Zowie?"

Eventually Marion took Zowie into their bedroom and Corinne

returned to her room. Now was the ideal moment for David to make his entrance.

David finally came into the living room, dressed in a kimono. Angie snuggled up next to him on the couch. She looked adoringly at him and stroked his hand. The roles they had elected to play with each other that evening were man of the house and loving wife.

David emptied a vial of cocaine onto a mirror and chopped it into lines. Using a hundred-dollar bill, he snorted a line or two.

He enjoyed the drug-taking ritual, chopping the cocaine and deciding how big each line should be. He especially liked the fact that he controlled the stash and could decide if and when to offer Zanetta a line. Angela neither took drugs nor drank. The cocaine binge between David and Zanetta would last fifteen hours.

Even when he was relaxing, David had an agenda; there was always a scenario, a script to act out, with David triumphant at the third-act curtain. Looking back on that meeting Zanetta realizes that Bowie had several intentions. He wanted first-hand confirmation from an eyewitness of what he had been told was going on in the MainMan offices. He was also engaged in a subtle but deadly war with Defries. Now David wanted to win Defries's right-hand man over to his side; he wanted Zanetta to work for him and not Defries.

"Every day I wake up to face a nightmare," David began, "a nightmare I don't understand. I once had a dream, and Tony had that dream. It's a dream we shared."

He looked knowingly at Zanetta. His dream automatically was everyone's dream, his quest a mission shared by all who knew and loved him.

"But I had to do my part," he continued. "I had to create; I had to do my work. I've done my part, haven't I? I've upheld my end of the bargain. I don't understand why he has done this."

Overcome by confusion, he paused. "Is this the time to *abandon* me?" he finally asked. "Is this the time to abandon the dream? This is the moment that is supposed to be triumphant." It was impossible not to believe along with him that he was a victim of a colossal betrayal.

"Z, I don't have a dollar in my pocket," he said incredulously. "It's ridiculous, laughable, a bloody nightmare.

"When Tony spoke to Angie like that he was meddling in my

personal life," David declared. "I don't advise him on the subject of Melanie's spending. Where does he come off telling Angie how to spend her money? He's crossed his boundaries with that one. He's in charge of my business, not my personal life or my work. All I know is I don't have the money to give Angie to spend while he has all the money in the world to give to Melanie."

Angela looked lovingly at her champion. "I was never so insulted in all my life," she said sadly. "He really hurt me." They cuddled up to each other. They looked so childlike and wounded they could have been posing for an orphanage poster.

Although they slept in separate bedrooms Angela and David had enormous loyalty, neither tolerating criticism of the other. In the proper mood they could give stunning performances of husband and wife. They acted the roles so well they convinced not only everyone around them but also themselves that they were deeply in love.

"I can't get through to Tony on the phone. I can't see him. He doesn't have time for me or my career. He's too busy getting the price of gold, too busy worrying about how many nights I'm going to play and counting heads. Everything, *everything*, has a dollar sign on it. It's diabolical!"

There was a pause. He stared at Zanetta. "Z, I feel very alone. I feel totally defenseless."

Zanetta was touched by David's surprising display of emotion. He replied, "I'm willing to do anything I can to help. I can talk to Tony for you."

"You're the only one I can rely on. You're the only one in that office I can trust, whom I can expect to give me answers about what's going on.

"I'm financially dependent on Tony. I have no idea what I've got, I don't know what I'm worth. I don't know who's paying for everything. Where's the money coming from for all the projects? Who's paying for the Wayne County film? Who's paying for the Broadway production of *Fame*? Who's paying for Mick Ronson's campaign? Who's paying for Dana's campaign? Who's paying for the billboards?

"Half this company is mine, but I have no say in anything. I don't know what's going out, I don't know what's coming in."

"David," Zanetta said, "your deal is no secret. You are to receive fifty percent of the profits—after your expenses are deducted—of the monies generated by you and you alone. You own no portion of MainMan. MainMan belongs exclusively to Tony."

It was as if David had erected a soundproof booth around himself. His look grew determined, and he jutted out his jaw. "I don't understand," he said. "Tony and I are partners. our agreement has always been fifty-fifty."

"You own fifty percent of your income after all expenses are deducted. Tony is under no obligation to pay you anything other than your salary and to support you, your family, and your staff. The money you generate is MainMan income not Bowie income. It remains MainMan income until Tony decides to distribute it. You have given him permission to use this money to develop other acts and to build MainMan. All your money goes to him, and he has total control over it. You have never had any control over your money."

"I own fifty percent of *MainMan*."

"That's not your agreement. You own no portion of MainMan."

"I know I own fifty percent of the company." Nothing could make him change his mind.

"Surely you always knew what your deal with Tony was," said Zanetta.

David looked confused. To admit that he had not known the truth was to admit that he had behaved irresponsibly, to admit that he was less than perfect. "I never understood it," he said stubbornly. "I know I own fifty percent of MainMan."

Once again Zanetta told him the exact terms of his deal. "David, it's the deal you made. You could always have renegotiated it; you can still renegotiate it."

"I own fifty percent of MainMan, I know I do."

"If you think Tony's cheating you, hire an accountant and audit his books. See where the money is going. Decide which expenses you think are legitimate." Zanetta was talking to a wall. David stared silently into space.

"If you have suspicions about anything, hire a lawyer and conduct a full investigation," urged Zanetta.

Bowie didn't want lawyers and accountants. He wanted to maintain his fantasy that Tony had become involved with him out of love and a belief in his talent, not as part of his empire-building.

It was almost dawn but the cocaine had filled David with speedy energy.

Angela curled up on David's lap and fell asleep.

Later, while Angela dozed, the two men watched the sun rise over Manhattan. Everything seemed peaceful and happy for a few moments. Then David again became crestfallen. "How did it come to this?" he asked quietly. "Why did it come to this? It shouldn't have. You know it shouldn't have. I don't understand any of it."

David hated emotional displays. Now there would be no more of them. Immediately after his all-night outburst with Zanetta, he pushed his problems with Defries out of his mind, and plunged into work, his usual pattern.

In July he was going to mix *David Live*, the recording of the live performance of the Diamond Dogs tour in Philadelphia. Then in August he was going to Sigma Sound in Philadelphia to begin another album. During 1974 an astonishing twenty-four hit singles had been recorded at Sigma, each becoming a rhythm-and-blues hit first and then crossing over to the pop charts. Sigma, the home of Kenny Gamble and Leon Huff's Philadelphia International Records, was America's most successful black-owned music company after Motown. At Sigma David would make American music with American musicians. He would enact the role of an American pop-soul singer and would produce an *American* hit. Then America would be at his feet.

Then at the end of August he was going to Los Angeles to finish the Year of the Diamond Dogs tour. Seven nights, beginning on September 2, had been booked at the vast Universal Amphitheatre. After that the show traveled to twenty-five cities, ending on December 1 in Atlanta.

Since his arrival in New York City in April, his schedule called for him to work nonstop for eight months. He had taken on an exceedingly strenuous work load, and he loved it. The conventional rules were always to be violated. He was "special"; he did not have to do what ordinary mortals did. He did not have to sleep or eat; his body could endure superhuman amounts of strain; he could produce more work more quickly than anyone else. The first leg of the Year of the Diamond Dogs had left him exhausted, but rest, good food, or a vacation were out of the question. The answer was more work and more seclusion—the choice Ziggy Stardust would have made.

During July, as usual he slept until late afternoon. In the early evening, surrounded by his ever-protective "family"—Corinne, Jim James, and Stuie George—he wafted through the lobby of the Sherry Netherland to his MainMan limousine to head downtown to Greenwich Village to Electric Ladyland Studio to mix *David Live*. One night Bette Midler dropped in to chat. They gossiped about rhythm-and-blues music, calling it the only music that was "real," and David reiterated his joy about going to Sigma to make some R and B of his own.

Periodically Norman Fisher was summoned to the Sherry Netherland to replenish David's cocaine supply. Fisher always brought along a tantalizing book, picture, or set of photographs. David was easily fascinated by unusual images, and he lived in a world of people whose pleasure came from pleasing others. Norman Fisher, with his coke, his gifts, and his ability to spin out a series of gossipy tales, mainly about New York media figures, was one of the great pleasers. He eagerly paid admission to David's inner circle by giving away lots of coke and entertaining the always charming but always somewhat distant rock star.

David had a streak of paranoia, and under the influence of cocaine it increased. The increments were slow and subtle. He told his video cameraman John Dove he couldn't get up on stage because he was too fatigued by the whole bloody process. He couldn't go out on the street because he'd be mobbed. He was trapped in the hotel and would go crazy unless he had something to do.

Dove perceived David as exceedingly normal. And in the confines of the MainMan suite, the exhausted, ultrapolite rock star was so persuasive he did seem normal—unless one dared step out of the picture long enough to look closely at how David chose to deal with both his exhaustion and his fame. Except in David's hyperactive mind, there were no mobs waiting to besiege him at every fork in the road, and New Yorkers, by nature, allow stars to wander the streets and go to public places without giving them too much of a hard time.

David loved the myth of enormous fame and the problems that came with it. Yet the part of him that masked his insecurity with an ironclad shield of omnipotence dreaded the fact that the public might discover him as life-sized and not mythic at all. In private, he chose with Dove to act out the polar opposite of his public persona, "just plain folks."

What David really wanted Dove to do was extend David's knowledge of video. But he didn't want to ask directly; Dove had to be seduced into playing the role of teacher. So he set up a situation in which Dove believed he was rescuing David from "going crazy" by teaching him about video.

David was fascinated by special effects. He wanted to create unusual and original video images and he needed to learn about fades, dissolves, and superimpositions. He wanted to take the special effects in his brain and convert them into video images that he could whirl, stretch, twist, distort, hurl into space, or divide into myriad fragments.

During July Ava was summoned whenever David wanted to spend the night with her. He also enjoyed the role of rebellious child. At one time, he discussed his every professional move with Tony Defries. Now he made his own decisions and discussed nothing with his manager. He wanted to go to Sigma Sound in August, and would go to Sigma Sound. He wanted to work with the guitarist Carlos Alomar, and Alomar was hired. David seemed optimistic, productive, and happy. He believed in those illusions and infused his small world with them.

Bosom Buddies

Angela and Dana Gillespie were bosom buddies. Angela was living at the Sherry Netherland, and Dana frequently trekked over to the hotel to visit her. Tony Defries had given Dana a Polaroid camera. Soon Dana was photodocumenting everything she saw.

One night she was hanging out with David when Mick Jagger came to visit. Jagger enjoyed palling around with other stars. On his arm was David's old friend Bebe Buell, with whom David had had a brief affair at the outset of Tour Two.

They sat around drinking and relaxing. Eventually the beauteous Bebe sprawled out on the couch, her head resting on Mick's lap.

Just then Dana got up, went into the bedroom, and returned with a pair of benwa balls. Available in most sex shops, they were two metal balls attached to a vibrating mechanism that were reputed to increase orgasmic pleasure.

David, who loved to play the observer watching as the theater of life parading by him, egged Dana on.

Dana turned on the vibrator. The balls made a whirring sound.

All eyes were on Bebe. David's had the eager-little-boy expression he had used to try to coax the drag queen into having sex with Ava.

Bebe looked at the pulsating balls. She didn't know what the balls did, but whatever it was, she didn't want it done to her.

Jagger knew Bebe was a passionate girl, but she was not kinky. He jumped up and stood protectively between her and Dana. Despite Jagger's gesture, Bebe still felt trapped, and Mick sensed her increasing nervousness.

"Come on, darling," said Jagger to Buell. "We're gonna go now."

The last thing Bebe heard as the door shut was the sound of the benwa balls whirring in Dana's hand.

A couple of nights later Jagger came back. This time Tony Defries showed up with Dana Gillespie. There was small talk, but David and Mick were restless. It was a hot summer's night, and they were in the mood for some adventure. Ava's name was thrown around, but the idea of repeating the sexual experiences they had already had with her did not thrill them. They needed new blood. Other names were bandied about, but none proved satisfactory.

Then Defries announced that it was time for him to go, and got up and left.

August 11–18, the eight days David spent at Sigma Sound, exceeded his wildest expectations. For starters, the studio itself exuded the euphoria that exists only in a pop-record boom town where each day a new hit seems to appear as if by magic. Sigma's music was sugar-coated, thumping rhythm and blues glossed to a shiny, slick perfection. The R-and-B feel of the records appealed to blacks; the glossiness appealed to whites. Everyone, it appeared, loved "the sound of Philadelphia." In this atmosphere Sigma's highly professional staff radiated warmth and self-confidence; a "can't-miss" feeling pervaded the entire operation.

At Sigma David instantly set about creating a new family. Supportive, devoted, and under his control, it was his kind of family. They included guitarist Carlos Alomar and his wife, vocalist Robin Clark. Alomar, in his early twenties, was a caring man with absolutely no music-business slickness about him. His buxom wife Robin was the epitome of earth mother. Thoroughly devoted to each other and very much in love, Carlos and Robin had grown up together in Queens along with their best friend, Luther Vandross. Carlos had invited Luther to Philadelphia. The minute Robin and Luther saw each other they burst into song. It took only a few minutes of their vocalizing to persuade David to hire Vandross and his vocal group to sing on the album, with Vandross doing the vocal arrangements.

The opportunity to work with David amazed Carlos, Robin, and Luther, kids who had been scooped up and dropped down at Sigma, the hottest recording studio in America. It all intimidated them. No expense had been spared to make them comfortable and happy. Dozens of fans maintained a twenty-four-hour vigil either outside the studio or in front of the hotel. They had never worked with a star who inspired such devotion. It was magic, and the big break they had been waiting for.

Over and over again people suddenly found themselves cascaded into the unreality of Bowie's orbit. The response of Carlos, Robin, and Luther was the only response they knew how to make: to make the best music they could as fast as they could make it.

Because he had heard that Frank Sinatra did not record his vocals until after midnight, David refused to begin singing until two or three in the morning. He was convinced that copying the behavior of such a mythic figure as Sinatra would ensure his own mythic status. Also, at that time the studio would be empty. No one could witness him performing vocals that might not be perfect. Often he worked through the night, not leaving the studio until the next morning.

A day or two after his arrival at Sigma, David ran into the Three Degrees, three attractive young black women. He chose the most flamboyant. He put on his most inviting smile; his conversation was sprinkled with wit and flirtation. He didn't say much, but every word and gesture indicated the promise of excitement and sexual adventure.

Because of his publicity, women expected to meet a freak. Instead, a surprise awaited them, a surprise that knocked them off kilter. Here was a man with ruby red hair and alabaster skin who spoke to them in a husky, honied voice. He accented his conversation with dramatic gestures with his long, sensual fingers. Used to being treated like sex objects, they sensed they were in the presence of a gentleman. David leaned over and whispered sweet nothings in the girl's ear. She was trapped in the illusion that she *was* special. David's charm made women feel wonderful.

It was an easy conquest, sweeter because it had been accomplished in front of the other musicians.

Ava watched from the distance, and wondered why she put up with David's sexual shenanigans. "There's something about David that hypnotizes and takes over," she said.

The next day David and Ava were back together. They had an arrangement. If David kept an affair secret it meant he had some feeling for the woman. Otherwise he had a friendly discussion with Ava about the one-night stand and gave her an evaluation of his partner's sexual performance. Ava did not have to give David the third degree about the Three Degrees. After he described her sexual acrobatics Ava knew that at least in this instance she had nothing to worry about.

At midweek Cherry Vanilla and Norman Fisher came to Philadelphia, and Fisher eagerly refilled David's cocaine bottle. Then Angela arrived. Believing that Ava's presence might prompt Angela to throw one of her legendary tantrums, it was decided to have Ava remain in seclusion until Angela left.

Angela was in her visiting housewife mode. Her husband could have been an out-of-town buyer she was visiting on the road. She was dressed plainly, wore no makeup, and spoke in a flat voice. As "Mrs. Bowie, Housewife from Beckenham," she was, as usual, superb in the part.

David played his Sigma tracks for Angela. One of them, "Can You Hear Me?" was a love song. She tensed. The Iceman never wrote love songs. There had to be something going on behind her back. Didn't they have an arrangement? Weren't they always to tell each other about their sexual escapades? David had written a love song for someone for whom he had some *feeling*, feeling he did not have for her. Otherwise he would have told her about the woman with whom he was sleeping in Philadelphia.

Some inner divining rod enabled Angela not only to know when David was sleeping with someone else, but also to be able physically to locate the other woman. She got up, walked slowly to Stuie George's bedroom door, opened it, and came face to face with Ava, who was keeping Stuie company. Instantly the housefrau became a blob of helplessness. David had not told her he was bringing Ava to Philadelphia. A lie of omission was still a lie.

But Angela could never accuse David of deceit. Nor could she cry out and hurl abuse at him. Her mission was to protect and promulgate his aura of perfection. So she became a panicked little girl and dashed into the hotel corridor.

Tony Zanetta was heading toward his room when Angela ran past him. He knew there was trouble, and he turned and followed her. Angela threw open the door to her room and headed for the window. She was going to stage a Great Suicide Attempt. She would be a human sacrifice on the altar of David Bowie. Zanetta grabbed her by the waist and wrestled her to the ground.

He held her tightly until she calmed down. He had learned the technique working with emotionally disturbed children when he first came to New York City. Angela collapsed and fell asleep.

When David heard the story, he rolled his eyes heavenward and said nothing. It was as if he were counting silently to ten in the hope that the incident would disappear. It took only a few seconds before it was out of his mind, and he moved on to something else.

That night, riding in his MainMan limousine with Ava, he said, "Angie and I are going to break up. I'm sick of this situation. You and I are together. The thing between Angela and me is just not going to work."

Ava assumed that she was going to replace Angela, which made her even more devoted to David. Angela left the next day, disappearing as quickly as she had arrived. Whenever she called David and Ava answered the phone, Angela would bellow, "Who is this?"

Then when David took the phone, she would become hysterical. David's response was to say nothing. She was a nuisance, and nuisances were to be ignored—until the right moment. When that moment came, they would be instantly and totally erased.

In eight days, nine tracks had been completed for the album tentatively entitled *Dancin'*. They included "Young Americans," which would become the actual title track of the album. The pace had been astonishing, and on the last night David put on his ad man's cap and decided to perform some market research.

The fans who had been keeping a twenty-four-hour-a-day vigil outside the studio and hotel were invited to the studio to hear the album. David wanted to see if they would get up and dance to *Dancin'*.

While the tracks were being played he moved freely among the kids, asking their opinions and listening intently to their responses. Then they began to get up and dance. He was ecstatic; it was a moment of genuine triumph. Here were young Americans dancing to "Young Americans"—exactly what he had hoped for.

CHAPTER 22

Hollywood

More than any other city in America, Los Angeles, center of the film and television industries, thrives on hype. Everyone, it seems, no matter what his occupation, reads the daily trade papers *Hollywood Reporter* and *Daily Variety* to see which stars were being hyped that day. The two major daily newspapers, the *Times* and the *Herald Examiner*, are viewed as ideal places to plant show-business stories. Most radio stations feature gobs of show business news and gossip; the evening television news shows shamelessly feature show-business items as their lead news stories, treating them as if they were international events of historical significance. In Los Angeles a good hype is discussed over breakfast and during drives along freeways. Hype is a way of life.

On David's behalf the MainMan machine was a hype factory run riot. Five months of relentless propaganda had paid off: David's seven nights at the Universal Amphitheatre beginning September 2 were sold out. Finally, after an absence of eighteen months, L.A. was going to have its opportunity to see Bowie. Programmed to perceive David as the Man Who Was Always Changing and who had changed the face of rock and roll by audaciously mating rock to theater, L.A. was primed and ready.

Fame and success are the only things that matter in this sunbaked Southern California city. Its gods and goddesses are stars. The only thing L.A. cares deeply about are the hit-makers and the size of their hits. David's ability to ring up huge ticket sales qualified him as a major hit-maker. He was the new god in town; the city couldn't wait to worship at his feet.

___

On August 24, six days after he finished his work at Sigma Sound, David boarded the train for the three-day ride to Los Angeles. He couldn't wait to get to the West Coast. Hollywood would always be his symbol of America, the America he had seen in movies when he was a child.

He viewed his first trip to Hollywood to promote *The Man Who Sold the World* in the spring of 1971 as preparation for his conquest of America. The trip had so invigorated him that he returned to Beckenham and wrote *Hunky Dory* and *The Rise and Fall of Ziggy Stardust and the Spiders from Mars*.

The second time David went to Hollywood, he went as Ziggy Stardust, the rock star he had invented so that he could become a star. On his third trip, he *was* Ziggy Stardust and *had* become a star.

By this trip, his fourth, another illusion had already taken shape. Ziggy would die, to be replaced by David Bowie, film star and director. The fact that he was so adored and his life seemed so charmed convinced everyone around him that he was always right no matter what he did. He liked it that way.

David adored symbols. To him success in Hollywood symbolized success in America. He believed that Hollywood was the most "plastic" place on earth, a factory town that manufactured and sold images. The plasticity intrigued him; he loved the idea of creating and manufacturing different images of himself. Here was the perfect place to fabricate the images, which could then be churned out and sold.

Going to Hollywood conjured his favorite Hollywood image: James Dean. He planned to cast himself as Dean. He would color his hair darker, take to wearing James Dean–style glasses, and go about striking James Dean-ish poses. Dean's image seemed to fit David's definition of the American male: sensitive and vulnerable yet macho and detached, androgynous and sexually appealing to both men and women. And Dean was so wonderfully tragic—exactly the way David wished to be perceived.

David was staying at the Beverly Wilshire Hotel because MainMan believed it exuded a feeling of affluence. Besides, the Beverly Hills Hotel had banned all rock stars after a suite had been demolished during a rock star's wild party. (It also found Tony Defries far too demanding a guest, and after his last visit had banned all MainMan personnel.)

The Wilshire demanded and got an extra $5,000 to hire extra security to protect David. Nonetheless, throughout his month in Los Angeles, groupies clawed their way into the hotel and scampered up and down the back staircases; some even made it into David's suite by scaling the balconies over the driveway until they reached David's balcony.

The musicians and roadies working on the tour were staying at the Sunset Marquis, a small rock-and-roll oriented apartment-hotel in West Hollywood. The tour members nicknamed the Wilshire "the Castle" because that's where the prince was staying; the Sunset Marquis became "the Plantation."

At the Wilshire David told Zanetta that he didn't want to go through the next three or four months of the tour encumbered by the giant set. He became very excited as he explained that he was into something new, and his new material didn't fit with the old set. Nor did he want to be pegged as a "theater artist," and the show he had been doing was much "too Broadway."

"I want the focus of the tour to be on music and not on theater," he continued. "So I want a clean, elegant image. A simple white background. A couple of levels. We can use slides and projections against that background to give the show some color."

As it happened, a gap had developed in the tour. Just that day seven dates had been canceled after it appeared that a promoter had refused to meet Defries's exorbitant financial demands. Now when the engagement at the Universal Amphitheatre ended on September 8, the show would play San Diego, Tucson, Phoenix, and wind up in Anaheim on September 16. The next date would be St. Paul on October 5. Everyone would be stationed in L.A. for the seventeen-day break between Anaheim and St. Paul.

"That would be the ideal time to change over to the new set," said David, handing Zanetta some sketches he had made on the train. They consisted of a white backdrop with him stage center at a microphone.

"I've made Carlos Alomar a member of the band; I want the backup singers out here to rehearse. I also want Ava on the tour, Z, you take care of it."

In the past whenever there was a change of plans either David or Defries would have convinced the other that it was the other's idea. Each wanted control, but without the responsibility for the outcome. Now David was calling all the shots by himself. He was going to prove he did not need Tony.

David had two reasons for abandoning the lavish set. First, his experience at Sigma convinced him that he had become a vocalist, an *American* pop-soul singer who had Number One hit records in America. Pop-soul singers did not put on extravaganzas like the Year of the Diamond Dogs.

But there was a deeper reason. Even though his interest in German expressionism had been the inspiration for the complicated Diamond Dogs physical production, it had been commissioned by MainMan operating on behalf of Tony Defries. Thus David viewed Diamond Dogs as a MainMan production. By dispensing with the set, he could symbolically castrate Defries. It was an act of open rebellion by a child who couldn't bring himself to cut the cord completely with his symbolic father.

He couldn't bring himself to tell Defries directly of his plans. He had persuaded Zanetta to go on the road so that Zanetta could be his spokesperson whenever information had to be conveyed to Defries. In the past Zanetta spoke for Defries; now he spoke for David. But Defries couldn't have cared less. He had no real desire to talk to David and was only too glad to speak to Zanetta in David's place. Zanetta had become their human telephone.

Zanetta knew that Defries would be infuriated by David's decision to abandon the set. But Defries, great actor that he was, would never let on. Defries had spent $400,000 to create the set in the first place; he expected the investment to pay off during the second part of the tour, which was expected to gross $3.7 million and net $537,000. MainMan's international press campaign had been a success; Defries was getting extravagant offers for the Year of the Diamond Dogs from every major European city.

As soon as Zanetta returned to the Sunset Marquis he called Defries to give him the news.

Defries thought it was a mistake, and that David was jumping too far ahead of himself without allowing the audience to catch up.

He had never liked the set in the first place, but all the publicity had made the show a must-see. Twenty-five American cities were awaiting it and no one knew how they would respond when David turned up with a white backdrop doing R-and-B versions of the David Bowie songbook. Then Tony shrugged it off. If that was what David wanted, that was what he was going to get.

In Hollywood, stars wanted to get to David to discover the secret of his magical hold on the public; movie producers wanted to check him out to see if he was right for the movies; an even greater army of male and female groupies was eager to claw its way into his hotel suite to discover his charms for themselves. A very few made it past the Beverly Wilshire security desk, Corinne, Stuie George, and Jim James.

The first to succeed was Marc Bolan, who was also staying at the Wilshire.

Bolan arrived with his girl friend, Gloria Jones, the black backup singer he later married. Meetings between David and Bolan were always interesting. Bolan's ex-wife, June, had been the source of much of his strength, as Angela had been the source of so much of David's. Bolan had replaced June with a black woman; David hadn't replaced Angela, but Ava was waiting anxiously in the wings.

The King of Glitter Rock and the King of Glam Rock were exceptionally cordial to each other. It was one of those deliciously ironic moments. After David had so consciously modeled himself after Bolan's splashy glitter image, Bolan had been replaced by David. Bolan had three times attempted to conquer America and each time failed; the hoopla surrounding David's arrival in Los Angeles made it appear that he was conquering America much the way the Beatles had, something Marc had never been able to accomplish.

Bolan was every inch "the Porky Pixie" the English press had labeled him. Bloated, fat, and very unhappy, he was still his arrogant self. Dropped by Warner Records, he was searching for a new American record deal and planned to attempt another tour of America.

Bolan was someone to take pity on, and when people were in trouble, David slipped into the role of wise father. The way he had been counseled by his father, Ken Pitt, and Tony Defries was the way he dealt with the lost children around him. He enjoyed playing daddy with Bette Midler, who could bring out a fatherly impulse in him, as could Ava.

Acting gentle and wise, he told Bolan how American audiences needed an American Hollywood-style image to which they could relate. They also needed an American sound; he suggested Bolan try R and B. They did not discuss Bolan's album, *Zinc Alloy and the Hidden Riders of Tomorrow*, which many critics felt had been Bolan's desperate attempt to regain his fame by cashing in on *Ziggy Stardust and the Spiders from Mars.* Nor did they discuss Bolan's last English tour, in which he attempted to duplicate Bowie's theatrics. At the end of the show Bolan had risen from the floor of the stage and had beaten a dummy amplifier with a whip until the amplifier exploded.

David wished Bolan, his whip, and his exploding amplifier well. They parted the best of friends.

The second person to get to David was Alan Yentob, a young, intense BBC filmmaker. On the spur of the moment Defries had agreed to allow Yentob to make a TV documentary about David in Los Angeles. Yentob had hired a crew and was ready to shoot. The only thing he did not have was David's cooperation.

At first David refused to meet with Yentob. The film had been Defries's idea, not his. Corinne and Zanetta pleaded with him. His response was the same as to any activity that involved strangers and forced him to put on a public mask. He turned childlike and demanded to be coaxed.

"Now?" he pleaded. "Doesn't he understand how much work I have to do? I just can't do it."

When they were at their wits' end he capitulated, and a plan was worked out. Zanetta would have lunch with Yentob and prepare him for David's arrival. David would meet them in the restaurant and not in the suite so that David could escape if he hated Yentob.

Two hours after Zanetta and Yentob sat down, David sailed into the restaurant. He was radiant and beautiful, every inch the star. All smiles and charm, he graciously took his seat and said, "All right. What do you have to say to me? What are you trying to sell me?"

It was a direct, funny opening, and Yentob liked him immediately.

It took David only a few minutes to agree. It would be a serious film called *Cracked Actor* after the song on the *Aladdin Sane* album. Yentob explained that he viewed the film as a study of a significant artist. It would deal with the great themes in David's life: his ability to create alter egos and present them in the context of rock and roll, and his vision of America as the source from which all contemporary myths sprang. Yentob pushed all the right buttons.

It would begin, explained Yentob, with a "plaster life cast" being made of David's face. All David had to do was sit still for one interview. Film editors would flesh out the show with interviews with fans, footage of the Year of the Diamond Dogs, and shots of

David riding in his MainMan limousine. The idea of a film about David Bowie in Hollywood was irresistible to David.

During the next three days, all of the major players in David's life gathered in Los Angeles. Even though they were his intimates, their paths rarely crossed. As usual, however, they were the more flamboyant actors, creating the ongoing drama that always surrounded David, who always chose to be a Buddha, the beacon of calm in the eye of the storms created by others.

First, Angela, Marion, and Zowie checked into the suite below David's. Defries and Melanie checked in. Defries insisted on staying in "the designer suite," so named because its walls were plastered with fashion sketches by prominent designers. Then Dana checked into the Wilshire, amid trunks filled with tight miniskirts, blouses with plunging necklines, and the ravishing gowns Angie had commissioned for her.

Dana was in Hollywood under the instruction of Defries. In a world in which image was everything, she was there to be seen. It was her job to look glamorous and sexy, lie alluringly by the pool, and look stunning in public. She was also going to host a tea party for the press. Every time she bent down to pick up the teapot the press would have a view of her magnificent breasts. Most of all, she was to spend whatever was necessary to be a MainMan "artiste" in good standing. In his own childlike way Defries was punishing David by flaunting the fact that his old girl friend had replaced him as Defries's favorite child.

As soon as she hit L.A. Angela assumed one of her favorite roles: Mrs. Bowie, the Superstar's Wife. She was going through a Grace Kelly period. She looked soft, and her hair was its natural ash blonde, grown to her shoulders. At first she wore a series of pretty sundresses. Then suddenly she decided to go Hollywood—she wanted to look like a "raving dyke" with a "big cock." Bowie's hairdresser, Jac Colello, slashed off her hair and dyed it platinum blonde, giving her the appropriate "butch look."

Playing the role of Mrs. Bowie to the hilt, and having a ball at it, she roamed Rodeo Drive with a vengeance. No $300 pair of underpants was left unpurchased; anyone with her was showered with lavish gifts. By nature Angela was generous to a fault, and had no difficulty using David's money to play tooth fairy. She dined at L.A.'s most expensive restaurants—Mr. Chow was among her favorites—and she boogied the night away at Studio One, the Sombrero revisited. She could be wild and bawdy there; surrounded by gay boys she was in her glory. She also visited the Plantation to hobnob with the workers and held court by the pool, making sure everyone was happy and relaxed. A group of gay groupies had followed David to L.A. and had checked into the Sunset Marquis. The closest they could come to him was Angela, and they fawned all over her; in return she played hostess, making sure their glasses were always filled and they had plenty to eat and drink.

During her stay in L.A. the Iceman had no patience for her, and she did not care to spend much time with him. She was there to have fun, not to play mommy.

Corinne Schwab never wore makeup and dressed plainly. She was about business and had the look of an office worker. Everyone made the mistake of not taking her seriously.

She lived at the Plantation. Every morning she got up at eight, pulled herself together, and headed for the Castle to spend her day keeping people away from David and coaxing him to do the things he resented doing but that were important to maintaining and increasing his success. Her day often didn't end until one or two in the morning.

She began most days with coffee poolside, accompanied by a crying jag and threats to quit. Tears streaming down her face, she complained that she had no life of her own and was very lonely in Los Angeles; either Angela or Tony had been rude to her; no one, including David, appreciated her. She wanted reassurance that she was needed and loved and was also essential to David's success. It was a terrible job, but she was glad to do it because David was so wonderful, and she loved him so much. Yet he paid so little attention to her. The dilemma set her brain on fire.

Corinne's theme song was "To know him is to love him." She sang it nonstop, and everybody in her immediate vicinity tapped their toes in time to the music. But they didn't really love him the way she did, and they certainly didn't want to be at his beck and call twenty-four hours a day. By default there was only Corinne, and by her mere presence every day she gained a little more power.

All she had to do was hang in and eventually there would only be her. Then he would *have* to pay attention.

Everyone seemed to be an actor and continued to play his part to the hilt, ignoring the fact that the curtain was inevitably going to ring down. And when it did the few smart ones—those whose self-reliance outweighed their addiction to the dumb show—would survive. The others would fall by the wayside.

Ava arrived on September 3, the day after David's opening night, and checked into the Sunset Marquis.

Surrounded by Angela, Ava, and Corinne, his harem was complete.

Then suddenly, out of nowhere, Iggy Pop appeared. He had been out of contact with David for over a year, and things seemed to have gotten worse for him. He looked like a ragamuffin. Iggy demanded money, food, and a place to sleep.

It was clear that Iggy admired David, but he was committed to upstaging him at every turn. Iggy could be a spontaneous madman; by nature David was overcontrolled. But David was fascinated by Iggy. Here was the real thing, not an actor who had invented a persona for himself, but a living, breathing example of the American rock-and-roll ethos. Iggy's on-again off-again struggle with drugs gave him the appearance of a doomed, tragic figure. His eyes may have been wild and his manner outrageous, but he was the classic victim.

By taking pity on Iggy and becoming his symbolic big brother, David enhanced his own feelings of nobility. Following David's lead, everyone was quite nice to Pop.

Meanwhile, Iggy roamed the Plantation, stealing small items from the rooms. Angela, who perceived him as a genius and, therefore, someone who could never be refused, summoned up her mother performance, allowing him to crash in her suite at the Castle. Later, David became especially magnanimous, and Iggy began to sleep in Stuie George's room in David's suite.

Corinne's last duty before each show was to stock David's suite with food and drink. Anyone who dropped in after the performance was to find a lavish display of refreshments. David never touched any of this food. Whenever the suite emptied, he ate by himself. He did not like to have other people watch him eat. As "artiste" and "alien being," he was beyond all mundane concerns.

Iggy did not share these pretensions. He liked to get on the phone in David's suite and have room service deliver enormous amounts of food. He devoured the food in front of David. Once he lifted his T-shirt and rubbed leftovers all over his body. David remained calm while "the Ig" did his routine. It was a waiting game. If he waited long enough Pop would be brought under control.

The Amphitheatre concerts were an amazing series of triumphs. The Hollywood elite was there in full force with the biggest furor created by Diana Ross. After her stunning movie debut in *Lady Sings the Blues*, everybody who was anybody in Hollywood referred to her as the "Queen of the Lot." When the queen arrived, there was pandemonium. Ross really knew how to make an entrance: preceded by a film crew and surrounded by cameramen and guards, she glided to her seat. Her shimmering floor-length gown picked up light, and her sparkle could be seen all over the house.

The Jackson Five also turned up. Their presence intrigued David. According to Bette Midler, they made the greatest American records. The previous March their record "Dancing Machine" had made it to Number Two on the *Billboard* chart. David was curious about thirteen-year-old Michael Jackson. Observing Michael close up might give him clues to enable him to enact his version of the teenage hit-maker.

As it turned out, Jackson was also intrigued by David. Any imaginative young singer had to be bowled over by David and the Day of the Diamond Dogs. Nine years after Bowie and Jackson first met, when Angela saw the Jacksons' Victory Tour in the summer of 1984, she observed, "It looks as if Michael unwittingly modeled his androgyny on David. He's doing his version of Ziggy Stardust up there." As David copied others, he also became a source from whom others borrowed freely.

One night Raquel Welch came to the show. Her entrance was surprisingly low key. Accompanied by Madeline Kahn, Welch was nothing like her sex goddess image. She was simply made up and wore an attractive rhinestone-studded T-shirt and denim jacket; Kahn, however, attempting to be the epitome of glamor, was dressed in a ball gown.

Dotted throughout the crowd on these nights were such film directors as John Avildson, Paul Mazursky, and Colin Higgins, there to size up David for the movies.

The only sour note came from Bob Hope, who lived near the Universal Amphitheatre and complained that the sound kept him up at night. Hope was such a powerful Hollywood figure that on succeeding nights the volume was turned down so that the comedian could get his rest.

David's "dressing room" was actually a suite of small rooms in a trailer behind the amphitheatre. Famous visitors dropped by before, during, and after the show. David was secure in a tiny room of his own at the end of the trailer. He greeted the few who were granted admission one at a time. It was easier to get an audience with the pope.

These visits confirmed to David and those around him that he had become a great Hollywood star. By leaving directly after the show, he missed Diana Ross's backstage visit. Ross asked if she could use David's john, and David's hairdresser, Jac Colello, stood guard at the bathroom door.

Around the pool at the Plantation the next day, the staffers kept repeating, "David was fabulous last night! Even Diana used his john!"

When Raquel Welch came back, David had not left yet and, as was the custom, she was kept waiting until David felt prepared to see her. "You look nothing like your pictures," she said sweetly to Angela.

Angela, whose look was always changing, never looked like her pictures. Nevertheless, all her insecurities came to the surface, and she began to fume. Did Raquel think her pictures were ugly? Or was she ugly in real life as opposed to her pictures? She became so upset she couldn't speak, turned on her heel, and marched away.

Finally, Corinne appeared from the bowels of the trailer to announce, "Miss Welch, Mr. Bowie will see you now." Welch was allowed a private fifteen-minute audience with David.

After Welch met Defries, an appointment was made for her to come to the Wilshire to discuss management with him. Such was Bowie's impact on Hollywood that stars like Raquel Welch were entertaining the notion of becoming MainMan "artistes" so that they, too, could synthesize contemporary music and theater under the aegis of Tony Defries, whom the press had labeled "the mysterious Svengali" guiding Bowie's spectacular career.

In Hollywood, by virtue of the Year of the Diamond Dogs,

Defries had taken on a special glow. He was the premier producer of a revolutionary new kind of concert event, one that combined music and theatrical production techniques never seen before; even more significantly, he was the producer of an event that was generating lots of money. In a city in which only the bottom line counts, Defries was perceived as a brand-new power broker.

During the week Welch came to the Wilshire to meet with Defries. Once again, she was casually dressed and simply made up.

Welch's approach to her career was a serious one. She explained that she had fifteen good years left in which to work; she wanted to do work for which she would be taken seriously, to expand into the cabaret field, launch a recording career, and develop on her own a series of suitable film projects. She was interested in having Tony Defries manage her for recording and live appearances.

Defries had a plan. He suggested that Welch become a spokesperson for cancer research.

She looked puzzled.

Defries explained that the cancer people would put up the money for her new endeavors. She could donate her services to cancer and they would pay for her new act. She wouldn't be at risk personally for any of the costs she incurred while creating her new image.

Even though she saw him a few more times, Welch did not sign with Defries and become the "cancer woman." She liked him and his odd style of dealing with the realities of show business. Years later, she looks back at that moment and recalls that she did not go with Defries because she found the rock-and-roll environment in which he was traveling "too funky."

"I've never been funky," she says of herself.

Not everyone who got backstage to see David was a star. One of his visitors was a well-known L.A. figure whose face was perpetually twisted into an eager grin. He was the type of character who could exist only in Los Angeles. He was rich and loved to be around rock-and-roll stars. They made him feel young. He got backstage simply by giving cocaine to the guards. In Los Angeles, a supply of cocaine gets anyone in anywhere.

When he met David, he slipped him a vial of "merk," three grams of medicinal cocaine. It was the best cocaine David had ever had. David's benefactor never had trouble getting backstage again.

As expected, the press reception to the show was spectacular.

Dedicated fan Robert Hilburn wrote in the *Los Angeles Times*: "Bowie is, by far, the most arresting figure to enter pop music in the 1970's and, I have a suspicion, he still is a long way from his peak."

On September 5, the fourth night of the L.A. run, David began to introduce his new songs with the backup singers accompanying him. Ava had suffered from terrible stage fright that night.

"I can't play in front of all those people," she told David.

"Yes, you can. I'll help you. You'll be able to," he replied.

During the show he headed toward her, smiling entrancingly. His seven spotlights followed him. Then he began to sing along with her into her vocal mike. Suddenly, Ava was sharing the spotlight with him. It was incredibly exciting, and seemed to fulfill David's prophecy that he would make her a star.

"That night is the best memory I have of my experience with David," she recalls. Onstage David was generous and caring; offstage he was totally self-involved. "As an artist he was totally a different person," she adds. "And I loved him and I still do."

The results of the musical transformation would do much to enhance his myth, but would also contribute to his personal misery.

During the performances Alan Yentob's film crew ground away, photographing the concerts, and interviewing fans.

Comparing Ziggy to Jimi Hendrix, one fan said of Ziggy, "He's like a rock-and-roll star who gets too big for his britches. He gets really, really immensely popular, and because of this he gets kind of very corrupted, and it becomes his downfall. . . ."

The Bowie caught by Yentob's camera really was the "cracked actor" of the documentary's title. David wore his tinted James Dean glasses, a fur-trimmed coat, and a fedora pulled down over his eyes. He looked frail, sickly, spooky, and alone. The most unnerving scene of all pictured David pressing himself back into the seat of his MainMan limousine while he traveled across the desert. One of his favorite records, Aretha Franklin's "You Make Me Feel Like a Natural Woman," blared from his cassette player. Next to him, Corinne, grinning sweetly, bopped in time to the music. It looked as if David were trying to disappear into the seat. His isolation was painful to watch.

During his on-camera interview, he was diffident and manifested a spaced-out quality, relying on the pretentious, existentialism-flavored rhetoric that had gotten him through other interviews. In an interview, David said, "A lot of my space creations are in fact facets of me. I have since discovered—and I wouldn't admit that to myself at the time—that I would put everything, just make myself a little kind of up-front personification of how I felt about things. . . . they're all facets of me. . . . I got lost at one point and I couldn't decide whether I was writing the characters or whether the characters were writing me, or whether we were all one and the same."

It was the beginning of his public stance of rock star as victimized drug burnout, Ziggy Stardust–like shadow mask that he believed would create the illusion of authenticity.

After two days of working with Yentob David grew bored. He didn't have to say anything; Corinne erected her impenetrable shield, and Yentob was cut off. The show would be pasted together from the interviews with David and the concert footage.

The nights at the Amphitheatre continued to be shining examples of Hollywood glamor, but the days at the Wilshire were far from glamorous. Production coordinator Fran Pillersdorf went there one day to visit David. "Corinne and Stuie were holding down the living room," she recalls. "I remember I had to go to the bathroom and decided to go past David's bedroom. If a room can give off a sad vibration, that was the one. It was dark in the middle of a bright California day. There were bottles and cocaine from the night before, and there was David lying in the dark room with the door ajar. He was bone tired and freaked out."

Few rock stars have been photographed more often than David Bowie. He insisted that every change in his appearance be documented by the still cameras. Now, he wanted new stills to accompany the release of *Young Americans*. The jacket of the album would represent Bowie as a star in the "old Hollywood" tradition; the press photos would represent his "new Hollywood" look, based on photographs of James Dean.

Terry O'Neill was assigned to shoot these pictures. The session was to take place in the Playboy Building on Hollywood Boulevard.

Before it, while Jac Colello was doing his hair, David's eyes drifted to the window. He was staring at the gas station across the street.

"That station's going to blow up," he announced ominously.

"Sure, David," said Colello as he turned on the blow dryer.

David was not kidding around. "That station is going to blow up!" he repeated emphatically. It was as if he could see into the future, even make the explosion happen through his powers of concentration.

Suddenly, smoke began to billow up from across the street.

"Go to the window," ordered David, "and tell me everything you see." Colello looked out at the thick black smoke. "It's getting worse," he said.

The coincidence was enough to trigger the imaginations of David's small group. Not only could David see the future, but he was also in danger. There *was* going to be an explosion. He could die!

Overcome by panic, they formed a protective net around David and fled from the studio into the street.

At a moment like this, the only thing to do was make a quick getaway, but David's limousine wasn't there. David turned ashen. There were some kids sitting in a car parked outside the building. Corinne dashed over to it.

"We've got to get David out of here," she said frantically. "Can we use your car?"

The kids were thrilled to have David Bowie in their beat-up Volkswagen. As they pulled away from the curb, flames shot up and engulfed the entire gas station. They all knew it was a matter of seconds before the explosion.

Lost in thought, David sat back against the seat. "David thinks he has these special powers," recalls Jac Colello. "He was really shaken up. Corinne and I were really totally freaked out. It was really scary."

CHAPTER 23

Soul Man

On September 9 Defries checked out of the Beverly Wilshire and returned to New York. Delighted to be on his own, David gave a sigh of relief. Dana also checked out. While David adored her, she was now Defries's favorite child. Her departure also pleased him. Angela remained behind, but she was too busy having fun to make David enact the role of loving husband. He was glad not to be coerced into a role that he resented.

He was in a merry mood as the Year of the Diamond Dogs set out for San Diego, Phoenix, Tucson, and Anaheim, the last concerts to feature the giant set. He was with family, *his* family.

In the audience at Anaheim Stadium were such diverse stars as Elton John, Desi Arnaz, Sally Kellerman, and director John Carpenter. But there was one star there whose presence eclipsed that of everyone else. All the tour members were on tenterhooks. Would she come backstage to meet David? They need not have feared; nothing was going to stop Elizabeth Taylor.

Surrounded by seven male escorts, dressed in a flamboyant purple caftan with a huge diamond ring planted brazenly on her finger, Taylor sailed past Stuie George, past Jim James, past Corinne, and headed straight for David. Bodyguards and retainers meant nothing to her. She was a force of nature.

For a second David was taken aback. But he quickly assumed his Prince Charming mask, attempted to match the dazzle of her ring with some dazzle of his own.

Despite Taylor's fame and glamor, her style that night was not at all grand. She was really "just plain folks," and he did "I'm just a normal guy." By the time they were done, they had convinced each other that they were dear old friends.

◇ David and Mick Jagger, 1974 (*Dana Gillespie*).

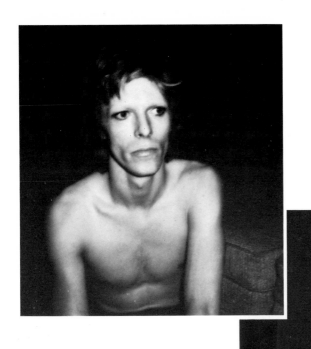

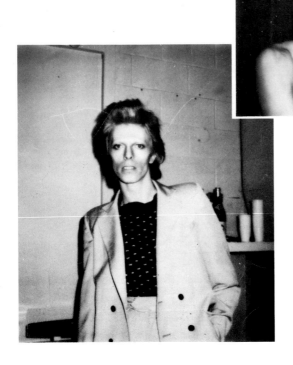

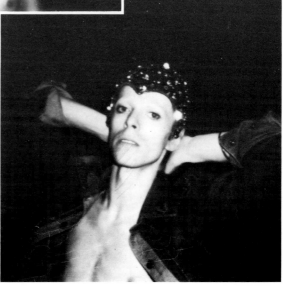

◇ Bowie trying out new looks,
1974 (*Dana Gillespie*).

◇ Freddi Burrett, David's "pretend" lover, the costume designer who helped develop the Ziggy Stardust look (*Dana Gillespie*).

◇ David's son Zowie at the Sherry Netherland in New York, 1974 (*Dana Gillespie*).

◇ MainMan vice president Jaime Andrews and David's personal assistant Corinne Schwab, 1974 (*Dana Gillespie*).

◇ Cherry Vanilla, former Madison Avenue·ad executive who headed MainMan's radio, television, and film department (*Dana Gillespie*).

◇ Geoffrey MacCormack with Gui Andrisano, the backup singers for the Diamond Dogs show, 1974 (*Dana Gillespie*).

◇ Bowie's long-term producer Tony Visconti (*Dana Gillespie*).

◇ David being made up for the Diamond Dogs television commercial, 1974.

◊ David with Tony Zanetta and Cherry Vanilla, who produced the commercial (*James J. C. Andrews collection*).

◊ Ava Cherry in Cherry Vanilla's unreleased video for "I Am a Laser" (*James J. C. Andrews collection*).

◊ Bowie on the *Diamond Dogs* set, 1974 (*James J. C. Andrews collection*).

◊ Painting by Guy Peellaert commissioned for the *Diamond Dogs* album cover but not used (*James J. C. Andrews collection*).

◊ MainMan's million-dollar campaign: billboards for MainMan artistes David Bowie and Mick Ronson on the Sunset Strip, Los Angeles, 1974 (*James J. C. Andrews collection*).

◇ Bowie and Vandross turn ''Funky Music'' into ''Fascination'' (*Tony Zanetta collection*).

◊ Bowie rehearses "Soul Train" in Los Angeles. From left, Mike Garson, Bowie, Pablo Rosario, Luther Vandross, and Ava Cherry (*Tony Zanetta collection*).

◊ David with Ronnie Spector and Iggy Pop at the party after the Thin White Duke performance at Madison Square Garden, 1976 (© *Andrew Kent, 1976*).

◊ David and Coco Schwab on their way to Europe, 1976 (© *Andrew Kent, 1976*).

◊ Bowie in a sailor cap during his 1978 world tour (*Paul Fusco/Magnum*).

◇ Carlos Alomar, Bowie, and unidentified musician during the Serious Moonlight tour in Washington in 1983 (© *Gamma, Liaison G. Mathieson*).

◇ An unglamorous Bowie snaps photogs in 1984 (© *RDR Productions, 1984*).

◇ Bowie at a press conference in New York in 1984 (*Ebet Roberts*).

Two weeks of rehearsals had been scheduled in Los Angeles before the tour was to go back onto the road on October 11. This would give Bowie, the musicians, and the vocalists time to get used to the new white backdrop, the new costumes designed by Freddi Burrett in New York City under David's direction, and the new songs.

During the first rehearsal, Elizabeth Taylor, escorted by her hairdresser, sauntered into the studio and plunked herself down beside David's hairdresser, Jac Colello. She was wearing a different violently colored caftan and a different huge diamond ring. She also had a bottle of Jack Daniels from which she occasionally took a sip. Unlike David, who made careful choices before he launched a conversation, Taylor chattered away with everyone who approached her. Warm, friendly, and unpretentious, her manner enabled people to transcend their awe. Her rehearsal visits soon became part of the regular routine.

Bowie's social skills were instinctive. Somehow the person he was with believed he had been given precisely what he wanted. David sensed that Taylor had to be reassured about her beauty and talent, but he also sensed that if he made himself too available she would lose interest. Both stars had an instinct for playacting, demanded the world be run strictly on their terms, and were easily bored. So they both set out to be scintillating.

Ava was very impressed by Elizabeth Taylor. She recalls, "We were rehearsing, doing vocals, and she was just sitting there. David kept going over and talking to her. He was really impressed. He was really playing up to her, he was kissing her. He was doing a whole number."

Then the next night David's manner changed abruptly. Observed Jac Colello, "Liz would try and talk to David, but David was too busy rehearsing. So she just sat there watching."

Like everyone else who came into David's orbit, Taylor was hooked. At four in the afternoon, as soon as Taylor awoke, she started her "morning" by calling David at the Wilshire. They had long conversations, with Elizabeth doing most of the talking while David supplied witty rejoinders during pauses. David also performed one of his favorite roles: sister. They talked about clothes, makeup, hairstyles, as well as the history of Hollywood. Elizabeth also discussed her long string of illnesses and her endless marital difficulties.

She invited David to appear in her new film, *The Bluebird*, an adaptation of Maurice Maeterlinck's fairy-tale play. In it she would play four characters: Mother, Maternal Love, Witch, and Light. The film would be shot in Russia, the first Soviet-American co-production in history.

No sooner had Elizabeth extended the invitation than the offer was leaked to the press. David loved all the attention Taylor was giving him, but he was also suspicious. While he prided himself on his ability to manipulate the press, he knew he was no match for Elizabeth Taylor. She was a great star in the classic tradition, and her every move was news. She was always in the headlines.

His appearances at the Universal Amphitheatre had proved that he was the hottest new star in Hollywood. Elizabeth Taylor was a middle-aged woman with nine flop movies in a row, whose days as the queen of box office had long been over. Yet she had made it seem that she was doing him the favor by inviting him to be in *The Bluebird*. Although he was not sure, David believed that she was using him to get publicity for herself and create the impression that she was a contemporary of America's brightest new rock superstar. She fascinated, amused, and scared him.

Despite the fact that the last thing he wanted to do was make his movie debut by going to Russia to co-star with Elizabeth Taylor in some obscure movie, he continued to be wonderfully charming to her. One of his ambitions when he got to Hollywood was to become a film star and director. He believed that Elizabeth's attentions were a signal to the film industry that he was movie material.

It was also another slap in the face of Tony Defries, and that pleased him no end. For a year Defries had been working with CMA's Stevie Phillips to find David a suitable movie role. All David had to do was turn up, and none other than Elizabeth Taylor dropped a movie offer on his plate, another demonstration that he did not need Tony Defries anymore. He had become *Bowie* and didn't need anybody anymore.

One night Taylor invited him to a party at her house. When he returned early in the morning Ava was waiting up for him. He had not slept with Elizabeth; David craved attention so much that he could never have kept that a secret. But he had had an adventure in the house. When he went to the bathroom, the bathroom doorknob had come off in his hand. He had become so embarrassed he didn't dare tell Elizabeth. But it had proved how "plastic" the house was and served as a symbol of the plasticity of Hollywood and, therefore, of America.

Even though he was reclusive by nature, David's friendship with his new "best friend" encouraged him to venture out of his suite at the Beverly Wilshire, first to another party to which Elizabeth invited him. He acted the role of "bright new star," and with Elizabeth by his side, it was a role in which he was comfortable.

That party was a birthday party for Ricci Martin, Dean Martin's son, held at the home of Martin's estranged wife, Jeanne.

When David entered the room, his eyes roamed over the crowd searching for Elizabeth. On one side of her stood Elton John; on the other side stood John Lennon. As soon as she spotted David, she beckoned him over.

"David, do you know John?" she asked.

"No. But I've always wanted to meet him."

David stared into John Lennon's eyes; his smile was bewitching.

Despite Lennon's fame, he was fascinated by other stars and had been eager to meet Elizabeth Taylor. He had also listened to David's records and was well aware of the impact David was having in Los Angeles. He was a very funny man, as was David.

David, John, Elton, and Elizabeth settled down to amusing each other. They traded quips back and forth, each trying to outdo the other. Soon, they were all roaring with laughter. Then it all became too much for David, and he began to feel claustrophobic. He said goodnight, and everyone assumed he had left. Later that night, Lennon, who at the time had left Yoko Ono and was living in Los Angeles with his assistant May Pang, wandered into the back of the house. John and May found David and Elizabeth sitting together on a couch in a deserted room, staring into each other's eyes and whispering to each other. Lennon and Pang both felt as if they had invaded a secret meeting place.

Taylor spotted them. "May, John," she called out, "come join us."

John and May sat down with them and the laughter started all over again. By the time the evening was over David and John had promised to see each other again.

The two-week rehearsal period proved especially joyous for David. He loved working with his new musicians and backup singers. The sensation that he was in charge of the show and was its one and only director also invigorated him. And he adored his new "soul man" Shadow, and worked hard to lower his voice so that it would sound dark, husky, and black.

While songs like "Space Oddity," which might reflect back on Ziggy Stardust, were dropped from the show, only four new tunes were added. The songs to which Ronno had given an English blues-rock feel and had then been subjected to jazz-Latino stylings were now converted to funk by Carlos Alomar.

David had become the rock music equivalent of his old mentor Lindsay Kemp. Kemp, heading his own company of actors performing mimes he created, had cast himself in the once great English tradition of actor/manager. David believed he was his own actor/manager, but unlike Kemp, who was also in charge of the business end of the company, David studiously avoided the business details of the forthcoming tour.

David never expressed affection in public. This time, though, he really did love his new musical "family." The only way David knew how to show his love for his new family was by allowing them to share the spotlight with him. So each would get a solo spot. It was the same sort of onstage generosity that had propelled him to share his spotlight with Ava Cherry at the Universal Amphitheatre.

An Englishman with no real experience in the world of rhythm and blues was hardly the best choice to put together a slick, sassy, R-and-B revue. David had attended a performance or two at America's premier black variety house, the Apollo Theatre in Harlem. Apollo performances were notorious for their length and energy. The black audience worked hard for its money; it demanded—and received—an enormous amount of entertainment in return. David gleaned the surfaces of things, using them as sources for his work. His few visits to the Apollo and the help of guitarist Carlos Alomar and vocalist Luther Vandross were all he believed he needed to create his own version of "A Night at the Apollo." His egoism blinded him to his inexperience in this area. And there wasn't any objective input. Once upon a time he had had Angela and Defries. On the Year of the Diamond Dogs, there had been Jules Fisher, and others. Now there was no one.

There wasn't a white English rock musician alive who didn't fantasize about being a get-down black soul man. David was the only one of them, however, who had the courage to act out that fantasy in front of the press and public. Emphatically professional, the group delivered the goods as best they could as they set out creating the "black-and-British" show. Whatever "the Bossman" wanted they were there to give him.

David also evolved an interesting new look for his new persona. He wanted something original but with mass appeal. Androgyny, otherworldliness, and stating that one is homosexual could make one famous, but that kind of fame was the death knell to the radio air play in America that resulted in a hit record. What could be straighter than a soul man?

First he had his hair dyed a gleaming orangey yellow. Then it was cut longer in the front and somewhat shorter in the back. Finally Jac Colello brushed it tightly across his forehead and used huge amounts of hair spray to keep it plastered down.

David's costume consisted of baggy trousers held up by brightly colored suspenders, an extremely short tan and brown jacket cut tight at the waist, buttoned over a blue shirt and a light necktie slightly loosened at the neck. He also carried a walking stick. When he made his entrance, a spotlight mounted on the apron of the stage would hit him from below, thrusting a huge silhouette of him against the translucent white backdrop stretched across the stage.

Part Edwardian dandy, part 1950s American teenager, the look reflected the fact that David had no notion whatsoever of what a soul man ought to look like. But David was convinced he was on the right track. As he had loved all his previous looks, he loved this look, and believed it was *the* look toward which he had always been striving.

Just before the end of the rehearsal period, it was decided that Corinne, who was at the breaking point, needed a short holiday. Angela and Jac Colello would take her to San Francisco for the weekend. Angela, as always good-hearted, loved the idea of playing Corinne's visiting nurse, and the two women got along well. Smart enough to know that a dose of her harshness would trigger one of Angela's outbursts, something David couldn't stand, Corinne always minded her p's and q's around the mercurial Mrs. Bowie.

As soon as they hit San Francisco, Angela encountered a sexy young rock-and-roller. A short while later, even though she was supposed to be looking after Corinne, she disappeared.

She returned two days later with an ingenious explanation for her absence. "Darlings!" she exclaimed. "You can't imagine what I've been through. This boy kept me locked up for two days. He held me at gunpoint. I was in great danger."

As always everyone roared with laughter.

Upon Angela's return, she and Corinne returned to Los Angeles. Corinne felt obligated to be near David, and Angela wanted to be in L.A. to celebrate her twenty-fourth birthday the next day. Colello remained in San Francisco.

A day or two later he received an urgent call from Corinne. Elizabeth Taylor and David were going to be photographed together for *People* magazine. Jac was needed immediately to do David's hair.

He hurried back to Los Angeles, and the next day he and David went to the simple white Bel Air house in which Taylor was living.

It was decided to photograph the two stars in the garden. Taylor would sit regally on a rattan garden chair while Bowie stood behind her, one hand resting affectionately on her shoulder. After a while Elizabeth sailed out of the house looking ravishing.

David and Elizabeth's familiarity with each other seemed to reflect the fact that in many ways they were each other's mirrors. Both were very late to every appointment; both had staffs to pick up after them; both were coquettes who exuded enormous sexuality and seemed used to sexual conquest as a symbol of power. But they were gentle with each other. It was as if two great warriors had met, each of whom respected the other.

The shot was set up. Taylor played the eternal beauty; Bowie the handsome new man about town. Both caressed the camera with their eyes. They looked striking together, the exotic collision of two larger-than-life myths.

They were both expert image-makers. Taylor projected another facet of her mystique: not even the most exciting new rock star of the 1970s could resist her orbit. David was pleased because this was another career move he had made without Tony Defries. Being side by side with the greatest movie star in history seemed to him to demonstrate they were equals.

CHAPTER 24

Breaking Away

I t was the most illusory tour of all.

Launched in St. Paul on October 3, 1974, Tour Five was scheduled to set down in Indianapolis; Madison, Wisconsin; Milwaukee; Detroit; Chicago; then back to New York City for five nights at Radio City Music Hall; and on to Cleveland; Buffalo; Washington, D.C.; Boston; Pittsburg; Philadelphia, winding up in Atlanta on December 1.

For the most part David operated in a state of bliss during the first five dates. Entranced by his new musicians and backup singers and enamored by his new soul-man persona, more than ever he loved getting up on stage each night. This was *his* tour, and *he* was calling all the shots.

The cracks in the actor's exquisite armor would not wrench open until he returned to New York City at the end of October. So far he had avoided any contact with MainMan, but when he got to New York he would be reminded that he was not his own man, but a MainMan "artiste," the one to turn a large profit and the one MainMan chose to ignore. He would also be reminded of his financial relationship with Tony Defries. No matter how hard David worked, Tony had legal control of all of his money. Although he worked for MainMan, MainMan did not work for him but for Defries. He would also receive the worst critical drubbing of his career.

The audience in Indianapolis on opening night was splattered with glitter-rockers, the audience who waited expectantly for its spaceman hero to arrive. Few rock stars have ever had so many fans who insisted on copying his look. David had become the first great pop hero of the "Me Decade."

A cheer went up as the lights dimmed, and the audience sat forward. A murmur of surprise greeted the twelve musicians and singers, nine of whom were black. For the most part the ensemble looked chubby, odd, and out of place.

The show began with a long funky version of "Love Train." The audience became restless and stayed that way until intermission. The audience was still very puzzled.

After a half-hour intermission, David's entrance was preceded by a five-minute soul rave-up by the musicians and singers. Then he bounded out, bristling with nervous energy. His vision of soul man was an athletic one. He raced from one side of the stage to the other and fell to his knees to rock back and forth in time to the music as he growled "Rock and Roll With Me." Soul also meant sexuality and he punctuated some songs by hunching over and grabbing his crotch while his face was transformed into a mask of ecstasy. He accompanied his new husky, deep soul-man's voice with a wide range of facial expressions. One minute his tightly closed eyes registered anguish and pain, the next minute he exhibited wide-eyed glee. His hands moved in large arcs as if he were a preacher and his audience a congregation.

The audience ate it up. Before the first number was over they were already rushing down the aisle to the footlights. They lifted their hands in supplication, their eyes begging him to reach down and bless them. It was exactly the reaction the MainMan staff had initiated and David had demanded during Tour One. But now he was doing it on his own.

As David sang he reached out to graze their fingertips with his. They were beside themselves. Whether they really liked the music was beside the point, and in any case not a question they would have pondered. David was a mythic figure, and they were cheering the fact that they were in the presence of the myth. Most had not seen Ziggy Stardust, nor would they see the Year of the Diamond Dogs. They hailed him as much for what he had already done and they had missed as for the performance he was giving them that night.

Things were going less well offstage.

Ava was concerned that David might decide to try heroin under the influence of groupies hanging around the tour. "I gave David pep talks," she recalls. "I thought he needed people to care that he didn't mess with that, that it was a bad trip."

There was a surprise visitor in Detroit, the fourth date of the tour. David's venerable Hollywood benefactor had arrived, his pockets bulging with cocaine. Under the influence of this exceptionally pure stash, David's version of Ziggy Stardust came vividly to life. He listened to the radio and heard a news story about a flying saucer that supposedly had crash landed, and he said that he already knew about it.

That night he came late to the theater, carrying an ounce bag of cocaine, which got spilled all over the dressing room. During the performance the stagehands rolled dollar bills into cylinders and crawled around the floor snorting it up.

"I'll just get another bag," David announced merrily.

On stage that night David told the audience about the flying saucer, and extraterrestrial creatures in general, indicating that he was on intimate terms with these beings from another time and place. He was disappointed that no one around him seemed interested.

After the show, he stayed up to two in the morning, talking fervently about three-inch spacemen.

Meanwhile Jac Colello was also having problems with Corinne. He believed that she had begun to fall in love with him. "She would get mad if I was going out while she was stuck in the hotel room alone," he recalls. "She felt I should be with her at all times. I used to have to sneak out of my hotel room or lie to her."

A pattern was forming. Eventually even David would, on occasion, have to find ways around Corinne's enormous displeasure when she felt that those she loved were trying to desert her.

In Chicago, the next stop on the tour, David and Ava toured the city's hot spots after his shows. Chicago was Ava's hometown, and she was glad to be back. With David's permission she did a number of interviews. In the Chicago press, she was "local girl made good."

One night they went to the Playboy Mansion to shoot pool and hang out with Ava's friend Claudia Jennings, a ravishing Playmate of the Year. Also with them was Ava's gorgeous sister, Tandalaya Shimek.

That night they were also supposed to have dinner with Ava's parents. Scheduled to arrive at Ava's home at ten, they turned up at three in the morning. Ava's parents didn't seem to mind. They were thrilled to see their beloved daughter, who was doing so well. She was performing in a show that was the hottest ticket in Chicago; she was featured in all of the newspapers; her boyfriend was the sensation of the 1970s.

David was intrigued by Mrs. Cherry, a handsome, stylish woman dressed in an elegant suit for the occasion. He also loved being welcomed to the home of these warm, friendly blacks. After an enormous meal of pot roast, collard greens, and corn muffins, "He took out a vial of coke and started doing it at the dinner table," Ava recalls. "My mother and father pretended as though it didn't happen. They were very cool. My father was so nice to him; my mother liked him so much."

Acceptance by Ava's parents convinced David that he was finally an authentic soul man.

Guitarist Carlos Alomar had quickly developed real respect for David, who had obviously done his homework. One day on the road he opened up "two trunks filled with a record collection of all the R-and-B going all the way back to the 1940s. He had more R-and-B training than I had. My training started at the Apollo, which was present-day music. I never had a chance to go back. I had to learn the stuff that was happening now.

"His stuff went all the way back: Cab Calloway up to early Dionne Warwick."

But the reviews were mixed. The critics who loved David applauded the transformation; those who didn't were appalled. The promoters were in an uproar. They had booked the Year of the Diamond Dogs and got a soul revue in its place. Without a hit record or the giant set, they were afraid the show, especially on Defries's extremely stiff terms, was not going to sell out.

Oblivious to it all, David was as pleased as punch. He had done it on his own, with no visible help from Tony Defries.

Whatever David thought he was accomplishing by his acts of independence on the road, he received neither praise nor blame from Tony Defries on his return to New York to play Radio City Music Hall at the end of October. Defries transcended his problems with David by making himself invisible. There were neither phone calls nor visits.

Nonetheless, Defries's control was evident from the moment David arrived in New York. While David was on the road, the MainMan suite at the Sherry Netherland had been relinquished. Unused for three months, Defries had given it up in one of those frequent power plays he called "economy moves." Even though David was ensconced in a lavish suite at the Hotel Pierre, the message was clear.

The only thing that seemed to concern anyone at MainMan about David was that he keep touring. A tentative itinerary of his first South American tour had even been drawn up. On January 10 he was scheduled to set sail for a twelve-day trip to concert dates in Rio.

David had been scheduled to play three shows at Radio City, November 1, 2, and 3. They had been quick sellouts, and so Defries had added two more nights at the beginning of the engagement; David's new opening date was October 30. No amount of advertising had filled the house for the first two nights. Privately the promoters voiced the opinion that David had come back to New York too soon after his two performances at Madison Square Garden. There just weren't twenty-five thousand fans in New York City willing to pay Defries's exorbitant ticket prices for Bowie's pop-soul revue only four months after seeing the elaborate Year of the Diamond Dogs. A hit record would have provided the promotional oomph to make all of the shows go clean, but David was still working on his new album. It was as if they were all chasing their own tails, but David was the one who was going to have to go on stage to play to empty seats, the thing he detested more than anything else.

Though he said nothing, Defries's attitude implied that David's inability to sell out the five shows was a reflection of his failure as an artist, an attitude that was picked up by the MainMan staff. A feeling of failure also permeated the atmosphere at the Music Hall. Attuned to subtle nuances, David sensed that he was being perceived as a failure. That made his own sense of failure rise to the surface. He did not have a hit record, had no control over his money, and Tony Defries was ignoring him.

A week before the opening night, a twist of fate occurred that made the New York media skeptical about David, his constantly changing personas, and MainMan's arrogant hard-sell.

ABC-TV screened an hour-and-a-half special on the Hammersmith-Odeon "Retirement Concert" of the year before. Despite David's endless noodling with the sound track, the sound had been terrible; and a few foolish moments had occurred on screen that had nothing to do with David. In addition, during "Suffragette City" the censors, reflecting network television's squeamish attitude toward rock and roll, had bleeped the words "Wham, bam" because they suggested sexual intercourse. David ended up singing, "Bleep, bleep, thank you ma'am." The word "suicide" was bleeped from "Rock and Roll Suicide," forcing David to sing, "I'm a rock and roll bleep." Probably the feeling was that after a Canadian adolescent hanged himself after watching Alice Cooper enact an onstage suicide, the word itself might be enough to inspire members of the viewing audience to take their lives.

At the end of the tape, David said those famous words, "Well, thank you. This is my last concert, not only for this tour, but forever."

The lie did not matter to the fans who would flock to the venerable hall during the forthcoming week. But it convinced the press that David was an opportunist who would—and did—say or do anything to become famous. David's "retirement" had been part of Defries's strategy, but David would be held responsible for it; Tour Five had been entirely David's creation, and he would be held responsible for it too.

The New York opening was a difficult one. The sound system at Radio City Music Hall was muffled. After the brouhaha over the sound at the beginning of the Year of the Diamond Dogs, one would have expected never again to encounter sound problems. Also David was hoarse, and from the stage he could see the empty seats.

This performance, designed to incite a frenzied response from the extremely willing crowd, was the most maniacally energized of the tour. "David was really wired," recalls percussionist Pablo Rosario. "He was doing too much cocaine. He looked like a tiger in a cage going from side to side of the stage."

There were those in the audience who emphatically disliked Bowie's latest incarnation. During the set a voice rang out, "Get off the stage." A few minutes later the heckler called, "We want our money back. We want Ziggy Stardust."

David turned to backup singer Gui Andrisano. "David made milk look pale," he remembers.

Lindsay Kemp was in the audience. In his typical dramatic fashion he likened David to a Christian martyr. David was sacrificing his rock singer self so that he could go on to the next phase of his work.

David was delighted with Lindsay's mixture of Christian symbolism and symbolic death and rebirth. For the moment he seemed to believe it was true.

After the show David and Zanetta returned alone to the suite at the Pierre. It seemed so anticlimatic. There was no party to refuse to attend, no people coming to the door to whom they could refuse admittance—none of the events that had marked previous opening nights.

David sat crumpled up on the couch, presenting himself as an icon of exhaustion.

"It was humiliating to open to an unfull house," he said. "The press was there, and it looked like I couldn't sell New York."

He was right. In certain ways he was instinctively shrewder than Defries.

Zanetta sensed that they were both bored. David needed some new audience members in the room; neither his "servants" nor his "family" satisfied him anymore. Finally the phone rang. Alice Cooper and a rock music journalist friend were in the lobby. Cooper seemed the ideal new blood. David signaled to Zanetta to have them come up.

It was an interesting encounter. Although David had adopted Alice's theatrics as his own, he resented the inevitable comparisons. He felt obliged to "father" Alice, as he fathered other confused stars such as Marc Bolan and Bette Midler.

"I've abandoned theatrics," he said quietly. "It gives me more options. It's easy to get trapped by your stage presentation; the secret is to find a way to move on."

Cooper, riveted by David's quiet intensity, listened carefully. They made a very odd father-son combination.

Zanetta excused himself for a minute to go down to the lobby for a pack of cigarettes. In the lobby he ran into Lance Loud, the son of television's extraordinary Loud family. At that time Loud was writing about rock music for *Circus* magazine. He was with Janis Cavasso, whom David had met at the beginning of U.S. Tour One. Zanetta invited them back to the suite.

Zanetta loved to play Tony Defries. David was an enthusiastic audience for these loud, forceful "I-have-the-courage-to-say-anything" demonstrations. Tonight, in his manic boredom, Zanetta felt like needling Alice. David was always receptive to a bit of theater.

"Alice, what you are is a vaudevillian," began Zanetta. "You'd be great on television, you could be a comedian. David, on the other hand, is a great 'artiste.' Alice, you're 'show business.' David has made an art out of performance."

It was a statement typical of the arrogance of MainMan officers. David smiled, liking what he had just heard. Then he echoed Zanetta.

"You could have a brilliant future in television," he said politely. "You are a great comedian."

Janis Cavasso stared skeptically at the pair. She found it hard to take seriously anyone who insisted on being treated like a god and who had retainers to fawn over him, pay him compliments, and refill his glass when it was empty.

Since there were two reporters in the room, this encounter would inevitably wind up in print. David fixed Alice with a penetrating stare and continued to offer career guidance. He explained that his current entry into rhythm and blues allowed far more freedom than the rigidity of his theatrics. He said he always gave great performances, which he sometimes turned into fantastic events.

He spoke with so much charm that everyone seemed to agree that he *was* great and fantastic.

He told everyone that his public demanded that he be invincible.

Then he got up and tried to turn on the videotape unit. He fumbled; simply turning on the switch seemed to be difficult for him. Everyone involuntarily leaned forward as if collectively they could will the machine to go on. Finally his image flooded the screen.

David's guests had been transformed into David's audience. They did not know that every performance was videotaped, and that David studied himself on television after each of his shows. They watched David enjoying himself on screen. His self-absorption was hypnotic.

Eventually Alice Cooper and his journalist friend said goodnight and left. David turned to Janis Cavasso. He wanted to do a little market research.

"Did you see the show?" he asked.

"Yes." He looked at her expectantly.

Cavasso, not a member of David's inner court, had no difficulty speaking her mind. "R-and-B is not exactly my taste," she announced. "I don't like the way you're presenting yourself."

This was a first. Her honesty inspired his honesty in return.

"I don't know why I got into it. I'm not into it either," he confessed. "It's not my best presentation."

"Why did you do it?"

"I wanted a hit," he admitted. "I hadn't been making any money for all the hard work I'd been putting in. I've been in this business twelve years and I still haven't had a big hit record in America."

He collapsed back on the couch. "I'm tired from working so hard," he added, suddenly vulnerable.

"The cocaine doesn't help," said Janis. "Tonight you might as well have taken a vial on stage."

"Well, it's always around."

"You don't have to do it."

David liked Janis. He liked the fact that she had no trouble telling the truth. It was a relief to meet someone who didn't want something from him.

"Will you be my friend?" he asked shyly.

They spoke for another half-hour, and then Janis and Lance decided that it was time to go. Finally everyone left together. It was after four in the morning. "By the time we left he didn't feel as much of a mess as he had when we got there," Cavasso recalls.

It should have been a night of triumph. Yet, when it ended, David was alone.

The press reaction to the New York shows was savage, especially in the music magazines that had supported him so unquestioningly from the days of the first Ziggy Stardust tour. *The New York Times* proclaimed the show "disappointing," adding that David had "looked self-consciously uncomfortable without routines to act out. . . ." Another daily newspaper declared that the evening "was like a huge, sumptuous birthday cake made out of cardboard with a hollow center."

Hit Parade commented, "Bowie isn't a rock and roller anymore, and except for a brief moment or two when I caught the old glint in his eye, he's not worth seeing in concert." *Creem* labeled David "Johnny Ray on cocaine singing about 1984," and described him as a "pastyfaced snaggletoothed little jitterbug" performing "a weird and utterly incongruous melange of glitter sentiment, negritudinal trappings, cocaine ecstasy, and Vegas schmaltz."

Another critic dismissed the show as "The David Bowie Minstrel

Show," adding that "his continual changes have become arbitrary, relying on a smug sense of staying ahead of the game, regardless of how shoddy it may seem."

David, who read every word written about him, did not comment about these reviews, behaving instead as if everything were fine. Those who knew him well knew that two things were going on at once. Part of him so believed in his own ascendancy that he really did not care about the reviews; they were a momentary setback, an annoyance to be forgotten as quickly as they were read. Another part of him was deeply hurt by them—to be so overwhelmingly rejected was a penetrating wound. But his acting skills masked the wound. Hardly anyone could see the cracks.

CHAPTER 25

The Martyred Star

On November 6, two days after the Music Hall engagement, the tour resumed in Cleveland. During November it traveled to Buffalo, Washington, D.C., Boston, Pittsburgh, Philadelphia, Memphis, and Nashville, ending in Atlanta on December 1. Even though almost all these concerts were sellouts, dates scheduled for the Nassau Coliseum on Long Island, as well as large concert halls in Norfolk and Tuscaloosa, had to be canceled because of lack of business.

After the shows, David had Corinne summon a few members of the company to his suite. He wanted to poll everybody about his situation with Defries. These meetings made the musicians very uncomfortable. David sat tensely on the couch, his face a mask of distress and pain, while he called for opinions. He wanted those around him to verbalize what he was thinking; eventually he would say the words himself.

Recalling these sessions, Gui Andrisano says, "Nobody wanted to go unless everybody was going because it was too intense. He was having conflicts with himself, he was having conflicts with MainMan, the show wasn't brilliant, it wasn't getting great reviews.

"So after a full day of that, when you are summoned to his room, you don't want to be there. You want to forget it because it was not fun."

On November 11, two weeks after its release, *David Live*, the live recording of the Year of the Diamond Dogs, received "gold" certification—proof of David's ability to sell albums without the enormous MainMan push. He was a real star now, no doubt about it. His albums went gold as soon as they were released, and he could draw audiences large enough to fill arenas. The record-buying public was ready for a Bowie hit single; all he had to do was supply the right record. A hit single would clinch the fact that he was a real star in America, that he had not failed despite his problems with MainMan, and that Tour Five had been the proper career choice despite the bad reviews.

He was convinced he would have that hit. He had no other choice.

Broadway legend has it that the only place to gather to wait for the opening night reviews is Sardi's, a restaurant in the theater district, the walls of which are plastered with caricatures of Broadway stars past and present. It was inevitable that MainMan would select Sardi's for its opening night party after the opening of its Broadway production of *Fame* on November 18, 1974.

The venerable restaurant had never seen anything like it. Limousines disgorged prominent underground characters dressed in their most flamboyant finery and glitter-rockers who shimmered from head to toe: a constabulary of people who were pleased—even honored—to be identified by the apellation "freak."

The group was served Sardi's best food and champagne. Despite the fact that some of them were not unfamiliar with either food stamps or welfare, the guests had no problem acting out *noblesse oblige*. They made small talk and called each other "darling," and made sure the waiters kept their glasses filled.

The reviews were terrible. Clive Barnes wrote in *The New York Times*: "It was 'Fame' but not fortune that gratuitously opened at the John Golden Theater last night. The best part of this limp rag of a comedy based on the life and times of Marilyn Monroe came at intermission." The play closed the same night.

Tony Defries was not fazed at all. The party was lots of fun, and the show's failure represented a loss of only $250,000. In the MainMan scheme of things, an amusing party was worth that and more.

Ingrassia though was deeply hurt by the bad reviews he had just received.

Defries brushed them aside. "What do you want to do next?" he asked his "artiste."

David said nothing about *Fame*'s failure. He was too controlled, too well-mannered to gloat openly. Nonetheless, on the contrary, these events provided him with extra fuel for the role of Martyred Star.

His day began at four in the afternoon with orange juice, coffee, and cocaine. Overcome by the realization that he was one of life's victims, a feeling of deep sadness accompanied his ablutions. Then he headed for the concert hall and transformed himself into a hyperactive soul man, followed by another long night. Someone—Ava, Corinne, Zanetta, Gui, Geoffrey—always had to be with him.

Throughout the tour Defries kept his distance, but that did not mean that he wasn't thoroughly involved in the business end of things. After tickets had been printed for the engagement at Philadelphia's Spectrum Theater, he decided he wanted to raise the ticket prices by $2.00. The standard ticket price in Philadelphia at that time was $6.50; the Bowie concert was scaled at $7.50; Defries wanted to raise the price to $9.50.

The Spectrum Theater, a long, narrow hall, had terrible acoustics, and most of the seats had no proximity to the stage. Nonetheless, Defries wanted to scale 90 percent of its eleven thousand seats at the top price. He was interested in generating an enormous gross and then taking one third of it—instead of the customary 15 percent—as a nonrefundable guarantee.

The local promoter, Rick Green, battled back and forth with Defries. Defries's response was to eliminate Green and go to another promoter. With the new promoter he capitulated on the size of the advance as well as the scaling of ticket prices. This was Defries's way of having fun, and far more entertaining than soothing a dependent, upset star.

The concert in Atlanta on December 1 marked the end of Tour Five. The feeling in the last few cities had not been one of triumph and success, but of tentativeness. This did not seem like a tour that was ending, but merely petering out. But Zanetta decided to throw a farewell party for the musicians, vocalists, and crew after the last concert. As concerned in his own way about public gestures and image as were Bowie and Defries, the MainMan president thought that David should bid his colleagues a public farewell. David agreed.

It was to be a small, private affair. All of the banquet rooms at the Hyatt-Regency Hotel were booked, so they rented a one-bedroom suite. During the afternoon, as Zanetta came and went setting things up, he noticed two beefy men in their midthirties hovering in the hall. They were wearing ill-fitting hippie clothes and looked very peculiar. Zanetta thought nothing of it. In this world everyone looked strange.

The tour personnel began to filter slowly into the party a little after midnight. Tired as well as glad the tour was over, the group was subdued. David arrived an hour later. Bodyguard Stuie George and chauffeur Jim James were assigned the job of monitoring the telephone and the door; this get-together was for "family"; their orders were to allow absolutely no one else into the suite.

David's mood usually set the tone of those around him, and his strangeness and unhappiness as the tour wound down had inspired uneasiness in everyone else. While he did not go out of his way to speak to anyone, he was cordial and friendly when people came up to him.

A little while later the phone rang. The caller described himself as the hotel's night detective.

"The party's too noisy," he barked. The complaint was ignored; the party was more like a wake than a celebration.

There were more calls from the night detective. Then there was a knock at the door. One of the two men who had been roaming the halls earlier told Stuie George that the party was too noisy.

"You've got five minutes to break it up," he announced.

Zanetta went to the door.

"I'm the house detective" the man said. "I want this room emptied in five minutes."

They argued back and forth, Zanetta getting annoyed. As the official representative of MainMan on the road, he found it intolerable that some "house dick" had the presumption to challenge him.

"I've had just about enough," he roared as he attempted to slam the door. The detective jammed the door with his foot. Whipping out a police badge, he said, "You're under arrest." He shoved Zanetta out of his way and burst into the suite, followed by eight or ten policemen, all of whose guns were drawn.

"Line up facing the wall," ordered the "house detective," really an undercover vice policeman. "Put your hands against the wall. Each of you is going to be searched."

Everyone but David did as he was told. Excitement flickered in his eyes. He was toying with the idea of disobeying orders, an action that would automatically result in his arrest. Being arrested was part and parcel of the image of a rock star ever since the drug trials of Mick Jagger and Keith Richards in June 1967. Ever the actor in public, he politely but firmly refused to face the wall and allow himself to be searched.

His action surprised and confused everyone. Used to seeing him as the sheltered star whom everyone protected, no one expected that in a situation like this he would break through the protective shield around him. Yet here he was speaking for himself, even going a bit too far in his desire to be assertive.

David wasn't arrested; Zanetta was.

The next day Zanetta was bailed out of jail, and he and the musicians flew back to New York City. David returned by car, a twenty-hour trip, and checked back into the Hotel Pierre. As soon as he hit the hotel, Norman Fisher was summoned to the suite. David was exhausted, but Fisher's cocaine provided him with the necessary energy to keep going. The next day, studio time was booked at the Record Plant, where he and Tony Visconti would do the final mixes of the *Young Americans* pop-soul album. Even more important, with no tour to distract him, he had no more excuses— the time had come to deal with Tony Defries and MainMan.

His solution was typically indirect. The fantasy that preoccupied him was to become a film director. He and Defries had music business problems. If David left the world of music, Defries and his problems would simply disappear.

He plunged again into the making of his movie based on *Diamond Dogs*. This was the story of three drag-queen divinities who ate the flesh of babies and of their encounter with the martyrlike Bowie, an "intergalactic communicator" who saved humanity by allowing himself to be literally absorbed into their flesh.

It was impossible for David to spend all his waking hours in a hermetic world devoted to realizing his fantasies. Once again the conversation about Defries that had begun six months before, on the day after the last performance of the Year of the Diamond Dogs, was initiated; once again David polled people about his future course of action. He spoke to Bette Midler, Ron Delsener, and Mick Jagger, among others. He believed that Jagger sent him messages on Rolling Stones LPs. He listened carefully to their records as if they were codes that, once deciphered, would give him clues about the direction to take in his music. A Jagger lyric that talked about "working so hard/working for the company" stuck in his mind. Jagger was jibing him about being a "company man" whose work benefited MainMan. He was upset that his situation with Defries, by its incorporation in the song, might slip into the public mythology about him.

David had finally begun to accept that he—not Tony—was paying for his luxurious lifestyle.

"Tony has apartments and houses and cars," he said repeatedly. "All I've got is a hotel bill of twenty thousand a month that I'm personally paying. Every time I order a cup of coffee, it costs me five dollars," he gasped. "I'm being ripped off. I've got to get out of here."

Word was conveyed to MainMan that David was unhappy about his living arrangements at the Pierre, and MainMan vice-president Jaime Andrews organized a search for less expensive accommodations. Only by turning to the enemy could David's problems be solved; the fact that he needed MainMan's help to solve his problems with the company stood in direct contradiction to the web of drama in which he had encased himself. It was a detail he overlooked.

December was shaping up as a series of rehearsals for a man who lived life by acting it. There was a bottom line, and only David had a sense of it: He wanted to return to Los Angeles. That was where the movies were and where he believed his future lay. It would also provide an escape from New York, the seat of Tony Defries's "empire" and a city that served as a constant reminder that Defries was failing him because in some way he had failed Defries.

Just before the tour had ended a request for an appearance by David had been made by the talent coordinator of Dick Cavett's talk show. The request was forwarded to Zanetta, who passed it on to David without consulting Defries, who was out of the country at the time. Ordinarily David would have turned it down; he had not wanted to do the "Omnibus" documentary about him in Los Angeles, and only vigorous persuasion had gotten him to change his mind.

But this time he was eager to do the show. He liked the fact that Defries was not involved in the decision; it was another example of his acting as his own manager.

After telling interviewers during Tour Five that his pop-soul show had been his presentation in concert of the "real" David Bowie, stripped clean of all theatrical artifice, he viewed the Cavett show as a way of beaming this real Bowie into millions of homes. Finally America would meet the man cleansed of his self-protective shadows.

The Cavett taping was scheduled for one in the afternoon. This was like five in the morning for David. He was tired and needed quiet around him. He studied himself in the dressing room mirror and began to collect his energies. He was like an actor gathering his resources in order to make his entrance. As the time for the taping arrived he grew calmer, while everyone else grew more nervous.

Just before he went on camera, he reached for the cane that he had used once or twice in concert. This was a subtle indication that he was going to "act" his appearance.

The cane gave him something to toy with while Cavett interviewed him in between the three songs he would sing. The focus for his nervousness, it helped him create the illusion of a distracted, tormented creature. His unhappiness was brilliantly demonstrated by his obsessive fiddling with the walking stick.

In addition to props, actors also give physical expression to the nature of the character they are playing. One actor might chew gum to demonstrate that his character is relaxed and laid back, another might adopt hair tugging to illustrate that his character is a nervous wreck. David chose a loud sniffing sound with which to dot his conversation, a signal to those in the know that he was a cocaine user of magnitude.

This was his version of the fall of Ziggy Stardust. The "real" David Bowie turned out to be his portrayal of a vulnerable performer who, under the pressures of his career and fame, had become rock's answer to Judy Garland.

One of the ways David entertained himself was by pushing everything too far. But his need for self-dramatization was inexorably leading him to the place he most feared. What would he do when he was *really* naked and vulnerable?

Defries summarized the Cavett appearance his own way. He felt that if an artist couldn't exploit the rights to what he creates, it's better never to hear from him at all. The observation was accompanied by only the slightest trace of annoyance.

During December, when David wasn't in the studio putting the finishing touches on *Young Americans*, he pursued his obsession with his movie, which dealt with Ziggy Stardust and three drag queen divinities. He decided to use three friends as character studies: Cyrinda Foxe, the girl friend of New York Doll David Johansen, who had accompanied him on portions of Tour One and had been his co-star in his first American-made video; Donyale Luna, the black model who had been eager to become a MainMan 'artiste'; and Tally Brown, a rotund Off-Off-Broadway actress.

In order to observe them firsthand as source material for his script, he would have a dinner party for them at the hotel. As his guests, they would never know they were under observation.

The party was merry. The women dressed carefully for the occasion. Foxe was earthy and streetwise; Luna, spacy and shy; Brown, regal and very grand.

David smiled warmly, listened carefully, and was utterly charming. The minute it was over he scooped up his sketch pad and began to draw. He was happy the way children are when they do something naughty and get away with it. He worked through the night. This is it, he thought, this is the project that will free me.

The Break

Also during **December**, two large talent agencies, International Famous Agency (IFA) and Creative Artists Management (CMA), merged to become the giant-sized International Creative Management (ICM). The merger meant nothing to David, yet because of it he would not only have to find someone to replace Tony Defries, but would also have the opportunity to make his first movie.

Michael Lippman had been a junior agent at CMA. Convinced he would not benefit as a result of the merger, and might even lose his job, he left the agency to join a Los Angeles–based entertainment law firm. Now he had to prove that he could attract major clients to the firm. Intrigued by David from the first day he had met him in Los Angeles during U.S. Tour One, he desperately wanted David to head his client list. He knew David was unhappy with Defries and sensed this was the perfect moment to strike.

In England, Mick Jagger's film agent at CMA, Maggie Abbott, was also concerned about the impending merger. Unlike other film agents she believed that rock stars could make the transition to dramatic films, and had developed a reputation as a renegade in the conservative film business. She knew that after the merger she would be replaced by IFA's staff of agents. So she cleared out her files and arranged to take her client list with her.

She too was eager to put together a series of new deals that would make her attractive to other agencies. She learned about a film project called *The Man Who Fell to Earth*. It would be directed by Nicholas Roeg, who had already directed Jagger in the film *Performance*.

"Is Jagger right for the title role?" Abbott asked Roeg.

"He's too strong, too positive," replied Roeg. "I want somebody

who looks as if he hasn't any bones in his body. I want Peter
O'Toole."

"David Bowie's the man for you!" she exclaimed.

"Who's that?" asked Roeg.

Abbott's work was cut out for her. She would have to convince
Roeg and his producer, Si Litvinoff, to hire David and also convince
David to do the movie. She was a buddy of Angela's and was sure
Angela would help. Once again his wife's ability to network people
was going to have a substantial effect on David's career.

A film project as unconventional as *The Man Who Fell to Earth*,
involving an eccentric film director and an exceptionally trendy rock
star, was exactly the kind of thing that most appealed to Maggie
Abbott. It was the sort of project that would lend credence to her
image as the "renegade" agent. It was also precisely the right moment
to put together such a deal. She was about to set out on her own
and wanted to announce a series of flashy new projects.

Dana Gillespie had a short engagement at Reno Sweeney. When
it came to an end, Defries decided to drop Wayne County and Ava
Cherry from the MainMan roster. Zanetta, a friend of County's, had
planned to work with the underground drag-rock performer but
instead had gone on the road with Bowie. Dropping Wayne County
appeared to be Defries's long-range response to Zanetta's decision.

His reasons for dropping Ava also seemed clear.

On December 19 a memo was circulated around the MainMan
office: "Last night, the 18th, final mixes were completed for 'Fascination,' 'All You've Got to Do Is Win,' and the remix of 'Win.'
Visconti says Bowie intends these to be his next three singles. . . ."

The first side of the album was finished. Three nights at the
beginning of January were scheduled for a twenty-four-track mix of
the album; four more nights would be devoted to the remix of the
album's second side. It was scheduled for completion on January 12.

Ava was periodically called at her MainMan apartment and summoned to the MainMan suite, to spend the night with David. What
she found when she got there was a man growing increasingly dependent on cocaine. "Mostly he would stay up for five days at a
stretch. He wouldn't answer the phone or talk to anybody," she
recalls.

"He would be busy working—painting, playing with his video

equipment, and tooting. He'd be busy but he'd be blown out of his mind."

Almost no one could crash through the security net that sur-rounded David. John Lennon, whom he adored, was one of the few. David had called John and invited him over. John arrived at the hotel with May Pang, the personal assistant with whom he was living during his eighteen-month separation from Yoko Ono. David played them his *Young Americans* tracks, showed them his video equipment, and told them about his *Diamond Dogs* movie. Impressed by David's output they returned the next night. Once again they heard *Young Americans*. The same thing occurred the third time they came to visit.

A night or two later John called David. Paul and Linda Mc-Cartney had dropped into the Upper East Side apartment he was sharing with May Pang, and John thought it would be fun if they all came over to visit David.

"David really wasn't friendly with Paul and Linda," recalls Ava. "There was this very tense feeling. Every time Paul started to say something, Linda would jump in and not let Paul talk. I also don't think she liked David very much, and the feeling was mutual."

David insisted on playing his *Young Americans* tracks for Paul and Linda. His insecurities and egoism surfaced easily, and they took the form of a market research survey. He eagerly solicited opinions, his neediness suggesting that he would accept only total enthusiasm.

When the tracks were done, he played them again. Before David had a chance to play the tracks a third time, Paul snapped, "Can we hear another album?"

David began the album again.

"It's great!" John exclaimed irritably. He suggested they hear another album.

David seemed stunned for a second. "Pick any album you like," he said.

Pang selected an Aretha Franklin record.

"Excuse me for a second." David got up and fled from the room.

Pang looked at John. "I think you hurt Bowie's feelings," she told him.

"Oh, no," interrupted Linda. "That's just the way he is."

That night as soon as John and May returned to their apartment,

John received a telephone call from David. They spoke quietly for quite some time.

After he got off the phone John told May, "David did feel really hurt when I asked him to change the record. He was very upset. I kept tellin' him I didn't mean it that way."

A day or two later Michael Lippman arrived in New York. He called the Pierre, and David agreed to see him. Lippman carried with him a batch of movie scripts. They were his credentials that he was from the world of movies.

All agents are salesmen, and Lippman had a pitch. He lived in *Hollywood*, he was a *Hollywood* agent and lawyer, he understood how the movie business worked.

Lippman's visit proved that David's personal magic was still working. Someone *had* arrived to pave the way for his next major transformation, the one that would enable him to become his *real* self.

Hollywood has always been reluctant to hire rock stars to appear in movies. Even Mick Jagger's attempted transition to dramatic films had resulted in two failures, *Performance* and *Ned Kelly*. Lippman was too young and inexperienced to have the clout to fight Hollywood's resistance to rock stars. David's persistent image as a gay space-rocker didn't help any, and he didn't even have a Number One record.

Still, it was the kind of meeting that played straight into David's fantasies. Lippman was gentle and eager to please, and was in no way threatening. He was a true fan with a passionate interest in David's career.

After Tony Defries David didn't want another strong, independent person in a position of control. From that moment on the control was always going to reside with him.

During Christmas week David announced that he really had decided to leave MainMan. Now was the perfect time for him to strike—Tony Defries, Dana Gillespie, Geoffrey MacCormack, and Gui Andrisano were all vacationing on the island of Mustique, known as Princess Margaret's secret hideaway.

He announced to Pat Gibbons, Corinne, and John Dove, "This rocker ain't gonna roll no more."

With the coast clear, he scheduled an appointment with Ken

Glancy, president of RCA Records. It was a most important meeting. He wanted to have his monies paid directly to him, not to Defries.

A firm believer in the power of his image, it was imperative that he dress carefully for the occasion. John Dove recalls, "A lot of emotion was associated with this because none of us knew what was going to happen. I remember David put on a French sailor suit. Blue bell-bottoms with a pinafore and, I swear to God, a little blue beret with a red bobble on it. This was his suit to go up to RCA and do business."

At RCA David learned that his royalties could not go directly to him, but could be put in escrow until he resolved his difficulties with Defries.

News of the meeting reached MainMan immediately. In the MainMan tradition, as the story of the meeting circulated, it grew increasingly dramatic. MainMan bookkeeper Jude Bartlett recalls one version, "David showed up an hour late and then he collapsed. He just sort of keeled over. He was really in bad shape. RCA was very freaked out about it."

Another version of the story put the blame on, of all people, Dana Gillespie. The story went that Dana was upset that David had become a star and she hadn't. She wanted to punish Defries and knew that if she removed him from the picture Bowie would be forced to take action. So she lured Defries to Mustique. Then David needed money, but MainMan would not advance him any cash without Tony's approval. He had tried unsuccessfully to reach Tony on Mustique. He had gone to RCA, which also refused him money because of the extravagant advances the company had already made to MainMan.

The story continued. RCA couldn't wait to turn the tables on Defries by showing David the books. At the meeting Bowie had learned that the company had advanced him anywhere from $3 to $7 million, proof, so the MainMan employees believed, of Defries's genius. By spending that much money on an artist, a record company was forced to promote him in order to protect its investment.

Finally, they believed that David's assistant Pat Gibbons had withdrawn his life savings of $2,000 in order to bail out David.

On Mustique Dana was by Tony's side when he did not take David's calls. It seemed to her that he was too distressed by David's behavior even to come to the phone.

Interestingly, despite all the rumors about the size of RCA's expenditures, recently deceased MainMan president Jaime Andrews pointed out that Tours Four and Five had proved splendid promotional ventures. Enough records had been sold to wipe out David's debt to RCA. At the time that David made his move at RCA he was finally in a profit position with the company for the first time in his American recording career.

Other unconventional English music acts like Roxy Music had been unable to crack America because their record companies had not been encouraged to go overboard. Defries's ability to work RCA had given David the ability to sell large numbers of records in America.

The moment was an ironic one, and all David had to go by was his intuition and his belief in himself. That intuition told him to get out.

After Defries's holiday was over, David, full of dread, agreed to meet with his manager. Position, as always, was of extreme importance. David had to go to the MainMan townhouse; Tony would not come to him.

Ostensibly the purpose of the meeting was for the two men to talk through their problems and arrive at solutions. Nothing could have been more impossible. At this point, in his mind David was living in the future and had already left MainMan. His pattern was to get rid of something once he did not need it anymore. His two previous managers had been discarded when he found replacements. Tony had promised to make him a star, and he was a star. The time had come to move on; he believed he *had* moved on.

David didn't really want to resolve his problems with Tony. He was playing out the drama of victimized rock star and suffering the fate that inevitably befell a Ziggy Stardust–like character. That drama provided him with far more excitement than would a series of realistic negotiations.

He sat on an overstuffed chair at one end of the large elegant living room, and Tony sat at the other end of the room. The manager sipped coffee and puffed on a cigar. Occasionally they stared out the bay window at the beautifully landscaped garden.

Characteristically, Defries did not admit that there were any problems at all. As far as he was concerned they were a step away from "world domination." Defries had fulfilled his end of the bargain brilliantly. He intimated that David had been extraordinarily unsuccessful before his intervention; with Tony had come the only satisfactory record deal of David's career, and that deal was continually being improved. David had become an English superstar as well as a major star in America.

None of the six months of drama in David's life about this meeting surfaced at this low-keyed, peculiar encounter. David volunteered a complaint; Tony ignored it, speaking majestically about the success they had achieved and the even greater success that loomed in their futures. Voices were never raised; there were no recriminations.

His trips to the bathroom became increasingly frequent; he never did coke in front of the paternal Defries. Every time he left the room a look of shock crossed Tony's face. David was doing cocaine in *his* bathroom. He was appalled.

David was unable to articulate most of his list of complaints. After all, Defries had removed all day-to-day worries, leaving David free to create. He had not only been supported financially, but Defries had also supported him by giving him the artistic freedom he craved. He had been gay and he had been black and in neither instance had he received any flack from Defries. They had formed a partnership so that David would become the "greatest entertainer of the century." It had been an adventure the payoff of which was glory. Trivia such as cash flow paled next to their quest and its fulfillment.

David might have demanded that the business end of their relationship finally be put on an even keel. How much had he really earned since becoming a client of Defries? What could he expect to earn in the future? How had Tony disbursed the funds? Did any of these disbursements violate their agreement? How much money did David have at that moment?

But those were questions he could not ask. What he wanted was for Tony to second-guess what was on his mind. But Tony was too preoccupied with himself to consider for a second what was going on in David's mind.

As always, Defries's laissez-faire attitude placed him above recrimination, making it virtually impossible to challenge him. His manner suggested that if David was unhappy and wanted to leave, that, too, would be quite all right with him.

Money would remain the symbol of David's discontent and the

substitute for the pain caused by Defries's insensitivity. David refused to feel pain and chose to erase the past rather than become upset by it. Defries's insensitivity to David's personality had set up a situation in which David had only one choice: He had to go.

The meeting took two hours, one of the shortest they had ever had. While in the past they had spent hours on a single detail of their venture, they now had very little to say each other.

Their parting was cordial but subdued. Both agreed that things would work out and there was nothing to worry about.

After David left, Defries remained convinced that there were no problems. After all, David finally was selling records.

On the ride back to the hotel David said, "When you're there, you don't know what you're doing. When you're out of there, you realize you've been had. You come out thinking everything was solved. But nothing has been solved. You get talked out of what you want to do, and Tony makes it seem like the best thing to do is to do it Tony's way. You have a beef. Somehow the beef becomes very trivial, and when you come out nothing is changed."

At the end of December, Jaime Andrews rented David a town house in the Chelsea section of Manhattan. Even though MainMan paid the rent, David told everyone that he was moving there "in order to hide out from Tony Defries."

CHAPTER 27

The House on Twentieth Street

"What would make me happy is to be an artist living in a garret, in a cold-water flat somewhere, as long as I could afford art material," David told John Dove as soon as he moved into his new home.

The name given by David's inner circle to this new home was "the House on Twentieth Street." David didn't know that he would live there less than three months before realizing his fantasy of returning to Hollywood. Nor did he know that he would grow to believe that the house was haunted and demand that its evil spirits be exorcised; a year after David left the house a mysterious fire would gut its insides, and it would remain deserted and in disrepair for the next eight years until new owners took it over in the spring of 1985.

It was a small three-story house directly across the street from an Episcopal church in the middle of a tree-lined residential block. One couldn't guess from the pretty facades of the neighboring houses that many of them were rooming houses for retired sailors. It was the least likely place one would expect to find David Bowie.

There was almost no furniture in the two small parlor-floor rooms, one of which was used as an office. A staircase led down to the combination kitchen and dining room in the basement. The only furniture in the room was a big round table. Three tiny bedrooms made up the second floor. All the walls on the third floor had been removed, creating a large and modern space, as if a contemporary loft had been plunked down in the middle of the house. There was a large hole in the middle of the ceiling. One could see up into the attic, which David used as his bedroom.

309

For the most part the house felt spare and transient. The fact that some floors had been renovated while others had been left untouched gave it a distinctly schizophrenic feel. It was perfect.

Into the house moved David's family of the moment: Zowie and Marion, Corinne, and Geoffrey MacCormack. This was the first time Corinne had lived under the same roof as David. As the days progressed she would function increasingly as David's full-time "wife," controlling every aspect of life in the house. Even when one realized that Corinne was doing exactly what David wanted, David was so adored he was never held responsible for any of her actions.

On January 1, 1975, Ava's rent ran out at her MainMan apartment, and David invited her to move into the House on Twentieth Street. The invitation delighted her, but from the day she arrived she sensed that Corinne did not share her delight. Corinne had waited a long time to live with David. The last thing she wanted was to be living with David and his mistress.

Angela was living in her own MainMan apartment, five blocks from David's house. She made periodic forays to the house to "organize" the activities. David remained aloof; he knew that if he ignored her long enough she would eventually flee. Angela had money problems too. After spending a small fortune to decorate her apartment, she discovered as the first of the year rolled around that Defries was not planning to pay the rent. The rent would have to come from David, but David's cash flow had been frozen by RCA, and MainMan was still paying his bills, and was not going to subsidize Angela's extravagances.

Angela fled and flew back to the house on Oakley Street, taking Marion and Zowie with her. As soon as she hit London, she resumed her role of "Mrs. Bowie, Superstar's Wife." Dancing the night away at Tramps was far more fun than hanging around the morbid House on Twentieth Street or haggling about the rent on a New York apartment.

During David's stay at the house he manifested a number of personalities. Some people saw him all day and never sensed that anything was bothering him; he was traveling in a wave of euphoria. Acting as if he were free of Defries and MainMan, he finally— *finally*—was going to be his *real* self: an artist in a garret. A very few were subjected to his private expressions of despair. He was one of life's lost victims. This was Ziggy Stardust: abandoned, impoverished, terrified of a future that seemed out of control. Both parts were acted to perfection; he believed everything he said and did as he was saying and doing it. Often, when visitors discussed their encounters with him, it was as if they were speaking about different men.

A tiny room on the second floor was assigned to John Dove as his working quarters. Every day David and Dove sat down in earnest to prepare David to write and then direct his *Diamond Dogs* movie. Dove found a film historian who taught at the New School. He was invited to give David a personal tutorial in film history. Dove also rented a series of old films, which they watched together while David took copious notes.

David's favorite film was still Fritz Lang's *Metropolis*. He and Dove watched it ten times. There are a number of reasons why David responded so completely to it. It has enormous visual appeal, and was directed with a painter's eye for composition and staging. It is also nonlinear: characters appear and disappear abruptly, and often their behavior is inexplicable. None of this fazed David. The movie seemed to make perfect sense to him.

Finally David and Dove were ready to write. According to Dove the film was going to be about a nuclear holocaust. "There were a lot of people who were really going through things that reflected what used to be done before the war. The world was filled with 1984-style conformists. They were the living dead. But everybody was into some kind of dust that went up their noses that was driving them nuts. It was a question of time before the living zombies were destroyed by the dust." It was David's personal *Metropolis*.

Soon after David moved into the House on Twentieth Street, John Lennon and May Pang came to visit. John Dove was introduced as "David's video man and the man who was writing his film for him."

Dove was flattered, and the flattery would make him even more devoted. Dove was always surprised by what he considered David's "lack of ego." After all, he was merely David's "organizer," and David was "the creative source."

David's seductiveness again enabled him to initiate discussions that had specific appeal to the person on whom he was focusing his gigantic concentration. He appealed to Lennon's social conscience by discussing video as a political tool.

John Lennon visited the house a few more times; then David and Ava paid a visit to John and May's Upper East Side apartment.

John told David about the UFO May and he had spotted from the terrace. He went out on the balcony to show David how close the UFO had come. Never one to be outdone, David responded by telling John about his experiences as a UFO observer for an English UFO magazine.

"They saw things nobody else saw," recalls Ava. "May and I were laughing; we didn't see the things they saw. We had a very good time."

Soon after the move to the House on Twentieth Street David finished *Young Americans*. Typically, this should be the moment when David would suddenly have an inspiration and feel compelled to make changes. *Young Americans* was no exception. He suddenly decided he wanted to do a Lennon-McCartney song on the new album, and he knew his good friend John Lennon would participate in the session. He called John, who eagerly agreed to come to the studio.

While David was out of the room John picked up his guitar and started to play a riff based on Shirley and Company's "Shame, Shame, Shame," a record that was currently climbing the charts. Bowie's guitarist, Carlos Alomar, picked up the riff, and the two men played together.

"What are you doing?" asked David on his return.

"We're playing 'Shame, Shame, Shame,' " John replied.

David listened for a second, went out and returned a half-hour later. "Shame" had become a lyric he called "Fame." John was amazed at the speed with which David had worked.

Carlos Alomar recalls, "Lennon's tiny little voice was already on the acoustic guitar track. 'Fame' was originally 'Foot Stomping,' which we did on the tour. David had recorded my chord changes and riff, and he hated it. He took out the lyrics and ended up with the music and cut it up on the master so that it would have a classic R-and-B form. He's a perfectionist and experiments with the original tape, running it backwards, cutting it up, doing things on the master as opposed to recording them live. 'Fame' was totally cut up.

"When we had the form of the song he wanted, he left. I stayed behind and overdubbed four or five different guitar parts on it. He listened to it and said, 'That's it.' "

It was a classic Bowie synthesis. The elements included a performance by John Lennon, a current R-and-B hit, an R-and-B standard, William Burroughs's cut-and-paste technique, David's anger at Defries, and Alomar's superb studio technique.

Although David had had a number of invitations to visit Defries at the MainMan estate in Greenwich, he had turned them all down. It was as if he didn't want to know how well Tony really lived. But now that he had convinced himself that his association with MainMan was over, he was ready to make the trek to Connecticut to see for himself. A visit to Defries's baronial manor would be the last piece of evidence he needed before he officially severed all ties with MainMan.

After the meeting in Greenwich each man had a distinctly different reaction.

David said that he had told Defries that everything was over and that Tony had agreed, saying, "Fine. That's it."

According to Defries, David had told him that he wasn't leaving.

Defries did say, though, that he had told David that if he did leave, he needed to find a new manager that was "just like Tony." He explained to David that he needed a strong manager because David could not discriminate between those ideas that would further his career and those that were mere distractions. David's personality and career demanded a director he could not seduce, someone who would focus his energies toward realistic, achievable goals.

It was the last thing David wanted at the moment.

During Ava's first few weeks in the house she and David had never been happier.

David never talked about his past. He liked to give the impression that as Minerva had sprung fully formed from Zeus's head, he had descended upon planet Earth from some imperial future world. Ava loved her parents but David told her he felt nothing for Peggy, and could not remember the date of her birthday.

But now, relieved to be rid of Defries and overwhelmed with glee about the fact that he was taking charge of his own life, he was willing to talk. His work with Dove on the *Diamond Dogs* film and with John Lennon in the studio seemed proof that his talent was his trump card. From the beginning, his belief in his own talent had always gotten him through.

Ava asked him about Angela. "He told me that he loved her but he wasn't in love with her," she recalls. "Even though he was with me he still gave her a certain amount of respect. He told me he wanted to get married. He even said, 'When I divorce Angie, we're going to get married.' He told me many times that he loved me."

But the second meeting with Defries changed everything. This one got to David. "I never saw him so upset as when that happened. I didn't know what to do. I was there to try and comfort him, but what could I do?" said Ava.

Defries had seemed to have been rejecting David even though David had done his very best. Childlike feelings surfaced, and he became devastated, frightened, and angry. David would have to crush those feelings, crush quickly in order to move forward.

To add to David's personal confusion, at the beginning of January the Led Zeppelin tour had settled down at the Plaza. The Rolling Stones were planning a tour, and Mick Jagger was impressed by Zeppelin's success. He was eager to see how their tour was being run and operated. David, who made Mick's quests his own, became intrigued also.

In his hotel room Jimmy Page studied footage shot by underground filmmaker Kenneth Anger, which would comprise portions of a film Anger called *Lucifer Rising*. The film was reputedly Anger's personal homage to Satan. On and off for three years Page had been scoring the film; its original composer was Mick Jagger.

David was curious about Page's film project. What he learned over the next few days had all the ingredients to fuel his hyperactive imagination. It was common knowledge that Page was infatuated with the body of work created by Aleister Crowley. He owned Crowley's mansion on the shores of Loch Ness in Scotland, and his collection of Crowley memorabilia included manuscripts, first editions, hats, canes, paintings, and robes. Known as "the Great Beast" and "the Wickedest Man in the World," Crowley had been dead for twenty-eight years. Nonetheless, his writings, which emphasized sex, drugs, and drink as the sources of spiritual power, had great resonance for certain rock stars. It was because of Page's study of Crowley that rumors had spread that Led Zeppelin (with the exception of bassist John Paul Jones) had made a pact with the devil in order to achieve its success.

Aleister Crowley's beliefs encompassed methods by which a person could gain complete control over the universe. Promiscuity and the use of drugs like cocaine could be justified as means to that end. It was another version of David's beloved Ziggy Stardust/alien theory, perfect for someone who propagated the notion that he was otherworldly.

Crowley instructed his disciples to disengage themselves from the physical sensations, thoughts, and worries of everyday life. One had to learn to transcend one's surroundings; everything that existed in the moral world had to be banished. By nature David always ignored the preoccupations of everyday life. Instead he devoted himself wholeheartedly to making his fantasies reality.

Crowley's magicians were to be bisexual, giving them the wisdom and power to dominate both sexes. It was a concept David understood well.

He forged a link between Crowley's precepts and his own brief flirtation with Tibetan Buddhism during the 1960s. Buddhist doctrine enabled one to transcend one's reality; Crowley enabled one not only to transcend that reality, but to control the universe in the process.

The Stones found Kenneth Anger sinister. They believed they had evidence that Anger, a disciple of Crowley, could accomplish tasks impossible for a normal man. Originally Anger wanted Jagger to play the title role in *Lucifer Rising*. He was attracted to Jagger because of his aura of power.

Jagger had bowed out of the project. A pragmatist, he, too, was fascinated by power and deeply interested in the ways that individuals, audiences, and even societies could be controlled. But he was able to separate image from reality. Performing "Sympathy for the Devil" and wearing a satanic T-shirt was one thing; it created a mystique and sold records. But devoting all of one's energies to a mystical film about Satan was quite another matter.

After Jagger left the project Anger replaced him with Jimmy Page. Page's study of Crowley had apparently provided him with an especially strong aura. An aura is believed to be a magnetic sphere that surrounds one's body. It is composed of three fields comprised of bands of different colors. The size of the bands and the brilliance of their color reflects the degree to which an individual is a master and in possession of power. Meditation and visualization are the techniques that enable one to create an aura of power.

David was entertained by the discussion of Mick Jagger's and Jimmy Page's powerful auras.

A few nights later one of the Rolling Stones, Jimmy Page, and David's Los Angeles friend with all the coke came to the House on Twentieth Street. Though he was his polite self, David was wary of Page. He was used to groupies and hangers on, but Page had another master. He was not someone who would fall instantly under David's spell.

Ava says David and she were blasted out of their minds.

Occasionally during the evening, the conversation touched on the subject of the occult. Whenever the power of the guitarist's aura was mentioned, Page remained silent but smiled inscrutably. It seemed that he did believe he had the power to control the universe.

David's smile never faltered but the attention paid Page rankled him. Finally it got too much for him, and he left the room. During his absence Page accidentally spilled his drink on the silk pillows on the floor.

When David returned, he looked at the stained pillows and erupted in a fury, one of the very few times he allowed his emotions to explode in public. He directed his anger at Ava since it was bad form to mistreat a guest.

"These are my beautiful pillows," he screamed. "How could you?"

"I didn't do it," blurted Ava.

David couldn't hear. He berated her mercilessly until she burst into tears. Page sat silently through the diatribe, a slight grin occasionally flickering across his face, as if he had masterminded the whole unpleasant moment.

Out of the corner of his eye, David spotted Page's grin. It dawned on him that he had been duped, something he couldn't stand. He wheeled around and faced the guitarist.

"Why didn't you tell me you were the one who did it instead of letting me blame Ava?" he shouted. Page remained silent, indicating he could transcend earthly moments like this one while David could not. David grew even angrier.

"I'd like you to leave," he ordered. There was a window open in the room. "Why don't you leave by the window?" he said evenly.

He stared at Page, focusing all his concentration on him. His eyes seemed to be ordering Page to go to the window and jump. He would prove he had the more powerful aura.

Page stared back at David. The room was silent as the two men sat staring at each other.

Ava couldn't stand the feeling of menace and danger that permeated the air. In that strange moment it seemed possible that something terrible might happen during this psychic battle.

Finally Page stormed out. When Ava and David next ran into Page at a party, David became so upset that he had to leave the room.

That encounter with Page, as silly as it was, demonstrated the dramatic side of David's nature that people like Jimmy Page might really have supernatural powers that he could not defeat. Another new drama was launched that night. By the time it was over the House on Twentieth Street would have to be exorcised because of the belief it had become overrun with satanic demons whom Crowley's disciples had summoned straight from Hell.

CHAPTER 28

The Telegram

D avid needed a lawyer. The only lawyer he knew whom he felt he could trust was Michael Lippman. On January 20 he called Lippman at his Los Angeles home. The next day Lippman was on a plane to New York City.

David told Lippman, "Don't worry about money. We'll make it up. The future is what we're counting on. Get me free."

His attitude about his financial affairs with Defries would remain unswerving throughout the following year. Money did not matter. He did not need Defries anymore. It was time to move on. What mattered to David was that Tony Defries be erased from his consciousness. David had a consistent pattern: once a firm decision about the future was made, the past was to be forgotten, eventually to be rewritten in light of current events. He did not want to challenge or threaten Defries, he only wanted to eliminate him from his consciousness.

With the elimination of MainMan David would have absolutely no means of support. The only place to turn was RCA Records.

Lippman scheduled a meeting with RCA's top brass.

With Lippman by his side David eloquently pleaded his case. It was his job to convince the executives that his MainMan days were behind him; by inference their continued financial support of David would ensure all of their rosy futures.

The MainMan phenomenon had to be puzzling to all of them. Despite RCA's advances Defries never seemed to have any money on hand. His frequent trips to RCA were essential to keep his venture afloat. David, who also spent money recklessly, never had any money either. So he would go to Tony for money, and Tony would go to RCA. The record company had been trained to expect Defries to ask for money, but they were unaccustomed to David appearing to ask for money on his own behalf.

RCA decided to give David an "unofficial advance" against future record royalties. David was about to deliver *Young Americans*, and RCA did not want to do anything that would encourage Defries to move against the album. But David also had to be kept happy and solvent so that he could continue to make records. At that time he was responsible for 4 percent of all of RCA's record sales in England, and had established RCA UK as a major force in the English music business.

While RCA appeared magnanimous, it was merely advancing David his own money. David had launched a new record company debt.

RCA also agreed to rent a one-bedroom suite for David at the Algonquin Hotel, which he could use as his office. Corinne, Pat Gibbons, and Lippman would use the suite as their headquarters. At this time David officially hired Gibbons away from Defries. It was Gibbons's reward for his loyalty. David also seemed to think that Gibbons's defection to his camp would show Tony that he had someone by his side who could inform him about the inner workings of MainMan. Defries hardly knew Gibbons was gone.

David asked Lippman to explain his contractual arrangements with Defries. Finally David said he understood. Lippman had no idea how many times the agreement had already been explained to David.

Next, a telegram was dispatched to Defries on David's behalf; Defries was informed that his and MainMan's services were no longer required.

Defries appeared unfazed. No one at MainMan seemed to take the telegram seriously either; the empire would run without David. Defries dispatched a telegram to David putting him on suspension. He tried to call David—not to woo him back, but to tell him what dangers lay ahead of him. Even without David as a client, Defries couldn't resist the opportunity to offer advice about "the long term" for David, but David refused to take his calls. He wanted to believe Defries had been erased.

In London Angela was in the middle of a new affair.

David was pleased when she called him with the news. Toward the end of January she made her television debut as a guest on a popular English talk show, "Russell Hardy Plus." The reason she was invited on the show was simply because she was "Mrs. Bowie." She was becoming an ersatz celebrity. An intelligent woman, Angela knew that being a media figure whose only claim to fame was a marriage that was not working was no way to become famous. But she could not help herself; her gift seemed to be to inspire and entertain others.

On the TV show she wore a strapless gown designed by Natasha Kornilof. Every time she lifted her arms, her tiny breasts popped out of her dress. The effect amused her but Russell Hardy was nonplussed.

Ironically, *Cracked Actor*, Alan Yentob's documentary about David's experiences in Los Angeles the past summer, aired on English television the same day. British viewers could either see Angela's flat chest or watch a wraithlike David being driven in his MainMan limousine across an endless stretch of American desert while Corinne bopped to an Aretha Franklin tape.

After seeing *Cracked Actor*, Maggie Abbott knew that only David could be *The Man Who Fell to Earth*. When Nick Roeg saw the show, he agreed. "He exudes such a wonderfully perverse nonhuman quality," he told Abbott.

Angela loved the idea of the project. She got David on the phone and used her most dignified, maternal voice to describe the movie. He sensed immediately that it was right for him. Angela's instincts on his behalf were often superb. Once again, she had come to his rescue, this time getting him precisely what he wanted, an opportunity to escape from the music business into the world of film.

Abbott flew to New York to meet David. Used to the good-natured jocularity that surrounded Mick Jagger, she was taken aback by the "uncomfortable tension" that pervaded the House on Twentieth Street. David was spending most of his time at the Plaza hanging out with Jagger and Led Zeppelin. He was also keeping extremely odd hours, staying up all night putting the finishing touches on *Young Americans*. Abbott felt that he was living unnaturally; the feeling in the house reeked of isolation and temporariness. The great days of MainMan had come to an end for David, and nothing had replaced them. He was trapped in a vacuum of his own isolation.

Finally Abbott sat down with David. He couldn't wait to play "Fame" for her.

She knew that since David had been conditioned to think of himself as unapproachable, inaccessible, and noncommittal she had to be strong with him. What she did not know was that he had already investigated Roeg's work and had learned of his three films, *Walkabout*, *Performance*, and *Don't Look Now*. Roeg was no conventional storyteller; he jumbled time, and used obscure symbols as well as the drama of ritual. It was the kind of pretension and self-conscious intellectuality that David adored. Roeg was an "artiste" as he was; he had also directed Mick Jagger in *Performance*, a very strong point in the director's favor.

David ignored business realities and thought neither about how resistant Hollywood might be to his entry into the movies (Mick Jagger had *not* become a movie star after making *Performance*) nor that Roeg had directed three commercial flops.

It would take Abbott some time to realize how much luck had been on her side. She had visited David at one of the most unprotected moments in his career. Tony Defries would never have permitted such a meeting to occur. The only film project he would have considered was one that could be described as "major." He would also have demanded a very "major" fee. It was another stroke of good luck for David, one of his many famous "planned accidents." While he desperately wanted to make a movie, until that moment his career had been set up so that no realistic movie project would have been permitted to move forward.

A day or two later David called Abbott to say he wanted to make the movie. Abbott called Nick Roeg and Si Litvinoff, who flew to New York. Abbott brought Roeg to the House on Twentieth Street, where David kept them waiting for eight hours. He had no sense of time; the world always seemed to him to come alive when he made his entrance.

What director would trust such a man? None, perhaps, except Nick Roeg. After several long meetings Roeg was convinced that David was The Man Who Fell to Earth.

As far as David was concerned he was going to Hollywood to make a movie. Abbott, Roeg, and Litvinoff now had to convince Hollywood that David Bowie was enough of a star to carry his own film.

After an eighteen-month separation, John Lennon returned to Yoko Ono in February of that year. Unused to being back at the

Dakota, he tended to pop out of his apartment. He either secretly visited May Pang, who had been his mistress, or dropped in on old friends. One night he turned up at the House on Twentieth Street.

David and Ava were there with Jac Colello. Later Bette Midler came by with Bob Dylan. The group sat up through the night drinking and talking and having a good time.

David was in high spirits. He was delighted with his new album, excited about his movie debut, and pleased to have been asked to present the Grammy Award for Best Female Soul Artist at the ceremonies, which would be televised nationally on March 1.

Aretha Franklin was a shoo-in to win the award. It was something that David was really looking forward to. Aretha Franklin was the Queen of Soul, and he loved her records; his appearance on the same stage with her seemed to validate his belief that he had become a soul artist himself.

At the Dakota one night, David announced to Ava, "I'm hungry. Cook me some food." Ava got up and headed in the direction of the kitchen; she planned to scramble him some eggs.

Yoko stared defiantly at David. "Wait a minute," she said firmly. "Hold up. No. You don't ask her. You don't say, 'Cook me some food.' Why should she have to cook your food? She's not a slave. Why should she have to cook your food?"

David responded evenly to Yoko, but she would have none of it. She launched into a monologue about woman's liberation, repeatedly accusing David of being a chauvinist. Her intimations that he was less than perfect riled him, and he responded to her with equal force. He really wasn't used to anyone talking back; nothing he said could silence Yoko.

Through it all John roared with laughter, obviously entertained by his wife's fearless, aggressively outspoken stance.

"David was mad," says Ava. "When we got home, I got it. He was not the kind of person that would fight in public; David never fought with people. He would just say something that would cut them so low that they would just shrivel up in a cocoon and die."

The mood was high on March 1. At the Dakota, Yoko Ono arose to a breakfast of caviar and yogurt while Jac Colello cut John Lennon's hair. In her small Greenwich Village apartment Bette Midler camped in front of her mirror in the comic hat adorned with a copy of the Del Vikings' single "Come Go With Me." In the House on Twentieth

Street David thought about what he would say when he read the nominations for Best Female Soul Singer.

On stage that night David smiled happily as he announced Aretha Franklin's name. Franklin took to the stage to accept her award. She took one look at David and quipped, "I'm so happy I could even kiss David Bowie."

That one remark, delivered over national television, made it clear that David was still being perceived as a rather repulsive future-world space-queen. His concentrated efforts to change his image seemed to him to have blown up in his face.

The next time Ava Cherry put an Aretha Franklin record on the turntable David flew into a rage and broke the record in half.

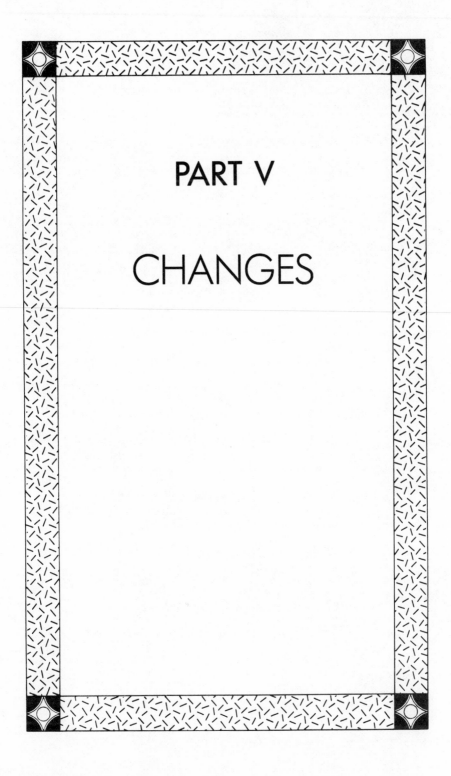

PART V

CHANGES

Exorcism

Nick Roeg had a three-picture deal at Columbia Studios that gave the studio first crack at financing his next projects.

Roeg, Si Litvinoff, and Maggie Abbott headed to the studio to report on their meetings with David Bowie. They brought a budget for the film; according to their figures it would cost $1.3 million.

The meeting was chaired by David Begelman, Columbia's president, and Begelman's head of production, Peter Guber. Begelman and Guber were less than enthusiastic. For starters, the script lacked a strong, clear story line. The explicit sex and degenerate feel of Roeg's *Performance* had shocked its distributor, Warner Films, and had been held back for release for two years while the studio employed seven different editors to recut and restructure the film both to tone it down and to make it more comprehensible.

Begelman and Guber refused to spend a cent more than $1.1 million (quite a low budget) on Roeg's new film and were afraid that a movie already budgeted at $1.3 million would ultimately cost even more.

They were also extremely wary about David.

"He's not a name. He won't draw at the box office," said Begelman.

"Can he act?" asked Guber.

Abbott fought a hard battle on David's behalf.

"The budget still bothers us," said Begelman at the end of the meeting. After much hemming and hawing Columbia finally passed on the project.

As the days wore on into March David grew moodier. "Young Americans," the title track of his new album and the single he had selected to be the front runner, was not climbing the charts fast enough to suit him. Defries had slapped an injunction on RCA in an attempt to stop them from releasing the album because it had been delivered by David and not by MainMan; after three days the injunction had been lifted but it was an indication that freedom from Defries might be just another illusion. There was still no word from Hollywood about *The Man Who Fell to Earth*.

But Norman Fisher appeared regularly to hold his hand and keep his coke bottle filled. The cocaine gave him the energy to push on, yet he was feeling increasingly insecure.

One evening Bette Midler came to visit. Ava sat in the room across from them while David and Midler spoke softly to each other. She could pick out only a few words.

"You must change your strategy," David said to Bette as they discussed Bette's career.

Then they got up and left the room. Ava became very suspicious. She could not resist following them. In the hallway David wheeled around and screamed, "Don't! Go away!"

Stunned, Ava stumbled downstairs. She sat alone in the kitchen, weeping. A little while later Bette came downstairs and sat beside her. "I know how you feel," she said gently. "Just calm down. You've got to understand what he's going through. I understand how you're suffering; I know how a man can make a woman suffer."

Ava smiled gratefully. Those were the first really kind words that had been directed at her during the days in the House on Twentieth Street.

A small English film company, British Lion, was interested in financing *The Man Who Fell to Earth*. They wanted to co-produce it with Columbia by supplying the overages that had made Columbia so nervous. Columbia passed on this plan too, so British Lion was left to raise all the financing on its own. A negative pick-up deal was made with Paramount to the effect that Paramount would pick up the production costs of the film in return for distribution rights. The deal would allow the project to go forward but proved not to be a good one. British Lion had failed to secure a guarantee from Paramount. When Paramount saw the first cut of the strange film, it recoiled in shock, and British Lion found itself having to foot the bill with no distributor in sight.

Meanwhile, the unpleasant incidents continued. Alice Cooper's manager, Shep Gordon, was dating a beautiful black girl named Winona Williams. When Gordon was out of town, Williams gave a party in Gordon's plush duplex.

When David and Ava arrived at the apartment, Bette Midler, Bob Dylan, and the members of Manhattan Transfer had already arrived. But what really interested David was Winona Williams.

Ava sat alone brooding while David unleashed all his high-voltage charm on his hostess.

Later everyone went upstairs. David played *Young Americans* for the guests. Dylan said he thought it was terrible and David got very upset.

Ava was paralyzed. Finally she got up and peaked into the bedroom. David and Winona Williams sat alone. While David wept, Winona consoled him. David's upsets had become a tactic to ensnare Winona. It was as if a new sexual conquest would mitigate the damage Bob Dylan had done to his public image.

British Lion's budget was so tight it could afford to pay David only $50,000 for his appearance in *The Man Who Fell to Earth*. Maggie Abbott knew it was an unsatisfactory figure. Even though David was not a bona fide movie star, he had to be paid something approaching a movie star's salary. In Hollywood, where above all else illusion and image counted, it had to look as if a real star had been hired for the film. The only way that could be accomplished was by getting David more money than he was really worth at the time.

The relentless agent had a brainstorm. She convinced RCA Records president Ken Glancy to invest in the film. RCA's contribution would be considered an advance against a Bowie sound track and would be paid to David as an acting fee even though it would guarantee that he would score the movie. The film and the record company monies would provide David with a fee of around $200,000, which Abbott considered respectable.

Abbott was feeling very pleased with herself when Michael Lippman called.

Zealously guarding what he believed were David's best interests, he said, "I read the script and I don't understand it at all."

"Michael, you don't have to understand the script," Abbott snapped. "The director understands it, the producer understands it, I understand it. You're a lawyer. It's not your job to understand it."

"I think David should get six hundred thousand dollars and ten percent of the gross."

Lippman had his first star and he wanted to make a really large deal for him.

"This is David Bowie's first movie. He doesn't deserve that kind of deal. The budget is small. I'll get him points and the sound track. There will be money stacked all over the place. So don't talk that kind of money to me."

The two former CMA agents battled. Finally Abbott prevailed and a deal was ready to be made.

After observing Corinne in action with David, Abbott believed that David found it essential to have her around. Abbott negotiated a deal not only for David but also for Schwab. Corinne would receive a salary, and personal and travel expenses.

Over the next few months, when Abbott called, she would find Corinne refusing to put her calls through to David.

He was going to be a movie star. The past was behind him, and his break with his former "father" was complete. That left only two people to be erased: Ava Cherry and John Dove.

Dove had been a daily visitor to the house, working side by side with David. They appeared to be best friends, and Dove adored him.

Whenever David was in the mood, he picked up the telephone and summoned Norman Fisher to bring over a stash.

One day Dove urged him to be more discreet. Before his days at New York University, he had been in the intelligence division of the army. He explained how easy it would be for the government to tap David's phone and use the information against him. David listened carefully, smiling gratefully at Dove.

Soon thereafter, Dove was erased. Later word reached him second-hand that David had come to the conclusion that Dove was a CIA agent. It was much easier for David to have the fantasy that he was the victim than to thank Dove and say goodbye.

That left Ava.

The MainMan staff liked to hang out at a notorious drag queen bar called the Gilded Grape. A rumor started that one of the most visible queens was rich. A MainMan staffer had seen "her" open bankbook in her purse and saw a balance of $100,000.

In MainMan's typical fashion, as the rumor went round the office it underwent an amazing transformation. Ava Cherry's name was substituted for that of the drag queen. Ava had saved every cent that MainMan had given her and was loaded.

Then the rumor was whispered to Corinne.

"Where did you get all that money, and could you show me the bankbook?" demanded David.

Ava insisted that she had no money, which was the truth, but David refused to believe her. After his experience with Tony Defries he would always be easily upset about money.

"Any time Corinne wanted to manipulate him or get rid of somebody she began to tell him that they were ripping him off," Ava recalls.

One day the two women came face to face. Corinne told Ava that David didn't love her anymore, that it would be easier if Ava just *went*.

David explained to Ava that he had to go to Hollywood to make a movie but that he would come back to her.

"I love you," he said tenderly. "I'll be back." It seemed impossible at that moment to know whether to believe David or Corinne.

Several days before David left for L.A. Ava discovered that while she had been out, her things had been searched. Worst of all, pictures of David and her had been ripped up. Pieces of photographs littered the floor.

"Why are you doing this to me?" she blurted to Corinne. "What have I done to you? What have I ever done to hurt you?"

"David's going to L.A. tomorrow. That's the end of you. The slate had to be wiped clean."

"Is that what David said? Are these David's orders?"

Corinne tossed her a contemptuous look. "He doesn't love you anymore. You've got one option and one option alone: You must go. And I want you to be quick about it."

David had structured his world in such an airtight way that even his mistress was afraid to ask him directly if Corinne was acting under David's instructions. Corinne was the part of David's personality the existence of which he refused to acknowledge.

Ava had no money and no apartment. Her relationship with David had left her homeless and penniless. She went to the phone and called her best friend, Claudia Jennings, in Los Angeles.

"After what you've been through you need a vacation," Jennings announced. "I'm coming east and we're going to go to the Bahamas to have some fun."

They were beautiful young women, and when something didn't work out there was always a new adventure waiting for them. Claudia did not tell Ava that the Rolling Stones were recording in the Bahamas. Perhaps unconsciously she realized that David deserved to be punished, and the best way to do it was to thrust "David's woman" under the nose of his "best friend" Mick Jagger.

Ava and Claudia made their escape to the Bahamas, where they encountered the Rolling Stones. David and Geoffrey boarded the train for Los Angeles. Corinne was left behind to take care of any unfinished business.

This was David's sixth trip to Hollywood. On his previous trips he had been inspired to create Ziggy Stardust, was proclaimed a star, had launched his pop-soul career, and had become an *American* performer. Now he would become a movie star.

Sensitive and vulnerable, macho yet detached, irresistibly androgynous as well as wonderfully tragic, he was everything—no, more than—James Dean could ever have hoped to have been.

Filming would not begin for three months. He had plenty of time on his hands. Nothing could be more dangerous to someone whose imagination would demand that he could not be *The Man Who Fell to Earth* on screen unless he assumed the role in real life. The time had come for the man acting the role of a real life Ziggy Stardust to cast Ziggy Stardust in the role of the Man Who Fell to Earth.

The journey to Los Angeles found David homeless for the first time in his twenty-eight years. For once there was neither a male protector nor a nurturing mother figure to control the environment for him.

Many upsetting factors played on his mind. Defries had proved uncontrollable; he was penniless; MainMan had not really been his and was now ignoring him.

It was March, and he had three months to prepare for *The Man Who Fell to Earth*, the kind of challenge that at the best of times made him feel vulnerable and in danger of failure. The cocaine abuse had raged for almost a year. David had been known to stay up as many as five days and nights in a row. He was open to intense feelings of anxiety, irrational fears, and paranoid thoughts.

Becoming *The Man Who Fell to Earth* dictated that he act out in his real life the most extreme expression yet of alien behavior, at the same time removing himself from it and watching himself as if he were in a play.

His incredible strength and energy came from an ability to distance himself. Never had he been more helpless; paradoxically, never had he been stronger.

In L.A., he went first to the house of a friend, musician Glenn Hughes. But Hughes had to leave town to go on the road with his band, Deep Purple, almost as soon as David arrived, and David was on his own. For company he had best friend Geoffrey and Glenn's houseman, Phil.

He started seeing a black singer and the venerable Los Angeles supplier of medicinal cocaine who had again begun to play groupie/drug supplier to David's English rock star prince.

Corinne was still in New York, and David needed mommy. So while he was with the black vocalist, he also turned to Angela. His calls to her at the House on Oakley Street often lasted for hours.

Leee Black Childers was one of Angela's house guests again. Angela reported to Childers that David didn't seem to make much sense and didn't seem to know what was going on.

After the phone calls Angela usually burst into tears. David was clearly in awful shape. He was calling out to Angela without asking her directly to come to Los Angeles.

Angela knew that she would go to him; she always went to him. But life in the House on Oakley Street was lots of fun, and she was having a ball.

One morning Childers awoke and found Ryan O'Neal lying beside him. O'Neal and Jim Capaldi had visited the night before; they had played guitar, sung songs, and drunk wine. O'Neal became tired and went to sleep. Angela thought it hilarious to toss the actor into Childers's bed without O'Neal's knowing it.

She appeared, all smiles. "Wake up boys," she boomed. Childers and she screamed with laughter. What healthy all-American boy wouldn't want to wake up next to delectable Ryan O'Neal?

"I was a perfect gentleman," says Childers, his voice tinged with regret.

Evil lurked in Glenn's house, and David had to do something about it. He covered the walls and windows with drawings. Pentagrams, symbols of protection in the practice of Magick, were drawn everywhere. But it was not enough.

Nancy and Michael Lippman came to the rescue. They moved him into a little bedroom in their house on King's Road above Sunset Boulevard.

Reflecting the sunny personalities of the Lippmans, the house was one of the bright, sunny Spanish-style haciendas so common in Los Angeles. There was light everywhere except in David's room. He never opened the shades, and soon the floor was cluttered with scraps of paper on which were scribbled notes and bits of lyrics. Books dealing with occult and mystical religions lay everywhere. Ashtrays were always overflowing; cartons of Gitanes cigarettes were piled against one wall, and clothes, scripts, and records were strewn everywhere.

David drew pentagrams and scribbled variations of the word AUMGN as a way of protecting himself. Aleister Crowley had expanded the Buddhist OM into a bastard version, AUMGN. Crowley believed that his mantra provided the ability to grab control of the universe. When things were so much out of control, nothing less would do.

David also began to store his urine in the refrigerator (Crowley had also saved his bodily fluids so that no other wizard could use them against him).

It was a new role. Now Michael Lippman, instead of Tony Defries, watched from the distance.

Corinne, whom Geoffrey MacCormack had taken to calling Coco, wanted to quit, but Michael Lippman talked her out of it. It was an action he would grow to regret.

One night David sat silently on the couch and seemed confused. He spent a lot of time playing with a piece of string. Periodically he got up and looked out the windows to see if anyone was lurking in the darkness. He searched the house for intruders. He stared at the phone knowingly, suggesting that he knew when it was going to ring.

There were moments that night when he seemed to go into a trance, sitting lost in thought and shaking his head in disbelief. When he suddenly came to life, everyone else did too. His cloistered Los Angeles family seemed to exist only to suit his moods.

One name was off limits during the sporadic discussion: Tony Defries. No one was allowed to say it, but if David mentioned Tony, then people were allowed to talk about him.

A bowl of cocaine rested on the coffee table. It was kept filled; David tested it with alcohol and water to confirm its purity.

David had begun to look terrible. He was exceptionally thin and pale. His skin had a greyish hue and he sniffled incessantly. His hands shook. He never took off his bolero hat, which had little balls dangling from it.

David wanted to perform a spell to remove the evil influences he believed were being directed at him. The enemy wizard's name was to be written on a piece of paper. When the proper candle burned down to the name, a psychic mirror supposedly was formed with the evil forces rebounding off the name on the paper.

The spell had to be performed at the stroke of midnight. David missed his cue, and a ritual was instituted. Now the name had to be written with a special quill pen and dove's blood ink, a mixture of "dragon's blood," cinnamon, bay, alcohol, gum arabic, and rose oil.

Salt was sprinkled in the corners of the room to absorb the evil energies that threatened him. David took his quill pen, dipped it in the dove's blood ink, and carefully wrote a name. The paper was folded properly, and the candle was lit. Maybe that would save him.

At the end of their Caribbean holiday Claudia Jennings brought Ava Cherry to Los Angeles. Ava was still nursing her wounds, and Claudia wanted to keep an eye on her.

Ava asked Michael Lippman to tell David she was in L.A. and passed on her phone number. Two days later he called and invited himself over.

By nature Claudia Jennings was a rescuer. She had rescued Ava and now felt compelled to save David. She felt he was paranoid, and she invited him to move in with her.

She had to leave the house she was in. David instantly left the

Lippman house, and he, Ava, and Claudia moved to Robert Wagner and Natalie Wood's Century City apartment. As he had done years before when leaving Ken Pitt's, he took his toys—a stereo system, portable keyboards, and tape recorders—with him.

David's behavior unnerved Ava. She suspected that David and Claudia had become lovers. In the mornings she would find them deep in conversation in bed. Claudia explained that she was merely trying to figure David out.

David was equally suspicious about Ava and Claudia. "What are you two always whispering about? Why do you go into the other room and talk alone? What are you two talking about?" he nagged.

There was a great deal on David's mind, but worst of all was Tony Defries. He brooded incessantly about him, always ending up weeping. Negotiations to settle his MainMan contract were approaching. The issue was upsetting and threatening, and he didn't want to deal with it.

One day he announced, "I've got to get out of Los Angeles because these people are after me."

"Who are they?" Ava asked. He was holding a glass, which suddenly crumbled in his hand.

He was terrified and confessed that an underground witchcraft cult was after him. He believed he was in grave danger. Then the television and stereo began to turn on and off, seemingly of their own accord.

David told Ava that a girl friend had given him a magical bracelet, which he was wearing. Ava threw the bracelet away.

Meanwhile David continued to investigate the practice of white magic. He painted a pentagram on the inside of Ava's hand in order to protect her. When she was in the bathtub he incanted a spell over her.

It appeared that David had encountered a small group of people who practiced Crowley's Magick. He believed their leader was Ken Anger, and that Anger was after him. Anger vigorously denies this; he says he's never met David Bowie. David had heard that Anger was angry at Jimmy Page, and he seemed to have become his own version of Jimmy Page as victim.

Despite his distress, the productive David kept on working, going into RCA's West Coast studios to work with Nina Simone, whom he had met in New York.

Neither David nor Ava had any money, so Claudia supported

them both, paying for their food and taking them out to dinner. She also took them to the Playboy Mansion to visit her friend Hugh Heffner.

Ava began to feel the walls closing in on her. She sensed that David's entire L.A. family—Michael Lippman, Geoffrey Mac-Cormack, and Corinne—wanted to get rid of her. She was still so entranced by David that she didn't stop to ask herself if they were doing his bidding for him, if a replacement had been found for her—namely Angela, whose arrival in Los Angeles was imminent.

Then one day David was gone, back to the Lippmans' house. He left behind a $2,000 phone bill, which Claudia was forced to pay, and his toys, which he wanted back.

When Angela arrived, she took charge and was eager to set up a new nest for David and look after him. As she had done before during their marriage, she went house-hunting and settled on a house with a pool on Doheney Drive—the House on Doheney.

It was imperative that David buckle down to *The Man Who Fell to Earth*. Angela felt he was being a prima donna. She also disliked director Nick Roeg, who she says came to the House on Doheney one day with David's leading lady, Candy Clark, and "sat in the living room telling Candy to get to know David better."

One day Angela looked outside. It was bright and sunny, without a cloud in the sky, but rain poured down on the House on Doheney, and only on the House on Doheney.

It was enough to make David turn white.

"I'm glad it's not me they're after," thought Angela as she marched in and out of the front door and shook off the rain.

Apparently this house was also haunted, and Angela didn't deny the truth of it, saying only that David "was definitely the victim of certain unscrupulous people's practice of the black arts."

David murmured that he believed one of his many Los Angeles girl friends was trying to have a baby with him to offer up to Satan. It was as if he was the Rosemary of *Rosemary's Baby*, and the baby was destined to be the Anti-Christ.

He told Angela that he was going to be destroyed on Walpurgis Night, May Eve, April 30, one of the eight times a year that witches gather to celebrate their magical powers.

The only solution, he believed, was to perform an exorcism that would remove the evil forces from the House on Doheney. David needed a white witch to give him instructions about performing the ritual.

Angela called Kathy Dorritie, who recommended white witch Wally Elmlark, who had written a pop witchcraft column for the teen fanzine *Circus*. David had met her in 1972 when she was recording with Robert Fripp in London.

When David called Elmlark in New York City, she had an explanation for everything. David was a walk-in, a visitor from outer space. He was an alien being living in a human form. David's mission was to change the consciousness of the world. It was a hard task; walk-ins often dulled their pain with drugs, sex, and alcohol.

David understood.

Elmlark added that walk-ins were always at war against the forces of evil. She compared David to two other musician walk-ins, Jimi Hendrix and Marc Bolan. Evil had destroyed Hendrix, while Bolan and David were both in great danger. Elmlark said that successful walk-ins had only five years before their inevitable destruction.

David was stunned. On *Ziggy Stardust* he had written that Ziggy had only five years to live, five years before he became a rock-'n'-roll suicide. And Tony Defries had repeatedly said that a rock star's longevity was five years.

"My five years are about to run out," he told Elmlark. "I'm in great danger." Elmlark agreed that an exorcism had to be performed and detailed the books, herbs, potions, and spells needed to accomplish the ritual.

Angela's response was annoyance. She couldn't bear to see David moping around; she hated the way Corinne, Geoffrey, Nancy, and Michael fawned over him. She thought his fears of the devil were nonsense, but she knew David hated being contradicted. As always, she became mommy. If David wanted an exorcism, he would have one, a four-star exorcism organized by his Nama-nama.

She took to the phone with a vengeance. For three days she called frantically all over Los Angeles. Soon every available piece of information on exorcism had been gathered. David took the books and skimmed them.

What madness! Angie thought. He's flirting with his fantasies of congenital insanity again; he's busy pretending he's Ziggy Stardust and practicing his own fall; he's getting ready to be the Man Who Fell to Earth and is making believe he's an alien.

The talk about the impending settlement with Tony Defries filled the air. David didn't like the discussions. It would be wonderful once and for all to exorcise Defries and the bad memories of the past. An exorcism was a wonderful way of eliminating the demons that were plaguing him.

But to Angela, it was all playacting. She knew how much David loved the drama inherent in ritual. She believed the scene was being set for a real-life performance David couldn't wait to give.

When the exorcism night arrived, Angela called Wally Elmlark and handed David the phone. The witch told him to surround the room with salt to purify the space and absorb all the negative influences in the air. She then told him to burn blue and white candles. The blue would avert the evil in the house; the white symbolized purity and offered protection. Then the ceremony could begin.

Salt was sprinkled and the candles lit. In New York City, Wally Elmlark's floor was decorated with a huge pentagram. She and a group of her friends stepped inside the design. The witch directed them to focusing their energy to raise a Cone of Power, whose purpose was to protect and save David Bowie.

In Los Angeles, David turned to a *Thesaurus Exorcisonorum*, a thousand-page catalog of exorcisms. An exorcism is usually performed by a Roman Catholic priest. David had decided to be his own priest. He would exorcise himself.

"I cast you out, unclean spirit, along with every satanic power of the enemy, every specter from Hell, and all your fellow companions . . ." he began.

Angela paced restlessly.

It went on and on. Finally, David paused. Much to Angela's chagrin he suddenly began again.

By the time it was over everyone believed the water in the pool was bubbling, and that a loud explosion had occurred.

David was ready to become the Man Who Fell to Earth.

He would still feel safe only hiding behind a self-made shadow. But now he seemed to believe he could control those shadows, slipping them on and off at will. But, Tony Defries was gone and he believed he was free.

Angela didn't see any change at all in his behavior. If anything, he seemed worse after the exorcism.

———

Until there was a settlement, RCA would withhold David's royalties. There was around $800,000 in escrow monies. Neither Defries
nor David had any cash flow, and it was in the interest of each that
they settle their differences. But Defries enjoyed complicated negotiations and long discussions. During negotiating sessions he seemed
to want to pontificate about everything, and no one knew how to
hurry him along.

The presence of Michael Lippman offended Defries, and he refused to speak to him. Defries sent word to David to hire a really
brilliant lawyer, but David ignored the message. He seemed un-
willing to deal with these business problems; he wanted them to
disappear.

Lippman tried to bring David up to date, but David listened
half-heartedly. He wanted magic; he wanted the past erased.

There were fears that the matter would wind up in the courts,
where Defries seemed capable of dragging it out forever.

When it became clear that David was not going to fight Defries,
things moved with amazing swiftness. RCA, acting for David and
Defries, added up the bills to arrive at a net figure. Expenses were
jockeyed back and forth, and RCA awarded MainMan $800,000,
$600,000 of which was earmarked for bills of expenses accumulated
by David and Defries's MainMan adventure. The remainder was
divided equally between them.

The settlement really did free David, but gave Defries a substantial stake in David's future.

According to Jaime Andrews, David and Defries remained co-
owners of David's MainMan catalog, giving Defries 50 percent forever of the songs and masters that would prove the most commercially viable of David's career. Defries was also to share in the royalties
of David's work until the end of 1982. All told Defries was going to
receive around 17 percent of new recording royalties for the next
seven years, as well as around 25 percent of David's new publishing
monies and around 5 percent of David's live appearance earnings. It
seemed the settlement of someone who didn't want to fight, and who
needed to keep the money flowing.

Those were not the only business matters to be put to rest during
the days that followed. The English courts awarded Ken Pitt a
15,000-pound settlement on his commissions. Essex Music also stepped

forward. Defries had fought David's deal with Essex. Now Essex wanted its contract honored. A settlement was reached with them; they would be David's copublishers on an agreed-upon number of new songs. David's commitment with Essex would not be satisfied until sometime after 1984.

It was in the midst of all this unhappiness that David's dream came true. *Young American*'s first two singles had failed to reach the Top Ten. Then, on June 2, a third single, "Fame," was released. Radio programmers loved its infectious, throbbing rhythm track, and it broke like wildfire. It was going to go all the way. At long last David could feel he was the pop idol of his dreams.

He boarded the train to New Mexico to begin shooting *The Man Who Fell to Earth* a bona fide American pop star.

CHAPTER 30

"Can He Act?"

In New Mexico the past was banished and David was at his most impressive during the filming.

Some days he had to be in the makeup room at four in the morning, and he arrived without a whimper. The process took three or four hours, and he sat through it calmly, everyone marveling that he never complained while latex glue was fastidiously applied to his head, body, and fingernails. He seemed to enjoy the transformation to an alien being.

On the set he proved curious about the moviemaking process. He asked questions and listened intently to the answers. It was like going to a new school; he became an eager schoolboy. Determined to be line perfect, between shots he rehearsed and ran lines with Candy Clark.

A suitcase of reading materials accompanied him to New Mexico. When he wasn't rehearsing or filming, he read, took movies, and painted—bright, psychedelic swirls of color.

New Mexico proved to be an eerie location, full of exotic visual spectacles that caught everyone's eyes. Near the location lived a number of government scientists, all moonlighting on their own projects. David was taken with a group of men who claimed they were creating multidimensional holograms.

His character, James Newton, fit him like a glove. *The Man Who Fell to Earth* tells the story of an alien who comes to earth to find water to save his planet from drought. Newton became very much David's persona, convincing, low-keyed, and occasionally very touching.

Nick Roeg and Candy Clark were having a love affair, and Roeg's attention was focused on Clark. At the same time Claudia Jennings was dating executive producer Si Litvinoff, and her appearances on the set caused a stir. She was a famous *Playboy* playmate.

David didn't seem to mind the lack of attention. Geoffrey had traveled with him, and they appeared to be such close friends Candy Clark thought they might be cousins. Corinne was also there every minute of the shoot, making sure no outsiders got through and that every one of David's phone calls was screened.

The cast and crew marveled at her protectiveness.

During Angela's visit to the set, she began to grasp that she was being replaced by Corinne. Angela was unaccustomed to being challenged by Corinne who was now standing up to her. According to Angela Corinne was behaving "like a moody bitch with no respect who was flexing her muscles."

Angela stormed off to the hotel, got drunk, and befriended two girls and two boys who had traveled all the way from Philadelphia to meet David.

"You look like you just got out of bed," said David when he saw her.

"I did," she replied, saying that she had been in bed with one of the female fans.

It could have been true or more of Angela's shock tactics, but David and Corinne were upset and embarrassed by the news.

"How could you?" asked David.

Angela announced that what was good for the goose is great for the gander.

It became clear to her that she had been summoned to the set because she was an excellent cook, and David wanted her to prepare his meals during the filming.

According to Michael Lippman, Nick Roeg pressured him to pressure David to compose the sound track for the film. David at that time did have the Number One single in the country. The plan was to record the sound track, which would spin off a number of "Fame"-like hit singles. Everytime one of them was played on the radio the film would get a free plug. David would play these songs during his concerts. The concerts would be used to promote the album and the film.

Working until dawn for five nights, David composed sound track material, then went to the set and shot all day.

One morning he had to play his first scene with the experienced actor Rip Torn. He was so tired he could hardly stand up, and the scene wasn't working. Si Litvinoff ground up some No-Doz so that it looked like cocaine. David snorted it and came to life.

Back in Los Angeles Angela assumed the role of David's spokesperson. Again, he appeared in his wonderful guise while she played the role of holy terror. She knew he was exhausted and wanted further recording of the sound track postponed so that David could have time off.

But the machinery had been set in motion. CMA was instructed to book a worldwide tour for David, including the Wembley dates Defries had been endeavoring to book. Lippman modified the deal so that David would be guaranteed 30 percent of the gross instead of 90. At capacity the promoter would make some money; and David would make a great deal. Still the promoters would be at little risk and with a deal like this, it was a way of making sure David could be booked everywhere. Finally he would have a giant-sized tour to match his enormous publicity.

Then it was decided not to use his music on the sound track. Everyone loved David's score, but it was not the stuff of hit singles.

No one said it outright, but a tour was being booked to promote a sound track album that wasn't going to be made. A studio album had to be created to justify the tour, and this album had to have a hit single. The pressure was on him to make hits and, once again, David felt unprotected and left open to rejection if he didn't come through.

During this period he wrote a three-page screenplay. In it a series of buildings age and then become enormous teeth. A person appears trapped inside the mouth of a giant. It was as if David were trapped by the success of his hit single "Fame" and pressure to sustain it.

Upon David's return to Los Angeles after the location shooting was completed, studio time was booked at Cherokee Studios, and David began recording *Station to Station*. Glenn Hughes was by his side a great deal of the time, and David wanted him to sing on the album. But Glenn's band, Deep Purple, objected. Then David told Glenn he wanted to produce a solo album with him, which pleased Glenn very much. Glenn felt even closer to David and grew even more protective.

Often the recording sessions were closed, and only one person was allowed in—the venerable L.A. figure with the vials of "merk."

Despite his presence, *Station to Station* proved to be one of the finest LPs of David's career. It extended the electronically oriented white soul on *Young Americans* with the music rooted by Roy Bittan's piano and Carlos Alomar's guitar.

Superficially the disk is an electronically oriented continuation of the white soul introduced on *Young Americans*. But nothing David did before or after sounds like this album, and no references to old personas appear. Even though David had no loyalty to any style, he automatically referred to himself. Yet it seems that the disk belongs to Bittan and Alomar and the parts they wrote for themselves.

The ten-minute title track sets the tone with a funny, marvelous couplet about the return of the Thin White Duke. Here David repeats his tendency toward mythical self-pretension, but this time it's a grim joke.

Alomar's acoustic and electric rhythm guitars are potent enough to distract the listener from the sentimental lyric during the steel-edged tribute to Angela, "Golden Years." Bittan's piano takes lead on the LP's most captivating song, the Huey Smith–derived "TVC 15," and provides a link to the early rock-and-roll sound David once attempted. "TVC 15" had no intended lyrical meaning, which makes it a joy. This was the first Bowie lyrical throwaway. While mood always took precedence over content in David's songwriting, never before had he so successfully put together a group of meaningless sounds that sounded so right. By keeping his lyrics in the background and allowing his words to work as sound, David had created the album many consider his finest. And it did have a hit. One single, "Golden Years," climbed to tenth position on the charts.

Money had always been the issue. From that day in the mid-1960s when the Lower Third refused to play, money seemed to be on everyone's minds. Often, money seemed more important than David.

Angela and Michael Lippman shared the same point of view. Corinne's actions reflected David's fears about money, and it seemed as if she was trying to eliminate everyone and have David totally to herself.

Corinne was in an ideal position because she never wanted money. Angela always needed money; the managers and musicians seemed ruled by it. The music publishers were always concerned about getting their money, as was RCA, which had reissued "Space Oddity" for the fourth time to capitalize on David's "Fame" hit. Only Corinne kept her hands clean.

The first to go was Geoffrey MacCormack, ostensibly because he couldn't bear to be witness to David's self-destructiveness. Lippman claims that Corinne turned David against Geoffrey at the time.

David's schedule was to put the finishing touches on the LP, announce the world tour by worldwide satellite television, attend Michael Lippman's Christmas party, then travel to Keith Richard's house in Jamaica to rehearse for the tour scheduled to begin on February 2.

On November 25, 1975, the day of the satellite broadcast, the Spanish government asked David to relinquish the satellite so that the death of General Franco could be announced to the world. He refused. It seemed more important for him to announce that he was going to return home to England and play there.

Just before Christmas an incoherent David called Lippman from the studio. Lippman couldn't make any sense of David's ramblings.

At Christmas Angela, Corinne, and Pat Gibbons gathered at the Lippmans. They all acted as if nothing were wrong. But David wasn't there, and Lippman couldn't get him on the phone. David just cut him off without any explanation.

During the ten-month Los Angeles period, David had made his film debut, completed a new album, and was about to embark on his first world tour. His business affairs were finally in some sort of order. He rushed to the train to see David before he left town.

"Hello," said David.

"Hello," said Michael.

"Goodbye," said David, and he stepped onto the train and was gone.

Lippman blamed Corinne.

Now, there was a new shadow, the Thin White Duke. To become the Thin White Duke David took the alienlike Man Who Fell to Earth to its extreme. From February to March 1976, David's Thin White Duke persona was scheduled to play thirty-three Canadian and American cities; David would perform thirty-nine shows.

The evening began with the 1929 Luis Bunuel–Salvador Dali surrealist film short, *Un Chien Andalou*, featuring an infamous collection of images that included the slitting of a young woman's eyeball. Salvador Dali's protégée Amanda Lear had turned David on to Dali, and he had learned his lesson well.

Onstage the movie screen was replaced by a black box drenched in harsh white light. A slow bashing rhythm began, and David appeared on top of a staircase at the back of the stage. He slowly descended the steps and marched toward the microphone at stage center.

He was dressed in black slacks, a stylish white shirt with French cuffs, a black vest, and a black jacket. The costume greatly resembled one he had worn in *The Man Who Fell to Earth*. His bleached-blond hair seemed pasted to his head. In this incarnation he was an ultra-stylish Euro-cabaret artist, the MC of *Cabaret*, a cabaret of his own creation.

As he stood stage center the throbbing synthesizer rhythms grew even louder.

During the entire concert he was on stage alone, the sole focus of a brilliantly hard-edged evening whose stark use of black and white reflected his interest in such old black-and-white movies as *Metropolis*.

The black stage design, illuminated only by overhead white flourescent lights and crisscrossing white spotlights, was reminiscent of Hal Prince's *Cabaret*, which he had seen as a teenager and which had its roots in Brecht's theater of alienation. Led by Carlos Alomar, the band remained offstage playing unrelenting techno-rock. This unlikely collage of sight, sound, and a solo artist's icy performing style came together seamlessly.

The fifth city on the tour was set for February 11, 1976 in Los Angeles. There Iggy Pop was enlisted as touring buddy and Geoffrey MacCormack's replacement. During David's stay in L.A. the previous June Iggy and he had recorded together. But Iggy had disappeared, to turn up days later as a patient at the UCLA Neuropsychiatric Institute, and David had visited him.

When the tour reached Rochester on March 21, David and Iggy were among a small group arrested on suspicion of marijuana possession. Felony charges were pressed in Rochester City Court. David pleaded innocent and was released on $2,000 bail. They were freed.

The press viewed David's persona on *Station to Station* as Aryan superman. As he had played Ziggy Stardust in his real life, he now seemed compelled to enact the Thin White Duke in public.

"I want to be prime minister of England," David announced.

Although he gave few interviews during the tour, those he did give found him irritable, delivering cryptic answers to simple questions and playing with a monkey doll he named Asshole.

Finally the American leg of the tour came to an end at Madison Square Garden on March 26. A small press reception was held afterward at the Penn Plaza Club. Bodyguards surrounded free-lance photographers attempting to take pictures of David and threatened to destroy their cameras. Some aspects of the MainMan myth-making procedure had been kept intact by David.

At the party David renewed his friendship with May Pang, whom he had met when she was living with John Lennon. Pang introduced him to Ronnie Spector.

Later that night there was a knock at Pang's door. She opened it and found Corinne and Pat Gibbons standing there.

"Where's David? He's got to take a boat to France tomorrow," said Corinne.

Pang dialed Ronnie Spector's number and gave Coco the phone.

The tour was scheduled to resume in Munich on April 7. With time on his hands before the Munich date David decided to visit East Berlin. In a woman's home he spotted a bust of Hitler and contemplated it in the style of Aristotle contemplating the bust of Homer. Photographs were made by tour photographer Andy Kent, who promised David the pictures would never surface. David was taken to Hitler's bunker and more secret photographs were taken. After viewing the bunker David turned and gave a one-armed salute. That, too, became the subject of a secret photograph.

At the performance in Berlin on April 10, the girls in the front row removed their furs and then their dresses, which they hurled on stage. As David sang they danced naked before him. It was exactly the response he most appreciated. Many years before when he was with Ken Pitt, Berlin had given him a king's welcome; now the gesture was being repeated. After the show he vomited.

In the audience that night was one of Berlin's most popular entertainment figures, Romy Haag, the proprietor and star of her own cabaret Chez Romy.

Romy Haag says she is a woman in the guise of a female impersonator. She was a great illusionist and had a striking image.

Haag was the epitome of glamour. Her face was a painted mask of chiseled beauty, and she was voluptuous and expensively dressed.

Her style was that of a European movie queen. She could have been Berlin's answer to Sophia Loren.

After the concert David and a small group went to Chez Romy for a party. Romy's audience was a fascinating mix of wealthy Europeans, tourists, German show-business types, cruising gays, and curious young heterosexuals.

That night Romy and her small company of "girls"—one the spitting image of Marilyn Monroe, took to the stage to do their show for David.

The performance was a brilliant one. Haag and her company lip-synched to a wide variety of music ranging from Marlene Dietrich numbers to rock and roll. Each was turned into a mini-production number. They were like music videos come to life years before such videos attained worldwide popularity. Each number was linked by a sound-effects collage that gave the show pace and flow.

At the end of the show Haag sang "My Way." She ripped off her wig, and her beautiful long hair tumbled to her shoulders. Then she took her hand and rubbed it across her face, smearing her painted red lips until her face resembled an open wound. As the audience gasped at the image, Haag fled from the stage.

After the show David went to Haag's dressing room.

"From the first moment, everything was clear. There is nothing to say. It was for sure. It was *wunderbar!*" Haag says.

They went to a smaller party at Romy's chic penthouse apartment, and when everybody left they were alone. As he had wooed so many before her, David turned his charms on her.

"David Bowie in my apartment, sitting on the bed playing love songs. *Wunderbar!*" recalls Haag.

When David discovered that Romy had none of his records, he became upset and made a call. The next morning a complete set was messengered to her.

Haag discovered that talking to David was like looking in a mirror. He seemed to understand her life, problems, and attitudes with a clarity and sympathy no one had ever manifested before. She perceived him as "a warm, sentimental man" and their encounter "like a fairy tale."

The next day, Coco called endlessly, but David didn't want to leave for his Hamburg concert. The show would be delayed two hours because of his lateness.

For the next month, he called Romy every day.

———

David had been advised to establish a Swiss residency. English stars often become residents of Switzerland to avoid England's exorbitant taxation. It fell to Angela to do the legwork. As she had found Haddon Hall she found a Swiss home for them.

During a break in the German tour, on April 14, David traveled to Lake Geneva, saw the house, went back on the road, returned to Switzerland on April 17, and then resumed the tour.

It was in Stockholm on April 26 that he told a reporter, "I think Britain could benefit from a fascist leader. I mean fascist in its true sense, not Nazi. After all, fascism is really nationalism. In a sense, it is a very pure form of communism."

Five nights, beginning on May 3, faced him at Wembley, with 300,000 tickets to be sold. Those around the tour believed he had used outrage to get publicity as he had often done before to ensure box-office success.

They knew David was apolitical and really didn't understand such concepts as fascism and nationalism. His curiosity about Hitler stemmed from his ability onstage to manipulate an audience in any direction he chose. It was clear to him that if a rock star had such power, a political figure like Hitler could—and did—get away with anything.

David's comments in Stockholm had made headlines in England, and six days later, when his train arrived at Victoria Station, press and fans mobbed him. His right hand seemed to have a life of its own as it jerked up in a Nazi-like salute.

"Publicity," explains Andy Kent, with David saying later that he was making a peace sign.

But as there were those before who had seen David slip in and out of Ziggy Stardust, it was clear that he was capable of clapping on the mask of the Thin White Duke. Did David really think he was a Hitler-like figure?

In the MainMan tradition the press had been used to sell out the Wembley concerts, but the press could be an enemy as well as a friend.

Peggy Jones read that her son had been compared to Hitler, and she didn't like it. Never one not to speak her mind, she phoned the *New Musical Express* to give an interview of her own.

The reporter came to her apartment, decorated with David's

record posters, a painting of David as Ziggy Stardust, and a huge poster of Humphrey Bogart.

Peggy's English sensibilities were offended. Saying that England would never become a dictatorship, she called David "a terrible hypocrite."

Then she said that after John had died, David had been generous to her, but that he'd only called her once in the last five years. The Christmas before, he'd sent her a mink coat, but as an old-age pensioner living on eleven pounds fifty a week, she had noplace to wear it.

The Wembley concerts gathered an illustrious crowd, with Mick Jagger and Keith Richards among those in attendance. One night Brian Eno came backstage, and David and he chatted about working together.

Glenn Hughes, David's old friend from L.A., was also there. The year before David had offered to produce an album with Glenn. But now David seemed uninterested in Hughes, who perceived that he had been replaced by Iggy.

"We loved each other," Hughes says of the relationship. "I literally emptied myself. I gave him everything. David drains people. I really let myself get drained emotionally."

The tour moved on to Rotterdam and then to Paris on May 17. David summoned Romy to Paris and moved her into his hotel room; Iggy Pop had the other bedroom in the suite.

In New York, RCA, exercising its right to release a greatest hits compilation, issued *ChangesOne* a mere three months after the release of *Station to Station*.

There were only two authentic hits on the album, "Fame" and "Golden Years," but the LP was enormously popular anyway. The music was all that was left of Ziggy, the pop-soul David, and the Thin White Duke. Many people had heard of these personas but had not had the chance to see them before David abandoned them. They would live only on compilation records like these and served as souvenirs of the Davids the public would never get to see.

ChangesOne also illustrated David's quest for a pop hit. The six-year journey between "Space Oddity" and "Golden Years" demonstrated that David had made significant progress as composer and vocalist. There was every indication he was beginning to hit his stride.

Exile

Myth has it that at the end of the Station to Station tour David exiled himself in Berlin for more than three years. In reality he had moved to his new Swiss home.

At the outset of the tour he had sued Michael Lippman, claiming that Lippman took 15 percent instead of 10 percent in commissions and was withholding $475,000 in assets that belonged to David. A court date was set, and David was to prepare to give depositions in Paris.

It was Angela's fantasy to have a new beginning in Switzerland. David and she went shopping for presents for Zowie for his sixth birthday on May 28.

They spotted a series of German expressionist etchings illustrating *The Cocaine Eaters.* The girls' hair stood on end, their jaws were tightly locked, their faces knotted into demented expressions.

"You know, we should buy these to remind you never to do that again," said Angela in her maternal Nama-nama voice.

But David seemed not to want or need a Nama-nama anymore.

The past was vomiting in his face. He was upset about the forthcoming depositions and afraid Lippman would make a fool of him in court. He feared he had been incorrectly advised and had made yet another mistake.

In his cuckoo clock chalet on six acres of ground overlooking Lake Geneva, he grew moody and uncommunicative. The only person he wanted to talk to was Corinne, now known to everyone as Coco. Angela couldn't bear to be left out, and his behavior drove her mad. According to Angela he seemed to be having a nervous breakdown.

The only thing for him to do was to flee, and he ran from Angela and the past. He headed for Paris and the Chateau d'Hérouville where he had recorded *Pin-Ups*. There he would produce a solo album for Iggy. It was titled *The Idiot*.

Angela demanded that Coco tell her where David was, but Coco wouldn't answer. Angela refused to accept that David might not see her.

In New York the past was playing itself out in the present with the opening of *The Man Who Fell to Earth*. John Philips was the musical director, not David, and the sound track was a hodgepodge that included electronic music by Stomu Yamashta, Gustav Holst's "The Planets," the Brothers Four's "Try to Remember," "Blueberry Hill," "True Love," and "Stardust." It was the kind of embarrassment David would feel compelled to erase.

A search for a distributor had led British Lion to Cinema 5, headed by Donald Rugoff. He thought the film was weird but that a young audience would like it.

Rugoff, who reportedly spent $800,000 to acquire the rights to the film, decided to test market it at Dartmouth College in Hanover, New Hampshire. Half the students loved the film, half didn't. Rugoff became nervous, and he solicited opinions from students, a film editor, a screenwriter, and a psychiatrist. The psychiatrist told him it was a disaster.

He cut twenty minutes from the film, much to the chagrin of director Nick Roeg, including a Bowie love scene with Candy Clark.

The film opened to reviews that were mixed but essentially positive. *The New York Times* labeled the film "a first-rate achievement," "absorbing" and "beautiful." David's performance was hailed as "stunning." But John Simon in *New York* magazine labeled David "an expressionless zombie," and the film "the work of a third-rate sensibility desperately aspiring to be second rate."

It did cult-sized business, grossing $4 million, but no evidence was offered that David had anywhere near the box-office appeal of a real movie star.

An attempt was made in Lausanne to settle the dispute between David and Lippman. They exchanged hellos, and then David became so uncomfortable he had to leave the room.

In Paris in September both men, surrounded by lawyers, made a court appearance.

"These are our problems. Let's settle this thing ourselves," said Lippman.

They spent ten minutes alone together to reach a settlement.

When it was over David burst into tears, as did Lippman. That was the last image each would have of the other.

The past had finally been replaced. Reborn yet again, David wanted to move on. He wanted to make a new album, and he wanted to work with Brian Eno.

Coco placed the call to Eno's management and negotiated the deal. Eno was advised not to become involved. David was trying to unravel the production secrets Eno had brought to the original Roxy Music albums. History proved that anyone who worked with David contributed to David's knowledge with David getting all of the credit. Such contributions were always absorbed into David's myth. Eno, uninterested in fame and glory, set out for the chateau.

Intelligent and soft-spoken, Eno had a precocious art-school background and had said that he went into rock and roll after he heard the Velvet Underground because none of the musicians could play.

On occasion, Eno wore huge blotches of rouge on his cheeks. With Roxy Music he epitomized glitter rock, playing the part of "intuitive woman" on stage, and he could be very free and witty about discussing his sex life with the press. He proudly declared that he had never had any venereal diseases even though his sex life was very active. He said he continually had himself examined for venereal disease and was always amazed when the tests were negative. He was also known to describe how he had once pulled the cartilage in his knee while having sex and that his excessive sexuality had caused a lung to collapse. Sex, he believed, was his own exhibition of craft, and he said he had even had himself filmed having sex because he thought his sexual skill should be documented.

Eno's musical ideas were equally precocious and avant-garde. He believed something musically interesting happened when a sound was "treated"—divided between two musicians playing the same sound. According to Eno, music should be intentionally confused and incoherent, and musicians should be brought together who would never play together in any other circumstance. Musical accidents were to be left in, and instruments that were grossly out of tune were often preferable to those in tune. If one liked a song by another composer, that song should be lifted without any hint of disguise.

One could also compose by a cut-and-paste method that combined the different songs of other people.

Eno was a visionary with one real message: take chances. He warred against image, which trapped a star and made him repeat himself.

The collaboration between David, with his ingrained pop sensibility, and Eno, a genuine avant-garde elitist, was the kind of juxtaposition that was one of David's creative hallmarks.

Their collaboration, *Low*, also provided a place for the *The Man Who Fell to Earth* score that had been so summarily rejected.

But at heart David had strong commercial instincts. The synthesis of avant-garde and pop sensibilities would become one of the hallmarks of 1980s postmodernism. David's sense that the avant-garde one day would be big business had led him to forge the trend. He had finally learned the art of being a step ahead, learned it so well, perhaps, that he was already two or three steps down the road. Now the world would have to catch up to him. The pop idol was moving into an art-for-art's-sake phase.

While David was in Paris dealing with Lippman, Eno studiously worked on the tapes, slowly making technological additions and trying to create better and better accidents.

During these recording sessions, Angela appeared at the chateau. She criticized Coco's handling of David's affairs, and David turned against her. Angela was being erased.

Then, in October 1976, David and Coco, with Iggy by their side, went to West Berlin. It appeared to Angela that the move was made to please Coco, who seemed to want to isolate David from the world.

In Berlin David seemed determined to play out his fantasy of being an artist. An apartment was found in a Turkish district in an area filled with workers and artists attracted by the large apartments and cheap rents. David's apartment was above a garage and next to a gay coffee house.

The coffee house was a meeting place for people of diverse backgrounds: radical lesbians, gays, anarchists, and left-wing philosophers. An air of sexual androgyny also hung over the place, something that David always found appealing. The atmosphere in the coffee house was volatile, and fistfights were not uncommon.

Soon David began coming in for late breakfasts. Usually Coco and Iggy's girl friend, Esther, staked out the place first. If it wasn't too crowded, Coco fetched David. Sitting side by side with the gays and arguing radicals, he ate meusli, chain-smoked Gitanes, and drank his coffee.

The Berliners tended to ignore David. Their curiosity concerned his politics—which had received international attention—not his celebrity.

At breakfast David always dressed down. He wore a worker's cap and ordinary, cheap clothing. Quiet and polite, he seemed like a melancholy, withdrawn Englishman. Iggy was the opposite. Usually boisterous, he often seemed drunk.

A small, quiet city, Berlin was still charged by tension. It was a city without a center because everything stopped at the Berlin Wall. The socialistic government had proved a great success, and the city was filled with two extremes, young people and old, both groups supported by the government. Surrounded by communist East Germany, the population seemed engaged in a state-supported twenty-four-hour-a-day party to demonstrate the nature of Western freedom. Wildness and decadence were in the air. There were sex bars and drag bars and no problem obtaining cocaine and heroin for those who wanted it.

In Berlin, it was easy to be a recluse or a maniac or both, depending on one's mood. It was an ideal place for an actor trying to devise a new life-script.

To Angela it was madness. She loathed the idea that David was setting up house for Coco. She couldn't understand why anyone would choose to live in a city just to be near drag queens, wake up in the shadow of the Holocaust, and eat meals consisting of brains, liver, and kidneys.

"I can understand the Third Reich from a design point of view," she says, "but to watch drag queens every night and disappear into the twilight of after-hours clubs does not seem like an escape to me."

There was bound to be an explosion, and when Angela came to Berlin there was. Coco now had permission to fight back, and she proved a worthy adversary. "I should have put a knife in her," Angela says, adding that she couldn't really upset David by hurting Coco if he cared that much about her.

Meanwhile Romy had her hands full with David. He turned up at night, came backstage, and was always depressed. Often he burst into tears, but would not tell her what was bothering him. The only things he talked about were his work and his ideas for the future. He refused to acknowledge feelings. Mute one minute, he became hysterical the next. One night he banged furiously on Haag's apartment door, but she sent him away.

To her David seemed to have two parts to his personality, "a macho guy that likes what every other straight macho guy likes" and "a child—a helpless baby." She believed his femininity took the form of a need for tenderness. He craved love and sweetness, and she wanted to give it to him.

But the helpless baby had taken control, and there was nothing she could do to help. Instead, "he was sleeping around with all the 'girls,' and he could have everybody. He was very depressed."

When Angela next visited David all hell broke loose. David went to the hospital, where the doctor thought he might be suffering from acute alcoholism. Coco usually disappeared during these visits— Angela was too volatile and unpredictable. But one night she called Angela at four in the morning. Her problems with David had reduced her to tears. Angela blamed Coco, and became enraged. She threw her bed out the window, set fire to her clothes, and left.

David did not seem able to take a firm position with Angela one way or the other and even seemed willing to consider reconciliation. Angela declared it was either Coco or her.

Then David brought Zowie, and his nanny, Marion, to Berlin. It was clear to Angela that her household had moved to Berlin and that her fantasies of a happily-ever-after life in Switzerland were shattered. But she didn't seem upset. She seemed to be enjoying her relationship with her current boyfriend and, without David to stop her, she finally became an actress. She was appearing in a lunch-hour political cabaret show called the Krisis Kabaret, which featured Angela's friend Gladys Shock performing an outrageous strip.

Finally David suggested divorce, and Angela and he celebrated the decision by making love.

Another new year meant another birthday, and on January 8, 1977, David turned thirty. Romy Haag and Iggy Pop were by his side.

A photographer took a picture of David and Romy, and David believed it was Romy's idea to exploit the occasion for her own publicity. He turned against her. From that moment on, whenever he stared at her his eyes were filled with hate. He seemed to be going out of his way to make her jealous. No matter what she said he wouldn't listen.

"It was the strangest love affair I ever had," she says.

A David Bowie album was scheduled to be RCA's Christmas 1976 release, but *Low* shocked the company. Almost the entire album was instrumental, and there were no conventional vocals. Where was the hit single? they wondered. Seven "fragments" made up the first side of the disk; four "extended pieces," including two written for *The Man Who Fell to Earth*, comprised the second side. While the fragments usually ran close to three minutes, the extended pieces were less than four, even softer in tone, and more overtly static than the fragments. What was the difference between a fragment and an extended piece, they asked. Everything on the LP seemed fragmentary and incomplete, as if David himself were a fragmented human being.

They listened again, searching for the hit. The instrumentals certainly didn't sound like hits. Spare and subtle, they leave much to the listener's imagination and have little sense of progression. These were intentional demonstrations of static music.

Trained to expect a different Bowie persona with each new disk, they couldn't find the new Bowie on this one. It was the onset of a new musical period for David and not his recasting of himself in his version of the Eno image. The cover illustration, another still from *The Man Who Fell to Earth*, demonstrated that David was still David, busy learning some of Eno's tricks during a low period in his life. At the same time he had begun to work through the role he believed would give him longevity: that of progressive musician.

The album's release was postponed to January—it certainly was no safe Christmas release, guaranteed to be purchased as a gift by Christmas shoppers—and the first-rate avant-garde rock "Sound and Vision" was issued as a single. The single would go to third place on the British charts, but it failed in the United States.

The album was met with a storm of controversy in the American press. David was a certifiable media celebrity, and, by now, every move produced an outburst of print. Many glitter-rock fans thought he was selling out, while purists were upset that Eno was working with rock's great poseur.

In many quarters *Low* was regarded as an Eno, not a Bowie, album. But the producer credit fell to David and Tony Visconti, with Eno co-author of only one song.

Its clearest antecedent was Eno's *Another Green World*, a consistently interesting demonstration of production values taking precedence over compositional values. But *Low*, an elaboration of static music that made it more accessible, was a bold, mostly successful attempt to integrate the musical worlds of David and Eno. David's vision of Eno had brought Eno into a pop context with nothing sacrificed.

On much of side one of *Low*, David sounds as if he's having fun, something he is not prone to do on vinyl. The unexpected lyrical playfulness of "What in the World" undercuts the coldness that pervades the album. For the first time in his musical career, songs appear in which the lyrics successfully carry the music.

Problems also abound. In "Always Crashing in the Same Car," machines are inserted merely for novelty value. Many of the songs are also subverted by the substitution of synthesizers for a live drummer. A warm body might have added a dose of immediacy to the austere, consciously subtle compositions.

Often the arrangements are exceptionally spare and offer little sense of progression. On such longer pieces as "Warszawa" and "Subterraneans" not enough happens during the five- or six-minute duration. Intentionally static, they could have benefited from that flesh-and-blood drummer.

Nonetheless, "Sound and Vision" and "Breaking Glass" are first-rate avant-rock. The result proved more compelling than Eno's solo experiments, and the disk marked a promising (if modest) new direction for David.

RCA's reticence angered David; RCA seemed to be warring against his creativity, with commercial gain its only interest. He took the position that *Low* was inherently commercial, and wanted RCA to sell the album. The company felt it was caught up in two very dramatic games of David's—an attempt to make people buy something they really didn't want and David's attempt to avoid the hit singles game that had proved so frustrating during the first seven years of his career. To them he seemed to want to become commercially unsuccessful and then wear that commercial failure as a badge of honor, like a leftover hippie.

RCA had also released Iggy's *The Idiot*, and a single, "China Girl." At that time David made the decision to play keyboard during Iggy's tour of England and America. As a mere sideman, David guaranteed Iggy the kind of large response he had never before received. It also provided an opportunity for David to recast himself as a musician. As he had worked through Ziggy Stardust by producing Freddi Burrett and began formulating his pop-soul excursion by producing Ava Cherry, he would practice a new shadow, that of musician, by appearing onstage as a boy in Iggy's band. It would prepare him to drop all personas when it came time for him to tour again.

England was in the throes of the punk explosion, and Iggy and the Stooges were considered one of the seminal bands in the punk music movement. By returning to England as Iggy's *auteur*, a background figure, never usurping Iggy's spotlight, David automatically created a new illusion: He was the father of one of punk's founding fathers. It was reinforced by the Ziggy Stardust haircuts affected by many punks.

A tour was booked for Iggy starting at Friar's Hall in Aylesbury, on March 1, 1977, ironically the scene of RCA's Ziggy Stardust junket. Because of David's involvement, three nights were booked at the Rainbow Theatre, where Ziggy had scored some of his biggest triumphs. They would go then to Canada and the United States and perform seventeen dates, ending at Santa Monica Auditorium on April 15, where Ziggy had had his first Los Angeles triumph. The persona of not having a persona was to be enacted in those very shrines where Ziggy had been most triumphant.

The series of concerts was triumphant. Working topless, scars painted on his cheeks, Iggy was even more menacing than usual, victim as well as victimizer. Once again he turned his pain and rage into theater. He crawled across the stage on all fours, snarled at the audience, and encored with "China Girl" as a props man held a yellow light under his chin and turned him the color of a bad case of hepatitis. It was a sublime rock version of Artaud's Theatre of Cruelty, starring a one-of-a-kind icon. The limiting minimalism of his music mated with Iggy's bravura theatricality showed the limits to which such an anarchic approach could be taken. The press agreed that the punks couldn't hold a candle to Iggy Pop, the real thing.

At the end of his English shows, hands reached up to Iggy. In typical fashion, he tried to bite the fingers of those who loved him.

It was all and more that David had asked for.

Before he left England for the United States, David spent a few days with Marc Bolan. Bolan was in his latest incarnation and had a new image for the late 1970s. His curls were gone, and he was wearing designer suits, the Euro-chic look David had pioneered during the Year of the Diamond Dogs in 1974. The look had become a hallmark of New Wave fashion statement.

Bolan was about to tour with the punk band the Damned and had taken to calling himself "the Godfather of Punk." It was another irony that Marc not only looked as David used to look, but that David was himself acting out the "Godfather of Punk" role onstage every night.

David was in wonderful spirits. When it came time to go to the United States, he suddenly discovered that the new persona-free David had even shed his fear of flying.

On April 15 Iggy's tour came to an end in Los Angeles. Its coda was a witty appearance on Dinah Shore's afternoon talk show. David and Iggy were exceptionally cordial and charming, and Iggy seemed to have learned a great deal from David about how to woo and win the press and public.

Shore, her face a mask of wonderment, asked if Iggy really had cut himself with broken bottles on stage. Iggy confessed to Dinah that he really mustn't have loved himself at the time. Dinah understood.

The tour over, David and Iggy returned to Berlin to record *Lust for Life*, a follow-up album to *The Idiot*. Meanwhile RCA released "Be My Wife," a second single from *Low*. It proved a failure.

David's follow-up to *Low* was *"Heroes,"* which introduced Robert Fripp into the Bowie-Eno association. Fripp, equally at home with pop and avant-garde music, understood that sparse guitar-playing was essential to Eno's technique because so much of Eno's approach depended on manipulation of the studio technology.

David, Eno, and Fripp loved to theorize and enjoyed calling one another charlatans. They entertained one another by conducting cliché-ridden conversations and had a wonderful time.

"Heroes" was again produced by David and Tony Visconti, but now Eno was co-author of not one but three songs.

RCA acted as if the LP had been made by charlatans. The entire second side of the disk seemed to the company to be *Low* outtakes, and the suspicion was that they were scraps recorded at the same time. The company believed it had gotten an LP of intentionally dissonant sound effects. Critics wondered if David was trying to emulate Klaus Nomi's performance art style and noted that Laurie Anderson had already accomplished musical suggestions of the feeling of movement on the "Transportation" section of her epic *United States*.

There was a wonderful title song on the album, "Heroes," with lyrics by David and music co-written by Eno. David's songs almost always maintained a distance from their subjects, but "Heroes" was astonishing in its warmth.

David and Eno both wanted to make a Big Statement about West Berlin. "Heroes" was especially effective because it dealt with two doomed lovers, (the only type of lovers David wrote about). The song told the story of lovers who lived on opposite sides of the Wall, and presented the clash of two moods, the fantasy of love, and the harsh reality of that towering wall.

David's hero can't give up the illusion, but also knows the truth, and his vocal delivery matched the passionate yet ironic lyric. Additionally, instead of stinging the listener, Fripp's lead guitar lines were caressing, and the backing vocals on the last verse of the song would prove the friendliest support David had ever allowed himself.

David finally had his first accessible song to convey a dose of genuine emotion.

Marc Bolan had capped his comeback with a six-week television series, *Marc*, and David went to England to debut "Heroes" on the show. During a finale jam Bolan slipped off the stage, and the duet was never finished. A week later on September 16, Gloria Jones ran her car off the road and into a tree. Bolan was killed instantly. The second of the three walk-ins Wally Elmlark had named was dead.

David went alone to the funeral, which was held at a synagogue in Golders Green. The altar was decorated with a huge swan made of flowers sent by Capitol Records to signify Bolan's big hit, "Ride a Pink Swan."

David sat directly in front of Dana Gillespie, whom he had not seen in three years. During the service she saw him weeping. It was the first time in all the years she had known him that she could recall such an honest outpouring of emotion. David always denied death; yet the fact that a peer he had known for fifteen years had died before his fair amount of time seemed a sobering reality.

During his stay in London he visited Haddon Hall. As he stood in front of the building where so many plans had been made and so many plots hatched, eight years before, the landlord appeared and handed him a bill for unpaid rent. It was more evidence that Defries hadn't really taken care of him, and that the past was filled with pain and had to be avoided.

The release of *"Heroes"* was accompanied by press and promotional activities in London, Paris, Amsterdam, and the United States. " 'Heroes' " was released as a single, followed by "Beauty and the Beast." Each just cracked the Top Forty in England.

While in New York, David recorded the narration for a new version of Prokofiev's *Peter and the Wolf*.

During an interview he dubbed *Low* and *"Heroes"* two volumes of a trilogy, which the interviewer noted had the appearance of "a clever afterthought." The journalist described David as "courtly, courteous, and decidedly distant," a man who was both "brilliant and manipulative." During the interview he would not talk about his sexuality; the past was over. The only time a hint of warmth occurred was when he talked about six-year-old Zowie.

As a Swiss resident David had to spend a required number of days in Switzerland each year. There he was visited by David Hemmings, who wanted David to co-star with him in *Just a Gigolo*, a film Hemmings would also direct.

It was set in the Germany of the 1920s and David would play a shell-shocked lieutenant returning home from World War I to become a gigolo dancer. His character also has a flirtation with Nazism and winds up at the end having a hero's funeral dressed in a Nazi uniform. It sounded as if it could be David's *Cabaret*.

To add to the enticement Marlene Dietrich had been offered the role of the Prussian baronness who runs the gigolo service. Dietrich, at seventy-seven, had not made a film in seventeen years. There was something irresistible about a legendary screen goddess, the mother of the sexually androgynous image, coming out of retirement to play a supporting role to David.

If that wasn't enough, Kim Novak, America's sex goddess of the 1950s, was going to be another of David's leading ladies, as was Synde Rome, an American-born actress living in Rome whom David had escorted to the Paris opening of *The Man Who Fell to Earth*.

The tone of the film reeked of irony. Of the script Hemmings said, "In the end all the characters opt for the easy way out. They all sell themselves."

David agreed to the project, which would begin shooting at the end of the year, in December 1977. It was reported that he had a financial interest in it.

Just before Christmas he taped a Christmas special with Bing Crosby; his old friend Twiggy was another of Crosby's guests. It was Crosby's last television appearance; within the month he was dead.

Angela's tendency was to live life as if it were theater, and now she gave one of her greatest performances. When she arrived in Switzerland with Zowie and Marion for Christmas, she was told to come to Berlin. She learned that Coco would be with her family, and that infuriated her. Zowie and Marion were sent to Berlin, and she flew to New York City and wound up staying with a friend Keeth Paul, a twenty-four-year-old sound man for the Heart-breakers.

Angela and Paul returned to Switzerland, where Angela heard that it had been reported to the press that she had abandoned Zowie. She needed money and decided to sell her side of the story to the newspapers. She sensed such public displays would mortify David.

When Tony Robinson of the *Sunday Mirror* arrived in Switzer-land, Angela seemed under heavy sedation. At four in the morning she got up, locked herself in the bathroom, and took sleeping pills. Then she went on a rampage and set out to destroy the house. She hit Paul on the knee with a rolling pin and then considered stabbing herself with a carving knife.

She fell unconscious and could hardly be revived. Then she pulled herself up and threw herself down the stairs. She had thrown herself down the stairs after her first night with David; her relation-ship with him was ending exactly the way it had begun.

Paul and Robinson took Angela to the hospital. When she re-turned to the house, she began divorce proceedings and reportedly asked for $2 million.

She said that she hadn't slept with David in five years, and that he refused to allow her to sign a recording contract.

Paul told Robinson that David gave Angela $40,000 a year and paid her rent and travel bills, around $75,000 a year. He said that she had spent $25,000 in Switzerland that year for taxis alone and took taxis to buy cigarettes and chewing gum.

In Angela's mind it was Coco, not David, who was to blame. She did not want to face the fact that David demanded someone at his side at all times, someone who could totally submerge herself to his needs. It was essential to him that he have his own one-person, adoring audience. That bored Angela and made her restless. Of all the people in David's life, only Coco seemed willing to go to the lengths demanded by David.

Angela went back to New York, where she again attempted suicide.

In Berlin, David put into motion the steps that would erase once and for all the woman who had done the worst of all: used the press as a means of retaliation.

In January *Melody Maker* reporter Mick Watts spent five days in Berlin on the *Just a Gigolo* set interviewing David. Watts was the reporter to whom David had given the notorious "I am gay" interview when he was launching Ziggy Stardust.

At that time David viewed himself as someone venturing into the arena of international filmmaking. He said that he had turned down an offer from Lina Wertmuller and wanted to work with Rainer Werner Fassbinder. He was also a working artist who brought Polaroids of his paintings to the interviews for Watts's approval. The paintings included self-portraits as well as portraits of Iggy Pop and Yukio Mishima.

David refused to discuss either his marriage or bisexuality.

"He also likes to control his publicity, and has become adroit in this. . . . It is the correct, approved David Bowie that must be presented to the public," wrote Watts.

David seemed ecstatic about working with David Hemmings, an experience that was proving far more satisfactory than his work with Nick Roeg. In professional situations he was again willing to do whatever was required of him, with no complaint.

As usual, his fellow actors were also treated respectfully. One day Maria Schell, who was appearing in the film with him, showed him a newspaper picture of her brother, actor Maximilian Schell, with Bianca Jagger. She laughed about the idea that they might be having an affair.

David responded discreetly. Just five months before, Bianca and David had been seen in Paris together and had gone to Spain on holiday. David kept it to himself.

He brought Kim Novak and David Hemmings to the coffee house next to his apartment. One cold January evening some rowdy skin-heads threw rocks into the windows of the coffee house. It was not the first time the windows had been broken; the student movements in Berlin had become increasingly violent, and acts of terrorism were becoming more frequent.

The owners decided to stage a party to last until dawn, when a repairman could be called. David heard the disturbance. He came downstairs, knocked at the door, and explained that he had been painting. Then he asked if he could join the festivities and was told he would be welcome.

He dashed upstairs, got his paintings, and brought them with him to show everyone. Then he handed over five hundred marks to pay for the broken windows.

David's neighbors noted that his depressions seemed even worse. He was spotted alone in a trendy café with his head in his plate. He seemed drunk. Occasionally, he cried out, "Please help me."

But he was left alone because he was David Bowie, and by nature Berliners are determined to respect others' privacy.

When the filming was completed, a world tour was announced.

A reporter asked why he had decided to return to the world's rock arenas when he had just used the public print forum to describe himself as an international film actor and aspiring painter.

His reply was succinct: "Very simple. I need the money."

The tour was scheduled to begin rehearsing on March 16, 1978, in Dallas. Nine days later it would move to San Diego, opening four days later on March 29 at the San Diego Sports Arena. Twenty-three American and Canadian cities were on the schedule. After a week's break, it would resume in Hamburg and travel to twenty-one more European cities, finishing up on June 29 at Earl's Court in London, where the worst Ziggy fiasco had occurred. In November it would resume in Australia, followed by Japan.

The sanest, best parts of David were in evidence throughout the tour. He was now Zowie's full-time father; in the process, he was emerging as an adult with real control over his own behavior.

The first half of the concert was devoted to music from *Low* and *"Heroes."* Carlos Alomar, who was to conduct the band using a baton, was amazed that David was going to present himself as composer and save his standard repetoire for the second half. The first half of the show would find David with a new shadow, working musician, a synthesizer player in a top-notch band that included Roger Powell of Todd Rundgren's Utopia on synthesizers and Adrian Belew of Frank Zappa's band on lead guitar.

His two costumes, featuring incredibly baggy pants—another look automatically destined to become a new wave fashion statement—were designed by Natasha Kornilof from his 1960s Lindsay Kemp days and were based on Jacobean models.

During the Texas rehearsal period the new musicians joining David's rhythm section, led by Carlos Alomar, discovered that David was in total control of every musical and production element. To everyone concerned he seemed to want to help people, needed to feel he had something to offer, demanded control, and also craved approval.

The musicians perceived him as down to earth, considerate, someone to be respected for his artistry and brilliance. He was a man who trusted his instincts and an erudite gentleman in the European tradition.

But he did not form fast friendships; he inspired fantasies. People felt compelled to pin their futures to his because he seemed such an unstoppable force. It was clear that he wanted to move on; the message was professionalism, and there was none of the 1960s camaraderie that marked bands of the past. The more people demanded of David and Coco, the less inclined they were to give. A job was to be done, and everyone was there to use his talents to the best advantage, to be useful in the best sense of the word and not become pals.

During the rehearsals, the band was given plenty of space for experimentation, and Alomar and Belew turned the claustrophobic sounds of the Bowie-Eno compositions inside out so that they soared. David experimented, made changes, and worked quickly and cleverly on his feet. He seemed at real peace with himself, a man unafraid to embrace and experience his fears so that he could discard them. Again, his calmness became a catalyst, inspiring others to do their best work.

Three relationships dominated his life—Zowie, Coco, and Iggy. With Zowie he displayed the warmth others rarely saw. He was clearly a good father and seemed to need to do the job properly just as he needed to be perfect on stage. Father and son loved each other very much.

Coco was perceived an alter ego. It was as if David and she had been married for a very long time. They seemed to trust each other totally, and each had an exceptionally strong hold on the other.

When the tour reached Australia, Bette Midler was in the same hotel. She told David she wanted to go to the zoo. During the excursion Coco never left David's side for a minute.

Iggy and David were best friends. David seemed to have created his best family of all.

Throughout, the key for David was always control. In Boston a rock flew over his head, hitting the keyboard and shattering five keys. There was a mad crush in the audience, and David took charge and stopped the show. In Detroit he walked off the stage because someone threw a roll of toilet paper at him. In New Zealand the audience seemed to be giving him the finger. He thought they were responding to his prior comments about fascism and he left again. If he wasn't totally in control of a concert, he refused to play.

One thing that really riveted him offstage during the tour was the television mini-series *Holocaust*. He stayed glued to the set. He seemed fascinated by both sides. Assuming the position of either side, he became an actor, playing all the parts vicariously and experiencing everyone's emotions.

Death seemed to puzzle him, and he appeared unable to accept the inevitability of dying. At the same time he was fascinated.

During the last European dates at Earl's Court, David Hemmings shot an enormous amount of film for a documentary, but apparently David and he argued and nothing came of the project. Sitting in the Royal Box during the performance was Peggy Jones. She would have nothing to complain about to the press this time around.

The problem with Hemmings could have been *Just a Gigolo*. After the tour had touched down in Berlin, David saw a cut of the movie with Manhattan Transfer, who had been invited to perform on the sound track. The movie was an incoherent mess, and David was mortified.

He described the film as "a cocaine movie." During dinner he grew unhappier. The film was so bad it could stop his career in its tracks. Those at the table perceived him as someone descending into overwhelming despair and self-pity.

Confronting failure was always very hard for him, and *Just a Gigolo* was a real fiasco. But it was not a heavily publicized Hollywood epic, and it disappeared from view after a few showings without tarnishing David in the public's eye. Yet it demonstrated again that his appearance in a movie did not automatically guarantee that a bad film would be rescued from oblivion.

The tour resulted in *Stage*, a two-record live album. RCA insisted that the two-record LP be counted as one record, and its release was delayed until the fall of 1978. The company knew it had its hands full again, selling a live recording promoting *Low* and *"Heroes,"* two LPs that had not delivered hits. The programming of the disks was disjointed and failed to give a suitable artistic history of David's progress. He seemed merely to be trying to follow contractual commitments.

But David had become a musician and had successfully proved that he could be "himself" on stage. It was a rehearsal for the long term. He needed a new recording company and a new beginning to capitalize on the major gains he had made in his lifelong quest to present the world with the real David Bowie.

From December 1978 until March 1979, David's life was a star's life, filled with travel and publicity to keep his name before the public. From Japan he returned to London, then to New York, back to London, to Wales, London, and New York. He made another trip back and forth across the Atlantic, and then went to Australia, back to London, and then to New York again.

Everywhere he went there were carefully selected interviews, press conferences, radio specials, and television appearances.

By March 1979, he was back in New York to finish mixing *Lodger*, the third Bowie-Eno collaboration.

On *Lodger* Eno's influence is so persuasive that some of the songs, especially "African Night Flight," don't even sound mixed, a tribute to Eno's aesthetic of capturing feelings but ignoring the big picture.

Influences also collide on the disk. The backing vocals on "Look Back in Anger" are derived from mid-period Beatles and disco with Alomar's guitar as anchor; "D.J." is about disco.

Interesting ideas abound on the LP but they remain unrealized. "D.J." and "Boys Keep Swinging" are funny, ironic jabs at musical and sexual mores respectively, but each seems unfinished. "Yassassin's" hysterical opening line—David emoting "I'm not a moody guy"—is counteracted by Eno's synthesizer backing; the intriguing dissection of domestic violence in "Repetition" dissolves into random images, and some spectacularly abrasive lead guitar bursts by Adrian Belew are buried in the muddy mix.

On *Lodger* David seemed more interested in writing songs than on the other two Eno collaborations. All ten tracks have lyrics. But the songs are more fragmentary than the long pieces on *Low*'s side two. "D.J." may offer a set of arresting images, but they never cohere.

David's three LPs with Eno contain some of the best (" 'Heroes' ") and worst ("The Secret Life of Arabia") songs David ever recorded. But even though the albums were grossly unpopular they declared that David belonged to a world unto himself. He did what he wanted when he wanted and defied classification. To his mystique was added another layer: He existed outside all business restraints. The sexual outlaw of the seventies had presented himself not only as a man whose constantly changing images were a declaration that artifice was the legitimate replacement for authenticity, but now as an artist-outlaw. Nothing that would follow these albums could ever be declared a sellout. The world David was manipulating was beginning to see the connections between artists and business, and new views were forming. Now artists could be avant-garde, hugely popular, and financially successful; it was possible for an artist to do strictly commercial work and not be considered a sellout. Making art for money seemed to have become an art form all its own.

What was emerging was the great theme of David's life. His ability to maintain emotional distance from himself and everyone else equipped him with the strength to survive, no matter what he put himself through.

Insecure? Yes. But also tough as nails. He had Peggy's hard skin but was blessed with the talent and ambition she lacked. The curse of his family had not destroyed him, although he responded to its drama with an actor's imagination. He was the one who was finally going to fulfill his grandmother's dreams.

He visited Hurrah, the new wave disco that was the first to feature rock videos of then current groups. It was becoming clearer that Defries had been right; video was the way to sell records.

In London at the end of April he appeared on "The Kenny Everett Video Show" to perform "Boys Keep Swinging" from *Lodger*. The director was David Mallet, whose experience in rock television reached back to the 1960s, when he came to America to work on *Shindig* and *Hullabaloo*. David knew that video could sell records in America, and went to RCA and received the funds to make three videos with Mallet, "Look Back in Anger," "D.J.," and "Boys Keep Swinging." For the last he became his version of Romy Haag and appeared as three startlingly different drag queens, ending the video with Haag's climactic gesture of smearing her lipstick all over her face. It was just as spectacular in David's video as it was on the stage of Chez Romy.

Lodger was scheduled for a late spring release. In almost five years it was the first new Bowie album with as many as ten vocal tracks. An internal memorandum was circulated through RCA in an attempt to stimulate excitement about the record: "It would be fair to call *Lodger* Bowie's 'Sgt. Pepper,' a concept album that portrays the Lodger as a homeless wanderer, stunned and victimized by modern life's pressures and technology," stated the memo. "It is absolutely necessary that you listen to *Lodger* until you *hear* it. The music *is* there."

In private the company seemed to detest the record. It appeared to demonstrate the law of diminishing returns, and the use of Eno as co-author of six tracks seemed formulaic. It was a record filled with colliding influences, such avant-garde hallmarks as unmixed sounds, fragments pretending to be songs, muddiness masquerading as instrumental clarity; middle-period Beatles backing vocals; and a preoccupation with the then-current disco sound.

Apparently an artistic dead end had been reached. "Red Money," the Bowie/Carlos Alomar collaboration that closes the album, did not feature Eno, and its last line was repeated several times. That line was : "Project cancelled."

David had already made the following comments to the press. "I've learned some of his [Eno's] methods quite thoroughly, and I'm fairly competent with them so I can utilize them on my own," he quipped to one reporter. To another he said, "I borrow and steal everything that fascinates me."

Even though RCA disliked *Lodger*, the videos were spectacular, and RCA decided to sell them as their major promotional tool. A four-minute collage of the many new video faces of David Bowie was offered to PromoVision Network and ran nonstop in one hundred key record stores across the country. It was also decided to hold video press and promotion parties across the country. The press would be used to sell David Bowie, video artist, and their articles about the videos would promote the LP. In New York a search was made for a suitable location for the press party. Two ballet schools and a mental institution were rejected before the Explorers Club was chosen.

David arrived almost three hours late to make a grand entrance and labeled his record "Dada-pop." Then everyone was led into a video room to watch the twelve minutes of video on a giant screen. The event was repeated in Los Angeles. Every important RCA branch office also had a viewing party in order to excite the local staffs.

Two years before MTV's debut, RCA had taken the lead in the rock video revolution and was attempting to sell David in the way that would eventually prove the most effective of all.

It still didn't change David's mind about the American division of RCA. In London he was a major star; in America, after all those years, he still couldn't get sufficient air play.

The New York company viewed him suspiciously. The Bowie-Eno trilogy was the stuff of rock music myths and a significant trailblazer. David had become one of the founding fathers of new-wave art rock. But the records didn't sell, and they knew David blamed them and used the press as a tool to humiliate them publicly.

Their dealings on a one-to-one basis were few and far between. Instead they dealt with Coco and Pat Gibbons, and Coco berated them mercilessly on David's behalf. They had never encountered such a fiercely outspoken *bête noire*.

Finally David appeared at a meeting with the Scotti brothers, an independent promotion team with stupendous success. They were tough-minded businessmen, while David played the artist. Everyone in the room knew that he was a brilliant innovator, but he seemed all posturing and defensiveness. No matter what anyone said, he deflected their words so that they were to blame. He had the capacity to make everyone feel that somehow they had failed him. His supreme aloofness accomplished one goal. When the meeting was over and he had moved on, those who stayed behind felt awful.

In New York that fall David continued to go to the new clubs. He loved to check out the trends. At Hurrah he met Jack Hofsiss, director of the Broadway hit *The Elephant Man*. Hofsiss, a charming, bright, talented young man, was looking for a replacement for Philip Anglim, the Tony Award–winning star of the play. David and he discussed the play, and David seemed intrigued as Hofsiss explained that the deformed elephant man must be played as a character and not as an attempt to grab audience sympathy.

They ran into each other again in a restaurant, and Hofsiss asked David if he would like to play the role. By this time David's curiosity was whetted.

He stayed in New York and met with Jack Hofsiss on the day after Christmas. David wanted to know if Hofsiss thought he would be good in the role, and the director explained that the part was similar to his *The Man Who Fell to Earth* character. Both parts were isolated individuals with otherworldly characteristics. David listened carefully. He knew he *was* the elephant man.

CHAPTER 32

Let's Dance

$\mathbf{A}$s David entered the 1980s, he was a man in search of freedom—freedom from Angela, RCA, and Defries.

Angela seemed the easiest to get rid of legally. The divorce decree became final on February 8, 1980. The divorce had been fought in the Swiss courts. Angela was represented by celebrity divorce lawyer Marvin Mitchelson.

David wanted custody of Zowie and presented sworn statements about Angela's conduct from such trusted sources as nursemaid Marion Skene, who loved Angela dearly but was ordered by David to tell the truth. Tony Visconti also traveled to Switzerland to stand up for David.

Angela's settlement was reported to be a lump sum of 30,000 pounds. She feels that Mitchelson did the best he could in the face of the evidence against her.

The thought that her marriage really was ending was so distressing to her that she says she numbed herself with drugs and also went to a psychiatrist. The psychiatrist shot himself before her second session.

David, meanwhile, buried himself in work and began a new album, *Scary Monsters*. *Scary Monsters (and Super Creeps)* appeared to be David's attempt to integrate the experimentation-for-its-own-sake aesthetic that permeated his work with Eno into a straight pop framework. The LP's back cover, butchered miniatures of his Eno album covers, lent credence to the theory that David was acknowledging rather than practicing his past incarnation in his current guise.

At its best *Scary Monsters* elaborates on the Eno format, taking an experimental sensibility and using avowed pop players to make it accessible. Carlos Alomar's rhythm guitar and George Murray's bass consistently blend to create the pulsing Eno-like sound that was missing on the Bowie-Eno collaborations. The other instruments, together with David's unusually committed vocals, build from rhythm guitar and bass, with each layer of sound enhancing rather than cluttering the mix. Within those layers are a number of spectacular instrumental performances.

The unheralded star of the album was Robert Fripp, who performs the most fully realized guitar playing of his checkered career. His brief metallic solo in "Fashion" sounds like a chain saw cutting barbed wire; his lead lines in "Teenage Wildlife" reveal a new-found warmth in his playing. Add Pete Townshend's cameo on "Because You're Young" and E Street Band member Roy Bittan's passionate arrangements and keyboard playing and the result is a musical aggregation that gave David far more focus than he'd ever had before. It's apparent that he was spurred on by the best band he'd ever fronted.

In America the LP did not really become David's reentry to the mainstream, but it proved that he could do it if he wanted. The album's influence outweighed its commercial life, spawning a pair of American A&R standards with "Ashes to Ashes" and "Fashion."

With "Fashion" David had a new-wave disco anthem. The young audience who had found their individual ways to clone prior Davids stomped to the rhythms of "Fashion" in new wave discos everywhere. The fact that the song was an ironic comment about them made the irony all the more delicious.

David also visited the Victorian London hospital in which the Elephant man, John Merrick, had lived. Never a man to waste a move, he would not have made the trek unless he was convinced he was going to do the part and had begun rehearsing it in his mind.

To supplement his income he did a Japanese television commercial, which was seen by a radical Japanese film director, Nagisa Oshima. Oshima is known to art-film buffs for *In the Realm of the Senses*, a graphic depiction of the erotic obsession and lovemaking of a Japanese couple. The film ended with the woman castrating her dead lover. Erotic excess had led to blood and death.

Oshima wanted to make an English language movie, *Merry Christmas Mr. Lawrence*. But he was also given to fantasy. His dream was to have Robert Redford appear in the starring role.

———

When Jack Hofsiss told Elizabeth McCann and Nelle Nugent, producers of *The Elephant Man*, that David Bowie wanted to play the role, their response was healthy skepticism. Visions of Ziggy Stardust danced before their eyes.

Their show was a hit, and their job was to protect it. The last thing they wanted was a rock star with a reputation for flamboyance failing in a difficult dramatic role. Such a failure would hurt the box office, and then their hit would be no more.

Hofsiss was dispatched to Los Angeles to work with David and to report back whether he really could cut the part.

Hofsiss's verdict was positive. McCann decided that David would have to break in the part on the road before attempting Broadway. After all, he was a rock star accustomed to playing in 20,000-seat arenas. Now he would have to scale down his performance to accommodate a 753-seat playhouse.

At a meeting with David, Nugent, a stylishly good-looking Broadway veteran known for her professionalism, gave David the facts. She wanted a four-week rehearsal period and a six-week road tour before New York. That would give him time to master the role, adjust to working with the other actors on stage, and also launch the requisite publicity blitz. But this blitz would be different, she explained. It would be "legit" publicity that created a new image for David, by means of which the press and public would perceive him as a serious actor and not a rock star having a frivolous moment. The message to be fed to the media was that David Bowie had gone legit—a perfectly natural part of his evolution as an artist.

David agreed, and a deal was negotiated with record-breaking speed, with David earning around 10 percent of the gross, the largest figure usually paid the most successful Broadway stars. It was a far cry from rock and roll, a back-breaking eight performances a week for a weekly fee in the range of $2,000, of which around $200 was to be paid directly to MainMan based on the then six-year-old settlement.

An Actor's Equity rule stated that alien actors could not replace Broadway actors, but it was circumvented by slipping David into a touring company contract and bringing the American actor playing the part into the Broadway production. Then David could legally be allowed to replace that actor.

Word spread through the New York company of the unusual casting, and the actors confessed their nervousness to Hofsiss. Their fear was that as a rock star David was used to running his own show and would not blend into a carefully rehearsed piece of ensemble acting. They were also afraid that he would spend all his time on stage facing front and not looking at them, as if he were singing a song. Hofsiss calmed them down.

But everyone wondered why David was doing it. David was the last person to level. He was charming and wonderful, but left no openings for deeply personal conversations. It appeared that his recording career was stalled, and he was looking for a way to extend his longevity. Broadway triumphs inevitably result in offers from Hollywood, and the belief was that David was also trying to establish the groundwork for a successful film career after having starred in two movie-box-office flops.

Before rehearsals began David called May Pang and invited her to attend the play with him. During the performance she noted that David mouthed each of Elephant Man John Merrick's lines as it was spoken from the stage. He was already line perfect. Hofsiss forbade him to see the show again. David was to create his own Elephant Man, not memorize and mimic the performance of another actor.

At rehearsals David was the essence of professionalism—on time, courteous, and respectful to everyone else in the cast. On the one occasion that he was late he apologized individually to every member of the company. In no time at all he seemed to have learned how to be a Broadway star in the classic tradition.

The role of John Merrick required him to contort his body into a twisted shape and keep it that way for two hours. The character also required a special voice, that of someone with no exposure to the world, and plagued by a terrible physical disease.

Neither gave him a problem. He appeared to be a perfectly trained mime and could make his body contort into the most difficult positions at will. In order to find the proper voice Hofsiss and he listened to tapes of cerebral palsy victims. It became clear that the proper vocal quality suggested an agile mind and a body that refused to allow words to be spoken at a normal rate of speed.

The only thing that unsettled him was that real acting demanded he reveal his inner self to the other actors on stage. He had to reach inside himself to dredge up feeling. Despite his discomfort he forced himself to become emotionally honest, and his performance became the most naturalistic of all those who eventually played the part.

While Philip Anglim's original Elephant Man had an intellectual austerity and did not seem sure of what was going on around him in the real world, David's characterization had a quality of the streets. It seemed impossible for him to fall into the trap of making the Elephant Man a pathetic creature because his acting suggested a man who had been around the block a couple of times.

At its heart, though, *The Elephant Man* is really a play about illusion. The Elephant Man wears neither grotesque makeup nor costume, but conveys his deformity through movement, voice, and the ability to suggest an illusion. No one understood such an approach better than David.

In keeping with his new legitimate image David had made an appearance on "The Johnny Carson Show" prior to rehearsals. Now his press agents got him a feature on ABC-TV's highly rated prime-time news show, "20/20."

David wanted to appear as an artist and asked that the interview be taped in a trendy Soho gallery. His paintings were flown from Germany to adorn the walls.

The interviewer wanted to know how it felt to be a homosexual and a father.

Again the past reared its head; again the press turned enemy. At all costs the press *had* to be controlled.

After a week's rehearsal in San Francisco with the national company David headed for Denver and his opening night on July 29. His first performance was unannounced, with David substituting at the last minute for the actor then playing the role. Its purpose was to distract the press, which seemed to be congregating in Denver from all over the world to cover David's legitimate acting debut.

On the night before the opening Coco and David had dinner with Hofsiss, and David was approached by two girls who recognized him. David sent Coco and Jack home by limousine; he would walk.

"You see how he is," Coco sighed as she leaned against the back seat of the car.

In the hotel Hofsiss realized that his star was loose on the streets of downtown Denver on the night before his first performance. He kept calling David's room until he got him on the phone.

Yes, he had gotten home safely, and yes, one of the girls was with him, and yes, he was going to be at the theater the next day at the top of his form.

An official opening night followed the preview. David was in terrific form, and the reviews were raves. The press also noted the fact that David's fans were in abundance, some even dressed in Ziggy Stardust drag. Producer Liz McCann noted that they seemed to have mirrors glued to their teeth.

A two-week engagement followed in Chicago. Again the reviews were spectacular. One night during David's curtain call a fan jumped on stage and seemed to be carrying a knife. A security man removed her so quickly no one quite knew what had happened. But the indication was that David would have to be zealously protected throughout the New York run.

Just before the play left Chicago for New York for rehearsals with the New York company and a week of previews, David thanked Nelle Nugent for suggesting he go on the road before braving Broadway.

"In two more weeks I'll really be ready," he said. He was.

David supplied a list of invitees for the New York opening night. Names were added to the list by his press agents. The producers added more names. While there was no way anything involving David was not going to be construed as an event, this had taken on a distinct coloration. The audience was going to be dotted with intellectuals and cultural celebrities. David had invited his Swiss neighbor Oona Chaplin to be his guest. The opening audience also included Aaron Copland and Christopher Isherwood (author of *The Berlin Stories*, which were the basis of *Cabaret*); Steve Reich sat behind Eno. A number of music and theater reviewers were also present, including Henry Edwards. It was an astonishing Broadway debut.

An elegant loft party was given afterward. In the MainMan tradition the press was barred. It only added more mystique to David's debut.

The rave reviews clinched it all, and the curtain never went up on an empty seat.

Before the opening a security check revealed twenty-seven different ways to sneak into the Booth Theatre. Four security men were hired, one to sit in the first row during the performance, a second in the wings, a third at the stage door, and the fourth in David's limousine. Each night the theater was also checked for bombs, and different routes were devised for David to make an uninterrupted getaway.

It seemed like a necessary set of precautions, and no one thought much about it. Besides, David seemed to have arrived with the best protection of all, Coco. At first people were puzzled by the service she provided. No one had ever met a star whose assistant worked a twenty-four-hour day. But Coco proved to be sensitive and intelligent. Because of the physical rigors of the role, David had to do a special warm-up before the show and a warm-down after it, and Coco got him to do it. She handled every difficult matter with ease, never interfered with the business at hand, and people became pleased to have her aboard.

The audiences were a mix of David's fans and people who might have been their parents, traditional middle-aged, middle-class Broadway playgoers. At the candy counter during intermissions the two groups often eyed each other suspiciously. But the fans, most of whom had never been to a play before, were genuinely touched by the message of *The Elephant Man*. It was a fitting irony that David, who had built so much of his career on masking his real self, would be in a play that stressed that the real man is the man beneath the superficial aspects of his appearance.

One night Ken Pitt came to the play. He was delighted that David had finally found a proper stage vehicle.

On another night, Peggy Jones was David's guest. He introduced her to every member of the cast and crew, and people enjoyed the opportunity of seeing David's boyish grin and his mother's proud smile.

During her visit to New York Peggy also had the chance to see her grandson again. Occasionally David brought Zowie to the theater with him, and one night the precocious eight-year-old tied an actor's legs together just before his entrance. David was flabbergasted.

Japanese film director Nagisa Oshima also saw the play. He had had no luck securing Robert Redford for *Merry Christmas Mr. Lawrence* and was considering David. After the performance he felt David might be too good for the film. They met anyway, and David expressed an interest in working with him.

Another visitor was German writer/director Herman Weigel. He asked David to do a performance cameo and appear on the sound track of *Christiane F.*, a film based on a German best-seller. The book dealt with the true story of a fifteen-year-old heroin addict who was a witness in a case involving a middle-aged man who sodomized minors. David was the girl's favorite rock star, and he agreed to do the film, a scene shot in New York that duplicated his 1978 Berlin concert appearance.

The semidocumentary was vivid and depressing but gave David an instant album to submit to RCA.

Of all his backstage guests, the one who caused the most commotion was Elizabeth Taylor. She was planning to make her Broadway debut in *The Little Foxes* and was anxious to see David on stage.

The two stars were scheduled to have dinner after the show at Sardi's. Shubert Alley had to be cordoned off so that they could walk from the theater to the restaurant. An enormous crowd formed to gawk as the pair led the procession.

At dinner Taylor brought David up to date on her illnesses and marriages. Then she looked over her shoulder and spotted Eddie Fisher.

She turned to David and said, "I haven't seen him since *Cleopatra*. Should I say hello?"

On December 8 May Pang heard the news of John Lennon's death on the radio. She had to call somebody—somebody who knew her when she was living with John and who had also loved John, someone who still treated her kindly despite the fact that John had returned to Yoko.

She called David's Chelsea loft and told Coco the news.

"You can't be alone," said Coco. "Come over immediately."

By the time May arrived Coco had located David, and he was on the way home.

That night David and May sat up together following the story on the news. Disbelief had settled in, and neither could really comprehend what had happened. It was the worst death of all.

That day Nelle Nugent phoned David to ask if he wanted to go on that night. He said that he would play and that he didn't want additional security.

Nugent found him an admirable man. She knew that he was grief-stricken, and she also knew that he knew that the show had to go on.

On January 3, 1981, David gave his last Broadway performance. In five months, even when he was very ill, he had gone on. Everyone agreed that he had been a star in the best sense of the word and had had the discipline to do eight hard shows a week with none of the problems far more experienced legitimate actors might have encountered in a similar situation.

A rock-and-roll star who viewed himself as a rock-and-roll actor had taken the unusual step of becoming the first rock-and-roll artist to master a dramatic Broadway role.

Finally, agonizingly, the Ziggy Stardust image had been erased.

During the preparations for *The Elephant Man* RCA released "Ashes to Ashes," David's first *Scary Monsters* single. Accompanying it was a striking Bowie-Mallet video with Mallet's lurid, brash trademark look stamped all over it. The video, a look at psychic decay, presented an exotic collection of David Bowies—clown, junkie, and lunatic—with each of its scenes introduced by David who held a tiny video screen. Yet again he appeared as the actor, acting out a life that could be recorded on videotape, and played back at will by the actor/participant.

Immediately on its release "Ashes to Ashes" shot to Number One in England. Its contemporary techno-rock sound accompanied by the appeal of the compelling video catapulted David back to commercial prominence in his native country. But in America, after nine years, RCA still seemed incapable of promoting a Bowie album without having David on tour. Two marketing strategies were devised. For the first time, in "Ashes to Ashes" David recycled one of his characters. The Major Tom of 1969's "Space Oddity" had become the junkie of 1980's "Ashes to Ashes."

RCA's advertisements heralded the fact that "Ashes to Ashes" picked up where "Space Oddity" left off. RCA took as its theme Defries's maxim about "the long term," and stressed that David had been a major rock star for eleven years. Full-page pronouncements declared that *Scary Monsters* was the latest release from a legendary rock star whose career was an ongoing demonstration of amazing longevity.

Additionally, without David to tour, the "Ashes to Ashes" video was sent across the country on a tour of its own. It was a brilliant ploy, and motivated journalists to rush into print to discuss the synergy between music and the imminent rock video revolution, and declare that if *David* was doing it, video had to be the next big thing. Once again, publicity was used to reinforce David's stature as rock music's great innovator. In the early 1970s such publicity had enabled David to capture the attention of the glitter-rock avant-garde. Now, the press positioned him as the leader of the image-conscious young people of the early 1980s.

Though *Scary Monsters*—the title seemed to indicate a tie-in with *The Elephant Man*, something David denied—climbed to twelfth position on the American pop charts, it did not deliver an American hit single. Again a portion of the blame had to be laid to RCA. In the early 1970s RCA's promotional forces were unable to persuade radio stations to give major air play to the King of Glitter Rock; at the beginning of the 1980s, RCA seemed to be having the same problem. Now it was not David's image but his sound that seemed too progressive.

Following "Ashes to Ashes," RCA tried again with "Fashion," another *Scary Monsters* single. The song dealt with a "goon squad" of the fashion conscious, those young people who live only to outfit themselves in whatever look is trendy. An ironic comment by David on those who copied his heavily publicized shifts of image, it became a popular new wave disco stomp with exactly the audience David was satirizing. It was the kind of delicious irony David really enjoyed.

Six months after the release of *Scary Monsters*, KROQ, an important Los Angeles radio station, converted to a techno-rock format. While David didn't have direct influence to get the air play he deserved, his indirect influence was great enough to cause a radio station to change its format. That, too, was the kind of irony David was all too familiar with.

After the release of *Scary Monsters* on September 12, 1980, David's job was to sit tight until 1983 when his contract with MainMan expired. Then he could reemerge with a new album and a world tour, and not have to pay MainMan any of the monies earned by his new music and concert performances. For the first time in his career all the money he earned finally would be his. But David also had to fulfill his contractual commitments to RCA before he would be free. By placing him on suspension for nondelivery, RCA was able to extend his contractual commitment until the end of 1982. Still David did not deliver any commercial new music during this waiting period, and RCA began to repackage records that had already been released.

Towards the end of 1981, the company released *ChangesTwo*, a second greatest hits collection. Since 1976's *ChangesOne*, there had been so few hits that selections were included from such old standby albums as *Hunky Dory*, *Ziggy Stardust*, and *Aladdin Sane*. *Fame and Fashion*, another repackaging, followed a year later. As a joke an RCA promotion man suggested that the disk be subtitled "David Bowie's All Time Greatest Hits," a reference to *Johnny Mathis's All Time Greatest Hits*, the best-selling greatest hits album in history. The joke was that David had only one hit. To the surprise of the promotion man, he was taken seriously, and the copy line went on the jacket of the record that contained twelve digitally remastered Bowie selections.

Tony Defries had preached a doctrine of waiting until there was a demand for one's services. While David waited, he turned his attention to television and films, making his dramatic television debut, followed by appearances in two dramatic films.

For London's BBC-1 he appeared in a condensed version of Bertolt Brecht's relatively obscure epic drama *Baal*, playing the title role, a bedraggled poet/singer/murderer. An EP of David's versions of five Brecht songs—could there be anything less commercial and more punishing to a record company that had not been able to find the way to sell the Bowie-Eno trilogy?—was delivered to RCA.

Playing Brecht's Baal seemed beyond David's reach, but the reviewers treated him kindly. No rock star had ever attempted such serious fare, and the fact that *David Bowie* had dared do it enabled him to transcend the normally objective critical response.

The Hunger, a horror film co-starring Catherine Deneuve and Susan Sarandon, followed next. David played a vampire, an eighteenth-century aristocrat who had been alive for over three hundred years. During the course of the film he had to age three hundred years, a makeup job that took four to five hours, and that harked back to the hours spent in makeup when he was transformed into an alien during *The Man Who Fell to Earth*.

David fascinated his co-actors. Out of character makeup, he was professional and engaging, but always his somewhat aloof self. Behind the wizened mask of a three-hundred-year-old man he turned warm and friendly. Life still seemed safer when lived behind a mask.

While Denueve, the icily gorgeous queen of French cinema, seemed to intimidate him, he became friendly with Sarandon, a brisk, outspoken, intelligent woman who expressed concerns about First Amendment violations and nuclear disarmament, and worked with the Imagination Workshop, a therapy unit for schizophrenics.

As usual Coco hovered by David's side during the filming, making sure his every need was anticipated, and that he was never left unprotected.

Despite David's convincing performance, *The Hunger* was just one more trendily decadent affair replete with graphic lesbian love scenes. Silly and pretentious, it seemed more like a feature-length send-up of a rock music video than anything else.

MGM had originally had grave objections about casting David because he had not proven himself a box office draw. *The Hunger* was not going to help on that score.

In the fall of 1982, production started on Nagisa Oshima's *Merry Christmas Mr. Lawrence*, with David and Tom Conti playing two English World War II POWs who fend off their Japanese captors. A brutal and confusing film, it could be viewed either as a meditation on the suicidally warlike nature of the Japanese or as the homosexual love story between a Japanese war camp commandant and David's POW.

The role of Jack Celliers gave David his first opportunity to play a flesh-and-blood human being, but Celliers's source of strength was not revealed until the film's conclusion. Then the audience finally discovered that he was sublimating the guilt he experienced when he abandoned his brother to the school bullies. The motivation was a weak one, and added to the film's unbelievability.

In the film's most powerful scene David plants a kiss on the lips of his sexually repressed commander. This act distracts the Japanese officer from the ritual execution of one of David's fellow POWs. David's punishment is to be buried up to his neck in a sand pit under the blazing sun. As shot by Oshima, the image of David, his one blue eye glinting under the sunlight, was as striking an image of the star as any that had yet made its way onto film.

Despite the wishes of producer Jeremy Thomas, Universal Pictures attempted to mass market *Merry Christmas Mr. Lawrence* in the

United States as "a David Bowie picture," and another box office failure loomed.

In six years David had made four films that had gotten some respectful attention from the press, but that had been commercial failures. These were a series of dramatic performances unmatched by any other rock star, as well as a reflection of David's view of himself as a film elitist and a major taker of chances, someone who makes special movies regardless of their commercial impact.

Yet the reality was that each film had been configured as a commercial project with the hope that it would be a hit; it was anticipated that David's presence would enhance the film's box office potential. Thus far that hope had not paid off. David's Ziggy Stardust image had set him apart from the mainstream. As that image had intimidated conservative radio, equally conservative Hollywood had also been put off, and remained put off. He had been consigned to character parts—the one who never gets the girl—usually in odd, independent productions.

In the early 1980s Hollywood remained wary. If David wanted his pick of scripts and the film career of the great international star spoken of so often by Ken Pitt and Tony Defries, he needed a more accessible image, and the hit singles that proved he was a substantial box office draw. Then he would have a shot at being a real movie star rather than a rock star who also made dramatic films.

Nonetheless, hits or no hits, in the early 1980s, the effect of his influence was felt everywhere. Nine years of innovation accompanied by unrelenting media coverage reaped their payoff in the world that had grown up under David's shadow. Such characters as Ziggy Stardust, Aladdin Sane, and The Thin White Duke had become a permanent part of rock mythology, and the waves of publicity accompanying each transformation had produced a generation who looked to David's manipulation of image as the source for its own experimentation.

Just as David launched his career by copying the Beatles, Rolling Stones, Bob Dylan, and Who, young English musicians and fans looked backward to copy the Davids of their childhoods. In the early 1980s everyone seemed preoccupied with image. David had always gone his way and, in the process, had taught himself how to anticipate change after change in the marketplace. Now the press credited him as the one man who seemed to know what the public wanted before they knew it themselves.

Nothing helped more than the arrival of MTV in August 1981. The twenty-four-hour music video channel devoured rock videos, and, by then, David and his video collaborator David Mallet had six terrific videos to their credit. Not just one David, but many, many Davids were beamed nonstop around the clock into people's homes. Viewers could see for themselves rock's man of a thousand styles and faces.

The message hadn't changed from the time David was in high school. Almost everyone had one role to play in life while David proved capable of playing so many different roles. That was his magic, and MTV emphatically reinforced his changeability to the vast video-rock audience. What Andy Warhol's career had taught David about pop and what Lindsay Kemp had taught him about the way to create theater by amalgamating bits and pieces from any and every source were being taught to the world by David via MTV. In places all over the world everyone seemed to be living his life as if it were theater, and the media credited David as the one responsible for this preoccupation with image and style. The message may have been Warhol's, but David had been his own medium.

Between films David turned his attention to plans for his come-back 1983 world tour. Research for the tour had been launched by his staff during the summer of 1980. David was curious about everyone who worked on the Rolling Stones' tours, among the most efficient and profitable in all of rock music. As his own manager David had decided that the time had come for him to make enormous sums of money. In the 1980s artists were supposed to be rich—very rich—and he was eager to join their ranks. Berlin's starving artist, formerly Bromley's pop idol, was about to evolve again, and cast himself in the role of international businessman.

The private David lived quietly in Switzerland where he copied Matisse etchings, and kept himself busy in bursts of creativity. But New York became the base for his transformation to businessman. He continued to live in his Chelsea loft, and those who came in daily contact with him inevitably mistook his surface affability for real friendship. Automatically they became protective. Again his personal style was marked by intensity and curiosity about whatever was going on. The fact that he was an especially nice man tended to obscure the fact that he had been trained from early adolescence to view himself as a star in the classic tradition.

After a career filled with staggering highs and devastating lows, this David had some real objectivity about himself. He was aware of his significance on the cultural horizon; his difference from any other rock star was proved by his ability to cross effortlessly back and forth between serious and mainstream culture. In the early 1970s he had viewed himself as actor working in rock and roll. Now he took himself very seriously as a mainstream artist.

As he waited for 1983 to arrive New York staff members were treated to aspects of David's philosophy that he had evolved over the years, especially his firm belief in the importance of image. Using real style as a weapon in aiding his credibility, whenever he set out to do his own business, he dressed impeccably. No matter what anyone expected when he met David Bowie for the first time, he met an immaculately groomed man determined to outelegant those he did business with.

Harking back to his days with Lindsay Kemp fifteen years before, he theorized that he really was a popularizer. It seemed to him that someone who incorporated innovations into his work was the one who achieved the commercial success.

At this time a deal was struck with United Artists so that David could develop his own film projects, something he had always wanted to do. But he seemed unable to devise cogent story lines or find anyone to invent conventional, workable plots for him.

This movie deal took him back to the 1960s when he so often lost his way trying to find the right form for his talents. Finally he repeated his pattern of turning to the past, and initiated a project discussed in 1975 with Si Litvinoff, producer of *The Man Who Fell to Earth*. The property was a novel, *Miracle Jack*, and David set to work developing it, even though he did not control the rights.

The project, and the movie deal, led nowhere.

The really important things in David's life were being dealt with intelligently and directly. His relationship with his son, now called Joey, was a good one. Angela observed that David was just too smart not to bring Joey up properly. And David and Joey loved each other very much.

As David's relationship with Joey had grown richer and deeper, he made peace with his own family. Peggy Jones was approaching seventy, and wasn't well. Old wounds healed as David took financial responsibility for her and tried to give her a pleasant life.

After his cousin Christine contracted cancer, he made a substantial financial contribution to her treatment. The only family member he seemed to avoid was Terry; Terry's ongoing mental illness was just too much to deal with.

Only one component of David's dream was missing, the enormous record sales that usually accompanied superstardom, and as 1983 approached he set out to achieve a huge new record deal, have hit records, and launch a breathtaking world tour with profits pouring in from everywhere. The picture would finally be complete.

David's first move of the new campaign was to ask his old friend Tony Visconti to produce his comeback LP. Then he met Chic producer Nile Rodgers in a New York club. It was another stroke of good luck, a planned accident, similar to his encounter with *Elephant Man* director Jack Hofsiss in a similar New York club situation. Rodgers was a certified hit-maker with a knack for creating danceable, catchy pop records that riveted the ear with pulsating rhythms. Among his biggest hits were Chic's "Le Funk" and Sister Sledge's "We Are Family." David's intuition told him that Rodgers was the man for him.

Rodgers was used to having total control in the studio, and working with musicians of his own choice. David's music director for eight years, Carlos Alomar, was called to play on the record, but was offered less than his usual fee. Alomar was a musician for hire, and always there for David at his agreed-upon fee. Offering him less ensured that he would not play on this record.

Alomar knew from his own experience that David's formula for musical changeability was a simple one. By using different musicians on each record and allowing them to make their own distinctive contributions, David guaranteed that each of his LPs would have a distinctly different sound. In 1978 David had originally told the press that he planned not to use Alomar on his world tour in order to get a new sound, but had then changed his mind. After nine years of working together Carlos was used to David's reversing himself on a moment's notice and erasing someone from his consciousness when he didn't think he needed him and then reinstating that person when he did need him. When Alomar was offered the opportunity to be musical director of the Serious Moonlight Tour at an attractive price, he was glad to accept. He loved David and loved playing with him.

Let's Dance had a spectacularly commercial sound. Sleek, danceable pop had been molded by Rodgers from the sets of unlikely juxtapositions for which David was known: imagistic ambiguous lyrics; the funky Chic sound; Rodger's horns section, a throwback to Louis Jordan's big band rhythm-and-blues sound; and the keening riffs of blues guitarist Stevie Ray Vaughn. David had made it a practice to hire guitarists who were not performing superstars in their own right, and had already worked with Adrian Belew, Chuck Hammer, and Robert Fripp. He repeated the formula on this disk by hiring Vaughan, at that time a relatively unknown Austin-born white Southern blues virtuoso. Conceptually, he believed that Vaughan's musical presence would give a "David Bowie meets B. B. King" feel to the disk, and he liked that very much.

Adding to the novelty Rodgers abandoned the synthesizer-based dance music pioneered on David's collaborations with Eno in order to make a dance record that didn't sound like a copy of the dance records currently being played.

In 1978 Donna Summer's "Last Dance," a cheerful, upbeat song, was America's Number One single. In 1983 David wrote "Let's Dance," a lyric that captured the underlying melancholy morbidity of a "last dance." But there was nothing melancholy about Rodgers's arrangement of the tune. The sounds of the Beatles (in the "Twist and Shout" "ah-ah-ah" opening), the World Saxophone Quartet (in the horn arrangements), and Chic (in the bass line and mix) came together seamlessly, and the result was a dance floor classic.

The sound of *Let's Dance* was pure Rodgers, an impeccable pop album that crossed barriers and appealed to a number of different audiences. While nothing on the record matched the flair of the title track, it did not matter. By choosing to work with Rodgers, David seemed to have come to terms with the compromises that were necessary to have a commercial hit. The compromises worked. For the first time in eight years he was headed for the commercial mainstream with an enormous success. Rock's great innovator was about to emerge from his hiatus in the role he had spoken of frequently in private— the great popularizer.

With the album in the can the time had come to conclude negotiations for the stupendous record deal David craved.

RCA was not the place to score that coup. In 1981 the RCA Corporation had lost $14.5 million; eventually $575 million would be lost in the videodisk-player business. It was not the moment for David to demand $17 million.

Besides, RCA knew David's sales figures. From 1977 until 1983 about one out of every two new Bowie records was returned from the stores unsold. As of June 1983, David had achieved the following net sales figures:

MainMan Albums

The Man Who Sold the World	207,302
Space Oddity	455,548
Hunky Dory	445,613
Ziggy Stardust	1,381,435
Aladdin Sane	531,862
Pin-Ups	421,247
Diamond Dogs	745,361
David Live	598,835
Young Americans	923,018

Post-MainMan Albums

Station to Station	552,791
ChangesOne	1,331,247
Low	265,906
"Heroes"	279,050
Stage	127,350
Lodger	153,364
Scary Monsters	347,413
ChangesTwo	143,994
Christiane F. (sound track)	26,156
Baal (sound track)	24,212

Of these nineteen albums recorded during an eleven-year period David had to his credit one platinum album (*ChangesOne*) and six gold albums (*Ziggy Stardust*, *Aladdin Sane*, *Diamond Dogs*, *David Live*, *Young Americans*, and *Station to Station*). "Fame" had been his sole gold single.

David's sales figures were astonishingly low for an artist of his stature and influence. With the advent of MTV and its insatiable appetite for new material, the music business was facing an enormous resurgence and was heading toward a moment when a single Michael Jackson album would rack up worldwide sales of 12 million copies. David wanted a megastar's advance despite sales figures that made such an advance seem unrecoupable. RCA passed.

The company hadn't heard *Let's Dance*, and RCA executives confided later that if they had, they might have made a substantial offer. However, a new recording deal was struck with EMI-Capitol estimated somewhere between $10 and $17 million. There were a number of reasons why EMI-Capitol was convinced David was worth that much money.

For starters the very length of David's career demonstrated real staying power, and it could safely be assumed that he was going to be around for many years to come. Second, 1980's *Scary Monsters* had been a big hit in England, an indication that David could have hits again. It does seem unlikely that EMI-Capitol would have made this deal without hearing *Let's Dance* and recognizing its commercial potential.

A further important reason was the prestige and mystique that surrounded David. He had the knack of getting attention. A whole new generation of stars reflected his influence. This influence also extended to the worlds of fashion and video. The English androgynous gender-bender look exemplified by Boy George and Eurythmics' Annie Lennox was traced directly to David's Ziggy Stardust look; in France the style was called "le look Bowie."

By signing David, EMI-Capitol, a label in search of a stronger roster of artists, was assured that many new acts would be attracted to the company simply because they wanted to be on the same label as David. It was the reason Mercury signed David in 1969 for $15,000, and the reason RCA signed him in 1971 for $75,000.

With EMI-Capitol's promotion department operating at a fever pitch, *Let's Dance* zoomed up the pop charts, spinning off three hit singles, "Let's Dance," "China Girl," and "Modern Love." Eventually it sold 5 million copies. As part of the promotion two sleek Bowie-Mallet videos were shot, and were aired around the world.

In 1969 David had turned his back on the hippie movement and created Hype, the antithesis of 1960s hippie authenticity. At the outset of 1983 he repeated the formula by rejecting the rock and roll outrageousness that he had inspired. He had taught himself how to be a step ahead and, to accompany his commercial success, he placed himself in the forefront of the new conservativism that was sweeping America. When he emerged to meet the press and to introduce the David Bowie of the 1980s, he was elegant, charming, and self-assured.

It was the conservative, aristocratic style and look of a classic star, and it harked back to Tony Defries's fascination with the Golden Age of Hollywood. At thirty-six, David's new shadow was the shadow of the star Ken Pitt knew David would become, and the long-term star Tony Defries so often spoke of. By nature such stars were publicly conservative, and their lives were free from scandal. It was at this time that David renounced homosexuality. "The biggest mistake I ever made was telling that *Melody Maker* writer that I was bisexual," he told *Rolling Stone*.

What a stunning reversal! Left unchallenged by the press all of David's statements were taken at face value, and this new assertion about his sexuality was not questioned by the press. Everyone was delighted to believe that he was, and always had been, heterosexual. So effective was his campaign on behalf of heterosexuality that, at the end of 1985, a New York gay newspaper, *The New York Native*, labeled him one of the most homophobic stars of the year.

He commented that Ziggy Stardust reflected his "lower self." The evolution of the unwaveringly heterosexual former King of Glitter Rock had led to a gleaming higher self. Being a good father to twelve-year-old Joey had transformed him into a completely normal man with a real sense of purpose. This David was an optimist who made friendly music. He was even a Redskins fan.

Credible, precise, intelligent answers to all the standard questions about his past were at David's fingertips, and no matter how many times he repeated himself, his comments sounded spontaneous.

"I wanted to be part of society again and not an alien freak on the outside which I'm very much not," he proclaimed to one reporter. "It's not hip to be cool," he told another.

This was the man of taste Ken Pitt had trained him to become, and the press loved the new self-presentation. David was labeled "the loveable alien." The former King of Glitter Rock, once the very symbol of rock and roll decadence, had anointed himself the Yuppie King.

Early in 1983 set designer Mark Ravitz was summoned to David's home in Switzerland to discuss the designs for the Serious Moonlight Tour. Ravitz had designed the Year of the Diamond Dogs in 1974. The two men had not seen each other in five years, and Ravitz found David concerned about business and a little insecure about his return to the concert stage, but he also seemed to have been through plenty and had a newfound sense of security about his role as a public figure. This new David kept his ski boots in the hall and drove his own car, a customized Volvo.

David wanted a simple set. The father of rock theatrics wished to present himself as a vocalist, yet another reversal. He showed Ravitz a rough model of the design. Onstage there were six columns as well as a large moon and a giant hand. The hand was adapted from the logo for *E.T.*, the most popular movie in history. The ad man in David had gravitated to this bit of motivational research, an identification with something his audience loved. How different from the mid-1970s when David appeared onstage in a giant-sized diamond that held him in its clutches and wouldn't let him go.

Musical director Carlos Alomar was responsible for arranging the thirty-five songs featured in the show, and creating a cohesive musical sound for the evening. When David came to rehearsals, the band had to be perfect so that he could effortlessly take center stage and polish his vocals. During the tour Alomar was also to serve as David's vocal adviser. Over the years David's voice had become reedier. This was the first time he would appear at outdoor festivals, and at times weather conditions would make it even harder for him to hit certain top notes and perform the breathy aria that was one of his stylistic trademarks. While recording technology could be utilized in the recording studio to give David's voice a high-pitched youthful sound, Alomar had to transpose these songs to a moderate range so that David's high notes wouldn't be all that high. In reality, David had a low voice with a flexible lower register.

A few musicians from the 1978 world tour were invited to join the Serious Moonlight Tour. This time they were offered around half their previous fees. Even though David was receiving $1.5 million for a single appearance at the U.S. Festival in northern California, an attempt was made to keep the musicians' salaries close to scale. Some declined because of the low fees; others settled for fair —though not generous—salaries. In rehearsals David provided them with a secret concept for their onstage appearance: they were supposed to pretend to be a 1950s Hong Kong bar band. Alomar's costume made him look like a rock-and-roll Gandhi.

The musicians, paid around $1,000 a week, received bonuses in the middle and at the end of the tour. They also traveled on a customized 707 jet with its own chef. There were videotape machines on board so they could watch their favorite movies. The tour bedded down in first-class hotels.

But the greatest pleasures happened onstage where David presented a polished version of his 1978 man-as-musician. Dressed first in a pale gray and then in a pale green suit, David presented two hour-long sets of fifteen songs each. His hair was dyed a brazen blond, the defiant color of movie stars like Lana Turner who when they entered their late thirties were determined to project an air of overwhelming youthfulness. Bronzer gave the illusion that David spent his days basking in the sun. The result was a healthy onstage glow. He looked wonderful.

The evening was a major retrospective of David's enormously varied body of work over a fourteen-year period, a musical everything-you-always-wanted-to-know-about-David-Bowie designed for the army of new fans who had never seen David before and weren't quite sure exactly who he was, but were eager to hear his new hits.

What they got was a warm and personable vocalist/songwriter backed by an expert band. For the most part David stood on the tip of the stage extended into the audience offering himself up as a legendary object to be worshiped and adored. The evening quickly became a ritual celebration of success, survival, ambition, talent, and agelessness. After twenty years in show business David received exactly the response he craved, a hero's welcome. These audiences worshiped success, and they worshiped him.

One critic wrote: "Making lots of dough is to the '80s what sex and political pessimism were to the '70s, what drugs and political activism were to the '60s. In that sense, Bowie's just a guy in tune with the times."

During the MainMan years David had acted Defries's role of great superstar, but finally he was having the success of an authentic superstar. The teenage fantasy of becoming a pop idol had finally become real.

David's tour staff knew that he was governed by one magic word, and that word was control. Coco collected every interview and concert review the second it was in print, and notes were made about details that contradicted David's new conservative image as well as any criticisms. Yet on occasion the past could not be silenced. The North American leg of the Serious Moonlight Tour was launched with a *Time* magazine cover story on July 18, 1983. In it Tony Visconti described David's marriage to Angela: "Thursday was gay night. David would go to a gay club, Angie to a lesbian club, and they would both bring people home they found. We had to lock our bedroom doors because in the middle of the night these people they brought home with them would come climbing into new beds, looking for fresh blood."

Instructions were issued to people in David's past to refuse all interviews. Anyone who did not comply was told that he would never again be spoken to by David.

It was clear that David and Coco were a team, with Coco there to make sure that David never met the world head on. The few who really got to know him sensed that he always harbored the fear that someone might betray him. The music business had also bruised him professionally, financially, and emotionally. He was wary, and was never going to be hurt again.

In August 1983 Serious Moonlight was scheduled to play two nights at Madison Square Garden. They sold out immediately. Fans posted stickers on poles and billboards all over New York begging David to schedule a third performance. When it was assured that a third performance would also sell out, it was added to the schedule. Six thousand of the best of the sixty thousand seats that had been put up for sale had been withheld to be sold to celebrities and important music business figures.

Tony Defries purchased thirty of these seats. During the show he observed that David had cast himself in another of his favorite roles, that of Frank Sinatra, and seemed to be walking through the show. But then again, he observed, David *never* sweated onstage. Defries maintained that David's fear of success was the reason it had taken David so very long to realize his commercial potential.

At the end of the show Defries commented that he was pleased that David was doing his old songs, a promotion for the catalog they co-owned. Ironically, there was only one EMI-Capitol album to promote, while there were many RCA albums that would benefit from the promotion and publicity surrounding the tour. Business *was* business, RCA had quickly issued *Golden Years*, which contained many of the most familiar songs David was performing during the tour. According to Jaime Andrews, even though David's and De-fries's settlement agreement had expired, Defries looked forward to realizing as much as $1 million that year as his share of David's earnings from the catalog promoted by the tour.

Despite the huge concert grosses, the real profits were to be derived from the merchandising industry that had grown up around touring since David's 1978 tour. David Bowie program books, T-shirts, sweatshirts, scarves, pin sets, badges, and posters were on sale everywhere. The show was filmed for an HBO special, and then released as home video. A tour documentary, *Ricochet*, was also re-leased to the home market.

Defries made noises about the videos, claiming that David had rerecorded master recordings that he and David co-owned. David was a terrific player, but so was Tony. And both really enjoyed the game. As David had gone on to score this triumph Defries's belief in his own long term had kept him financially secure. He was a happy man, content to create new MainMan families around himself, and roam the world in comfort and style.

Yet Defries had taught David that the present was always a rehearsal for the future. At the end of 1983, David had become *Playboy*'s Man of the Year. He was already thinking about 1986. At that time the rights to the valuable catalog of the many master re-cordings co-owned by David and Defries would revert back to them. Discussions were begun with RCA about a new deal. At the con-clusion of negotiations the many Davids of the past could be re-packaged and recycled all over again.

If life were fiction, the Serious Moonlight triumph would be the happy ending to David's story. But life goes on—and with it the inevitable highs and lows. While David waited for 1986, he faced the never-ending task of all stars, keeping his name before the public.

In the fall of 1984, *Tonight*, a follow-up to *Let's Dance*, was re-leased. The album featured "Blue Jean," a rock anthem in the style of "Rebel Rebel"; "Dancing with the Boys," an earnest attempt to amalgamate the popular Anglo-funk sound of the moment; and "Lov-ing the Alien," best described as David's homage to Bryan Ferry. The title track recycled an old tune by David and Iggy, and featured an impassioned guest appearance by Tina Turner. The rhythm-and-blues queen was on the verge of one of the great comebacks, but David, always a step ahead, got there first.

Tonight was a calculated attempt to appeal to the huge audience attracted by *Let's Dance*, but the record seemed like a tossed-off effort. Bits and pieces of David's versatility and originality were scattered everywhere, but the obligation to be an ongoing hit-maker had always been his *bête noire*. He seemed bored, and his attempt to duplicate his success as middle-of-the-road hit-maker produced one of his least compelling LPs.

Yet the record inspired David's entry into the long-form video pioneered by the John Landis–Michael Jackson collaboration, *Thriller*. *Jazzin' with Blue Jean* was directed by Julian Temple, who shared David's fascination with the mystique of rock superstardom. In the twenty-minute-long video David played two parodistic personas, rock superstar and nerdish fan. The video suggested that there really wasn't much difference between nerds and superstars, but that super-stars got all the rewards.

Jazzin' with Blue Jean was put into heavy rotation on MTV, but *Tonight*'s sales didn't approach those of *Let's Dance*. The mass audience proved fickle; without major hits they did not respond.

In the press David was portrayed sympathetically as a victim of his own success. The public was told not to expect an ongoing string of hits from him. David was an innovator and a hero, and entitled to do precisely what he wanted to do the way he wanted to do it. People like David Bowie lived to fulfill their personal expectations of themselves, and not to satisfy the demands made upon them by others. In 1984 David had become a media hero the press dared not criticize.

John Landis's success with Michael Jackson next encouraged David to make a cameo appearance in Landis's *Into the Night*. The film was a contemporary comic film noir that featured cameos by a horde of cult directors. Still, it went unnoticed. Another film appearance was in *Absolute Beginners*, Julian Temple's musical adaptation of Colin MacInnes's novel about growing up English during the 1960s. It is scheduled for release in the spring of 1986.

Still the past continued to rear its ugly head, and the result was the thing David most feared, newspaper headlines that presented an unflattering picture of the man whose current shadow glistened with love and success. During the spring of 1984 Angela stormed into New York. After the death of her father she seemed finally capable of turning her attentions to herself, and decided finally to begin the process of manufacturing herself as a pop star. She moved into a tiny four-room tenement apartment which she shared with her four-year-old daughter Stashia (Stashia's father was Andrew Lipsius, whose stage name was Drew Blood); Stashia's nanny; and two boyfriends, an employee at a local rock club and a teenaged musician she scooped up on the road. Irrepressible and looking wonderful, she confessed that she was still boy-crazy and announced during an interview that she had "always wished she had a big dick."

During that August Joey, twelve at the time, a handsome and precocious young man, came to stay, along with his nanny Marion. Even though the East Village apartment, painted fire engine red, was unair-conditioned and sweltering, Joey seemed to be having a wonderful time. Everywhere Angela went there was noise and people and excitement, and this apartment was no exception. It was another of her Haddon Halls, and Joey could see for himself what life was probably like when his parents were first married.

In the fall he began his high school education at the Gordonstoun School in a remote part of northern Scotland. Gordonstoun, an all-boy's school, stresses discipline, physical fitness, and academic achievement, and is known as one of the world's most challenging educational institutions. It is a place for special boys destined to lead special lives, and its best-known graduate is the Prince of Wales.

Angela, who never has a harsh word for anyone, said that time had healed the painful parts of her relationship with David. She remembered only how much she had loved him.

She formed a band, cut some singles, and made two rock videos. She also gave interviews. The ex–Mrs. Bowie was still Mrs. Media Heroine, and the press was eager to report her activities and remarks. Angela couldn't resist saying that every time David looked at Joey, she got even with David because Joey bore such a strong resemblance to her. She also complained that she was broke and had run through a $700,000 alimony settlement, and that her letters came back from Gordonstoun unopened.

David could do nothing to stem the wave of print that followed in Angela's wake. Nor could he control the reports of family tragedy that followed next. At the beginning of 1985 Terry Burns committed suicide by throwing himself in front of an oncoming train. It was Terry's third attempt in three years. A relative committed the worst crime of all and spoke to the *London Times*. According to her David had not seen Terry in ten years, and went to visit him only once in 1982 after the relative complained to the press. Both David and Peggy were portrayed as callous, unfeeling people when it came to Terry with David making promises to Terry he did not keep. It was as if nothing had changed in the Jones family in the twenty years that had passed since Terry first became ill.

David did not attend the funeral but sent flowers and a note.

Later that year, on July 13, David was one of the many stars who appeared at Wembley Stadium as part of the Live Aid Concert for the African Famine Relief Fund. In the two years since 1983's Serious Moonlight Tour, rock authenticity as exemplified by Bruce Springsteen and Tina Turner had made a staggering comeback. Rock stars were supposed to do long sets and work hard. It was a hot summer's day, and the onstage temperature hovered around 100 degrees. But when David hit the stage, the onstage temperature rose even higher, and David proved he could sweat with the best of them. His stirring performance of " 'Heroes' " was one of the highlights of the benefit.

Subsequently he and Mick Jagger teamed on a single and video of the Martha and the Vandellas' hit "Dancing in the Streets," with the profits earmarked for Live Aid. Over the years they had talked about doing a movie together, and one of the projects batted around was a remake of *Some Like It Hot. La Cage aux Folles*, *Victor/Victoria*, and *Tootsie* had made men in drag a popular film subject. At the moment David and Mick have a film project set up with MGM.

A guest appearance on *Private Dancer*, Tina Turner's HBO special, followed. The king of artifice had no trouble holding his own with the queen of authenticity.

Meanwhile, the success of *Let's Dance* and the Serious Moonlight Tour had finally caught Hollywood's eye, and David was being offered major scripts. But there was a new condition. He was expected to deliver sound tracks in the style of *Let's Dance* so that his new hits could be used to promote the films. His friend Ridley Scott wanted him to play a rock star and studio executives suggested that they would go so far as to supply composers so that David would deliver bona-fide hits.

Such offers were unacceptable to him. Nor did he want to play villains, and turned down an offer to play a villain in one of the James Bond series.

The film he did accept was *Labyrinth*, a $25-million film directed by puppeteer Jim Henson, creator of the Muppets, and produced by George Lukas. The screenplay was written by Monty Python's Terry Jones, and the visual style designed by fantasy illustrator Brian Froud, author of *Faeries*. David had only one of two speaking parts, that of a goblin king who traps a fourteen-year-old girl in a maze.

Labyrinth is scheduled to open in June 1986 accompanied by a gigantic promotional campaign in the style that Lukas had already mounted for his own *Star Wars* trilogy. In January a trailer was shown in movie theaters across America, and David's appearance was greeted with cheers. Posters announcing the movie began to appear in theater lobbies. The copyline read "Jim Henson, George Lukas, and David Bowie invite you to a world of fantasy and adventure."

It is the antithesis of films like *The Man Who Fell to Earth* and *Merry Christmas Mr. Lawrence*, a major studio film with an extravagant budget and enormous promotion. David's image of the moment found him fulfilling Ken Pitt's and Tony Defries's dream that he become a great international entertainer. If *Labyrinth* is a success, he finally will be a real movie star.

For David the thrust is always forward. But in their own ways every member of David's past has also moved on. For example, Graham Rivens is a happy man in Margate, Maggie Abbott is a successful agent, and Michael Lippman is a successful manager. In 1986 Craig Copetas published *The Billion Dollar Skim*, an investigative report about financial manipulations, and Ava Cherry sang backup on Luther Vandross's tour, and then made a solo recording deal. By coincidence she is signed to David's label, EMI-Capitol. Like Angela her memories of David are fond ones, and the thing she remembers most is how much she loved him.

Each remembers David as a man who never stood in judgment, but allowed a creative contribution to occur. David's singlemindedness about himself proved the catalyst for these bursts of creativity. The process seemed so magical at the time that each felt sprinkled by David's stardust, an experience each will never forget.

But that stardust has always really belonged solely to David.

"I'm smart enough to know my best bet in life is myself," he told the press at the outset of the Serious Moonlight Tour.

It's the way David felt from the time he was a teenager. The conviction was strong enough to convince anyone who met him to give his help in support of David's cause. Above all else, this was the belief that guaranteed David Bowie the long term.

Selected
Bibliography

Alterman, Lorraine. "Bye, Bye, Bowie." *Melody Maker*, December 23, 1972, Vol. 47, pg. 37.

Arieti, Silvano. *Creativity: The Magic Synthesis*. New York: Basic Books, 1976.

Aronowitz, Al. "The Super Pop Event." *New York Post*, September 29, 1972, pg. 32.

Arthur, J. "Hard Rockin' Mr. Bowie." *Record Mirror*, September 9, 1972.

Atkinson, Rick. "All That Glitters." *Disc*, January 20, 1973.

Bailey, Andrew, and Paul Gambaccini. "Big Private Party Caps Bowie's Final Night on Stage." *Rolling Stone*, August 16, 1973, Vol. 141, pg. 8.

――――. "Tears as Bowie Bows Out." *Evening Standard*, London, England, July 4, 1973.

Bangs, Lester. "Chicken Head Comes Home to Roost." *Creem*, April 1976, pg. 58.

――――. "Iggy and the Stooges: The Apotheosis of Every Parental Nightmare." *Stereo Review*, July 1973.

――――. "Iggy Pop: Blowtorch in Bondage." *Village Voice*, March 28, 1977, pg. 49.

――――. "The New Living Bowie." *Creem*, January 1975, Vol. 6, pg. 38.

Blake, John. "Back from Russia with Love." *Evening News*, London, England, May 12, 1973.

――――. "Kinky King of Rock." *Evening News*, May 12, 1973.

Bockris, Victor, and Gerard Malanga. *Uptight: The Velvet Underground Story*. New York: Putnam, 1983.

Bosworth, P. "Bowie: Is It All for a Lark?" *Melody Maker*, January 6, 1973, Vol. 48, pg. 35.

Brazier, C. "Bowie: Beauty Before Outrage." *Melody Maker*, September 4, 1976, Vol. 51, pg. 17.

Brown, M. "This Man Taught David Bowie His Moves." *Crawdaddy*, September 1974, Vol. 40, pg. 28.

Campbell, Jackie. "Rock Star Bowie Convincing as 'Elephant Man.' " *Rocky Mountain News*, July 31, 1980, pg. 79.

Cann, Kevin. *David Bowie: A Chronology*. New York: Simon and Schuster, 1983.

Carr, Roy, and Charles Shaar Murray. *David Bowie: An Illustrated Record*. New York: Avon Books/London: Eel Pie, 1981.

Cavendish, Richard. *The Black Arts*. New York: Putnam, 1967.

Charlesworth, Chris. "Bowie: Birth of the New Rock Theatre." *Melody Maker*, June 22, 1974, Vol. 49, pg. 3.

———. "Bowie: Ringing the Ch-ch-changes." *Melody Maker*, March 13, 1976, Vol. 51, pg. 16.

———. *David Bowie Profile*. New York: Proteus, 1981.

Childers, Leee Black. "On Tour with David Bowie." *Hit Parader*, December 1974.

Chin, Brian. "Bowie Sprinkles Stardust at the Garden." *New York Post*, July 27, 1983, pg. 25.

Claire, Vivian. *David Bowie*. New York: Putnam, 1977.

Clapton, Diana. *Lou Reed and The Velvet Underground*. New York: Proteus, 1982.

Cocks, Jay. "David Bowie Rockets Onward." *Time*, July 18, 1983, Vol. 122, pg. 54.

Cohen, Debra Rae. "David Bowie Takes On the Challenge of Being Himself." *New York Times*, May 15, 1983, Sect. 2, pg. 27.

Coleman, Ray. "A Star Is Born." *Melody Maker*, July 15, 1972, Vol. 47, pg. 43.

Connolly, Ray. "Wowie, Bowie." *Evening Standard*, London, England, February 3, 1973.

Copetas, Craig. "Beat Godfather Meets Glitter MainMan." *Rolling Stone*, February 28, 1974, Vol. 155, pg. 24.

Craig, James. "Bowie Goes North." *Record Mirror*, May 26, 1973, pg. 9.

Crescenti, Pete. "Ronson & McGuinn = Thunder & Byrd." *Circus*, April 8, 1976.

Cromelin, Richard. "Bowie: Time for Another Ch-ch-change." *Rolling Stone*, October 10, 1974, Vol. 171, pg. 10.

Crowe, Cameron. "Bowie to Tour: 'No Gimmickry.' " *Rolling Stone*, January 15, 1976, Vol. 204, pg. 12.

———. "Ground Control to Davy Jones." *Rolling Stone*, February 12, 1976, Vol. 206, pg. 78.

————. "Space Face Changes the Station; David Bowie Pulls a Lazarus." *Creem*, May 1976, Vol. 7, pg. 38.

Coxhill, Gordon. "Superstarman." *The Sun*, London, England, September 29, 1972.

Damsker, M. "Philly Stopover: Fans and Funk." *Rolling Stone*, October 10, 1974. Vol. 171, pg. 10.

Darter, Tom. *The Art of Electronic Music*. New York: GPI Publications, 1984.

Davis, Stephen. *Hammer of the Gods: The Led Zeppelin Saga*. New York: Quill, 1985.

De la Parra, Pimm Jal. *The David Bowie Concert Tapes*. Amsterdam: Pimm Jal de la Parra, 1983.

Duncan, Robert. *The Noise*. New York: Ticknor & Fields, 1984.

Dyroff, Dennis. "David Bowie, Strange Man, Hits Musical Big Time." *The Times Herald*, Norristown, PA, November 18, 1972.

Edmonds, Ben. "Mick Ronson, One of the Boys." *Creem*, January 1975.

Edwards, Henry. "A Growing Boy Who Gets Better and Better." *After Dark*, October 1973, pg. 39.

————. "Bowie's Back but the Glitter's Gone." *New York Times*, March 21, 1976, pg. 1.

————. "The King of Glitter Rock." *Entertainment Magazine*, May 1973, pg. 19.

————. "Rock and Rouge." *Hi Fidelity/Musical America*, October 1973, Vol. 23, pg. 95.

————. "The Rise of Ziggy Stardust." *After Dark*, October 1972.

Ewbank, Tim. "Pop Idol Bowie Gives Last Show." *Daily Mail*, London, England, July 4, 1973.

Feiden, Robert. "David Bowie Brings Back Style to Rock and Roll." *Record World*, March 3, 1973.

Ferris, Timothy. "Are You Man Enough for David Bowie?" and "The Iceman Having Calculated, Cometh." *Rolling Stone*, November 9, 1972.

————. "David Bowie in America." *Rolling Stone*, November 9, 1972, Vol. 121, pg. 38.

Fields, Leslie. "Seventies Style." *The Sunday Times*, London, England, October 14, 1978, pg. 17.

Finn, Deborah Elizabeth. "Moon and Gloom; David Bowie's Frustrated Messianism." *Commonweal*, September 9, 1983, Vol. 110, pg. 467.

Foster, Hal. *The Anti-Aesthetic*. Port Townsend, Washington: Bay Press, 1983.

Fox-Cumming, Ray. "Bowie Bows Out." *New Musical Express*, July 14, 1973.

Frame, Pete. *The Road to Rock*. London, England: Anchor Press, 1974.

Freedland, N. "David Bowie: It's Back to Live Dates, but Fame Singer Won't Fly." *Billboard*, January 3, 1976, Vol. 88, pg. 17.

Fricke, David. "David Bowie." *Musician*, December 1984, No. 74, pg. 46.

Frith, Simon. "How Low Can You Get?" *Creem*, May 1977, Vol. 8, pg. 56.

———. "Only Dancing—David Bowie Flirts with the Issues." *Mother Jones*, August 1983, pg. 3.

———. *Sound Effects*. New York: Pantheon, 1983.

Gaines, Steve. "Bowie Divines Doom in Moscow." *Circus*, August 1973.

Gerson, Ben. "Bowie's Martian Spiders Spin New World." *Boston Phoenix*, October 17, 1972.

Giangrande, M. "Take David Bowie for Instance: A Collector's Tale." *Stereo Review*, March 1976, Vol. 36, pg. 74.

Gillett, Charles. *The Sound of the City*. New York: Pantheon, 1983.

Goldman, Albert. *Elvis*. New York: McGraw-Hill, 1981.

Gussow, Mel. "Roeg: The Man Behind 'The Man Who Fell to Earth.' " *New York Times*, August 22, 1976, Sect. D, pg. 11.

Harrington, Richard. "The Fall and Rise of David Bowie." *Washington Post*, May 2, 1983, pg. B1.

Hauptfuhrer, Fred. "Rock's Space Oddity David Bowie, Falls to Earth and Lands His Feet in Film." *People*, September 6, 1976, Vol. 6, pg. 57.

Hayman, Martin. "Life and Times of David Bowie." *Sounds*, May 26, 1973.

———. "Outside David Bowie." *Rock*, October 8, 1973.

Hibbard, Don J., and Carol Kaleialoha. *The Role of Rock*. Englewood Cliffs, NJ: Prentice-Hall, 1983.

Hilburn, Robert. "Aladdin Sane Features a Broader Bowie." *Los Angeles Times*, June 3, 1973.

———. "Bowie Finds His Voice!" *Melody Maker*, September 14, 1974, Vol. 49, pg. 3.

———. "Bowie: Now I'm a Businessman." *Melody Maker*, February 28, 1976, Vol. 51, pg. 9.

———. "David Bowie Arrives with a Burst of Stardust." *Los Angeles Times Calendar*, November 5, 1972.

———. "David Bowie Has Dropped the Disguises." *Los Angeles Times*, May 29, 1983, Vol. 102, Sect. C, pg. 50.

———. "David Bowie Rated Top Recording Artist of '72." *Los Angeles Times Calendar*, January 7, 1973.

———. "David Bowie Rocks in Santa Monica." *Los Angeles Times*, October 23, 1972.

———. "Dylan Revue at Troubadour." *Los Angeles Times*, January 27, 1976.

———. "Pop Poll Points to New Leadership." *Los Angeles Times*, October 6, 1973.

———. "Rock Theatre of David Bowie at Long Beach." *Los Angeles Times*, March 12, 1973.

———. "RTR/A Different Way To Go." *Los Angeles Times*, February 1, 1976.

———. "Second Bowie Concert for Overflow Crowd." *Los Angeles Times*, March 3, 1973.

———. *Springsteen*. New York: Scribners, 1985.

Hodenfield, Chris. "Bad Boys in Berlin." *Rolling Stone*, October 4, 1979, pg. 41.

Hodenfield, Jan. "Iggy Stooge, I'll Stick It Deep Inside." *Gentlemen's Quarterly*, April 1971.

Hoggard, Stuart. *Bowie "Changes."* New York: Putnam, 1980.

Hollingworth, Roy. "Can Bowie Save New York from Boredom?" *Melody Maker*, October 7, 1972, Vol. 47, pg. 38.

———. " 'Ch-ch-ch-Changes'—A Journey with Aladdin." *Melody Maker*, May 12, 1973, Vol. 48, pg. 9.

———. "Drive Out Saturday." *Melody Maker*, May 19, 1973, Vol. 48, pg. 20.

——— and M. Benton. "Is Bowie Really Quitting?" *Melody Maker*, July 14, 1973, Vol. 48, pg. 8.

Holloway, Danny. "David Bowie—I'm Not Ashamed of Wearing Dresses . . ." *New Musical Express*, January 29, 1972.

Johnson, Derek. "Final Bowie Gig Filmed." *New Musical Express*, July 14, 1973.

Jones, A. "Bowie's Raw Power." *Melody Maker*, May 22, 1976, Vol. 51, pg. 35.

———. "The David Bowie Story." *Melody Maker*, May 1, 1976, Vol. 51, pg. 36.

———. "Goodbye to Ziggy and All That." *Melody Maker*, October 29, 1977, Vol. 52, pg. 14.

———. "Ronson: I'd Like to Kick Sense into Bowie." *Melody Maker*, April 5, 1975, Vol. 50, pg. 29.

Kamin, Philip, and Peter Goddard. *David Bowie: Out of the Cool*. Toronto: Musson, 1983.

Kavanaugh, Julie. "Nicholas Roeg's Time Machine." *Women's Wear Daily*, April 2, 1976, pg. 51.

Kaye, Lenny. "Smiling & Waving & Looking So Fine." *Changes*, October 1972.

Kelleher, Ed. *David Bowie*. New York: Chappell & Co., 1977.

Kent, Nick. "This Is America Special." *New Musical Express*, April 21, 1973.

Kirsch, B. "Midnight Special Shines with Bowie and Choreography." *Rolling Stone*, March 29, 1973, Vol. 131, pg. 16.

Kubernik, Harvey. "Fame at Last for Soulful Bowie." *Melody Maker*, October 25, 1975, Vol. 7, pg. 42.

Lasch, Christopher. *The Culture of Narcissism*. New York: Norton, 1979.

Lazell, Barry, and Dafydd Rees. *Bryan Ferry and Roxy Music*. New York: Proteus, 1982.

Leavens, Tom. "Making of a Pop Star 1973." Detroit, Michigan, *South End*, February 28, 1973.

Leogrande, Ernest. "Bowie Wows the Garden." New York *Daily News*, July 27, 1983, pg. 45.

Le Petit, Paul. "The Night Bowie Came to Kilburn." Willesden and Brent *Chronicle*, June 22, 1973.

Livingstone, David. "An Exquisite Legend in His Own Time." *Macleans*, September 19, 1983, Vol. 96, pg. 54.

Loder, Kurt. "Bowie's Main Man." *Rolling Stone*, October 25, 1984, pg. 17.

———. "Scary Monster on Broadway." *Rolling Stone*, November 13, 1980, pg. 8.

———. "Straight Time." *Rolling Stone*, May 12, 1983, pg. 22.

Lowen, Alexander, M.D. *Narcissism*. New York: Macmillan, 1983.

Lynch, Kate. *David Bowie: A Rock and Roll Odyssey*. New York: Proteus, 1984.

Mabbs, Val. "Ziggy's Back." *Record Mirror*, May 19, 1973.

MacDonald, Ian. "The Revolution Is Here . . . Doesn't Anybody Want It?" *New Musical Express*, March 17, 1973.

MacKay, Patricia. "Serious—and Stunning—Moonlight." *Theatre Crafts*, January 1984, pg. 17.

Mandel, William. "Bowie Creates a Musical Experience." *Philadelphia Evening Bulletin*, February 17, 1973.

Marsh, Dave. *Before I Get Old: The Story of The Who*. New York: St. Martin's, 1983.

———. "The Incredible Story of Iggy and the Stooges." *Creem*, May 1970.

Maslin, Janet. "A Rock Singer Takes Off as a Movie Star." *New York Times*, May 29, 1983, Vol. 132, Sect. 2, pg. 16.

———, and Leee Childers. "Going Apeshit from St. Marks to Staten Island with Iggy and the Stooges." *Changes*, December 15, 1970.

McCormack, Ed. "New York Confidential." *Rolling Stone*, August 20, 1973.

McCormick, Ruth. "Let's Act." *American Film*, September 1983, Vol. 8, pg. 29.

Melly, George. *Revolt in Style*. Middlesex, England: Penguin Books, 1970.

Mendelssohn, John. "David Bowie and Dee Snider: The Bizarre Passions They Can't Control." *Creem*, March 1985, pg. 49.

———. "David Bowie? Pantomime Rock?" *Rolling Stone*, April 1, 1971.

Miles, Barry. *David Bowie Black Book*. New York: Putnam, 1980.

Miller, Jim. "David Bowie's New Look." *Newsweek*, July 18, 1983, Vol. 102, pg. 76.

———. *Rolling Stone Illustrated History of Rock and Roll*. New York: Rolling Stone Press, 1976.

Mitgang, Herbert. "Author Who Checkmated Academe." *New York Times*, April 6, 1983, pg. C15.

Murray, Charles Shaar. "Aladdin Sane." *New Musical Express*, May 12, 1973.

———. "Back at the Dorchester." *New Musical Express*, July 29, 1972.

———. "David at the Dorchester." *New Musical Express*, July 22, 1972.

———. "Gay Guerrillas and Private Movies." *New Musical Express*, February 24, 1973.

———. "Goodbye Ziggy and A Big Hello to Aladdin Sane." *New Musical Express*, January 27, 1973.

———. "Let's Talk: A Conversation with David Bowie." *Rolling Stone*, October 25, 1984, pg. 14.

———. "Total Sensory Overload." *New Musical Express*, May 26, 1973, pg. 10.

———. "Won't You Come Home Dave Bowie?" *Creem*, March 1976, Vol. 7, pg. 22.

Musel, Robert. "Journey Through Siberia." UPI, June 20, 1973.

Nevard, Mike. "David Wowie." *The Sun*, London, England, April 26, 1973.

Newman, Alan. "The Return of Ziggy Stardust." *Daily Planet*, February 13–20, 1973.

Oldfield, M. "Up Pops Iggy." *Melody Maker*, July 22, 1972.

O'Regan, Denis, and Chet Flippo. *David Bowie's Serious Moonlight*. New York: Doubleday, 1984.

Padroff, Jay. "Star Shoots to Earth and Broadway." *New York Post*, September 24, 1980, pg. 27.

Paivo, Bob. *The Program Director's Handbook*. Summit, PA: Tab Books, 1983.

Palmer, Robert. "David Bowie." *Penthouse*, November 1983, pg. 118.

Pang, May, and Henry Edwards. *Loving John*. London: Transworld Publishers, 1983.

Pareles, Jon. "David Bowie Ponders His Newfound Popularity." *New York Times*, November 4, 1984, Sect. 2, pg. 25.

———. "Eno Uncaged." *Village Voice*, May 4, 1982, pg. 77.

———. "The Rock and Roles of David Bowie." *Harper's Bazaar*, May 1983, pg. 163.

Peacock, Steve. "Rock On Ziggy." *Sounds*, June 17, 1972.

———. "Under the Image." *Sounds*, October 21, 1972.

Petrie, Gavin. "Bowie Is End of an Era." *Disc*, January 20, 1973.

———. "Ziggy Stardust." *Disc*, September 23, 1972.

Philbin, Peter Jay. "In Long Beach—David Bowie Sings." *Los Angeles Free Press*, March 23, 1973.

Pitt, Kenneth. *Bowie: The Pitt Report*. London: Omnibus, 1983.

Pulin, Chuck. "Ziggy in NYC." *Sounds*, October 7, 1972.

Reed, Rex. "David Bowie: He Is FAR-Out." New York *Sunday News*, June 13, 1976, pg. 7.

Rice, Anne. "David Bowie and the End of Gender." *Vogue*, November 1983, Vol. 173, pg. 432.

Robinson, Lisa. "Bowie: 'I Am Not An Alien Freak.' " *New York Post*, July 25, 1983.

———. "Clockwork Orange in Black and White." *Creem*, May 1976, Vol. 7, pg. 48.

———. "David Bowie." *Interview*, June 1978, Vol. 8, pg. 28.

———. "David's the Darling of the City." *Disc*, October 7, 1972, pg. 11.

———. "Mick and Patti and David and Iggy and Bryan." *Hit Parader*, September 1977.

Rock, Mick. "Bowie Returns—On T.V." *Rolling Stone*, December 6, 1973, Vol. 149, pg. 18.

———. "David Bowie Is Just Not Serious." *Rolling Stone*, June 8, 1972, Vol. 110, pg. 14.

Rockwell, John. "Hunter/Ronson at the Felt Forum." *New York Times*, May 3, 1975.

Rolling Stone Editors, *The Rolling Stone Record Review*. New York: Simon and Schuster, 1971.

———. *The Rolling Stone Record Review, Vol. II*. New York: Simon and Schuster, 1974.

Rose, Frank. "Four Conversations with Brian Eno." *Village Voice*, March 28, 1977, pg. 69.

———. "Is David Bowie Coming to Earth?" *Mademoiselle*, October 1983, pg. 432.

———. "After the Wall." *Playboy*, July 1983, Vol. 30, pg. 26.

Ross, Ron. "David Bowie's Glamorous Career." *Phonograph Record Magazine*, October 1972.

Roxon, Lillian. "A Rock Happening: David's Debut." *Sunday News*, New York, NY, October 8, 1972, pg. 9.

Russell, Rosalind. "Bowie's Backup Men." *Disc*, July 15, 1972.

———. "David Bowie—Bent on Success." *Disc*, May 6, 1972.

———. "David Bowie, the Man Who Saved the Music World." *Disc*, September 23, 1972.

Saal, Hubert. "The Stardust Kid." *Newsweek*, October 9, 1972.

Sanchez, Tony. *Up and Down with the Rolling Stones*. New York: William Morrow, 1979.

Schaffner, Nicholas. *The British Invasion*. New York: McGraw-Hill, 1983.

Shapiro, Susin, "Down by the Old Mainstream." *New York Daily News Magazine*, July 24, 1983, pg. 8.

Shinfield, Barry. "The Prettiest Star." *Beckenham & Penge Advertiser*, London, England, June 28, 1973.

Shipman, David. *The Great Movie Stars*. New York: Da Capo Press, 1982.

Shore, Michael. *The Rolling Stone Book of Rock Video*. New York: William Morrow, 1984.

Short, Don. "Bowie Bows Out in a Pop Finale." *Daily Mirror*, London, England, July 4, 1973.

Shroyer, S., and J. Lifflander. "David Bowie Spaced Out in the Desert." *Creem*, December 1975, pg. 42.

Simels, Steve. "Bowie and Hoople and Reed." *Stereo Review*, February 1973, Vol. 30, pg. 92.

———. "Bowie: Three Ways, No Way." *Stereo Review*, February 1975, Vol. 34, pg. 52.

———. "David Bowie: No Honey, It's Not One of Those." *Stereo Review*, January 1973, Vol. 30, pg. 90.

Sinclair, Paul. *Electric Warrior: The Marc Bolan Story*. New York: Putnam, 1982.

Smith, Liz. "Keeping Up with Miss Jones." *Daily Mirror*, London, England, July 24, 1973, pg. 15.

Smith, Patti. "Heroes—A Communique." *Hit Parader*, April 1978.

Stein, Bruno. "U.F.O.'s, Hitler and David Bowie." *Creem*, February 1975, Vol. 6, pg. 52.

Sterritt, David. "The Furniture Music of Rock Star Brian Eno." *Christian Science Monitor*, May 3, 1984, pg. 1.

Thomas, Deborah. "Has the Star Gone Too Far?" *Daily Mirror*, London, England, May 22, 1973.

———. "King of Rock & Rouge." *Daily Mirror*, London, England, January 22, 1973.

Toepfer, Susan. "A Terminal Case of Cool." *Daily News*, New York, NY, November 27, 1977, pg. 23.

Townsend, Richard. "Remembrance of Things Past." *Sunday News*, New York, NY, September 5, 1976, pg. 9.

Tremlett, George. *The David Bowie Story*. New York: Futura Publications, 1974.

Truscott, Lucian K., IV. "Dylan Freewheelin' Through the Village." *Rolling Stone*, August 28, 1975.

Tyler, Andrew. "Just an Old Poser." *Disc*, September 23, 1972.

Valentine, Penny. "Bowie Coming Back to Life." *New Musical Express*, January 29, 1972.

Valiente, Doreen. *The ABC of Witchcraft, Past, Present and Future*. Custer, WA: Phoenix Publishing, 1973.

Van Matre, Lynn. "Driven by Change Rock's David Bowie Turns Actor." *Chicago Tribune*, August 3, 1980, Sect. 6, pg. 2.

Waddington, R. "Ziggy the Crooner!" *Melody Maker*, February 14, 1976, Vol. 51, pg. 13.

Wale, Michael. "David Bowie: Rock and Theatre." *The Times*, London, England, January 24, 1973.

Warhol, Andy, and Pat Hackett. *Popism*. New York: Harper & Row, 1980.

Watts, Michael. "Bowie: Funeral in Berlin." *Melody Maker*, January 29, 1977, Vol. 52, pg. 36.

———. "Bowie, the Darling Who Put Glam into Rock." *Melody Maker*, October 6, 1973, Vol. 48, pg. 37.

———. "Bowie: Waiting for the Man." *Melody Maker*, July 1, 1972, Vol. 47, pg. 28.

———. "Bowie's Last Tour?" *Melody Maker*, February 24, 1973.

———. "Bowie's Mainman." *Melody Maker*, May 18, 1974, Vol. 49, pg. 40.

———. "Bowie Today." *Melody Maker*, February 18, 1978, pg. 1.

———. "Confessions of an Elitist." *Melody Maker*, February 18, 1978, pg. 35.

———. "From Brixton to Berlin." *Melody Maker*, February 18, 1978, pg. 33.

———. "Lock Up Your Daughters, Iggy's Here." *Melody Maker*, April 1, 1972.

———. "Night of the Iggy." *Melody Maker*, February 12, 1972.

———. "Oh, You Pretty Thing." *Melody Maker*, January 22, 1972, Vol. 47, pg. 19.

———. "The Rise and Rise of Ziggy Stardust." *Melody Maker*, August 19, 1972, Vol. 47, pg. 8.

———. "Stranger in a Strange Land." *Melody Maker*, February 24, 1973, Vol. 48, pg. 3.

Welch, Chris. "Bowie A–Z." *Melody Maker*, May 12, 1973.

———. "Bowie and Bolan Get It On." *Melody Maker*, September 17, 1977, Vol. 52, pg. 16.

———. "Bowie's Free for All." *Melody Maker*, October 27, 1973, Vol. 48, pg. 3.

———. "Bowie: Myths and Mystique." *Melody Maker*, March 12, 1977, Vol. 52, pg. 14.

West, Mike. *Lou Reed and the Velvet Underground*. Manchester, England: Babylon Books, 1982.

Whitburn, Joel. *Top 40 Hits: 1955–Present*. New York: Billboard Publications, 1983.

Wigg, David. "Bowie's Last Binge." *Daily Express*, London, England, July 7, 1973.

Discography

David Bowie (Deram DES 18003)

Uncle Arthur; Sell Me a Coat; Rubber Band; Love You Till Tuesday; There Is a Happy Land; When I Live My Dream; Little Bombardier; Silly Boy Blue; Come and Buy My Toys; Join the Gang; She's Got My Medals; Maids of Bond Street; Please Mr. Gravedigger
Produced by Mike Vernon
Released in 1967

Man of Words, Man of Music (Mercury SR. 61246)

Space Oddity; Unwashed and Somewhat Slightly Dazed; Letter to Hermione; Cygnet Committee; Janine; An Occasional Dream; The Wild Eyed Boy from Free-cloud; God Knows I'm Good; Memory of a Free Festival
Produced by Tony Visconti
Released in 1970

The Man Who Sold the World (Mercury 61325)

The Width of a Circle; All the Madmen; Black Country; After All; Running Gun Blues; Saviour Machine; She Shook Me Cold; The Man Who Sold the World; The Supermen
Produced by Tony Visconti
Released in 1971

Hunky Dory (RCA LSP.4623)

Changes; Oh, You Pretty Things; Eight Line Poem; Life on Mars; Kooks; Quick-sand; Fill Your Heart; Andy Warhol; Song for Bob Dylan; Queen Bitch; The Bewlay Brothers
Produced by Ken Scott (assisted by the actor)
Released in 1971

The Rise and Fall of Ziggy Stardust and the Spiders from Mars (RCA LSP.4702)

Five Years; Soul Love; Moonage Daydream; Starman; It Ain't Easy; Lady Stardust; Star; Hang Onto Yourself; Ziggy Stardust; Suffragette City; Rock 'n' Roll Suicide

Produced by David Bowie and Ken Scott
Released in 1972

Space Oddity (RCA LSP.4813)

Re-release in 1972 of "Man of Words, Man of Music"

The Man Who Sold the World (RCA LSP.4816)

Re-release in 1972 of the Mercury album of the same name

Aladdin Sane (RCA LSP.4852)

Watch That Man; Aladdin Sane; Drive-In Saturday; Panic in Detroit; Cracked Actor; Time; The Prettiest Star; Let's Spend the Night Together; Lady Grinning Soul
Produced by David Bowie and Ken Scott
Released in 1973

Pin-Ups (RCA APL.I.0576)

Rosalyn; Here Comes the Night; I Wish You Would; See Emily Play; Everything's Alright; I Can't Explain; Friday on My Mind; Sorrow; Don't Bring Me Down; Shapes of Things; Anyway, Anyhow, Anywhere; Where Have All the Good Times Gone?
Produced by Ken Scott and David Bowie
Released in 1973

Diamond Dogs (RCA APL.I.0576)

Future Legend; Diamond Dogs; Sweet Thing; Candidate; Sweet Thing (reprise); Rebel Rebel; Rock 'n' Roll With Me; We Are the Dead; 1984; Big Brother; Chant of the Ever-Circling Skeletal Family
Produced by David Bowie
Released in 1974

David Live (RCA CPL.2.0771)

1984; Rebel Rebel; Moonage Daydream; Sweet Thing; Changes; Suffragette City; Aladdin Sane; All the Young Dudes; Cracked Actor; When You Rock 'n' Roll With Me; Watch That Man; Knock on Wood; Diamond Dogs; Big Brother; Width of a Circle; Jean Genie; Rock 'n' Roll Suicide
Produced by Tony Visconti
Released in 1974

Young Americans (RCA APL.I.0998)

Young Americans; Win; Fascination; Right; Somebody Up There Likes Me; Across the Universe; Can You Hear Me; Fame
Selections produced by Tony Visconti, Harry Maslin, and David Bowie
Released in 1975

Images 1966–1967 (London BP .61829)

Two-record repackaging of *David Bowie* with additional material.
Rubber Band; Maids of Bond Street; Sell Me a Coat; Love You Till Tuesday;

There Is a Happy Land; The Laughing Gnome; The Gospel According to Tony Day; Did You Ever Have a Dream; Uncle Arthur; We Are Hungry Men; When I Live My Dream; Join the Gang; Little Bombardier; Come and Buy My Toys: Silly Boy Blue; She's Got Medals; Please Mr. Gravedigger; London Boys; Karma Man; Let Me Sleep; In the Heat of the Morning
Selections produced by Mike Vernon and Tony Visconti
Released in 1975

Station to Station (RCA APL.I.1327)

Station to Station; Golden Years; Word on a Wing; TVC 15; Stay; Wild Is the Wind
Produced by David Bowie and Harry Maslin
Released 1976

Changesonebowie (RCA APL.I.1732)

Space Oddity; John, I'm Only Dancing; Changes; Ziggy Stardust; Suffragette City; The Jean Genie; Diamond Dogs; Rebel Rebel; Young Americans; Fame; Golden Years
Released 1976

Low (RCA APL.I.2030)

Speed of Life; Breaking Glass; What in the World; Sound and Vision; Always Crashing in the Same Car; Be My Wife; A New Career in a New Town; Warszawa; Art Decade; Weeping Wall; Subterraneans
Produced by David Bowie and Tony Visconti
Released in 1977

"Heroes" (RCA AFL.I.2522)

Beauty and the Beast; Joe the Lion; "Heroes"; Sons of the Silent Age; Blackout; V-2 Schneider; Sense of Doubt; Moss Garden; Neukoln; The Secret Life of Arabia
Produced by David Bowie and Tony Visconti
Released in 1977

David Bowie with Eugene Ormandy and the Philadelphia Orchestra/ Peter and the Wolf (RCA Red Seal ARL.I.2743)

David Bowie Narrates Prokofiev's *Peter and the Wolf*; Benjamin Britten's *Young Person's Guide to the Orchestra*
Produced by Jay David Saks
Released in 1978

Stage (RCA CPL.2.2913)

Hang Onto Yourself; Ziggy Stardust; Five Years; Soul Love; Star; Station to Station; Fame; TVC 15; Warszawa; Speed of Life; Art Decade; Sense of Doubt; Breaking Glass; Heroes; What in the World; Blackout; Beauty and the Beast
Produced by David Bowie and Tony Visconti
Released in 1978

Lodger (RCA AQL.I.3254)

Fantastic Voyage; African Night Flight; Move On; Yassassin; Red Sails; D.J.; Look Back in Anger; Boys Keep Swinging; Repetition; Red Money
Produced by David Bowie and Tony Visconti
Released 1979

Scary Monsters (and Super Creeps) (RCA AQL.I.3647)

It's No Game (No. 1); Up the Hill Backwards; Scary Monsters (and Super Creeps); Ashes to Ashes; Fashion; Teenage Wildlife; Screaming Like a Baby; Kingdom Come; Because You're Young; It's No Game (No. 2)
Produced by David Bowie and Tony Visconti
Released 1980

Changestwobowie (RCA BOW LP 3)

Aladdin Sane; (On Broadway); Oh, You Pretty Things; Starman; 1984; Ashes to Ashes; Sound and Vision; Fashion; Wild Is the Wind; John, I'm Only Dancing; D.J.
Released 1981

Christine F. (Sound track) (RCA ABL.1.4239)

V-2 Schneider; TVC-15; "Heroes/Helden"; Boys Keep Swinging; Sense of Doubt; Station to Station; Look Back in Anger; Stay; Warszawa
Released 1982

David Bowie in Bertolt Brecht's Baal (Sound track) (RCA CPL 1.4346)

Baal's Hymn; Remembering Marie A.; Ballad of the Adventurers; The Drowned Girl; The Dirty Song
Released 1982

Bowie Rare (RCA PL 45406)

Ragazzo Solo, Ragazza Sola; 'Round and 'Round; Amsterdam; Holy Holy; Panic in Detroit; Young Americans; Velvet Goldmine; Helden; John, I'm Only Dancing; Moon of Alabama; Crystal Japan
Released 1983

Let's Dance (EMI-America AML 3029)

Modern Love; China Girl; Let's Dance; Without You; Ricochet; Criminal World; Cat People; Shake It
Produced by David Bowie and Nile Rodgers
Released 1983

Golden Years (RCA AFL 1-4792)

Fashion; Red Sails; Look Back in Anger; I Can't Explain; Ashes to Ashes; Golden Years; Joe the Lion; Scary Monsters (and Super Creeps); Wild Is the Wind
Produced by David Bowie, Tony Visconti, Ken Scott, and Harry Maslin
Released 1983

Ziggy Stardust—The Motion Picture (Sound track) (RCA CPL2 11862)

Hang Onto Yourself; Ziggy Stardust; Watch That Man; Wild-Eyed Boy from Freecloud; All the Young Dudes; Oh! You Pretty Things; Moonage Daydream; Space Oddity; My Death; Cracked Actor; Time; Width of a Circle; Changes; Let's Spend the Night Together; Suffragette City; White Light/White Heat; Rock 'n' Roll Suicide

Produced by David Bowie and Mike Moran
Released 1983

Fame and Fashion (RCA AFL1 4919)

Space Oddity; Changes; Starman; 1984; Young Americans; Fame; Golden Years; TVC 15; "Heroes"; D.J.; Fashion; Ashes to Ashes
Released 1984

Tonight (EMI-America SJ-17138)

Loving That Alien; Don't Look Down; God Only Knows; Tonight; Neighborhood Threat; Blue Jean; Tumble and Twirl; I Keep Forgetting; Dancing with the Big Boys

Produced by David Bowie, Derek Bramble, and Hugh Padgham
Released 1984

Acknowledgments

We are grateful to all those who consented to be interviewed for this book, including Maggie Abbott; Carlos Alomar; Jeanna Andrews; Gui Andrisano; Ken Anger; Joey Arias; Ron Ashton; Tom Ayers; Jude Bartlett; Toni Basil; Rodney Bingenheimer; Eli Bird; Meg Bird; Angela Bowie; Dore W. Broderick; Gustl Breuer; Janis Cavasso; Ava Cherry; Leee Black Childers; Candy Clark; Marilyn Cohen; Jay Cocks; Jac Colello; Charles Comer; Craig Copetas; Tom Cossie; Cameron Crowe; Bob Davis; Jules Fisher; John Dove; Danny Dragon; Paul Feegon; Cyrinda Foxe; Danny Fields; Mike Garson; Benoit Gautier; Dana Gillespie; Stu Ginsberg; Rick Green; Richard Gurchick; Romy Haag; Carol Hill; Jack Hofsiss; Glenn Hughes; Peter Hunsley; John Hutchinson; Mel Ilberman; Dennis Katz; Jack Kreigo; Chris Langhart; Grelun Landon; Martin Last; Michael Lawrence; Michael Lippman; Little Richard; Si Litvinoff; Lance Loud; Max McCaree; Melanie McDonald; Lori Maddox; Ann Magnuson; John Mendelssohn; Jaime Mosedale; Robby Monk; Raquel Narvaez; Nelle Nugent; Ron Oberman; Brooks Ogden; Linda Palermo; Will Palin; D. A. Pennbaker; Martin Pierrepoint; Gail Parento; May Pang; Fran Pillersdorf; David Platz; Mark Ravitz; Steve Reich; Scott Richardson; Mick Rock; Nicholas Russiyan; Pablo Rosario; Mick Ronson; Sue Fussey Ronson; Bernard Roth; Bob See; Heather See; Dick Shepard; Gayle Smiff; Susan Smith; Ray Stevenson; Linda Stein; Sylvain Sylvain; Dennis Taylor; Twiggy; Michael Todd; Raquel Welch; Barbara Wilksinson; Stevie Ray Vaughn; and Pat Wadsley.

We thank also those who spoke to us off-the-record.

Special thanks must be given to our English friend Kevin Cann, Special Features Editor of *Starzone*, the superb English-based David Bowie fanzine (P.O. Box 225, Watford, Herts., WD1 7QG, England). Kevin made available to us his complete copies of his interviews, and they proved of great help. Kevin is the author of *David Bowie—A Chronology* (Simon & Schuster: 1983), a must for any Bowie fan.

419

He also provided an introduction to Ken Pitt, one of the seminal figures in David Bowie's life. Ken graciously allowed us to interview him, and it was our pleasure to speak at length with him. Ken is the author of *Bowie—The Pitt Report* (Omnibus: 1983), a book which provided the factual basis for our history of the early years of David Bowie's career. In his introduction Pitt writes that he wished to supply future researchers with "reliable source material." His book is a treasure trove of information about these years, and is also highly recommended to all Bowie fans.

We are also grateful to the intrepid Dorothy Sherman for providing access to her unpublished history of Iggy Pop as well as the research notes she gathered while preparing her manuscript.

Michael Shore, author of *The Rolling Stone Book of Rock Video* (Rolling Stone Press: 1984), was especially helpful in the area of rock video.

Additional research was supplied by Charlotte Nugent; Ian Blair; Joseph Bivona; Madeleine Bocchiaro; Jimmy Gitterman; Anthony Ingrassia; Chris Karatnsky; Barbara Pepy; Susan Smith; Doris Toumarkine; Pat Wadsley; John Wilcock; and John Walker (whose survey of Bowie's early recordings in *Trouser Press* was especially definitive).

Clerical assistance was provided by Jan Acker; Chris Carter; Toby Fitterman; Kathy Inglesias; Nursa Miller; and Carolyn Shookhoff.

Special commendations must go to two close friends who lived through the experience with us: Joseph Melnyk and Myrna Zimmerman, and especially David Rockwell; as well as the manuscript's "godparents" Paula and Rod Steiger.

The spiritual beacon that guided the project to completion was one of the great healers of our time, Dr. Eugene E. Landy. Inspiration was also provided by the healing process of Dr. Jac Conaway; Dr. Ria Eagan; Aleta St. James; Steve Hymowitz; and Leonare M. Tint; and Dr. Baron Shopsin.

At the time we commenced work James J. C. Andrews was the president of MainMan. Jamie gave unstintingly of himself to the project and to everything else he did. As the book neared completion he succumbed to pneumonia. Those who knew him will always miss him.

Ultimately three people were most important of all: Reid Boates, Cynthia Merman, and Renée Sacks. Their suggestions and support were the bedrock upon which this project was built. They are our "heroes," and we can never thank them enough.

Index

421